Julia Davis

In Their Own Words
How Russian Propagandists Reveal Putin's Intentions

With a foreword by Timothy Snyder

UKRAINIAN VOICES

Collected by Andreas Umland

50 *Serhii Plokhy*
    Der Mann mit der Giftpistole
    Eine Spionageschichte aus dem Kalten Krieg
    ISBN 978-3-8382-1789-5

51 *Vakhtang Kipiani*
    Ukrainische Dissidenten unter der Sowjetmacht
    Im Kampf um Wahrheit und Freiheit
    ISBN 978-3-8382-1890-8

52 *Dmytro Shestakov*
    When Businesses Test Hypotheses
    A Four-Step Approach to Risk Management for Innovative Startups
    With a foreword by Anthony J. Tether
    ISBN 978-3-8382-1883-0

53 *Larissa Babij*
    A Kind of Refugee
    The Story of an American Who Refused to Leave Ukraine
    With a foreword by Vladislav Davidzon
    ISBN 978-3-8382-1898-4

The book series "Ukrainian Voices" publishes English- and German-language monographs, edited volumes, document collections, and anthologies of articles authored and composed by Ukrainian politicians, intellectuals, activists, officials, researchers, and diplomats. The series' aim is to introduce Western and other audiences to Ukrainian explorations, deliberations and interpretations of historic and current, domestic, and international affairs. The purpose of these books is to make non-Ukrainian readers familiar with how some prominent Ukrainians approach, view and assess their country's development and position in the world. The series was founded, and the volumes are collected by Andreas Umland, Dr. phil. (FU Berlin), Ph. D. (Cambridge), Associate Professor of Politics at the Kyiv-Mohyla Academy and an Analyst in the Stockholm Centre for Eastern European Studies at the Swedish Institute of International Affairs.

Julia Davis

IN THEIR OWN WORDS
How Russian Propagandists Reveal Putin's Intentions

With a foreword by Timothy Snyder

Bibliografische Information der Deutschen Nationalbibliothek
Die Deutsche Nationalbibliothek verzeichnet diese Publikation in der Deutschen Nationalbibliografie; detaillierte bibliografische Daten sind im Internet über http://dnb.d-nb.de abrufbar.

Bibliographic information published by the Deutsche Nationalbibliothek
Die Deutsche Nationalbibliothek lists this publication in the Deutsche Nationalbibliografie; detailed bibliographic data are available on the Internet at http://dnb.d-nb.de.

Cover photo: ID 9157855 © Pavel Losevsky | Dreamstime.com

ISBN-13: 978-3-8382-1909-7
© *ibidem*-Verlag, Hannover • Stuttgart 2024
Alle Rechte vorbehalten

Das Werk einschließlich aller seiner Teile ist urheberrechtlich geschützt. Jede Verwertung außerhalb der engen Grenzen des Urheberrechtsgesetzes ist ohne Zustimmung des Verlages unzulässig und strafbar. Dies gilt insbesondere für Vervielfältigungen, Übersetzungen, Mikroverfilmungen und elektronische Speicherformen sowie die Einspeicherung und Verarbeitung in elektronischen Systemen.

All rights reserved. No part of this publication may be reproduced, stored in or introduced into a retrieval system, or transmitted, in any form, or by any means (electronic, mechanical, photocopying, recording or otherwise) without the prior written permission of the publisher. Any person who commits any unauthorized act in relation to this publication may be liable to criminal prosecution and civil claims for damages.

Printed in the EU

Contents

Foreword by *Timothy Snyder* 13

Preface 17

Russians Praise Trump, Taunt Zelensky, as Ukraine Signs On to Peace-Plan Proposal 19

Russia's State TV Calls Trump Their 'Agent' 23

Did Russian Prime Minister Medvedev Drop a Grim Hint About Putin's Latest Power Grab? 27

This Is the Real Goal of Putin's Propaganda Machine 31

Can Trump's Art of the Arms Deal Get More Stupid? The Russians Are Loving It 39

'America's Dying': Russian Media Is Giddy at Chaos in the USA 45

Russian Media Is Rooting for Civil War in America: 'The Worse, the Better' 49

Russian State Media Roots for Violence as America Counts Its Votes 53

Russian Media Is Angry and Desperate Over Biden Win 57

Russian Media Wants Moscow to Grant Asylum to Trump 61

Russian Media Mourn as Putin Acknowledges Biden's Win: But Say Trump 'Burned' U.S. on His Way Out 65

Putin Gleeful After Trumpsters' Violent Insurrection 69

Russian Media: 'Traitors' Like Alexei Navalny Deserve Death 73

Russian Media Pushes the Lie That Capitol Rioters Were Antifa 77

Top Kremlin Mouthpiece Warns of 'Inevitable' War With U.S. Over Another Ukraine Land Grab 81

Russian State Media Gears Up for a War 'Against the West' 85

How Putin Made a Fool of Tucker Carlson 89

Russia Targets Fox News Fans in Bid to Become the World's Anti-Woke Capital.. 93

State TV Host Mocks Black January 6 Cop in 'N-Word' Fueled Rant.. 97

Russia Is 'Enjoying' America's Failure — and Cozying Up to the Taliban 101

The Russian Public Is Being Primed for Another of Putin's Wars.. 107

Russian State TV Drops Deranged Love Letter to Its Darling 'Trumpushka'... 111

Russian Citizens Are Now Being Prepped for Nuclear War........ 115

How Tucker Carlson Is Boosting Russia's New Propaganda War.. 119

Trump's Mega-Fans in Moscow Declare They're 'Ready to Elect Him Again' 123

Welcome to the Fantasy World Where Putin Already 'Won This Round' 127

Russian State TV Is So Ridiculous Right Now It Looks Like a Farce 131

Kremlin TV Asks 'Where's the Champagne?' as Ukraine's Kids Are Prepped for War.. 135

Putin's Own Minions Are Exposing Him for the Liar He Is 139

Sanctioned Russian TV Host Cries About Losing His Italian Villa 143

Kremlin TV Tells Ukraine to Listen to Fox News Guest and Kneel to Putin... 147

Russian State TV Just Blew Up Putin's 'Nazi Ukraine' BS........... 151

Even Russian State TV Is Pleading With Putin to Stop the War 155

Wild Kremlin TV Hosts Threaten the U.S. With Nuclear Strikes Unless Sanctions End and Reparations Are Paid 159

Kremlin TV Descends Into Screaming Match Over Putin's War Failures 163

Putin's Minions Demand Grotesque 'Rewards' for Mass Killers in Ukraine 167

Russia Airs Its Ultimate 'Revenge Plan' for America 171

Putin's Stooges: He May Nuke Us All but We Are Ready to Die 175

Putin's Puppets Admit Their Army Has Been a Total Embarrassment 179

Kremlin TV Betrays Darling Trump in Crazed Defense of Putin's War 183

Kremlin TV Names the Country Putin Will Invade Next 187

Putin's Lap Dog Humiliated by Fed-Up Guest on His Own Show 191

Team Putin Dishes on the Moment They Could Win It All 195

You'll Never Guess the Lie Putin Has Come Up With Now 199

Putin's Lies Have Kremlin TV Flailing and Fighting On-Air 203

Kremlin TV Says if Putin Ran For U.S. President, He'd Win— and Trump Would Be His Veep 207

Putin's Pals Furious Younger Russians Don't Want to Die in Ukraine 211

Russia's Panicked Confession: This Is What Scares Us Most 215

Kremlin TV Desperately Wants You to Move to Russia Right Now 219

Putin Cronies Threaten 'Hundreds' of American Coffins on Live TV 223

Team Putin Admits Their Worst Case Scenario Is Coming True 227

Team Putin Threatens Maniacal Response to Bitter War Losses 231

Putin Crony Belts Out Song in Cringey Push for More Russian Troops 235

Team Putin Begs Rich Russians to Help Save His Failing War ... 239

Russia Desperately Tries to Sell Its Ukraine War Draft as Citizens Flee 243

Putin Crony Says He Drafted Russian 'Kill List' of Western Officials 247

Team Putin Wakes Up We Never Should've Laughed at Ukraine... 251

Kremlin TV Exposes the Real Goal of Putin's 'Revenge-Bombs' 255

Top Putin Lackey Urges Russians to Choose Violent Death Over War Defeat 259

Putin's Top TV Puppet Threatens 7 Countries With Air Strikes After Poland Blast 263

Kremlin TV Stars Combust as Russians Admit War Is Aimless... 267

Putin's Cronies Turn on Russian Elite in Paranoid War Frenzy.. 271

Russians Fear They'll Soon Be Starving 'Like North Koreans' ... 275

Putin's Henchmen Threaten 'Tens of Thousands' of Dead U.S. Troops 279

Putin's No. 1 Cheerleader Rips into Russia's War Failures 283

Gloom Envelops Putin's TV Propagandists 287

'Morality Shouldn't Get in the Way' — Russia's Genocidal State Media 291

Team Putin Melts Down Over International Arrest Warrant 297

God's Propagandists 301

Russia Laments the Loss of Tucker Carlson 305

Married Putin Stooge Accused of Hiding Kids With Secret American Lover 309

Team Putin Spars Over Baffling Russian 'Victory Plan' in War 311

Russian State TV Anchors Aghast That Putin Didn't Kill Prigozhin 315

The Kremlin Has a Batshit New PR Position: There Was No Armed Mutiny 319

Kremlin News Stars Unravel in Post-Mutiny Television Fiasco 323

Top Putin Crony Curses Audience and Berates Colleague On-Air 325

Kremlin Flacks Tease Next 'Global' Targets of Putin's Wrath 329

Putin Stooge Loses It When Confronted About Prigozhin's Death 333

Who Assassinated Prigozhin? Duh, the English 337

'Woe to My Enemies' Rages Russia's Mouthpiece-in-Chief 341

Russia Lauds North Korea's 'Square-Headed Dude' and His Pauper Legions 345

Putin's Pals Brag: Elon Musk 'Really Is Our Agent!' 349

'Only Good News Today' — Russia's Propagandists Delight as Israelis Die 353

Russians Divide Over Terrorist Attack on Israel 357

Putin Flack Claims 'Ethnic Cleansing' of Jews on Kremlin TV ... 361

Israel Conflict Rekindles Russian Antisemitism 365

Women Enter the Putin Regime's Crosshairs 369

Give the Kremlin an Inch and it Will Take Half of Europe 373

Reality Check for Putin as Russians Get Damn Tired of War 377

Putin's Pals Think the GOP Just Won Them the War in
Ukraine 381

'Shocking' Reality of Ukraine Blowback Hammers Putin at
Home 385

Putin's Sham Election Rivals Can't Even Keep a Straight Face .. 389

Kremlin Cronies: Putin-Tucker Interview Will 'Blow Up' U.S.
Election 393

Putin Nearly Bores Tucker Carlson to Death With Two-Hour
History Lesson 397

Tucker Carlson Misses the Bullseye 403

Putin Says He Was Not Impressed by Tucker Carlson 407

Putin's Pals Link Death of Alexei Navalny to Tucker Carlson
Interview 411

Putin Plants 'Info-Bombs' 415

Russia Issues Chilling Warnings to Navalny's Widow 419

Putin Inc. Fears Navalny Even Beyond the Grave 423

Trump is 'Unhinged' But We Love Him, Say Kremlin
Mouthpieces 427

Putin's Friends Celebrate Re-Election With Photos of Mass
Hanging 431

Moscow Terror Attack: A Lie Too Good to Waste 435

Kremlin Glee as US Dithers on Lifesaving Ukraine Aid 439

Whiplash as Russia Toasts Derided Marjorie Taylor Greene as Their Top New Hero 443

Putin's Propagandists Rage Against the Republican 'Betrayal' .. 447

Afterword 451

"Julia Davis's work has long been obligatory reading for anyone who seeks to understand Russia. Her new book now provides a chronological account of how the Kremlin's most popular propagandists shaped the agenda and prepared the Russian population to accept the liquidation of their own opposition, the invasion of Ukraine, and the genocide of Ukrainians."
  —Anne Applebaum, author of *Gulag: A History* and *Red Famine*

"This collection of articles provides analysis of Russia's domestic and international propaganda, with an unmistakable trend. State-controlled propagandists cultivate popular opinion well in advance of what the government is planning, including but not limited to the invasion of Ukraine and interference in foreign elections. Outrageous and unlikely propaganda narratives have a tendency to become a reality, months and years later. These narratives are replete with warnings of what the Kremlin would like to do in the future—ignoring them might prove very costly in the long run."
  —Admiral James Stavridis,
  16th Supreme Allied Commander of NATO and author most recently of *2054* a novel of geopolitics and artificial intelligence

"Few in the West have ever experienced the bizarre and dehumanizing propaganda that now dominates all Russian media. Julia Davis, however, has kept a steady eye on this electronic madness and this book is a must-read for anyone who wishes to understand the darkness that has overtaken Russia."
  —Tom Nichols, Professor Emeritus, Naval War College

Foreword

Russian propaganda is in the shadow of America. Whereas the America only covers Russia when there is something to cover, and sometimes not even then, Russian propaganda television starts every night from the premise that whatever has happened is America's doing. This does not reflect reality—or a typical American's experience of reality. It does reflect the problem that Russian propaganda is meant to solve. Since Vladimir Putin is the boss of bosses in an oligarchical regime where domestic policy is impossible, the propagandists must direct attention to the world beyond Russia in a way that makes Russia's leadership seem righteous.

Russian propagandists do this in the confidence that no one beyond Russia is watching, but Julia Davis has been. From this collection of her articles, we can understand the propagandists' job description, but also the tensions they feel when the outside world causes them problems. Their basic posture is that America is in a constant war with the Russian Federation. Because Russia cannot fight and cannot win any actual war of that description, the propagandists are most comfortable when America is turned against itself. They talk almost never about Russian domestic politics, but obsess over every piece of evidence of American domestic weakness.

Donald Trump is their favorite weapon against America. Trump is described as a friend and ally, "our Trumpushka" and "Donald Fredovych". Out of office, he is described as Russia's great hope. He is "sorely missed"; Russia is "ready to elect you again". Russia's propagandists had no trouble predicting that Trump would try a coup when he lost in 2020, because that is a familiar sort of behavior to them. They rejoiced when he did, because they thought that this could lead to a civil war in the United States. Their coverage of Trump's coup attempt was at first highly positive. When it failed, a very awkward pivot was made to the position that it had all been some sort of provocation by the Democrats.

One of the things that Russian propagandists expect not to be noticed, but which is brought home here, is that they believe that

Trump is an idiot. Of course, it's hard to see, from their perspective, how they can believe anything else (except, perhaps, that he is a traitor, as also sometimes hinted). In their public worldview, destroying the United States is the main aim, and here is an American who follows their talking points.

The same goes for Tucker Carlson. He is celebrated on Russian television, of course, and his clips replayed. But Russian propagandists naturally think anyone beyond Russia who is on their side must not be very bright, and they cannot quite stop themselves from saying so. It is the one point on which they are completely sincere.

It is important to note, and Julia Davis gives us all the details, the hypocrisy of the anti-American pose. A leading Russian propagandist sent his girlfriend to America to give birth so that his child would have US citizenship. Propagandists are clearly personally hurt by sanctions that separate them from their property in the European Union or make it harder for them to travel abroad. They send their children to study and work in the West, they don't have any real animus towards the West. This is, I think, one more reason why they can't resist thinking of Americans on their side as idiots.

When Putin ordered a full-scale war on Ukraine, the propagandists suddenly had a problem. Before the attack, as we are reminded in this book, there was great confidence among Russian propagandists that Ukraine would fall to Russia in "two days" or even "ten minutes." But when Russia actually did undertake a full-scale invasion of Ukraine in February 2022, it set off a chain of events that the propagandists found hard to master.

For one thing, they had been cut out of the loop. The invasion was meant to be its own propaganda, a "special military operation" that overthrew the Ukrainian government in three days, followed by a victory parade and a warm welcome by the Ukrainian masses. This did not happen, and was based upon a worldview (Putin's) that was both obviously wrong and impossible to criticize.

Russian propagandists switched immediately to the comfortable idea that the war was really against America, and that America had initiated. Rereading Julia Davis's essays, I was struck by how quickly this happened — within a few days.

The Ukrainians themselves had to be dehumanized. This was a direct consequence of the senselessness of the war. Russians had to be made to feel that they were somehow superior, and that war had some kind of logic. The premise of the war, as Putin had made clear, was that there was not really a Ukrainian state or nation; this was all a conspiracy, and would collapse immediately. If, as it emerged, more Ukrainians defended themselves than expected, that did not mean that Ukraine was real; it just meant that logic of the special military operation, killing the elites, had to be extended ever further downward into the population.

As Julia Davis shows, Russian propagandists use openly genocidal language over and over again, urging the extermination of vermin, worms, demons, zombies, etc. Putin's grotesque "denazification" framing of the war is genocidal. If all Ukrainians are defined as Nazis by nature, then it is right to kill them all. The "Nazi" claim has never had anything to do with political reality (the actual fascists, the ones in Russia, are calling for genocide), and always had everything to do with justifying that murderous project. After the Hamas attack on Israel, there was a split in the Russian media elite between Russia's non-Nazi fascists and the Nazi ones. This too is chronicled here.

When reading Julia Davis's essays carefully, it becomes clear that America is not just needed as a propaganda target, but as a de facto ally, called in by the propagandists to correct the (unmentionable) mistakes made by their own (supposedly infallible) dictator. Russia needs Trump because it cannot manage on its own. Trump allows them to claim that everything is America's fault and that this is confirmed by America's own leadership. And then everything can go on in Russia as before.

Russia needs America to bail it out of its war with Ukraine. When you read Julia Davis's summaries of Russian propaganda day after day, it is abundantly clear that the propagandists themselves (despite all of the bluster) are aware that the war did not go according to plan, and indeed is going very badly. Again and again they are put in impossible positions: when Ukraine takes territory; when Russia fails to take territory; when more Russians have to be mobilized; when Yevgeny Prigozhin tries a coup. They cannot criticize Putin, and they know that Putin cannot win unaided: and so they root for his allies abroad.

This itself is worth emphasizing, at a time when many Europeans and Americans seem to be asking how Ukraine can win. The answer is simple. Ukraine can win if Europeans and Americans believe it can, and continue to help. Ironically, that emerges quite clearly from these pages. Russia's propagandists know this. They are relying entirely on their own domain, that of discourse.

The war is not going well for Russia on the actual battlefield. The Europeans and the Americans are bearing essentially no costs. But if they can somehow decide that they are weary, Russia can win.

Russia can't win its own war, is propagandists' evident conclusion, but America can win Russia's war for it. America is of course not all-powerful, as the Russian propagandists claim to believe, but on this point they are right. Their discussions of Ukraine, like their discussions of Russia and everything else, focus entirely on what is happening inside the United States. The regime they serve, and the senseless and genocidal war it began, can be bought some time, if and only if the United States fails to support Ukraine. And so the heroes of Russia's war, in Russia's own propaganda, become the Americans who support it.

Timothy D. Snyder
Yale University,
New Haven, CT

Preface

This abbreviated anthology of articles illuminates a fascinating time in modern Russian history, through the lens of analysis of Moscow's propaganda tactics. The Kremlin's cadre of state-controlled propagandists is tasked with laying the groundwork for the actions planned by the regime of Vladimir Putin and Russian state-controlled media provides crucial clues about sinister goals that the government is planning to pursue: from election interference to invasions, with the end goal of a new world order — with Russia at the helm.

This journey starts with a pre-invasion assumption that the West is incapable of a strong stance or international unity in opposing Russian aggression against the neighboring countries. Putin's propagandists cheer for war against Ukraine, predicting it would be quick and victorious — and the response from the US and allies would be limited to some mild sanctions, à la Crimea. Misreading the ability of the West to unite against Russian aggression and miscalculating Russia's capabilities in confronting determined Ukrainians, Russia ended up in a quagmire of its own creation.

Putin's decorated propagandists find themselves facing unpleasant consequences — with the possibility of future scrutiny and potential prosecutions for their proactive incitement of genocide.

They unravel, along with the Kremlin, having to tell multiple conflicting stories, condemn the same players they used to lionize and facing the possibility of a civil war in Russia — and not in Western countries, as they've so frequently predicted and openly wished for. Backed into the corner, they resort to nuclear threats and demand even more blood from Ukraine, whose only crime is its desire for democracy and freedom.

Russian propaganda is a weapon of a murderous regime in its pursuit of global domination. Understanding it is a key to analyzing the aspirations of the Kremlin and the methods it uses with the goal of controlling the minds of domestic and international populations.

In a 1948 speech to the British House of Commons, Winston Churchill said, "Those that fail to learn from history are doomed to repeat it." Modern history is unfolding before our eyes. Look through the window of the state media's house of mirrors to decipher what Putin's Russia would like to do—not only to Ukraine, but to the entire world, if the West allows the Kremlin to get away with it.

Russians Praise Trump, Taunt Zelensky, as Ukraine Signs On to Peace-Plan Proposal

"Trump let Zelensky down. Three times he told him: 'Go meet with Putin,'" gloated one prominent Russian TV host.

Originally published by *The Daily Beast* on October 03, 2019

Existential dread washed over the face of the president of Ukraine, Volodymyr Zelensky, as he sat next to the American president during their joint press conference on the sidelines of the U.N. Donald Trump, as the face of Ukraine's most powerful ally in its struggle against Russian aggression, was telling him: "I really hope you and President Putin get together and can solve your problem."

Having lost more than 13,000 people in an ongoing conflict with its belligerent neighbor, Ukraine was now being told to make a deal with the aggressor, because—according to President Trump—"President Putin would like to do something."

During the same conference, Zelensky pleaded with Trump for help with returning the territories occupied and annexed by Russia, and, egged on by Trump—and contrary to the facts—complained that Europe wasn't doing as much as the United States to help Ukraine. In reality, European institutions spent nearly double the amount supplied by the United States: $425.2 million in 2016-2017, as compared to $204.4 million spent by the U.S.

While that disclosure infuriated Ukraine's European allies, Trump in the now infamous July 25 phone call with Zelensky blamed Ukraine's troubles on the Obama administration, dismissively concluding "it's just one of those things" and directing Zelensky to ask for more help from Europe. Since the call's release, Ukrainians have nicknamed their president "Monica Zelensky," as a jab referring to his part in the ongoing impeachment proceedings against Trump.

Backed into the corner and seeming to stand alone there, Zelensky made a step toward a deal with Putin by officially signing up Ukraine to the Steinmeier Formula. The agreement provides the pathway to a summit that would bring Zelensky face-to-face with Russian President Vladimir Putin, French President Emmanuel Macron, and German Chancellor Angela Merkel.

Russia demanded written codification of the Steinmeier Formula by Ukraine as a key precondition to the next Normandy summit. It interprets the clauses of the Minsk "accords" (agreements between the Ukrainian authorities and Russia-backed separatists) in line with Russia's preferences and therefore enjoys the Kremlin's seal of approval.

The formula further calls for elections to be conducted under the supervision of the Organization for Security and Co-operation in Europe (OSCE) in the territories held by Russian-backed separatists in the Donbas region of eastern Ukraine. It was signed on October 1 by representatives of Ukraine, Russia, the separatist pseudo-republics of Luhansk and Donetsk (LPR and DPR), and the OSCE in Minsk. Kremlin spokesman Dmitry Peskov described the signing of the Steinmeier Formula agreement as a "positive" development.

Senator Konstantin Kosachev, chairman of the Federation Council's foreign affairs committee, who is under U.S. sanctions for "worldwide malign activity," said the signing represents "without a doubt, a victory for common sense and an overall success." In stark contrast to Russia's jubilation, hundreds of Ukrainians in Kyiv have protested, demanding "no capitulation" to the Kremlin and its proxies.

The most controversial aspect of the Steinmeier Formula is that it provides for local elections to take place in the occupied parts of Ukraine before Kyiv has control of the border and prior to the withdrawal of the Russian-backed forces. This condition doesn't seem to match up with Zelensky's understanding of the agreement. After signing on to the Steinmeier Formula, the Ukrainian president declared during a news conference that the elections would not be held "under the barrel of a gun" and would take place only when no troops remain in the separatist-held areas.

"What Ukraine was so afraid of has happened... Zelensky doesn't understand what he signed," concluded Vladimir Solovyov, the host of the nightly *The Evening With Vladimir Solovyov* on Russian state television.

The heads of Russia-backed separatist pseudo-republics in eastern Ukraine openly proclaimed in a public statement that "the Kyiv authorities won't get any control over the border" and vowed that LPR and DPR will make decisions "about integration with Russia" of their own accord. "Forget about controlling the border, once and for all," exclaimed political scientist Sergey Kurginyan, appearing on *The Evening With Vladimir Solovyov*.

During a panel discussion at the Russian Energy Week forum, Putin said that Zelensky "will have to decide how the relations between Ukraine and Donbas will develop," pointedly referring to Ukraine's own region as a separate geopolitical entity. Putin opined that Ukraine "did much better when it was a part of the Soviet Union, along with Russia." Appearing on Russia's state television program *60 Minutes*, Oleg Nilov, member of the State Duma of the Russian Federation, asserted that Ukraine was "forced to sign" the Steinmeier Formula—and proceeded to threaten the country with "the Israeli formula" of taking all the land Russia wants, if Kyiv reneges on the deal.

"Come back to the Soviet Union," urged Karen Shakhnazarov, CEO of Mosfilm Studio, appearing on *The Evening With Vladimir Solovyov*. The talk-show host Solovyov concurred and reminded the guests that the USSR was originally formed by a treaty that united the Russian, Ukrainian, Belarusian and Transcaucasian republics.

"Trump let Zelensky down. Three times he told him: 'Go meet with Putin,'" said Olga Skabeeva, the host of *60 Minutes*. During the same program, Nikolai Platoshkin, head of the International Relations Department at Moscow University for the Humanities, predicted that once all the "formulas" have been exhausted, LPR and DPR will ultimately become a part of the Russian Federation. Skabeeva concurred: "The sooner the better." She surmised: "After his 'triumphant' meeting with the American president, Zelensky had no choice but to lie back and enjoy it... We know what happened in the United States. You have nowhere left to go."

Russia's State TV Calls Trump Their 'Agent'

Russian commentators note, rightly, that "sooner or later, the Democrats will come back into power," and they're already joking about offering Trump asylum.

Originally published by *The Daily Beast* on December 16, 2019

Sometimes a picture doesn't have to be worth a thousand words. Just a few will do. As Russian Foreign Minister Sergey Lavrov returned home from his visit with President Donald Trump in the Oval Office last week, Russian state media were gloating over the spectacle. TV channel Rossiya 1 aired a segment entitled "Puppet Master and 'Agent'—How to Understand Lavrov's Meeting With Trump."

Vesti Nedeli, a Sunday news show on the same network, pointed out that it was Trump, personally, who asked Lavrov to pose standing near as Trump sat at his desk. It's almost the literal image of a power behind the throne.

And in the meantime, much to Russia's satisfaction, Ukrainian President Volodymyr Zelensky is still waiting for that critical White House meeting with the American president: the famous "quid pro quo" for Zelensky announcing an investigation that would smear Democratic challenger Joe Biden. Zelensky hasn't done that, and as of now, no meeting has been set.

Russian state television still views the impending impeachment as a bump in the road that won't lead to Trump's removal from office. But President Vladimir Putin's propaganda brigades enjoy watching the heightened divisions in the United States, and how it hurts relations between the U.S. and Ukraine. They've also added a cynical new a narrative filled with half-joking ironies as they look at the American president's bleak prospects when he does leave office.

Appearing on *Sunday Evening With Vladimir Solovyov*, Mikhail Gusman, first deputy director general of ITAR-TASS, Russia's oldest and largest news agency, predicted: "Sooner or later, the Democrats will come back into power. The next term or the term after that, it doesn't matter... I have an even more unpleasant forecast for Trump. After the White House, he will face a very unhappy period."

The host, Vladimir Solovyov, smugly asked: "Should we get another apartment in Rostov ready?" Solovyov's allusion was to the situation of Viktor Yanukovych, former president of Ukraine, who was forced to flee to Russia in 2014 and settled in the city of Rostov-on-Don.

Such parallels between Yanukovych and Trump are being drawn not only because of their common association with Paul Manafort, adviser to the first, campaign chairman for the second, but also because Russian experts and politicians consider both of them to be openly pro-Kremlin.

Tightly controlled Russian state-television programs constantly reiterate that Trump doesn't care about Ukraine and gave Putin no reasons to even contemplate concessions in the run-up to the recent Normandy Four summit in Paris.

State-television news shows use every opportunity to demoralize the Ukrainians with a set of talking points based on the U.S. president's distaste for their beleaguered country. The host of *Who's Against* on Rossiya-1, Dmitry Kulikov, along with pro-Kremlin guests, took repeated jabs at the Ukrainian panelist, boasting about the meeting between Trump and Lavrov.

"There are no disagreements or contradictions between Trump and Russia," argued Valery Korovin, director of the Center for Geopolitical Expertise, appearing on the state-television channel Rossiya-24. Korovin insisted that the Democrats in Congress are the main antagonists in the relationship between Russia and the United States.

Dmitry Kiselyov, the host of the Sunday news show *Vesti Nedeli*, accused the Democrats of joining forces with Hollywood, carrying out various conspiracies in order to undermine Trump's popularity. Reporting for *Vesti Nedeli* from Washington, Mikhail

Antonov used the term "the Cold War," a fraught rhetorical twist to describe the clash between Trump and the Democratic majority in the House of Representatives.

Appearing on *Sunday Evening With Vladimir Solovyov*, Mikhail Gusman noted: "The scariest part of our relationship with America is that the level of trust between our countries, our governments, our political powers, is precisely at zero."

"But not between the presidents," chimed in the host.

Rudy Giuliani, acting as the president's personal attorney and determined to divert attention from Trump's impeachment to former Vice President Biden's alleged corruption, recently embarked on an "evidence-gathering" trip to Ukraine.

Shortly after Giuliani's return to the United States, Russian state television started airing video clips of his OAN (One America News Network) "documentary." It purports to prove Kyiv's meddling in U.S. elections and accuses former Ambassador Marie Yovanovitch of "lying under oath in Congress to whitewash [Joe] Biden's corruption." Giuliani's efforts on behalf of President Trump are bound to pay propaganda dividends for the Kremlin.

Putin has expressed undisguised delight with the crusade led by Trump and Giuliani to whitewash Moscow's interference in the U.S. elections and pin the blame on Kyiv. Last month, the Russian president smugly remarked "Thank God no one is accusing us of interfering in the U.S. elections anymore. Now they're accusing Ukraine."

Rossiya-1 reporter Valentin Bogdanov surmised that by now the majority of American Republicans believe that Ukraine interfered in the U.S. elections, with the show airing various clips from Fox News.

The absurdity of such claims spawned by the Russian security services puts the hypocrisy of the Republicans on full display. The Kremlin, having argued for years that democracy is a sham and the West is devoid of morals and principles, can now showcase the GOP as its "Exhibit A."

Appearing on *The Evening With Vladimir Solovyov* in October, political scientist Dmitry Evstafiev argued that Trump has to destroy the Republican Party in order to secure his own long-term survival. The impeachment proceedings seemed to expedite the process, with the GOP's self-immolation for the sake of its "Dear Leader."

Prompted by the head-spinning swerve of the Republicans, Tucker Carlson of Fox News even argued that, in the Ukrainian conflict, the U.S. should be taking the side of Russia. Kremlin-controlled Russian state media doesn't suffer from a similar lack of clarity.

Appearing on Solovyov's show, Semyon Bagdasarov, director of the Moscow-based Center for Middle Eastern and Central Asian Studies, exclaimed: "The United States is the enemy. It is our enemy. It is a hostile state that aims to destroy our country... We are at war!"

Did Russian Prime Minister Medvedev Drop a Grim Hint About Putin's Latest Power Grab?

Reading from Chekhov's "A Night in the Cemetery" on national television Tuesday, Dmitry Medvedev foreshadowed the upheaval to come with his government's resignation on Wednesday.

Originally published by *The Daily Beast* on January 16, 2020

At a celebration of the Russian Orthodox New Year on Tuesday, Prime Minister Dmitry Medvedev chose a grim message, the sarcasm of which left his audience on edge. But then, Medvedev probably knew what Wednesday would bring—the resignation of his entire government—and the audience did not.

On national television, the prime minister read at length from Anton Chekhov's story "A Night in the Cemetery," which suggests with ironic wit that celebrating the coming of the New Year is a foolish pursuit, unworthy of a properly functioning mind, since "every coming year is as bad as the previous one," and the newest year is bound to be even worse. Instead of celebrating the New Year, Chekhov wrote—and Medvedev read—one should suffer, cry and attempt suicide. Every new year brings you closer to death, makes you poorer, your bald spots larger and your wife older, he said.

Medvedev's sour greetings brought on some awkward laughs and sparse applause from confused Russian bureaucrats in the studio audience, most of whom remained stone-faced. The prime minister seemed nervous and almost dropped his papers at the end of the speech.

Then Wednesday dawned, and Russian President Vladimir Putin in his annual state of the nation address proposed a constitutional overhaul. It supposedly is designed to boost the powers of parliament and the cabinet, but more likely is intended to give

Putin, 67, a firm grip on the country for many more years, even decades, to come.

A few hours later, Medvedev submitted his resignation, and his entire cabinet submitted theirs as well. And while some of them may stay on, Medvedev, who once served a term as Putin's placeholder president, will move to a previously nonexistent post.

Putin offered the prime minister slot to Mikhail Mishustin, the head of the Russian Tax Service, who has been described as "the taxman of the future," digitally acquiring receipts of every transaction in Russia within 90 seconds.

It's unclear whether Mishustin will be a placeholder technocrat or assume other responsibilities currently known only to Putin. But in his annual address, Putin articulated the need to identify any persons with current or former double citizenships and foreign holdings, eliminating them from government service.

Mishustin might become instrumental in such a reshuffling of Russia's power elites, who are perceived to be unpatriotic by maintaining residences or bank accounts abroad. The added pressure will also give Putin further leverage over them.

In the past, Putin and Medvedev have choreographed moves that allowed Putin to remain in charge under different titles, swapping places to circumvent term limits.

This time around, Medvedev will assume a newly created position as the Deputy Chairman of the Security Council and all current ministers will remain in an acting capacity until a new government is appointed.

Meanwhile, the leader of Chechnya in Russia's volatile North Caucasus region, Ramzan Kadyrov has declared himself to be "temporarily incapacitated," relegating his duties to the current prime minister of Chechnya, Muslim Khuchiyev.

Putin's sweeping changes are widely interpreted as designed to weaken his successor, reshaping Russia's power structure in order to create additional opportunities for Putin's continued control over the government, even after the conclusion of his fourth presidential term in 2024.

Putin proposed amending the Russian constitution to expand the powers of the legislative branch and investing additional powers in the State Council, leading to speculation Putin is contemplating his future return at the helm of a newly empowered Parliament, after the expiration of his current presidential term.

Commentary on the Russian president's likely intention to carve out a new position for himself has been skillfully avoided by the Russian state media. Instead, Kremlin-controlled news outlets chose to focus on promised subsidies for families with young children, designed to address Russia's demographic crisis by boosting the birth rate, and the general claim that Putin has, as it were, made Russia great again.

On the Russian state television show, *The Evening With Vladimir Solovyov*, the host proclaimed, "The greatness of the country is indisputably tied to the name of Putin." Solovyov argued that the Russian president "restored respect" towards their country globally.

His take was echoed by the State Duma Deputy Chair Irina Yarovaya, who pontificated that Putin, having achieved his foreign policy and national security objectives, could now move on to his domestic agenda.

Yarovaya said, "We remember statements by [U.S. President Barack Obama] in 2014—very recently—that Russia is a regional power of minor importance. We remember all of that. We remember how the sanctions started. We remember how we weren't invited to the G8. And today there is a line of world leaders waiting just to talk to our president over the phone…"

The sanctions started and Russia was disinvited after it seized and annexed the Ukrainian peninsula of Crimea in 2014, then incited and abetted a separatist war in Ukraine's east. They were intensified after Russia's flagrant interference in the 2016 U.S. presidential elections.

Russian state media also highlight Putin's promises of socioeconomic largesse and his prediction that "Russia's economy will grow faster than the global average in 2021." During the last decade, the Russian leader has promised in vain that Russia will become the world's fifth largest economy by 2024. It is currently ranked as the 11th largest economy in the world, with a smaller GDP than that of California.

President Putin's current growth prediction is much more modest. It's still not realistic, but such promises had to be made as Russia's declining standards of living have led to political unrest and mass protests.

Without providing any direct answers as to his own plans, the Russian leader—who has now been in power for 20 years—created new venues for his continued reign in yet-to-be-revealed future capacities.

Amid all the uncertainties, maybe it shouldn't surprise us that Medvedev was reading Chekhov's story about a blind drunk civil servant who stumbles out of a New Year's celebration only to get lost in a graveyard—and then discovers in the morning he was somewhere else entirely.

This Is the Real Goal of Putin's Propaganda Machine

The Kremlin's minions may seem to push Bernie Sanders, Tulsi Gabbard—and Trump. But the bigger goal is to destroy faith in the whole electoral system.

Originally published by *The Daily Beast* on March 10, 2020

In Russia and abroad, the Kremlin's state media are waging info-warfare designed to undermine former Vice President Joe Biden while boosting Senator Bernie Sanders—and Rep. Tulsi Gabbard.

But Donald Trump is the intended beneficiary of the Kremlin campaign, and the ultimate goal is not to elect Sanders, much less Gabbard, despite militant messaging on their behalf. It's to discredit the democratic process as a whole. And that's where the English-language Russian state media take the lead.

For example, RT (formerly Russia Today) praised Gabbard (D-HI) for staying in the race—while demeaning Sen. Elizabeth Warren (D-MA) for sticking around in spite of low ratings—and described the whole electoral process as "a rigged game."

One of RT's offshoots, *In The Now*, claimed: "This nomination is getting stolen from Sanders, we are witnessing a robbery… Everything has already been done to make sure Sanders doesn't have enough delegates."

Describing all of the presidential candidates—except for Sanders—as "puppets," and the electoral process as the "smoke and mirrors show," *In The Now* host Anissa Naouai mocked Biden, razed Mike Bloomberg, blamed Warren for staying in the race too long to "keep delegates from Sanders… in a coordinated attempt to keep Sanders out." Naouai also proceeded to admit that she voted for Bernie Sanders, even though she doesn't think that he can win, essentially encouraging other American voters to do the same.

Russian state media specialize in rage-inducing coverage of the U.S. elections, aiming to prompt Americans to vote for the unlikely contender out of sheer spite at "the establishment," or to discourage people from voting at all.

While the methods utilized by the Kremlin's operatives have been somewhat modified since the 2016 elections, the aspirations remain the same. The main objectives include undermining public faith in the U.S. democratic process, stoking divisions, promoting unrest, and lobbying for the re-election of Donald J. Trump, whose presidency continues to be considered highly beneficial for the Kremlin.

A bipartisan report released by the U.S. Senate Intelligence Committee in 2019 found that in 2016 a Russian troll farm known as the Internet Research Agency (IRA) urged voters not to vote for Hillary Clinton, not to vote at all, or to instead vote for the Green Party's Jill Stein.

Jill Stein's 2016 campaign was heavily promoted by RT. One year earlier, she attended the dinner celebrating RT's 10th anniversary and was seated at the table with President Vladimir Putin.

In 2020, pro-Kremlin actors urge voters not to vote for Biden, not to vote at all, or to vote for Sanders. Curiously — but perhaps unsurprisingly — Jill Stein is rallying against Biden's nomination.

Pro-Kremlin media are not as dedicated as they were in 2016 to creating their own agitprop. Instead, they more frequently amplify select talking points by publicizing handpicked social media content and useful statements made by various analysts, writers and politicians, including President Trump.

Russian state media have been merciless when it comes to almost all of the U.S. presidential candidates, except for Trump, Sanders and Gabbard.

Tapping into Sanders' appeal with Hispanic voters, RT's Spanish-language outlets are targeting one of this key demographic with reports designed to boost his popularity, peppered with allegations of "rigged" U.S. elections standing in the way of his candidacy. The following is a small sampling of Russian state media talking points and conspiracy theories amid the ongoing flood of propaganda that is likely to intensify in the run-up to the U.S. presidential election in November:

Stay home, voting is pointless:

- RT: "Bernie or Biden—doesn't matter. Trump's election wasn't a glitch and the trends say he'll beat the Dems again... I didn't bother staying up late for Super Tuesday... The results really were a matter of indifference. Rather than being a glitch, Trump is actually a 'normal' president (if we ignore his orange colour)—so the usual rules and trends apply... Trump isn't unbeatable; only that, for him to be beaten, something out of the ordinary must happen."
- RT: "Do the Democrats really think they can beat Trump with this rogues' gallery of political hacks? If they aren't too young and inexperienced, like the ex mayor of South Bend, then they are too old and feeble-minded, like the lead candidate who just declared he was running for the US Senate. If they aren't a bald-faced liar, like a certain fake native American, they are a brutally honest socialist who freely admits he will confiscate your hard-earned earnings once elected."
- RT: "The DNC knows this presidential race is lost."

No one to vote for on the Democratic side:

- Sputnik: "Old Commie, Dementia Patient Walk Into Convention."

Elections are rigged:

- RT: "American politics is a Ponzi scheme..."
- Sputnik: "Trump Accuses Democrat Elites of 'Rigging' Primary Race Against Sanders."
- RT: "Fake JoeMentum: US media & Democrats are forcing a new pro-Biden narrative."
- RT: "Warren & Bloomberg lost big on Democrats' Super Tuesday—or did they? Supporters of Bernie Sanders have accused Warren of staying in the race as a 'spoiler,' to split

the progressive vote and harm Sanders in the race against the establishment favorite Joe Biden... If so, it would appear Warren succeeded, rather than failed, in her appointed task on Super Tuesday.
- RT: "Last woman standing. Tulsi Gabbard plays a rigged game."

Establishment conspires to control the outcome:

- RT: "Obama's 'hidden hand' in Biden's surge tells us all we need to know about what kind of president he'll be... Sanders might actually defeat Trump, claim the presidency and enact some of the policies that might seriously gut the US billion-dollar war machine... rejecting Sanders for a racist war-hawk like Biden makes little sense."
- RT: "Establishment Joe-mentum: Biden racks up Super Tuesday wins as party lines up behind him."
- Sputnik: "The Biden Bet: How Could Hillary Clinton Claw Her Way to the Presidency?"
- Sputnik: "Having served two presidential terms, Obama is not allowed to run again, but he could send in his wife Michelle... perhaps the DNC and Obama's real objective is for Michelle Obama to enter the 2020 race so Obama may once again gain control."
- RT: "Obama's national security and spying apparatus is only the latest section of the Democratic party establishment to line up behind Biden."
- RT in Spanish: "Sanders: Establishment strikes back... Javier Rodríguez Carrasco wonders if these results are decisive and if there is an orchestrated campaign within the Democratic Party to remove Sanders from the electoral race."
- RT: "What really matters [for the Democratic party] is not beating Trump, it's ensuring that the rich stay rich and the rest of us suffer."
- RT: "Trump serves the class interests of the Democratic establishment way more than Bernie Sanders ever could... They're fine with another Trump presidency... They don't

actually do anything. They are more threatened by Bernie Sanders than they are by Donald Trump. They're happy, they're perfectly fine with another Trump presidency."
- RT: "There is collusion between the DNC and the media."
- RT: "Pete Buttigieg was a manufactured candidate... dropping out in coordination with the Democratic party to help Joe Biden, same with Amy Klobuchar, and you also have Elizabeth Warren staying in the race in order to try to obstruct Sanders as a spoiler."

Biden's mental fitness is in question:

- RT: "The cantankerous and erratic candidate...mistakes, poor judgment...The septuagenarian has issued a string of insults and exhibited episodic aggression, erupting at the slightest challenges."
- Sputnik: "Joe Biden's once-moribund presidential bid came back from the dead in the past week, but there has also been an increasingly growing flow of questions regarding his mental health...cognitive decline... He appears to be suffering from brain damage... anticipate his complete mental collapse."
- RT: "The political lifer seems to be cognitively unraveling before the American public's eyes."
- RT: "Joe Biden, 77, a man who appears to be exhibiting all the trademark signs of senility."
- Sputnik: "Watch: A Proud 'Obiden Bama Democrat' Joe Biden Says 'We Can Only Re-Elect Trump': Joe Biden's never-ending flow of verbal gaffes is taking increasingly blatant forms and drawing more and more attention to his cognitive abilities."
- RT: "Trump really looks super presidential against Joe Biden... Donald Trump is the greatest president of my lifetime, and if anybody thinks that any of these democratic clowns—any of them—could have done 10 percent of what he's done for this country and the world, it's a delusion. The Democratic Party is dead. Moribund. Through. Pipe dream. Forget it. It's over. You have nothing."

Trump's corruption is a "hoax," Biden must be investigated:

- RT: "Will the pretense for the impeachment of President Trump, the elephant in the House hearings and Senate trial, ever get an actual hearing? Will the dealings of Biden's son Hunter with the Ukrainian energy giant Burisma, and the former VP's possible role in the arrangement, ever get addressed in the establishment media?"

Unrest, retaliation:

- Sputnik: "Bernie's Supporters Will Unleash Hell on DNC if It Deprives Him of Nomination Again: it's unlikely that Bernie's supporters "will tolerate this and go quietly" like they did in 2016... We could see a shakeup in the Democratic Party in the event they use the same machinations to deny Sanders the nomination, even a potential split of the party or a third party run by Sanders."
- Sputnik: "The vocal and energetic Sanders supporters... would either sit out or vote for Trump in protest of another Bernie loss."

One lesson from all this: In 2020, Americans should be well aware that by spreading divisive rhetoric, exacerbating internal divisions, and disseminating conspiracy theories they are helping Russia and not their chosen candidate.

Russia is highly proficient at harnessing the power of social media and audiovisual communications. RT seemed less than pleased with Twitter's decision to add a "manipulated" tag to a video retweeted by President Donald Trump and shared by his social media director Dan Scavino. The video was deceptively cropped, creating a false appearance that Biden had endorsed President Trump. It was also featured by RT's sister outlet, Sputnik.

RT's senior writer opined that "the entire argument that fake news or 'manipulated' social media posts swayed US elections has always been an insult to Americans' intelligence."

On the other hand, Margarita Simonyan, editor-in-chief of Rossiya Segodnya, RT and Sputnik shared her true opinion of Americans in 2017, when she said: "Their level of knowledge is lower than the baseboard... Americans have such low education and understanding of the world, so off the charts, it's way below the baseboard."

RT's main concern is clearly not with defending Americans from "insulting" labels on fake or manipulated media, but with the way such designations undermine the Kremlin's deceptive influence campaigns.

On their own turf, Russian state media pundits, experts and politicians openly admit that information warfare between the United States, the Soviet Union and subsequently Russia, has been going on for decades.

Appearing on the Russian language state TV show *The Evening With Vladimir Solovyov*, Konstantin Zatulin, a leading figure in Putin's United Russia party, said: "We waged this fight for many years, except it wasn't as technologically advanced. We had no Internet, or fast-acting Wikipedia, or the rest of it."

Another guest on the same show, Boris Yakemenko, asserted that World War III between the United States and Russia is already in progress and is playing out in the social media.

Analyst Dmitry Drobnitsky added that Russia should be proactive in fighting info-wars in the West: "If we say this is war, then using the analogies of WWII... we need to work behind enemy lines, where they least expect us." The host, Vladimir Solovyov agreed and said: "RT and Sputnik are working brilliantly."

The Kremlin enjoys the spoils of its info-wars, but fears reciprocity. Appearing on a state-run television station TVC, RT's Simonyan said that modern information warfare is no less important than nuclear weapons. She complained that the most watched TV channel in Russia is YouTube, which is controlled by the Americans. Anticipating the boomerang effect of Russia's info-wars abroad, Simonyan exclaimed: "They'll blow us up from within." After all, that's what the Kremlin has in mind for America.

Can Trump's Art of the Arms Deal Get More Stupid?
The Russians Are Loving It

Now that Trump reportedly is toying with a resumption of nuclear testing, the Kremlin intends to take full advantage.

Originally published by *The Daily Beast* on May 23, 2020

President Donald J. Trump has announced the U.S. intends to exit the "Open Skies" treaty. The 34-nation agreement allows the United States, Russia and other countries to conduct observation flights over each other's territories in the interests of transparency and international security.

Speaking to reporters, Trump said: "We're going to pull out, and they're going to come back and want to make a deal. We've had a very good relationship lately with Russia."

While the Trump administration is citing Russia's various violations of the agreement as the main reason for the U.S. withdrawal, Russian experts and government officials believe that the abrupt decision is rooted in Trump's desire to throw all international treaties out the window in pursuit of a bigger, better deal which he can claim to pursue during his election campaign even if it comes to nothing.

Such flippant methods may work for reality television, but tend to backfire in real life. Case in point, Trump's gambit with Iran, where U.S withdrawal from the nuclear deal led to the expansion of Tehran's nuclear stockpile.

Now that Trump reportedly is toying with the idea of resuming nuclear testing as well, the Kremlin intends to take full advantage of that harebrained idea.

Washington's approach reportedly is rooted in the flawed assumption that renewed nuclear testing would prompt the Kremlin to pressure the Chinese into joining a trilateral agreement with the United States and Russia.

This concept was dismissed out of hand by Russia's Deputy Foreign Minister Sergei Ryabkov. During an online forum conducted by the Gorchakov Fund, a Russian think tank, Ryabkov asserted that the Kremlin didn't intend to apply any pressure to China to please Washington.

Instead of playing along with Trump's dangerous brinkmanship, Russia may pull out of the Comprehensive Nuclear-Test-Ban Treaty altogether. Alexei Fenenko, an associate professor of global politics at Moscow State University, told the state media outlet RIA Novosti that such a withdrawal would be "beneficial for Russia, since the collapse of this treaty would cause colossal damage to the United States of America." State media outlet Vesti surmised that such a move would obliterate all of Washington's efforts and decades-long investments in the nuclear ban treaty.

As for the planned U.S. withdrawal from the Open Skies treaty, Secretary of State Mike Pompeo clarified that it is set to take place six months from now, on November 22, 2020, after the next presidential election in the United States.

In Russia, Trump's commentary and the timing of the intended withdrawal from Open Skies were interpreted as a sign that the move is merely political, with no tangible repercussions for the Kremlin. Russia's Deputy Foreign Minister Sergei Ryabkov mentioned that the Kremlin's exchanges with Washington were taking place via the traditional and non-traditional channels, but described the Trump administration's demands and ultimatums as "senseless" and "categorically unacceptable."

Russian state-owned radio station Vesti FM described Trump's dangerous flailing on the international arena as his desire "to play with toy soldiers."

The Kremlin's state media have grown used to laughing at Trump's irrational bluster. Appearing on the state TV show *60 Minutes* earlier this week, Elena Malinnikova, an infectious disease specialist for the Russian Health Ministry, said that Trump must really be taking the regimen of hydroxychloroquine, since it's known to cause psychotic side effects.

Trump recently sought to improve relations with Russia with a donation of U.S. taxpayer-funded ventilators, despite Moscow's claim that it already has more ventilators per capita than the United States.

In fact, Russian state media reported that the country is so flush with ventilators, it plans to start exporting them to other countries by July. Instead of eliciting gratitude, Trump's gift to the Kremlin only prompted more mockery.

The Kremlin is waiting for the November election, hoping it's guy Trump will win, and looking at the administration's announced policies through that lens.

Appearing on the state TV show *60 Minutes* on Friday, Oleg Nilov, member of the State Duma of the Russian Federation, said: "After the [U.S.] elections, the new political chapter will emerge in the United States of America. A lot of things will surface." He dubbed the Open Skies announcement a "pre-electoral move," and, referring to the U.S. president's remarks about good relations, joked that Trump thinks, "Everything is fine in relations with Russia, we [the U.S.] trust them completely and therefore, they don't need to be monitored."

Nilov's commentary prompted the experts and the host of *60 Minutes*, Olga Skabeeva, to chuckle. The possibility of genuine trust between the United States and Russia sounded too far-fetched to be taken with any degree of seriousness.

Skabeeva asked military expert Ivan Konovalov whether the U.S. withdrawal from the Open Skies treaty would hamper Russia's ability "to uncover important information about the Americans." Konovalov assured her that regardless of the treaty, Russia can continue to obtain the same data by utilizing its space operations.

Last year, the Defense Intelligence Agency noted that both China and Russia "have developed robust and capable space services, including space-based intelligence, surveillance, and reconnaissance."

The signatories of the Open Skies treaty include most of America's NATO allies — and Ukraine. Konovalov explained that the termination of the treaty wouldn't impact Russia, while at the same time it would harm NATO, Europe, and especially those countries on Russia's borders: the Baltic States and Ukraine. "They are losing much more," he said. "Ukraine participated in these flights since 2014. In spite of all of our disagreements and confrontations, Ukrainian officers and inspectors were allowed to enter our airspace along with Americans." America's allies "are losing because of this, the Europeans are losing."

Political scientist Vladimir Kornilov pointed out: "Trump is convinced this is a bilateral agreement, he isn't even thinking about other countries involved. It's funny."

Sergei Ryabkov, Russia's Deputy Foreign Minister, noted that the U.S. announcement about its intended withdrawal from the Open Skies Treaty came as a surprise to America's allies. He accused the Trump administration of lying about its reasoning for withdrawing from the treaty and added: "The United States is sowing discord and uncertainty among its allies... They are ignoring the opinion of NATO and other nations that are party to this agreement."

France, Germany, Belgium, Spain, Finland, Italy, Luxembourg, the Netherlands, the Czech Republic and Sweden jointly said they "regret" Trump's decision to withdraw from the Open Skies Treaty, calling on Russia to return to compliance with the agreement.

NATO Secretary-General Jens Stoltenberg, trying to smooth things over within the alliance, cited Russia's violations of the treaty, including "flight limitations over Kaliningrad, and restricting flights in Russia near its border with Georgia" and expressed hope that the agreement could be preserved if the Kremlin returns to compliance.

European Union foreign policy chief Josep Borrell said, "Withdrawing from a treaty is not the solution," adding that the EU "will be examining the implications this decision may have for its own security." The European Union on Friday urged the United States to reconsider its plan to pull out of the Open Skies Treaty.

As the Trump administration casts aside the concerns of the Europeans, the Kremlin intends to amplify "the lack of solidarity" exhibited by the United States towards its allies.

Russian Deputy Foreign Minister Alexander Grushko told the state media outlet TASS: "This move will not only worsen the situation with strategic stability and military security in Europe, but apparently it will also harm the interests of U.S. allies that are parties to this European agreement."

Trump's ability to sow that kind of discord among NATO allies is unquestionably appetizing to the Kremlin. Earlier this week, experts on the Russian state TV show *The Evening With Vladimir Solovyov* discussed Russia's preference for Trump's re-election, as opposed to the candidacy of former Vice President Joe Biden.

Andrey Bezrukov, retired intelligence service colonel who serves as an advisor to the president of Rosneft (the Russian state-owned oil company), and a member of the Presidium of the Council on Foreign and Defense Policy, explained: "I am often asked: 'Why is Trump better than, for example, Biden or Clinton?' The answer is simple. Because Biden or Clinton would act in support of [international] coalitions. It's the gathering of all forces against us into one group, one team. When Trump came, he destroyed that team."

So, from the Kremlin's point of view—in spite of Trump's mind-numbing arrogance and incompetence—his actions ultimately boost Russia's interests. In light of Trump's successes undermining transatlantic unity, the Kremlin has to be unquestionably rattled by the possibility he might lose the election in 2020.

Anatoly Torkunov, a member of the Russian Academy of Sciences and the Collegium of the Ministry of Foreign Affairs of the Russian Federation, offered fairly cogent analysis: "Even though the world system is less and less dependent on the United States and the results of their elections, we continue to carefully analyze the situation. At the beginning of the year there was more certainty. According to our experts, Andrey Bezrukov and Ivan Safranchuk, the outcome of the elections depended on two variables: the economic situation in the United States and the ability of the Democratic Party to mobilize its political base. Given that the economic situation was favorable and the Democrats could not recover from internal conflicts, the chances of the incumbent president to maintain his post were pretty high."

"The pandemic caused things to change," said Torkunov. "On the one hand, the United States is facing serious economic difficulties. On the other hand, the Democrats, at least the establishment of the party, rallied around their candidate, Joseph Biden. This reduces Trump's chances."

The Kremlin's apparent concern that its preferred candidate might lose in November explains the avalanche of anti-Biden coverage on Russia's English-language outlets, RT and Sputnik.

Kremlin-funded media are latching on to every distraction spawned by Trump's re-election campaign: Obamagate, Huntergate, Flynngate and whatever else may follow. The goal of undermining the American democracy continues to guide the Kremlin's actions and Trump's presidency still suits Putin's agenda to a "T."

'America's Dying'
Russian Media Is Giddy at Chaos in the USA

From the U.S. troop drawdown in Germany to Trump's refusal to slam Russia over soldier bounties, Russian state media is jubilant over America acting in the Kremlin's interests.

Originally published by *The Daily Beast* on July 30, 2020

This week, U.S. President Donald Trump reiterated his intent to move forward with reducing the U.S. military presence in Germany, without any consultations with Berlin. And even as members of the U.S. Congress and America's allies abroad expressed concerns about the drawdown, the Trump administration's decision brought joy to the Kremlin and Russian media.

Back in June, 22 Republican members of the House Armed Services Committee urged Trump not to go ahead with the move, stating in a letter: "We believe that such steps would significantly damage U.S. national security as well as strengthen the position of Russia to our detriment ... In Europe, the threats posed by Russia have not lessened, and we believe that signs of a weakened U.S. commitment to NATO will encourage further Russian aggression and opportunism."

German officials have called the move politically motivated. While Trump claimed that the drawdown was based on Germany not meeting the NATO target of spending 2 percent of its GDP on defense, Belgium and Italy—the two countries that will be receiving some of the U.S. troops from Germany—spend an even a smaller percentage on defense. The move will cost billions of dollars to the American taxpayers and undermine NATO alliances.

Meanwhile, when the intent to reduce the U.S. contingent in Germany was first announced, Russian Foreign Ministry spokeswoman Maria Zakharova said that the Kremlin "would welcome any steps by Washington to scale down its military presence in Europe," brazenly telling the United States to take home not only its troops, but also its tactical nuclear weapons.

The Kremlin-controlled Russian state media also sensed a precious propaganda opportunity. Sergey Brilyov, anchor of the news show Saturday Vesti on Russian state media channel Rossiya-1, pondered whether the controversial move by the Trump administration could be considered the proof that Russia no longer poses a military threat to Europe.

Kremlin spokesperson Dmitry Peskov used the same rationale today, when he claimed that Russia doesn't present any threat to European countries and "the fewer U.S. soldiers are on the European continent, the calmer it is in Europe." Russian Envoy in Vienna Mikhail Ulyanov speculated that the withdrawal of part of the U.S. contingent from Germany won't impact the country's security and Berlin is likely to even "benefit" from this move.

Unsurprisingly, Germany doesn't see it that way. Norbert Roettgen, the head of the Bundestag's Foreign Affairs Committee, warned on Twitter, "In withdrawing 12,000 soldiers from Germany, the USA achieve[s] the exact opposite from what [Defense Secretary] Mark Esper outlined. Instead of strengthening NATO it is going to weaken the alliance. The US' military clout will not increase, but decrease in relation to Russia and the Near and Middle East."

The troop withdrawal is just the latest piece of good news for Russia in its relations with the Trump administration.

When news broke of Russian bounties placed on the heads of American soldiers, followed by revelations that Russia and China have been hacking Western coronavirus research, it seemed that the die was cast and the sanctions against the Kremlin were all but inevitable. A chorus of experts on Russian state TV unanimously warned the audiences: There will be new sanctions.

But so far, the sanctions for the hacking of the coronavirus vaccine have been imposed solely on China. Other Russian pundits and experts accurately predicted that—unlike the Democrats—Trump and the GOP would single out not Russia but China as America's top adversary.

Therefore, instead of a stern rebuke, Russian President Vladimir Putin enjoyed a friendly phone conversation with Trump.

During their phone call, Trump didn't raise the issue of Russian bounties on American armed forces in Afghanistan, nor did he admonish Putin for Russia's hacking of the coronavirus vaccine research. Likewise, Trump didn't question the Russian president about his country's ongoing interference in U.S. elections and domestic affairs.

Instead of confronting Putin, Trump lashed out at Democratic Congressman Jerry Nadler (D-NY) about domestic antifascist group antifa, tweeting in part, "Jerry, blame it on Russia, Russia, Russia!" The unfunny punchline reaffirmed that Russian wrongdoing would continue to be swept under the carpet by the Trump administration — a signal that was enthusiastically received in Moscow.

"Trump is still ours," concluded Russian International Affairs Council expert Alexey Naumov. "Whew," theatrically exhaled the host of a state media news talk show *60 Minutes*, Olga Skabeeva.

"Trump is ours" is a familiar refrain in Russian state media. Its aim is twofold: mocking the inquiry into the Kremlin's involvement in the U.S. elections, while simultaneously emphasizing the inexplicable hold Putin seems to possess over his American counterpart. It's hardly humorous, in light of Trump's actions that consistently benefit Russia's agenda on the world stage. During the 2018 Trump-Putin press conference in Helsinki, the Russian president openly admitted that he wanted Trump to win the 2020 election.

Russian experts, pundits, and the Kremlin's bullhorns repeatedly reiterate that Trump is still the preferred figure in the upcoming presidential contest — as a "chaos candidate," dividing Americans domestically and causing international rifts within transatlantic alliances.

The weakening of the enemy is most certainly a coveted opportunity for Russia — and there is no doubt that the United States is seen as such by the Kremlin. Discussing the United States on Russia's state TV program *60 Minutes* last week, Alexei Kondratiev, member of the Federation Council on the Russian Federation's

Defense and Security Committee, emphasized, "They are our enemies, 100 percent."

During the same show, expert Alexey Naumov claimed that the world is witnessing the U.S. "in its death throes," as America's greatness and its global standing is in steep decline. "America is dying," announced host Olga Skabeeva.

Margarita Simonyan, the head of the state-funded TV channel RT, formerly known as Russia Today, was similarly blunt in her assessment. She told Komsomolskaya Pravda — a daily Russian tabloid newspaper — that America's complete disintegration would be highly beneficial for Russia.

Simonyan speculated that internal chaos would force the United States to focus on its own survival, allowing Russia and other countries to pursue their global aims unimpeded: "In order for them to leave us alone, it is necessary that they be terribly busy with their own internal problems." This perception falls in line with recent revelations that Russian intelligence services are using English-language websites to spread disinformation — undoubtedly, just a tiny snowflake on the tip of Russia's anti-Western disinformation iceberg. In the run up to the U.S. presidential elections, these efforts can be expected to intensify.

As for the weakening of NATO, Trump is essentially fulfilling Putin's wishes by ordering the drawdown of U.S. armed forces from Germany. The Kremlin is sure to exploit the fault lines in transatlantic relations between Western allies and widen the cracks at every opportunity, aided by the divisive actions of the Kremlin's unlikely comrade at the White House.

Russian Media Is Rooting for Civil War in America
'The Worse, the Better'

Originally published by *The Daily Beast* on September 16, 2020

There is no shortage of local topics that interest the Kremlin—from the poisoning of an inconvenient dissident to the events in neighboring Belarus and the ongoing battle against the coronavirus. In the thick of it all, America remains front and center of the Russian state media's steely focus. In Putin's Russia, U.S. President Donald J. Trump's rallies, events and press comments are viewed and reported with maniacal obsession.

Russian state media happily poked fun at the Trump campaign's use of a stock photo of Russian-made fighter jets, but aside from an occasional jab, Moscow's coverage of the Trump presidency closely resembles that of Fox News. State-controlled media's slant is a telling indicator of the Kremlin's leanings. To imagine the relationship between Russian President Vladimir Putin and his massive media apparatus, one may reference the coziness between Sean Hannity and Trump—and magnify that intensity tenfold, with directives flowing only from the top down. Obsessed with retaining his dominance and fully realizing the power of propaganda, Putin leaves nothing to chance.

Russian lawmakers, state media experts and pundits on tightly choreographed TV shows openly reveal that the Kremlin is still rooting for Trump. But Moscow has a growing concern that this time around, their preferred candidate might lose. Appearing on a state TV show *The Right To Know*, Margarita Simonyan, the editor-in-chief of the Kremlin-funded propaganda networks RT and Sputnik, said about Trump's chances of re-election: "I think Trump will lose, but then I think there will be a major blow-up from the standpoint of accepting or not accepting the outcome of the election. They'll be battling over that for a long time, who knows how it might end."

Having openly wished for Trump to drive the United States into civil war, Russian state media figures are now relishing that idea with renewed enthusiasm. They believe it would destabilize America to such an extent as to undermine its very sovereignty, thereby untying the Kremlin's hands to wreak even more havoc upon the Western world.

Appearing on Russia's state TV show *The Evening With Vladimir Solovyov*, analyst Dmitry Drobnitsky explained his belief that U.S. elections "can be considered America's internal affairs only up to the point when an actual civil war starts there." The idea of a coup d'état seems all but inevitable, Drobnitsky argued: "The loser in this election would be an idiot to accept the outcome."

Russian state media repeatedly echoed Trump, who is doing the Kremlin's bidding by attacking the legitimacy of the 2020 elections, falsely suggesting that mail-in voting is completely fraudulent, and that Democrats are rigging the process to falsify the outcome. There is no doubt that the Kremlin would align with Trump in case of a contested election, as the groundwork for accusing the Democrats of fraud has been laid in advance.

Russian state media analysts also make no secret as to the Kremlin's preferred candidate. Writing for the newspaper Kommersant, Dmitry Kosyrev, political columnist for state media outlet RIA Novosti, pondered: "Is Trump ours?"

This popular refrain can be interpreted in one of several ways: to signify Russia's hold over the American president, to express that Trump's position is in perfect alignment with that of the Kremlin—meaning, "he is on our side"—or to signal Russia's preference: "He is the one we choose." Kosyrev concluded that in the anticipated civil war in the United States, "it is better to remain neutral, but if we had to choose, then Trump is certainly ours."

There is a unanimous consensus among the pro-Kremlin analysts, all of whom uniformly reject the potential presidency of former Vice President Joe Biden. Analyst Mikhail Taratuta told Moskovsky Komsomolets, a Moscow-based daily newspaper, that Trump's re-election "would open a new window of possibilities" for Russia, as opposed to Biden's presidency, which would constitute "a serious situation" with "no chance of improved relations."

Russia's Federal News Agency (FAN), underwritten by "Putin's chef" Yevgeny Prigozhin, exclaimed: "Experts predict civil war in the United States following the presidential election." A political scientist specializing in America, Rafael Ordukhanyan, told FAN that "The USA has become a land of idiots," and predicted: "There will be civil war." He added: "We prefer Trump... he has an affinity for our president." Ordukhanyan recommended that Russia intensify its info-wars against the United States, in order "to showcase America's impotence on a global stage."

Broadcaster Vladimir Pozner surmised that the United States is on the verge of a civil war and added that in the past, America was loved, hated, or feared, but now it is merely pitied. He attributed the crisis to the words and actions of President Trump, who "lies with every breath." RIA Novosti ridiculed the idea of potentially awarding a Nobel prize to the president who is provoking civil war in his own country.

While some Trump administration officials urge the president's supporters to load up on ammunition and the president personally spreads fears of a potentially rigged election, the Kremlin's networks follow through with matching rhetoric in multiple languages. Moscow's state media outlets at home and abroad anticipate November mayhem in America, with the expectation that Trump and his supporters would eventually gain the upper hand. Russian analysts argue that facing electoral defeat, Trump will use his executive powers to mobilize troops into the streets, while pro-Trump militias will take matters into their own hands.

During his eponymous evening show, TV host Vladimir Solovyov described Trump's followers as "wealthier than BLM [Black Lives Matter]," "much better armed," "extremely aggressive and very active." Solovyov argued that facing the prospect of Trump losing the election, his armed supporters would head into battle to secure the White House for the benefit of the incumbent. A long and bloody conflict would inevitably follow, shattering America's stability and world standing — which would serve Moscow's interests to a T.

Discussing the upcoming November elections in the United States, Evgeny Popov, the host of state TV show *60 Minutes* said:

"There are more and more precursors of civil war." With great irritation, Popov complained that in spite of America's internal turmoil, U.S. nuclear-capable B-52 strategic bombers are still flying near Russia's borders.

Referring to Russia's anticipation of the impending civil unrest in the United States, State Duma deputy Aleksey Zhuravlyov retorted: "If things blow up like they should over there, there will be less flying."

He concluded with a simple view on events in America that is undoubtedly shared by the Kremlin: "The worse, the better."

Russian State Media Roots for Violence as America Counts Its Votes

Russian state media was thrilled over the undecided election, telling viewers to "get the popcorn ready" and hoping for American civil unrest.

Originally published by *The Daily Beast* on November 04, 2020

With tens of thousands of votes yet to be counted in the contentious U.S. presidential race, President Donald Trump falsely asserted election fraud and prematurely declared himself to be the winner Tuesday night—even though the final tally may take days to resolve, and even as Democratic candidate Joe Biden appeared to be surging on Wednesday morning. Meanwhile, the American election turmoil brought much joy to Moscow, with Russia seeing clear gains in its ongoing fight against democracy.

State Duma deputy Vyacheslav Nikonov, the grandson of the notorious Vyacheslav Molotov, predicted to the state media outlet Vesti that, regardless of the final outcome, half of American society will see the result as illegitimate. Nikonov falsely claimed that both presidential candidates claimed to have won, although the campaign of former Vice President Joe Biden made no such assertion as the votes are still being counted.

"This outcome of the elections is the worst scenario for America," Nikonov concluded. He mockingly urged the Russians to buy lots of popcorn, due to the "uncompromising divide in the well-armed American society." Russian state television started to announce upcoming TV movies by describing them as "the greatest show on earth, not counting U.S. elections."

Appearing on the Russian state media TV show *60 Minutes*, Alexei Naumov from the Russian International Affairs Council said about the American presidential elections: "The greatest political thriller of the year is upon us. Watch and enjoy. Nothing like this will ever happen again."

Russian state media has long predicted civil war and mayhem in post-election America. In the run-up to the presidential elections in the United States, the host of *60 Minutes* Evgeny Popov repeatedly asked pundits and experts, "Will there be blood?" Igor Morozov, a member of Russia's Federation Council, replied, "Yes, there will be blood. There is no way there wouldn't be."

Talking about the anticipated post-election violence between armed supporters of both candidates, Russian lawmaker Aleksei Zhuravlyov told *60 Minutes*, "What's not to like? It's excellent, if you ask me... I love it!"

Sergey Mironov, the head of Fair Russia political party and former chairman of Russia's Federation Council, argued that chaotic elections and the threat of violence in the United States demonstrate that America has lost its moral authority and can no longer claim to be the leader of the free world.

Appearing on *60 Minutes*, Igor Korotchenko, member of the Defense Ministry's public advisory council, argued that Russia should seize the opportunity to sell more arms to the countries trying to buck America's global leadership, while the United States is embroiled in an internal political battle.

While the undecided election and the possibility of post-election violence in the U.S. bring joy to the Kremlin, Russia certainly has a dog in this fight. Pro-Kremlin pundits, experts, and lawmakers are openly rooting for Trump's re-election.

Appearing on Russia's state TV show *The Evening With Vladimir Solovyov*, deputy dean of world politics at Moscow's State University, Andrey Sidorov explained, "We're certainly not indifferent as to who wins, because if Trump is re-elected, the same politics of chaos in America will continue. The United States undoubtedly will not be able to consolidate their allies... For us, Biden is the worst scenario."

Appearing on Russia's *60 Minutes* one day prior to the U.S. elections, lawmaker Leonid Kalashnikov mockingly described the electoral choice hanging in the balance between Trump as "the

Russian spy" and Biden as "the Ukrainian spy." Host Evgeny Popov played along: "We're for the Russian spy."

Kalashnikov concurred: "When something is good for you, don't search for something better. Let our guy, Trump, stay. We know and understand him well." Popov's co-host and wife Olga Skabeeva noted, "The left and the Blacks are protesting against our candidate Trump."

Putin's Russia did its best to help Trump win re-election, by disseminating the alleged sex-tape "kompromat" about Hunter Biden designed to harm Biden's candidacy. State TV hosts and pundits expressed deep frustration that, unlike in 2016, in 2020 the American media didn't fall for these disinformation tactics. Nonetheless, Trump's baseless claims of election fraud and premature declaration of his own victory spell out a hotly contested electoral process. Russian state media channel Rossiya-1 predicted a "prolonged political crisis" in the United States, which is beneficial for Moscow.

Co-host of *60 Minutes* Olga Skabeeva explained, "We're hoping that while they're dealing with their own problems, they'll have no time to impose any more Russian sanctions." Yulia Makarova, the host of a news show on the state media channel Rossiya-24, echoed the same expectation: "There is hope that after elections, the Congress will focus on internal affairs, and not on sanctions against Russia." Makarova said that the anticipated economic stimulus will weaken the U.S. dollar and echoed Bloomberg's prediction that in terms of the strengthened ruble, Russia would be the biggest beneficiary of Trump's re-election.

State media outlet RIA Novosti noted that a Biden presidency would lead to increased pressure against Russia. Channel Rossiya-24 predicted that Biden's election would increase the likelihood of new anti-Russian sanctions. On the other hand, the co-host of *60 Minutes*, Olga Skabeeva, described Trump as someone who is trying to destroy the American system—which suits the Kremlin just fine.

To help Russia's preferred candidate and discredit democratic elections, Kremlin-controlled state media outlets echoed Trump's baseless claims of election fraud.

RT editor-in-chief Margarita Simonyan even took to Twitter the day after the vote to spew the same complaints Trump has been making for weeks, if not months. "Neither free nor fair," Simonyan proclaimed, capping off a Twitter thread in which she alleged "numerous violations" and "numerous reports of corruption" without providing any specifics.

She also alleged "censorship on major media platforms," apparently in reference to social media flagging many of Trump's Election Night posts as "misleading" for his claims of a plot to "steal" the vote.

Similar efforts will undoubtedly unfold via Russia's underground disinformation channels, in anticipation of the final election results that may spell out trouble for Moscow's favored presidential contender.

Russian Media Is Angry and Desperate Over Biden Win

"What is the world coming to?"

Originally published by *The Daily Beast* on November 07, 2020

With Joe Biden declared America's newest president-elect, darkness descended over Russian state media this week. Pro-Kremlin news anchors, pundits and experts have long dreaded former Vice President Joe Biden's victory in 2020, having described it as "the worst scenario for Russia." As their nightmare became an inevitable reality, Russian state television shows were permeated with angry faces and raw emotions.

"Nothing will ever be the same... What are we witnessing? What is the world coming to? Not only this country, but the world?" mournfully asked Evgeny Popov, the host of Russian state media show *60 Minutes*. Panelists in the studio grimly outlined the bevy of consequences Biden's presidency may mean for the Kremlin.

Lawmaker Leonid Kalashnikov, who admittedly celebrated Trump's victory in 2016, said: "Unfortunately, Trump lost." Pontificating about what Biden's presidency will mean for Russia, Kalashnikov surmised: "Understandably, I have nothing to be happy about... All of us should be thinking: 'What is Russia supposed to do now?' Get ready to be disconnected from SWIFT [international banking payment system]? That Europe will line up along with their sanctions?" He warned fellow Russians about the wave of incoming consequences: "Trump lost, so it's time to get ready ... They will start fighting against us like they do in the Middle East."

Dmitry Abzalov, Director of the Center for Strategic Communications, concurred: "All of us are hostages of this situation ... Biden will come and punish everyone who acted against him."

"This whole time, we've been living with an illusion that Trump is ours," noted political scientist Ilya Graschenkov. Host Evgeny Popov corrected him: "Trump IS ours, but couldn't lift anti-Russian sanctions because of the legislation signed into law by Democrats."

Visibly irritated by the lack of deliverables from the Trump administration, combined with the surety of additional punitive measures anticipated from the incoming president, Popov exclaimed: "We spit on them both!"

Trump's presidency netted plenty of benefits for the Kremlin—from the weakening of transatlantic alliances and decline in America's global standing, to the deepening divide within the United States. But the Kremlin believed that the American president would pay off like a slot machine on a much bigger scale during his second term.

Disappointment with Trump's failure to lift the sanctions, recognize the annexation of Crimea, stop U.S. support for Ukraine and other perks eagerly anticipated by the Kremlin was threaded through the statements made by Russian lawmakers and political figures.

In his interview with radio station Echo Moskvy, politician Vladimir Zhirinovsky—who famously celebrated Trump's 2016 election by throwing a champagne party in Russia's parliament—bitterly complained: "Trump didn't do anything good for us ... In his election campaign, he promised to improve [relations], but in reality he did nothing, he didn't even come here. All U.S. presidents came to Russia and invited our president to their place in Washington, everyone except him. Donald Trump did not come to Moscow and never invited our president to Washington. Therefore, all we are left with are bad memories."

Discussing U.S. elections on *60 Minutes*, co-host Olga Skabeeva pointed out: "The last time we interfered, but not this time around." Writer Zakhar Prilepin noted that Trump should have been a better friend to Putin and Skabeeva enthusiastically agreed: "Then we would have saved him. Everything would have been fine."

While Russian experts and politicians are in mourning over Joe Biden's presidential victory, they managed to make a small amount of lemonade out of the shriveled lemons of Trump's waning presidency. Russian state media repeatedly aired Donald Trump's notoriously undemocratic press conference, wherein he baselessly trashed and undermined his own country's elections, describing the democratic process as unclean, untrustworthy and mired in fraud.

Russian propagandists amplified and embellished Trump's rabidly anti-American statements and false claims. Appearing on a radio show *Full Contact,* Margarita Simonyan, the editor-in-chief of state-funded propaganda networks, RT and Sputnik, disingenuously argued that the U.S. president's unsubstantiated claims of election fraud should be taken at face value simply because of his unprecedented access to information no one else is privy to.

Russian state media described the U.S. elections as a "bacchanalia," worse than contested elections in Africa or Belarus, and falsely accused the states of egregious "machinations and falsifications" designed to unseat Trump. The Kremlin's mouthpieces baselessly alleged that 11 million illegal immigrants, 1.5 million dead voters and an untold number of dogs—supposedly registered to vote by their owners—unlawfully voted for Biden. There is no evidence to substantiate any of these allegations, which are rivaled only by the U.S. president's bold-faced lie that he lost the race due to unproven, phantom "election fraud."

Andrey Kortunov, director general of the Russian International Affairs Council, noted in an interview with state news agency TASS on Saturday that prior to these elections, Americans never thought that their electoral system could be rigged.

Thanks to the barrage of allegations by U.S. President Donald J. Trump, that is no longer the case. Kortunov noted: "Whoever wins, the American political system has already lost. Voter confidence will have to be restored again, and what Trump is doing now—accusing the Democrats of very large-scale fraud—also undermines trust."

During Friday's broadcast of *60 Minutes,* co-host Olga Skabeeva claimed that at least half of America is now disappointed in the country's electoral system. Lawmaker Leonid Kalashnikov summed up the U.S. election debacle: "That's how you delegitimize a nation."

Discrediting the crown jewel of Western democracy has always been one of Russia's top priorities—and while he failed to come through on other fronts, Trump delivered a parting gift above and beyond the Kremlin's wildest dreams.

Russian Media Wants Moscow to Grant Asylum to Trump

Russian media and lawmakers are concerned about the future of the Kremlin's favorite U.S. president.

Originally published by *The Daily Beast* on December 09, 2020

Russian state media—a reliable barometer of the mood at the Kremlin—remains fixated on election-related events in America. Affectionately referring to Donald Trump as "our Donald," "Trumpusha" and "Comrade Trump," Russian lawmakers, experts and pundits repeatedly have expressed their concerns about the future of Moscow's all-time favorite U.S. president.

Co-host of Russian state TV news talk show *60 Minutes* Olga Skabeeva brought up the possibility that President Trump would end up seeking asylum in Russia to escape any prosecutions in the United States following the conclusion of his sole presidential term. Skabeeva emphasized that this was by no means a joking matter: "It's all very serious," she said, as she pondered out loud about the nature of criminal charges Trump might soon be facing.

Experts in the studio enthusiastically discussed the likelihood of Trump being charged with a bevy of offenses from tax evasion to fraud and sexual assault.

They concurred that Trump's presidential pardon would not help him in state cases, unlike the recently advanced constitutional amendment in Russia that secured lifetime immunity from criminal prosecution for the country's former presidents.

Russian President Vladimir Putin can relate to Trump on a very personal level—not only where it comes to a ruthless pursuit of power, but also with respect to the intense fear of accountability if that power was to ever slip away. While Putin's grip on Russia is feverishly safeguarded, Trump's fate is far from certain.

The rabidly anti-American military expert and member of the Russian Defense Ministry's Public Council, Igor Korotchenko, spoke out in Trump's defense with a passion that is drastically different from the combative rhetoric that traditionally accompanied his commentary about any other Western heads of state.

Korotchenko angrily—not to mention ludicrously—compared "poor Trump's" anticipated legal troubles to the Stalinist repressions of 1937. He argued: "Russia can offer political asylum to the persecuted former president of the United States, Donald Trump. But let him not simply arrive to Rostov or elsewhere, but also transfer his capital here and finally build his famous Trump City somewhere in our New Moscow."

State-controlled RIA Novosti opined that the looming threat of criminal prosecutions is the Democratic Party's way of "spitting at Trump on his way out."

Staunch Kremlin propagandist Dmitry Kiselyov's Sunday show *Weekly News* argued that for Trump, pardoning himself is a matter of survival. Full-throated support of the Kremlin-controlled state media is at odds with Trump's repeated mantra of being "tough on Russia."

To the contrary, in the land of Putin, there is a gnawing fear that things will get tough for Russia without Trump at the helm. Putin's refusal to congratulate President-elect Joe Biden is echoed by Russian lawmakers on state TV shows.

They believe that Trump will continue to unleash dirty tricks out of the Pandora's box of his shameless determination to stay in office even after being voted out.

Notorious politician Vladimir Zhirinovsky, who previously suggested that Putin should milk Trump like a cow before he is forced to leave office, enumerated actions he hoped Trump would undertake prior to his departure: recognize Russia's annexation of Crimea, leave NATO, withdraw U.S. troops from every place they're stationed worldwide, arrest disloyal U.S. state governors, refuse to recognize the outcome of the elections, force all states to conduct mandatory recounts, and induce Attorney General Bill Barr to pursue any actions that would benefit Trump.

"Trump is your creation," grimly noted the host of *60 Minutes*, Evgeny Popov, referring to Zhirinovsky's champagne-soaked celebration of Trump's 2016 election victory in Russia's parliament.

In response, Zhirinovsky argued that the current U.S. president was still capable of pulling off a fast one and staying in the office against all odds: "You don't know Trump, he has plenty of tricks up his sleeve and can still cause lots of damage to America and the entire world."

Zhirinovsky's stance appears to be in perfect alignment with Putin's deliberate delay in recognizing or congratulating the incoming Biden administration, since doing so might undermine the likelihood of extracting some last-minute favors from President Trump. "There is no need to rush," Zhirinovsky argued, "the 20th of January isn't here yet."

The Kremlin is in no hurry to congratulate Joe Biden with his return to the White House as president. Appearing on Russia's state TV show *The Evening With Vladimir Solovyov*, the deputy dean of World Politics at Moscow State University, Andrey Sidorov, predicted that the Biden presidency would spell out the consolidation of the entire Western world against Russia. Experts and lawmakers in Russian state media concurred that Moscow should anticipate additional sanctions in the near future.

"Biden is telling us that America is back. What does that mean for us?" asked *60 Minutes* host Evgeny Popov, noting Russia's inability to adequately retaliate against U.S. sanctions.

Deputy Speaker of the Russian State Duma (lower chamber of parliament) Pyotr Tolstoy responded with an ominous threat: "We're going to use their computers to make sure that people like Biden and his entire team will never again imagine that they have the right to world domination. We will unquestionably demonstrate it to them in years to come. Just wait and see."

Russian Media Mourn as Putin Acknowledges Biden's Win
But Say Trump 'Burned' U.S. on His Way Out

"He is discrediting the American electoral system," crowed one Russian TV host even as Putin acknowledged Biden's win.

Originally published by *The Daily Beast* on December 15, 2020

On Tuesday, the Kremlin finally acknowledged that U.S. President Donald J. Trump has been defeated by President-elect Joe Biden, by sending an official congratulatory message to the incoming American president. Russian state media immediately noted that Russian President Vladimir Putin was the last leader of the G20 to recognize Biden's indisputable victory.

Russian state TV hosts, pundits and lawmakers were also quick to point out the unusually dry language of Putin's greetings, noting that—unlike his prior telegrams to Trump and Obama—Putin didn't express any hope that U.S.-Russia relations might improve in the near future. "There are no hopes expressed in Putin's letter to Biden, none whatsoever," noted Olga Skabeeva, the co-host of Russia's state TV program *60 Minutes*. She added: "We're disappointed in Americans."

Describing American president as "our candidate Trump," "our friend Donald," "our Grandpa" and "poor, poor Trump," Kremlin-controlled state TV shows conceded that Trump's days in the Oval Office are numbered.

While the doom and gloom in Russian state media inevitably surrounded most discussions acknowledging Trump's electoral defeat, pundits and experts celebrated the bright side of their favored candidate's four-year reign.

"Mission accomplished," rejoiced Karen Shakhnazarov, CEO of Mosfilm Studio and an ever-present pundit on Russian state TV news talk shows. Appearing on state TV program *The Evening With Vladimir Solovyov*, Shakhnazarov opined that Trump's mission was to destroy the political system of the United States, and he successfully did exactly that.

In 2016, anticipating Trump's loss in the presidential election, Russian state media toed the Kremlin's line by laying the groundwork to assert that their favorite candidate lost solely because American elections are fraudulent and the entire system is rigged.

These claims were cast aside, since Trump was elected — even after losing the popular vote. In 2020, Trump and the GOP provided the Kremlin with priceless agitprop by making and supporting the same baseless allegations, voiced from the highest podium in the world: the White House.

Political expert Alexei Martynov, director of the International Institute of the Newly Established States, surmised during the broadcast of *60 Minutes*: "They burned the reputation of U.S. institutions during these elections." Political commentator Sergey Strokan concurred: "He [Trump] is discrediting the American electoral system." Evgeny Popov, the host of *60 Minutes*, grinned like a Cheshire cat: "Let's be glad about that." Deputy of the Russian Duma Alexei Zhuravlyov agreed: "I certainly am." He cheerfully concluded: "The worse for them, the better for us."

During the same broadcast, Popov pointed at the map of states supporting Trump's desperate plight of overturning election results: "Just look at this map, this is a real beauty. Exactly half of the country, divided. America is divided!"

The Kremlin's mouthpieces came to recognize the Republican party as their unusual bedfellows in helping to mar the crown jewel of the American democratic system and divide the society. Russian pundits inferred that they perceive the Republicans as fellow racists, who snapped into action to support Trump's attempts to remain in power, motivated by Biden appointing "non-white people" to serve within his administration.

Dmitry Mikheev, a former Soviet political refugee who worked as a researcher at the Hudson Institute, but later returned to Russia, claimed to be well familiar with American conservatives and their values.

Appearing on *60 Minutes*, Mikheev alleged that the Republicans were unsettled and spurred into action by the inclusion of minorities as Biden's top-level appointees: "The whites aren't being allowed in there. They [the GOP] got scared." The host, Popov, added: "And the head of the Department of Defense is Black. What is this? That must have been the red line."

Continuing the theme of alleged oppression of white people in America during the following day's broadcast of *60 Minutes*, co-host Olga Skabeeva repeatedly used offensive terms to describe African-Americans and later acknowledged: "This is some sort of a racist show."

Stoking racial tensions has long been one of the Kremlin's favored methods of sowing discord in American society, as confirmed in the Mueller report, noted by U.S. intelligence officials and concluded by the U.S. Senate.

The GOP's silent approval, while President Trump insulted minorities and vilified immigrants, worked even better than the Kremlin's most successful disinformation operations. The calls prompting further divisions and even violence were coming from inside the house — the White House.

Once the electoral votes came in and the Kremlin finally acknowledged the outcome, state media pundits predicted that the GOP would shortly follow suit.

With all respect due to the party that abandoned its own values in favor of the cult of personality and the pursuit of power at the expense of democracy, Russian International Affairs Council expert Alexey Naumov described Russian President Vladimir Putin as "the owner of Donald Trump" and "the main Republican."

Mocking the GOP, host Evgeny Popov, added: "Republicans, it's time to give up. Your owner recognized the outcome." Naumov added: "Your leader [Putin] already recognized Biden's victory — what are you, dog, waiting for?"

There is a grain of truth in every joke, since Senate Majority Leader Mitch McConnell finally congratulated President-elect Biden and Vice President-elect Kamala Harris — so late in the game that his belated acknowledgement came after the congratulations from Vladimir Putin.

Putin Gleeful After Trumpsters' Violent Insurrection

Bemoaning Biden's election, Russian state media talking heads consoled themselves with the thought that Trump fatally undermined democracy on his way out.

Originally published by *The Daily Beast* on January 08, 2021

Russian President Vladimir Putin was practically glowing while leaving a Russian Orthodox Christmas Eve service this Wednesday. Speaking to state TV reporters, he gushed about "the anticipation of a miracle" that can get a person through any rough patch in their life.

Putin wasn't talking about the United States, of course, but he might as well have been: America's outgoing president had just delivered the biggest Christmas present to the Kremlin imaginable by inciting a violent insurrection. Hundreds of Trump supporters descended upon the Capitol, launching a brazen attack that defiled the most precious symbol of U.S. democracy and attempting to overturn the outcome of an election in favor of their conspiracy-peddling idol.

Russian state media had played its own part in amplifying Donald Trump's baseless claims of electoral fraud and gleefully predicting that post-election violence would inevitably follow. "There will be blood," asserted Russian lawmakers and state media talking heads, a prospect they considered to be "excellent."

And indeed, there was blood. Vesti reporter Denis Davydov was embedded in the thick of it all, interviewing sweaty seditionists with bloody knuckles in between their attempts to storm Capitol Hill. "The United States never experienced anything like this," Davydov noted.

In his report for Vesti, U.S. correspondent Valentin Bogdanov asserted that the violence is not over: "While the Democrats gained control of Congress and the Senate, that doesn't mean they can control the minds of the people. January 6, 2021 is forever written into the American political calendar. For some, it's a dark date they will try to forget. For others, it's a day to remember — or perhaps to repeat."

Political scientist Yury Rogulyov told state media channel Rossiya-24: "The discontent will remain, the divisions will continue, but the big question is to which degree the Republicans will follow in Trump's footsteps. If they do it, the crisis will be extended and America's healing — if it's even possible — will take a long time."

Bemoaning Joe Biden's election, Russian state media talking heads consoled themselves with the thought that Trump had burned the United States on his way out by discrediting America's electoral system and democracy as a whole. The failed insurrection provided even more fuel for the fire.

Instead of condemning an attempted coup — stoked by blatant disinformation — Russian officials joined Trump and his Republican collaborators in trashing the integrity of the U.S. elections. Addressing the foiled coup, Maria Zakharova, official spokeswoman of the Russian Foreign Ministry, blamed the "archaic" electoral system and the U.S. media — and not President Trump's incendiary messaging.

Russian state TV outlets followed the official line with precision, defending Trump and baselessly maligning U.S. elections.

"Democrats are blaming Trump for undermining democracy, but democracy in the United States ended with the unverifiable, unreliable mail-in voting. Democracy ended with the archaic, non-transparent electoral system in the United States," claimed Igor Kozhevin, the host of the state TV news show *Vesti* on channel Rossiya-1. His program included clips from Fox News, whose messaging during the Trump years became almost indiscernible from Kremlin-controlled state media outlets.

But even Trump-friendly Kremlin media outlets were forced to acknowledge that the current U.S. president had squandered any legacy he might have had by repeatedly attempting to undo the outcome of the presidential election: "It's one humiliation after the next," surmised *Vesti*.

The program's U.S. correspondent, Valentin Bogdanov, predicted that Trump "may soon be declared insane, accused of being a spy, or thrown into prison."

State TV programs repeatedly brought up the possibility that Trump may end up seeking asylum in Russia, emphasizing that it's a very serious matter and not some kind of a sick joke. Kremlin-controlled media outlets pondered who will represent the Republican party in the next presidential elections, openly doubting that President Trump "will have the stomach for another run at the presidency" after his ignominious defeat in 2020.

Regardless of what happens to Trump, Russian propagandists find comfort in knowing that their favorite U.S. president's divisive rhetoric and deliberate disinformation have inflicted lasting damage on America—and cast a dark shadow on democracy, which used to be an example for other countries.

Russian tabloid Komsomolskaya Pravda argued: "The United States has long insisted that it is perhaps the only standard of democracy and order. But the inability of the American political system to transfer power peacefully and legally from one presidential team to another has torn the fragile veil from a failed example of democracy that has been carefully imposed on both Americans and the world."

Political scientist Igor Shatrov added: "The storefront is broken, shattered. It will be patched up, but the most valuable thing was stolen from the display: trust in American democratic institutions."

It's hard to imagine a bigger Christmas gift for Putin.

Russian Media: 'Traitors' Like Alexei Navalny Deserve Death

As Russia sentences Alexei Navalny to almost 3 years in prison, RT's editor-in-chief delivered a chilling message to the activist.

Originally published by *The Daily Beast* on February 02, 2021

Alexei Navalny, the main rival of Russian President Vladimir Putin who was poisoned with a deadly nerve agent last summer — allegedly by the FSB — was sentenced to 2 years and 8 months in prison (subtracting time served under house arrest from the total prison term of 3 years 6 months imposed by the court) over trumped-up charges by Russia's Federal Penitentiary Service.

Russian authorities alleged that by receiving medical treatment in Germany after being poisoned with the nerve agent Novichok, Navalny violated the terms of a suspended sentence in a contrived embezzlement case in 2014. Navalny's suspended sentence ended in June 2018 and his probation period concluded on December 30, 2020.

Nonetheless, the charging officials faulted Navalny for not returning to Russia immediately upon coming out of a coma, even though his medical treatment continued for months thereafter. Navalny returned to the country in mid-January and was immediately placed under arrest.

Appearing in court on Tuesday, Navalny pointed out that Putin himself knew where he was, having boasted about allowing the opposition activist to travel to Germany for medical treatment. Navalny's attorney, Vadim Kobzev, told the court: "The whole country, the whole world knew where he was." The New Times, an independent Russian weekly news magazine, aptly summed up the situation: Navalny is on trial simply for surviving the poisoning.

Speaking in court during Tuesday's hearing, Navalny outlined the true meaning of the proceedings: "They're imprisoning one person in order to scare millions of others."

If you ask Margarita Simonyan, editor-in-chief of the state-funded network RT that passes for news in the United States, prison is not a harsh enough punishment. Simonyan explained her shocking views during Monday's broadcast of *The Evening With Vladimir Solovyov* on Russian state TV channel Rossiya-1. "I'm proud of my Motherland," she exclaimed and argued that those who attempt to undermine the regime must be harshly dealt with and immediately imprisoned. Simonyan described Navalny as "a traitor of the Motherland."

She added: "We don't know who poisoned the Skripals [Sergei and Yulia] or [Alexander] Litvinenko, we don't know whether Russia did this or not. But let me say something savage and unpopular. Who were Skripal and Litvinenko? Traitors of the Motherland... And what large country would allow the traitors of the Motherland to walk around without punishment?"

Simonyan concluded: "I'll tell you a scary thing: if I found out and received the evidence that [the poisonings] were the handiwork of intelligence services against the agents of other intelligence services, I wouldn't mind that a bit."

The Skripals and Litvinenko were poisoned, allegedly by agents of the Russian state, in Britain. The former survived their poisonings while Litvinenko died in 2006 from radiation sickness.

During the same show, the host Vladimir Solovyov and various panelists referred to Alexei Navalny as "a traitor" and baselessly accused him of working for Western intelligence agencies. The inescapable conclusion is that the Kremlin's mouthpieces are laying the groundwork for justifying the fate that they believe awaits Navalny, however horrific it may be.

Navalny's biggest crime in the eyes of the Kremlin is symbolizing the idea that the people can choose a leader besides Putin, or to even have an option to decide for themselves. Russia's fearless opposition leader inspired multiple demonstrations against government corruption, which led to massive turnouts across Russia and ended with the arrests of an unprecedented 5,000 people, including 82 journalists.

Kremlin press secretary Dmitry Peskov rejected White House calls for Navalny's release and Secretary of State Antony Blinken's condemnation of a violent crackdown by Russian authorities against peaceful protesters.

"As to the statements made by U.S. representatives on the unlawful demonstrations in our country, I repeat that we are not ready to accept and listen to such statements of the Americans and will not do so," Peskov stressed.

Appearing on *The Evening With Vladimir Solovyov*, Dmitry Kulikov, member of a club of experts organized by the state TV network Russia Today, deciphered Peskov's message as he understood it. Kulikov explained that Peskov was diplomatically telling Blinken: "Get the hell out of here, we couldn't care less about anything you have to say about this. We will pay no attention to you anymore."

Gone are the days when experts on Russian state television adoringly recounted the signs of former U.S. President Donald J. Trump's apparent subservience to Russian President Vladimir Putin.

In contrast to calling Trump "ours" and lovingly referring to him as "Trumpushka," Russian state media personalities exhibit open hostility towards the newly elected U.S. President Joe Biden and his administration.

Russian state media accused Western countries, including the United States, of fomenting another "color revolution" in Russia—the prospect that clearly unnerved the Kremlin. Speaking to students in a televised exchange, Putin recounted various events in Russian history, such as the revolution of 1917 and the fall of the Soviet Union and cautioned against "destabilizing society and the government," which he said could make things go from bad to worse. Drawing the parallels to the revolution of 1917, Russian state television show *Vesti Nedeli* warned the viewers that revolutions inevitably end in "blood, bitterness and poverty."

Margarita Simonyan described the U.S. State Department's commentary about the Russian protests as "the funniest thing." She ludicrously described Russia as "the most liberal country" out of all civilized nations. "We need to be harsher," the head of RT argued, as she called on "brothers" in Russian law enforcement to crack down on the unruly protesters.

Simonyan scoffed at the demonstrators who dared to chant about the power of the people and retorted with a view undoubtedly shared by the Kremlin: "No, that's nonsense. You're not the power here."

Russian Media Pushes the Lie That Capitol Rioters Were Antifa

Russian media is gleefully peddling the fiction that Biden, not Trump, was behind the siege on the U.S. Capitol.

Originally published by *The Daily Beast* on January 15, 2021

In a last-ditch attempt to defend the outgoing U.S. President Donald J. Trump, Russian-speaking participants in the recent mob at the Capitol flooded the airwaves of the Kremlin-controlled Russian state television. They claimed that the pro-Trump insurrectionists were merely "peaceful demonstrators" and blamed "antifa" for the violence that took place in Washington, DC on January 6, 2021.

Russian state media propagandists and their mouthpieces apparently didn't get the memo that even the Republicans no longer pursue that false narrative. Congressman Kevin McCarthy spoke on the House floor ahead of a vote on Trump's second impeachment and asserted: "Some say the riots were caused by antifa. There is absolutely no evidence of that."

But the truth never stopped the Kremlin's propaganda networks from continuing to disseminate a convenient fable.

Russian-speaking eyewitnesses were shown intermittently — or some might argue interchangeably — with clips from Fox News, featuring Tucker Carlson, Marco Rubio and other Trump apologists.

Appearing on state TV channel Rossiya-24, two Russian-speakers living in the United States were identified as "those who participated in the events" on Capitol Hill and later took part in numerous shows on Russian state television. Anchor Stas Natanzon asked Elena Nikitskaya of Greenville, South Carolina and Alexander Schneider of Boston, Massachusetts whether they're facing persecution in the United States for supporting Donald Trump.

Sitting in front of a large flag that said, "Trump 2020: No More Bullshit," Schneider expressed his belief that Trump supporters are being unjustly oppressed. Nikitskaya joined the grievance chorus and described the alleged persecution of pro-Trump individuals as "tyranny." She made a flurry of appearances on various Russian state media outlets and told Russia's Channel One that all followers of Trump in the United States live in fear.

Nikitskaya's YouTube channel, replete with various conspiracy theories, gained notoriety after she posted a video of marching towards the Capitol and opined that Trump's followers would take Washington, DC in a matter of minutes if their leader gave an order to do so. Nonetheless, in her subsequent videos and multiple media appearances, the blogger conveniently—and baselessly—blamed omnipresent "antifa" for storming the Capitol.

She claimed that the police opened up the barriers and invited "peaceful protesters" like herself to enter in, trying to set them up: "It's as though the followers of Gestapo and Dr. Mengele decided to organize this tyranny against the people." At the same time, Nikitskaya denied ever entering the Capitol and, if so, could not have possibly witnessed the events she had described.

Nikitskaya complained of being hounded with threats of legal repercussions from callers who said that after watching her videos, they've reported her to the FBI. "It's scary to be surrounded by so many vile people," she grumbled. Nonetheless, the blogger expressed her intent to participate in future protests and demonstrations "to save our country from the usurpers of power."

Miami blogger Steve Doudnik appeared on Russian state TV news talk show *60 Minutes*, sitting in front of a U.S. flag emblazoned with the photo of Donald Trump and the logo of his presidential campaign.

On his way to the event, surrounded by dozens of other Russian speakers, Doudnik proudly exclaimed: "Our team is moving towards Washington, DC. We're ready, Russian speakers don't surrender! Everyone here can confirm this. We're for our president. I hope we will defeat those bastards."

On his way back to the hotel on the evening of January 6, with Nikitskaya by his side, Doudnik said: "We didn't see any antifa or

BLM [Black Lives Matter]" and added: "We're very disappointed. When the Capitol was taken, if Trump was there, there would have been a revolution."

However, during his subsequent state TV appearance, Doudnik denied taking part in the violent events of that day. He claimed that the police allowed "antifa" to break the windows, enter the Capitol and take selfies inside. He disingenuously asserted that having broken into the Capitol, "antifa" subsequently left and innocent Trump supporters "entered the trap," solely because they were "invited" to come in and the doors were already open.

Having described this surreal scenario, Doudnik proceeded to clarify that he was nowhere near the Capitol and found out what supposedly happened from fellow pro-Trump participants staying in the same hotel. He expressed hesitation to participate in any future marches or protests, fearing "arrests and repressions."

Irina Raskina, another pro-Trump marcher who traveled from Los Angeles to Washington, DC told *60 Minutes* that the storming of the Capitol "was an obvious set-up" and described herself as "the victim who was tear-gassed." Nervously drinking water, Raskina blamed "the left" and "antifa" for storming the Capitol and asserted that she had no plans to participate in any other marches or protests.

The co-host of *60 Minutes* Olga Skabeeva followed up to reinforce the official propaganda line: "Let's reiterate it one more time: Biden provoked the people to storm the Capitol in order to blame Trump?" "Isn't that right?" chimed in host Evgeny Popov. Raskina hesitated and stammered, seemingly realizing the outlandish message she was expected to deliver.

She reluctantly went along with a suggested shtick, unconvincingly blaming President-elect Joe Biden, his assistants and phantom "elements of the left" for the pro-Trump insurrection.

Back in the studio of *60 Minutes*, Konstantin Zatulin, a member of Russia's lower house of parliament, speculated that the storming of the Capitol was a "fake," created by the Democrats to set up Trump for another impeachment. Other panelists had a hard time not rolling their eyes, uncomfortably grimacing at such a ludicrous suggestion—because earlier during the same show Zatulin conceded: "Just between us, elements of incitement were obviously present in Trump's behavior."

The uncomfortable truth is hard to swallow, because on the reverse side of the coin, the thought of a violent mob storming the Kremlin or Russian parliament is not something that Russian President Vladimir Putin or his mouthpieces could ever attempt to praise or justify. Nonetheless, Trump remains the Kremlin's top choice for America's president—now and in 2024—therefore, the other side must be blamed for his crimes and misdemeanors.

Moscow's full-throated defense of Trump is not based on affinity or admiration. His scandalous persona, appearance, ignorance and subservience to Putin have been mercilessly mocked and kept on full display by Russian propagandists throughout the duration of his tumultuous presidency.

While Trump himself may be loathed or derided in Russia, his misdeeds are deeply valued, having caused incalculable harm to the United States of America. The blow that Trump's false claims have dealt to public trust in U.S. elections is a highly coveted prize that has been long pursued by the Kremlin. Internal turmoil caused by the outgoing U.S. president's relentless attempts to stay in power damaged America above and beyond the Kremlin's wildest dreams.

Appearing on *60 Minutes*, Deputy of the Russian Duma Alexei Zhuravlyov rejoiced that America could no longer be viewed as the paragon of democracy and openly stated that spilled American blood is viewed as a good thing, not only by him personally but also by the majority of his constituents. Zhuravlyov later noted: "They talk about us interfering—we'd be glad to interfere, but what's the point? What they're doing to themselves, we couldn't even come up with."

"Well done, Trumpushka," laughed state TV host Vladimir Solovyov during his show, *The Evening With Vladimir Solovyov*, making fun of the fact that Trump is the first U.S. president to be impeached twice during his one term in office.

"It's too bad that Americans haven't been watching our program," Solovyov said during another broadcast. He reiterated predictions that have been made on his show over the years: "Trumpushka will destroy your America."

Top Kremlin Mouthpiece Warns of 'Inevitable' War With U.S. Over Another Ukraine Land Grab

The head of the Kremlin-funded RT and Sputnik news agencies believes Russia will invade Ukraine, sparking a conflict with the U.S. that will force entire cities into blackouts.

Originally published by *The Daily Beast* on April 13, 2021

All-out cyberwarfare, nation-wide forced blackouts, and the targeted disruption of internet services—for one of the Kremlin's top propagandists, all of those tactics are fair game in what she describes as a fated war-to-come against the U.S.

"War [with the U.S.] is inevitable," declared Margarita Simonyan, editor in chief of the state-funded Russian media outlets RT and Sputnik, who believes the conflict will break out when, not if, Vladimir Putin moves to seize more territory from Ukraine.

As Russia's military buildup on Ukraine's doorstep mounts, Kremlin loyalists have been urging for even more overt aggression and bloodshed in the campaign to annex Ukraine's Donbas region. The only thing standing in the way, they say, is U.S. support for their beleaguered neighbor. NATO issued a statement on Wednesday demanding an end to Russia's troop movements on the border with the disputed territory of Donbas in eastern Ukraine.

It is the largest buildup of Russian troops since the annexation of Crimea in 2014. The U.S. underlined the statement this week by deploying two warships to the Black Sea.

On Tuesday, Russian Deputy Foreign Minister Sergei Ryabkov threatened retaliation. "We warn the United States that it will be better for them to stay far away from Crimea and our Black Sea coast. It will be for their own good," he said.

The escalation was foreshadowed on state television's *Sunday Evening With Vladimir Solovyov* over the weekend. Simonyan explained that it was time for Russia to gear up for a showdown against the U.S., and prophesized a kind of war driven by hacking, the forced disruption of internet access, the shutting down of power supplies, and an all-out offensive on U.S. infrastructure.

"I do not believe that this will be a large-scale hot war, like World War II, and I do not believe that there will be a long Cold War. It will be a war of the third type: the cyberwar," said Simonyan. She warned that—in this theoretical battle—the U.S. would plot to cut off the electricity of entire Russian cities. In turn, she speculated, Moscow would be able to force a blackout in Florida or New York's Harlem at the flip of a switch.

"In conventional war, we could defeat Ukraine in two days," Simonyan said, "but it will be another kind of war. We'll do it, and then [the U.S.] will respond by turning off power to [the Russian city] Voronezh," she said.

The top RT editor asserted that "[Russia] needs to be ready for this war, which is unavoidable, and of course it will start in Ukraine," arguing that the Kremlin is "invincible where conventional war is concerned, but forget about conventional war... it will be a war of infrastructures, and here we have many vulnerabilities."

Her solution consists of Stalin-type measures to eliminate "vulnerabilities" in the run-up to another escalation, emphasizing the need for a hack-proof, government-controlled internet. "We still don't have a sovereign internet, but God willing, we will," she said.

She wholeheartedly endorsed a suggestion from Vladimir Zhirinovsky, the ultranationalist leader of Russia's Liberal Democratic Party, who argued that all of Russia's opposition must be eliminated by May 1, 2021. With imprisoned opposition leader Alexei Navalny on a hunger strike—and suffering from severe health ailments after being denied appropriate medical treatment— the Kremlin seems to be firmly set on that course.

Simonyan argued that once Russia minimizes its vulnerabilities and renders Putin's opposition powerless—which she argued could happen in a matter of months—the Kremlin will finally be ready to annex Ukraine's eastern region.

"I've been agitating and even demanding that we take Donbas. We need to patch up our vulnerabilities as fast as we can, and then we can do whatever we want," she boldly proclaimed. The host, Vladimir Solovyov, wholeheartedly agreed: "We only lose if we do nothing."

He argued that by absorbing parts of Ukraine—or the entire country—Russia would be able to remove the zone of American influence further away from its borders.

As one of the Kremlin's most valued propagandists, Margarita Simonyan is notoriously close to the Russian president and has received multiple awards directly from Putin. After accepting one such award in 2019, Simonyan thanked Putin "for the most important reward in life... this honor to serve one's Motherland."

Her "service" has involved RT and Sputnik-driven disinformation operations aimed at influencing the 2016 U.S. presidential election, which she often boasts about by pointing to the inclusion of her name in various U.S. intelligence reports.

Russia's recent cyberspace activities seem to serve as good practice for the "inevitable war" foreshadowed by Simonyan.

Last year, six Russian intelligence officers were criminally charged by the U.S. for using the world's most destructive malware to force blackouts in Ukraine and damage the critical infrastructure of multiple countries, which caused nearly $1 billion in losses. On Monday, hackers operating from Russia targeted France's homeschooling platform.

The Kremlin is prepared to intensify its offensive against the West but fears the retaliation that would follow.

The idea of a bulletproof "sovereign internet"—completely under government control within Russian borders—is already on the books, with Moscow having introduced the idea as a preventive measure against retaliatory hacking attempts from other nations.

Simonyan argued that Russia will surely be able to exploit the U.S.'s "catastrophic" educational standards, and referred to American military analysts and specialists as incompetent and stupid. She heartily laughed about news that more than 200,000 U.S. service members experienced hearing loss due to defective earplugs.

"We can never come to any agreements with [Americans]," Simonyan said, arguing that instead, Russia can just as easily defeat the U.S. in a cyberspace war.

She added, mockingly, "We don't even need the nukes."

Russian State Media Gears Up for a War 'Against the West'

One Kremlin propagandist even suggested that the struggle for Ukraine will end in a "nuclear conflict" between Russia and NATO.

Originally published by *The Daily Beast* on April 05, 2021

Russia is gearing up for war again, local experts, state media propagandists, and government officials are all saying. The fight will begin once again on the real-world battlefield of Ukraine. But it will extend much, much further. And the real enemy? Thousands of miles from Kyiv.

"Everything will start in Ukraine," predicted Andrey Sidorov, deputy dean of world politics at Moscow State University, appearing on *Sunday Evening With Vladimir Solovyov* this weekend. "We will be forced to step onto the battlefield in a fight for which they think we're not ready," he added.

The host asked: "A fight against whom?" and Sidorov clarified: "Against the collective West."

The fear-mongering propagated by Russian state media aims to prepare the population for the consequences of the Kremlin's actions, while preemptively placing most of the blame upon the United States.

Russian experts fear that to make Russia pay for its election interference, hacking and other malign activities, the Biden administration might declare Russian President Vladimir Putin a "persona non grata," and impose a total trade embargo upon Russia. Preparing for the worst and never willing to admit responsibility for its actions, Russian diplomatic sources told TASS that Russia's ambassador to the United States will return only if "Americans do at least something" to normalize relations between the two countries.

The Kremlin commented with great alarm about the possibility of the United States establishing a military presence in Ukraine, although no such plans have been announced. "They want to destroy us," hyperventilated Dmitry Kulikov, appearing on *The Evening With Vladimir Solovyov*. "It's in their nature," agreed Solovyov, adding: "You can't turn a wolf into a vegetarian." The host further claimed that Russia "will be destroyed very quickly" if it "loses Donbas"—a Ukrainian territory that is not Russia's to lose or to keep—because "Putin's electorate won't stand for it."

Rather than to risk Putin's eternal presidency, Solovyov suggested that the fight over Ukraine's Donbas will end in a "nuclear conflict" between Russia and NATO. Senior military analyst Mikhail Khodaryonok, a former colonel from the Soviet air defense force, opined: "I think that any conflict could be stopped by the threat of at least a tactical nuclear strike from our side. The main question is how convincing our message will be."

Khodaryonok then proposed launching a limited nuclear strike in neutral ocean waters as a warning shot to the West. "Perhaps we should start by doing that right now," Solovyov suggested. "It's not only probable, but very likely indeed," Khodaryonok confirmed. The potentially devastating consequences of such a reckless approach didn't seem to bother the professional performers of Putin's propaganda machine.

"We've been in the state of Cold War since 2014, and have been following the formula of [Commander Mikhail] Kutuzov"—the Russian commander who repelled Napoleon's invasion—"I don't presume to win, I'll try to outwit." That is the policy of the Russian Federation that we've been implementing since 2014," said Andrey Sidorov on Solovyov's show.

Referring to Russia's annexation of Crimea, Sidorov outlined the Kremlin's strategy: waiting for Ukraine to make the first move, then promptly retaliate. (In reality, the Kremlin consistently blamed Ukraine for escalating tensions within its own territory, while feeding and arming the insurgency and prolonging the bloody conflict on its neighbor's land.)

In an ongoing ploy to eventually annex Ukraine's Donbas, Moscow proceeded to issue Russian passports to hundreds of thousands of inhabitants of Eastern Ukraine, with plans to flip more than one million Ukrainians to Russia's side. As a Russian proverb goes, "There is no free cheese, except for the mousetrap" and the passports came with strings attached.

Russia's proxies controlling the so-called "people's republics" in Eastern Ukraine have just commenced mandatory military draft. Russia's top propagandist, Dmitry Kiselyov, proudly announced the draft last Sunday on his weekly program, *Vesti Nedeli*. Recipients of Russian passports in Eastern Ukraine will be expected to fight and die for their new Motherland. Based on their recent passport applications, newly-minted conscripts won't be hard to find.

Seeking plausible deniability in an attempt to avoid the harshest U.S. sanctions, the Kremlin will most likely continue to fight the war against Ukraine via proxies. When the time comes, pro-Russian forces will stage a provocation and step in to "defend" Russian citizens from the Ukrainian government.

America's response to Russian aggression had been uneven under former U.S. President Donald J. Trump, with his administration sending weapons to Ukraine while Trump tried to make that aid contingent on political help against Joe Biden, his political opponent. State media experts acknowledged that things would have been quite different if Hillary Clinton won the electoral college—and not just the popular vote—in 2016.

"The same state of war that we have right now would have started within the first 6 months of the Clinton presidency," asserted Dmitry Kulikov—member of the Zinoviev Club, instituted by the Kremlin-controlled media giant Russia Today—said on Solovyov's show.

He added: "America was much stronger then." The host, Vladimir Solovyov, pointed out: "And Russia wouldn't have had four years." Kulikov emphatically agreed: "That's why they [Americans] are furious with Trump. He stole those four years from them and gave them to Russia and China."

Under Biden, such games appear to be over. Instead of laughing about Trump's embarrassing subservience to Putin, experts and pundits on state TV are grim-faced as they anticipate harsh measures against the Kremlin by the Biden administration.

Even Margarita Simonyan, editor-in-chief of the Kremlin-funded RT and Sputnik, whose bombastic anti-American rhetoric fills the air on multiple state media programs, admitted that Russia is not immune against U.S. sanctions.

Appearing on the talk show *Our Own Truth* that aired on television channel NTV, controlled by state-owned Gazprom Media, Simonyan conceded: "There could be sanctions that would cause us to end up living like we're in Iran... We have vulnerabilities, as you know."

Fears of additional sanctions are holding Moscow back from overt aggression, but the inflammatory anti-American rhetoric is being ratcheted up across all of the Kremlin-controlled state media. Duplicitous claims that Russia wants peace with America and loves its people are now being replaced with raw admissions of hostility and ill will.

The host of Russia's *60 Minutes*, Evgeny Popov, claimed that the Russians can't stand U.S. politicians, but love ordinary American people. He was cut off by his wife and co-host, Olga Skabeeva, who proclaimed with brutal honesty: "Let's be real, we don't love the American people either."

How Putin Made a Fool of Tucker Carlson

A clip of the Fox News host agreeing with Putin was played on Russian State TV where pundits and propagandists were thrilled by how easy it was to manipulate Carlson.

Originally published by *The Daily Beast* on June 21, 2021

President Vladimir Putin has pulled off a targeted propaganda operation against the U.S. that's so simple it never should have worked—and he did it in plain sight as part of the build-up to last week's summit with President Joe Biden. This weekend, Russia's favorite propaganda shows celebrated a job well done. State TV propagandist Dmitry Kiselyov asserted on his show on Sunday, "Biden should keep in mind that not only America is back, but Russia is back too."

The ploy began when Putin sat down for an interview with NBC's Keir Simmons. He directed the conversation away from his suspected involvement in the murders and attempted murders of his critics. Instead, he asked, "Did you order the assassination of the woman who walked into Congress and who was shot and killed by a policeman?" The Russian president was referring to Trump supporter Ashli Babbitt, who was fatally shot by a Capitol police officer as she tried to climb through the broken window of a door leading directly onto the House floor during the January 6 riots.

This line of attack was no surprise to people who follow Russian propaganda. It had been preplanned and foreshadowed by pro-Kremlin experts appearing on Russian state TV talk shows prior to the summit. "[Biden] is planning to tell us about Navalny and we will tell him about the woman shot on January 6 at the Capitol," explained Olga Skabeeva, the host of state TV show *60 Minutes*, on June 1.

Ten days later, Putin did exactly that in his NBC interview.

On June 16, with the world's attention fixed on the Geneva summit, the Russian president reiterated the same flawed premise during his press conference: "About my opponents being jailed or imprisoned. People went into the U.S. Congress with political demands. Four hundred people now facing criminal charges... On what grounds? Not quite clear... One of the participants, a woman, was shot dead on the spot. She was not threatening anything."

Putin's plot paid off in spades when Tucker Carlson played the clip of his comments to NBC on his show and expressed agreement. Carlson said, "Now, under normal circumstances, we would never play tape of a foreign adversary criticizing our government. But honestly, those are fair questions."

Without a hint of irony, Carlson added, "Vladimir Putin knows authoritarian systems very well, and he sees clearly what is happening in this country."

The Fox News host seemed to assume that an authoritarian adversary was providing this advice without an ulterior motive—and eagerly shared it with his American audience. His decision was cheered by pro-Kremlin propagandists in Moscow.

During his nightly show, *The Evening With Vladimir Solovyov*, host Vladimir Solovyov proudly surmised, "Putin knew whom he was talking to and his message was heard. This is Fox News and its very popular program—one of its highest-rated programs. Republicans listened and couldn't help but agree... Putin was heard and what he said hit the bullseye."

Russian political scientist Sergey Mikheyev enthusiastically replied, "This is a good illustration of the thesis as to whether we should be influencing public opinion in America. Yes, of course we should—of course! The question is how to do it and which resources to use. Without a doubt, we should be using any existing divisions. Sometimes I hear, 'What's in it for us?' and I will cynically tell you: whatever harms them benefits us. That is terrible but true."

Putin is already polling higher than President Biden among Trump voters, according to the recent poll by Economist/YouGov, which also found that Republicans viewed Russia as less of a threat than Democrats do. Now that Republican voters are increasingly influenced by conspiracy theories spread through the QAnon movement, pro-Kremlin propagandists seek to capitalize on that trend as well.

During the broadcast of his show on May 31, host Solovyov asked, "What if the heroic city of Moscow hosted a forum 'Free America' by American QAnon supporters, and their living expenses would be funded by the Russian government, how fast would we hear accusations of interference with their [U.S.] internal affairs?" RT's editor-in-chief Margarita Simonyan promptly replied, "We need to be doing that."

Carlson's commentary also flagged another line being pursued by Russian state propagandists. The Fox News host asked, "Who did shoot Ashli Babbitt and why don't we know?" Rossiya-1 probed that question, quoting Republican Congressman Devin Nunes in a state TV news show on June 11.

Russia's state media previously worked alongside the GOP in their attempts to unmask the Ukraine whistleblower whose revelations contributed to Trump's first impeachment. It would not be surprising if the Kremlin-controlled media yet again takes the first step to publicly finger the law enforcement officer in question, further inflaming political divisions in the U.S.

Russia Targets Fox News Fans in Bid to Become the World's Anti-Woke Capital

The Kremlin and its staunchest loyalists are touting Russia as a politically incorrect utopia—something they think Western conservatives can't resist.

Originally published by *The Daily Beast* on June 30, 2021

Galvanized by the results of recent American polls and the popularity of Russian President Vladimir Putin with Fox News and its audiences, the Kremlin is proceeding with a new charm offensive targeting Western conservatives. Russia cannot offer much in terms of gun rights, freedom of speech, or standard of living—at least not for those excluded from Putin's mob-like circle of trust. Rather, the Kremlin intends to attract Western converts with another type of currency—bigotry—turning Russia into the land of ultimate political incorrectness, the world's anti-woke capital.

On Monday, Russia's Foreign Affairs Minister Sergey Lavrov published an op-ed that left many readers scratching their heads. "In a number of Western countries, students learn at school that Jesus Christ was bisexual," Lavrov claimed. Aside from a single viral post on TikTok featuring the ramblings of a child, there doesn't seem to be any suggestion—much less any evidence—of such a curriculum actually being taught.

Far from simple non sequitur, Lavrov's musings seem to be part of a larger agenda. In fact, they appear to fit squarely within the strategy pursued by the Kremlin's elaborate propaganda ecosystem.

The topic of inappropriate lessons being taught in Western schools surfaced last week on the state TV show *The Evening With Vladimir Solovyov*. Margarita Simonyan, editor-in-chief of state media outlet RT, claimed to be personally helping multiple foreign families hoping to relocate to Russia. The reason for their desired move, Simonyan claimed, is what the children are being taught in school. Reminding the audience of Simonyan's status as a prominent Kremlin insider with direct access to the Russian president, host Vladimir Solovyov immediately hinted that Simonyan ought to speak directly to Putin to expedite the process.

Back in January, the spokeswoman for Russia's Ministry of Foreign Affairs, Maria Zakharova, told Solovyov that she has received a flood of inquiries from American Trump supporters imploring her to provide information about obtaining Russian citizenship. She seemed particularly impressed with communications from a certain blogger, who immigrated to the United States from the USSR and was now interested in going back to Russia, allegedly fearing "repressions."

Zakharova didn't specify whether she was talking about the Russian YouTuber who posted videos at the Capitol on January 6 and subsequently went on Russian state TV to blame "antifa" for the violence.

The Kremlin has long been toying with the idea of attracting Western supporters — and even potential émigrés — to side with Russia, and even move there. A stream of Steven Seagals would fuel Putin's claim that Western democracies have lost their credibility and appeal.

In 2018, a photograph of Trump supporters donning T-shirts that read, "I'd Rather Be A Russian Than A Democrat" was proudly showcased in Russian state media as evidence of the Kremlin's growing popularity with American Republicans. A recent opinion poll confirmed that Putin is more popular than President Biden among Republican voters.

Simonyan excitedly claimed: "More and more people see our country — and Putin as its leader — as the embodiment of the place they can run to, like the West used to be for former Soviets." She boasted that her media outlet receives plenty of support from English-speaking audiences, claiming that it proves the massive disenchantment of average Western denizens with their governments and popular ideologies.

Russia's approach to courting Trump supporters has proven to be quite simple: to appeal to their belief that so-called "political correctness" threatens their livelihoods and even their future. In coming up with their tactics, pro-Kremlin propagandists rely quite heavily on the material pumped out by Fox News, with clips featuring Tucker Carlson regularly appearing on Russia's most popular state TV programs.

Without even trying to conceal her glee about divisions in Western countries, Simonyan said: "What's happening there honestly brings me joy. For the first time in Russia's history — at least in the last 200 years — it has a unique opportunity to become a patron of its own homegrown ideology, which we couldn't accomplish with communism."

The head of RT explained the ongoing goal of state propaganda in detail: "Russia is becoming the last refuge of a normal person." She specified that a normal, "healthy" individual is someone who does not agree with liberal goals and ideas of Western countries, which she described as "totalitarian liberal fascism." "It's all such nonsense," she moaned, referring to American public discourse on cultural appropriation, systemic racism, and LGBTQ rights.

The host mockingly proposed the idea of a "heterosexual pride" event, and Simonyan enthusiastically played along. Disregarding damning statistics and contradicting RT's own reporting, Simonyan boldly claimed that absolutely no discrimination based on gender, ethnicity, race or sexual orientation exists in Russia. "We're different. I hope we will continue to be different," she proclaimed.

Other top propagandists like Dmitry Kiselyov have been drawing absurd parallels between the prosecutions of the Capitol rioters and the suicide of John McAfee, claiming that McAfee killed himself because he was so afraid of the corrupt U.S. justice system. "America forever lost its moral leadership in the world," he argued on his Sunday program *Vesti Nedeli*.

The program alleged that white people in America are being "shamed" and subjected to "mass humiliation." *Vesti Nedeli* showcased clips from Fox News featuring Tucker Carlson, who claimed that the critical race theory amounts to racism against white people. Earlier in June, popular tabloid Komsomolskaya Pravda opined that President Joe Biden "declared white Americans to be the main enemies of the United States" and vowed that Russia would not help the U.S. in its fight against the proponents of white supremacy.

Shortly after the Capitol riot, the host of the state TV program *60 Minutes*, Olga Skabeeva, described the death of Ashli Babbitt as an example of "the negroes lynching the whites." In the weeks following the attempted Capitol insurrection, Solovyov complained that unlike George Floyd, Babbitt wasn't buried in a golden coffin and pondered out loud why there was no movement entitled "White Lives Matter."

With Russia positioning itself as the anti-woke empire, it is ready to reel in more Western supporters by any means necessary. During Solovyov's show last Friday, Vitaly Tretyakov, dean of the Moscow State University's School of Television, suggested: "It's time to move on to more active measures — and I don't mean sending ships into their territorial waters. I mean sending political vessels. Do you want me to spell it out?" Simonyan quickly interjected, keeping her fellow propagandist from divulging too much. "No need," she said.

State TV Host Mocks Black January 6 Cop in 'N-Word' Fueled Rant

Russian state media has never been shy about its position on the January 6 Capitol riot, but current U.S. hearings have triggered a particularly vile wave of propaganda.

Originally published by *The Daily Beast* on July 28, 2021

Russian state media had a familiar—albeit repulsive—approach to coverage of the January 6 Capitol riot hearings. "The long-awaited first hearing in the United States was a total farce," said the scowling host of Kremlin-funded TV program *60 Minutes*, Olga Skabeeva. "Imagine that, a huge dark-skinned policeman, his name is Harry Dunn, got teary-eyed like a boy, because the protesters called him the N-word." She then proceeded to say the Russian translation of the word out loud, a common occurrence on Russian state television.

In Russian, both the N-word slur and the word "Negro" are translated as the same expression. Skabeeva has long-used it with obsessive insistence, often making other panelists uncomfortable while repeatedly acknowledging her awareness that it is offensive. Last year, Konstantin Zatulin, a member of Russia's lower house of parliament, pointed out that the word in question is deeply insulting and suggested she use the phrase "African American" instead. Skabeeva reacted with a grin and continued to use the same offensive term through many *60 Minutes* broadcasts.

The pundit's use of the word can't be chalked up to a cultural disconnect, either: The TV personality used to live and work in New York, alongside her husband and co-host Evgeny Popov. The cosmopolitan couple frequently vacations in Europe and longingly talks about their great time living in the U.S., only to return to

Russia to spout medieval views and nasty expressions while hosting their popular program.

Racist undertones permeated the rest of the coverage. Dmitry Abzalov, Director of the Center for Strategic Communications, falsely claimed that rioter Ashli Babbitt was "simply standing in front of the door" when she was shot and killed. In reality, Babbitt and others were attempting to breach a barricaded door inside the Capitol building. Disregarding the facts, Skabeeva harped on her favorite myth of reverse racism: "She was a white woman... shot by a Black policeman, and a Black policeman has the right to shoot a white woman." In January, Skabeeva had claimed that Ashli Babbitt's death signified that in America, "Negroes are starting to lynch the whites."

Congressman Adam Kinzinger (R-IL) also provoked the ire of Kremlin propagandists. "It's a pitiful sight," Skabeeva scoffed at the congressman's tears. She claimed that the first insurrectionist to be convicted of a felony, Paul Hodgkins, was sentenced to serve eight months in prison "simply for walking around with a flag." Hodgkins unlawfully entered the Senate chamber and pleaded guilty to obstructing congressional proceedings.

In a Newsmax appearance last week, Georgia congresswoman Marjorie Greene described the rioters as "political prisoners of war." Russian state TV followed suit: "The so-called terrorists are actually political prisoners," Skabeeva exclaimed on Wednesday.

She derided the Capitol officers as "talented actors," echoing a move by Fox's Laura Ingraham, who handed out mock awards for "best action performance" to the Capitol police officers testifying about the events of January 6. Yet again, Russian state television was in perfect harmony with Fox News.

The congruence of Kremlin-funded media's talking points with that of the Republican party position is remarkable. In May, Rep. Andrew Clyde (R-GA) downplayed the attempted insurrection of January 6, likening the violent mob who overran the Capitol to a "normal tourist visit."

On Wednesday, Russian state TV host Skabeeva claimed that the rioters were simply touring the building, "but the ticket counter was closed at the time," so they just went in. "No big deal," Skabeeva raged, "There was no need for the police officers to cry!"

She demanded that human rights organizations step up to defend America's "political prisoners"—a particularly callous demand, considering opposition activist Alexei Navalny is still rotting in prison.

Perhaps worth noting too is that, in August 2004, after a group of young people unlawfully occupied offices of Russia's Health Ministry for two hours and tossed a portrait of Putin out the window, multiple participants were sentenced to five years in prison for the "seizure of a government office and mass disturbances." Panelist Dmitry Galkin brought up the event for comparison's sake, but Skabeeva loudly interrupted him: "That's different! This was an excursion."

On the day of the insurrection, videos shown on Russian state television were a far cry from a harmless sightseeing trip. Russian state TV reporter Denis Davydov was embedded among the rioters, interviewing them and showcasing their bloody wounds on camera for Russia's news program Vesti.

Davydov featured the seditionists violently clashing with the police, and at one point exclaimed, "The protesters don't intend to retreat. The mob is crushing the police with their weight!" He described the rioters as "the rebels" and noted, "The United States never experienced anything like this!"

Only days after January 6, state TV featured Russian-speaking bloggers who participated in the events that day. The guests falsely blamed antifa for the horrendous violence, but there was no mention of a "peaceful tour" of the Capitol building. The narrative has since shifted, and as always, Russian audiences are expected to play along.

In recent remarks, President Joe Biden referred to the President's Daily Briefing and announced that Russia is already in the process of interfering in the 2022 elections in the U.S. and spreading disinformation. The content of Russia's foreign and domestic propaganda operations, including current coverage of the Capitol riot hearings, leaves little doubt as to which side the Kremlin will continue to support.

Russia Is 'Enjoying' America's Failure — and Cozying Up to the Taliban

"The Taliban made all the relevant promises to us, let's hope they will be fulfilled," the Russian ambassador to Kabul said on Monday.

Originally published by *The Daily Beast* on August 16, 2021

The fall of Afghanistan's capital city to the Taliban provided Russia's state media with plenty of opportunities to churn out streams of anti-American propaganda, all while cozying up to the extremist militant group.

Unfavorably comparing the U.S. pullout to the Soviet Union's inglorious exit from the country known as the "graveyard of empires," Russian government officials and state news outlets described the takeover as a total defeat for the mightiest nation on earth.

Appearing on the state TV show *60 Minutes* on Monday, political scientist Oleg Matveychev asserted that the U.S. withdrawal from Afghanistan is beneficial for the Russian Federation: "Russia's authority is on the rise... this situation is beneficial for us... America no longer matters." He added that Russia should continue to "quietly strangle the United States... which is what Putin has already been doing."

Russia's courting of the Taliban extended to the Kremlin's English-speaking media, with RT providing a podium to the group's spokesman on August 14, 2021, aiming to prove that the U.S. mission in Afghanistan amounted to nothing more than a waste of time and money. "Where did the money go?" asked Mohammad Naim, appearing on RT Arabic.

The Taliban spokesperson went on: "We want the countries who still don't understand the reality of what's happening on the ground in Afghanistan, those countries that came to Afghanistan 20 years ago, we want them to understand who represents the Afghan people...These countries have to understand the reality." Referring to the Afghan government supported by the U.S., Naim asserted: "Why are people forced to have something they don't want, something that contradicts the principles and values of the people?"

While western countries evacuated their embassies as Kabul was being overtaken by the Taliban, Moscow didn't feel the need to do the same. Nikita Ishchenko, spokesman at the Russian embassy in Kabul, told the state media channel Russia-24 on Sunday that Moscow had no intention of evacuating the diplomatic mission: "The situation in Kabul is tense, but there is no war in the city... There are no threats to the embassy, no evacuation is required."

With respect to Russia's relationship with the transitional government of Afghanistan, Ishchenko said that Russia is "very actively" involved.

The Russian embassy in Kabul told state TV Channel 1 that "everything is peaceful and everyone is calmly fulfilling their duties."

Currently, only the embassies of Russia and China are functioning in Afghanistan. Both are being guarded by the Taliban, Russian ambassador to Kabul Dmitry Zhirnov told state TV channel Rossiya-1. "We want Afghanistan to be civilized so that there is no terrorism, there is no drugs, so that human rights are respected. The Taliban made all the relevant promises to us, let's hope they will be fulfilled," the ambassador said on Monday.

In spite of the undisguised glee in Moscow caused by the U.S. exit from Afghanistan, the reality on the ground and the potential spread of terrorism in the region do present a cause for concern, even to the Kremlin. State TV host Skabeeva acknowledged: "We can savor America's failure, yes, perhaps we are enjoying it... but it will cause problems for Russia as well."

In July, Russian Foreign Minister Sergey Lavrov said that the withdrawal of the U.S. military forces from Afghanistan represents a total failure of America's stated mission. This outcome is exactly what the Kremlin has been urging Washington to accept.

The withdrawal, set in motion by the Trump administration, was always a thrilling prospect to the Kremlin.

In early 2020 the United States and the Taliban signed an agreement aimed at ending the war in Afghanistan. In February 2021, NATO alleged that the Taliban has committed serious breaches of the peace deal and the U.N. questioned the assassination spree targeting Afghan human rights defenders and journalists.

The Kremlin jumped to the Taliban's defense, with Zamir Kabulov, Russia's presidential envoy to Afghanistan, claiming: "The Taliban adhere to the agreement almost flawlessly... which cannot be said about the Americans."

Russian state media experts openly worried that the Biden administration might not follow through with the U.S. exit. Nonetheless, pro-Kremlin analysts were encouraged by the fact that the terms of the peace deal Trump signed with the Taliban placed President Joe Biden in a no-win situation.

Writing for state media outlet RIA Novosti, in February 2021 political analyst Pyotr Akopov pompously claimed that by pushing the U.S. to proceed with the troop withdrawal announced by Trump, Russia is trying to save America "from inevitable war and shame."

The Kremlin's real motives have long been in question, especially after reports that Russia has been arming the Taliban and its foreign military intelligence service offered bounties to the militants to kill American soldiers.

After the Soviet Union's humiliating departure from Afghanistan in 1989, Russia has been seeking to increase its influence in the region, while edging out the U.S. and NATO. Even though the Russian Supreme Court declared the Taliban to be a terrorist organization in 2003, Moscow embraced its representatives and frequently hosted them for consultations and negotiations. During one such visit to Moscow in July of this year, the Taliban assured the Kremlin of its intent to curb drug production and trafficking.

Participating in a webinar in July, Foreign Minister Sergey Lavrov described the radical group as "rational people." On

August 15, state media outlet Vesti credulously repeated the Taliban's promise "to respect the rights of women."

One day later, host Olga Skabeeva reported on the state TV show *60 Minutes*, "Sharia Law is being imposed by the Taliban across Afghanistan. The rights of women are already being limited." She added that in Herat University in western Afghanistan all women were forcefully removed, and all female teachers will now be replaced by males.

Skabeeva predicted that Russia will run into "colossal problems" in dealing with the new government in Afghanistan: "Some of the Taliban are giving us guarantees while others are cutting off heads." Skabeeva surmised: "We will have to deal with these terrorists. Perhaps we will even have to stop calling these people terrorists."

In addition to strengthening their geopolitical stance, the withdrawal provided priceless propaganda opportunities to undermine the idea of alliances between the United States and other countries. China's state-run Global Times discussed the U.S. withdrawal from Afghanistan as a signal to democracy activists in Hong Kong that they should not believe American promises to stand by their side. Likewise, Russian state media peppered its broadcasts with repeated warnings to Ukraine, claiming that at some point America will abandon the country, just like it did with Afghanistan.

"Americans are traitors, it's dangerous to be friends with them", asserted Olga Skabeeva during the broadcast of *60 Minutes* on August 3, 2021.

In a wider context, Russian government officials claim that the U.S. withdrawal from Afghanistan represents a global failure of democracy. On August 15, on his Telegram channel, Senator Alexei Pushkov called the events in Afghanistan "a revenge of history, religion, and ideology over modernity and globalism." Pushkov described this course of events as "dramatic, or even catastrophic" not only for the United States but also for the entire 'liberal world order.'

Pushkov concluded: "Now the United States is retreating, along with its doctrine, which for 30 years has been the basis of their policy of "exporting democracy." Russian state media outlets approvingly re-printed Pushkov's conclusions.

On Monday Skabeeva described the situation with the withdrawal as a major blow to the reputation of the United States—and democracy. She referred to the current atmosphere in Afghanistan as "total hell," drawing comparisons to the fall of Saigon in the final days of the Vietnam War. Skabeeva said, "August 15 can be officially considered the end of American hegemony and the end of Afghanistan as we knew it since autumn of 2001. We're watching the most shameful escape of world hegemon."

Appearing on *60 Minutes* last week, Igor Korotchenko, a member of the Defense Ministry's public advisory council, described the United States as a "dinosaur, whose time is up." Retorting to former U.S. President Barack Obama's description of Russia as a gas station, during the August 16 broadcast of *60 Minutes* Korotchenko gloated: "I don't want to stomp on the American flag, but America is no longer a superpower. It's a regional power. The United States of America is North America's gas station. American greatness is over... Russia's hands are untied to do whatever is necessary."

The Russian Public Is Being Primed for Another of Putin's Wars

The Kremlin's propaganda campaign at home is getting people ready for a 'reluctant' move into Ukraine.

Originally published by *The Daily Beast* on November 24, 2021

Domestic propagandists and state TV pundits are promoting the idea of an inevitable confrontation with the West as Russia's military posture grows increasingly hostile, causing major concern for its nearest neighbors and NATO. Ukraine remains the crown jewel for the Kremlin and the Russian public is being primed for the intended absorption of more territories under the umbrella of the Russian Federation, while NATO is being accused of fomenting the potential escalation.

Whether or not the Kremlin is planning to speed up its creeping assault against Ukraine's Donbas region in the near future is a mystery even to the most knowledgeable experts with close access to Russian President Vladimir Putin. Nonetheless, they eagerly fulfill the Russian leader's express intent to keep NATO—and the West in general—in a state of hypervigilance. Ukraine's non-affiliation with NATO remains at the top of the Kremlin's long wish list, with Putin demanding "serious long-term guarantees that ensure Russia's security" in the region.

The real issue is not that NATO presents an acute threat to the Kremlin, but rather that its involvement stands in the way of Russia swallowing additional Ukrainian territories. Putin's objectives with respect to subverting Ukraine remain the same, with two different paths to getting there: by securing Ukraine's submission and undermining its sovereignty through unwarranted concessions from the West, or by escalating Russia's military aggression.

State TV propagandist Dmitry Kiselyov—notorious for boasting that "Russia is the only country in the world that is realistically capable of turning the United States into radioactive ash" — explained that Moscow's moves are explicitly designed to affect the U.S. and NATO. On his Sunday show, *Vesti Nedeli*, Kiselyov said that Russia's tests of its Tsirkon hypersonic cruise missile and its recent anti-satellite test were "arguments" to reinforce Russia's "red lines" with respect to Ukraine. Kiselyov boasted: "By stepping over the "red line," NATO risks losing all 32 GPS satellites at once, which will blind all their missiles, planes and ships, not to mention the ground forces. Americans are paying attention to this — they can't afford not to."

State TV experts equivocate between two conflicting messages: on one hand, claiming that Russia is not planning to invade Ukraine, but then immediately pointing out that "the Ukrainian problem" could be solved "very quickly," due to Russia's superior military might.

They argue that the U.S.-led NATO needs to be taught a lesson and brag that "underpaid and underfed American soldiers" are no match for the Russians. Blustery proclamations are promptly followed up by the claim that none of the participants are interested in a hot war.

Igor Korotchenko, a member of the Russian Defense Ministry's Public Council and editor-in-chief of the National Defense magazine, said the military movements that concerned Western and Ukrainian officials served as an intentional signal, designed to elicit a reaction.

In a message addressed to U.S. Secretary of State Antony Blinken on the state TV show *60 Minutes* this Monday, Korotchenko said about Russia's military buildup: "If your satellites are seeing this, that means it is being shown to you. Any American military analyst at the Pentagon can tell you that. You don't know — and won't know — Russia's real plans and goals. Your HUMINT [intelligence gathered by means of interpersonal contact] is either blocked, neutralized, or is feeding you disinformation, in course of the operations conducted by Russian intelligence services. You need to relax and aim towards constructive interaction."

Calling out the U.S. for being concerned with Russia's activities, the rabidly anti-American host of *60 Minutes*, Olga Skabeeva, insisted: "Mind your own business."

However, Russian state media does not abide by the same principles, with obsessive interest in American elections and internal affairs, dwelling on everything from QAnon and turkey prices to the sentencing of Jacob Chansley and the acquittal of Kyle Rittenhouse. America is at the forefront of the Kremlin's attention, so resorting to provocation in order to be acknowledged as an equal and to extract concessions would almost make sense.

During a speech to Russian diplomats last week, Putin complained: " We understand that our partners are very peculiar and, to put it mildly, do not take all our warnings and talks on red lines seriously." He added: "Our recent warnings have had a certain effect, tensions have risen... It is important for them to remain in this state for as long as possible."

Russian state TV pundits and propagandists took Putin's message to heart and snapped into action. Appearing on *60 Minutes* the day after Putin's speech, Igor Korotchenko warned: "Let's be straightforward about it: World War III is knocking at our door. It will come from the direction of Poland and Ukraine."

Korotchenko argued that Russia can fight back against alleged Western provocations by demonstrating its military might: "We need to grab the West by the udders, they should feel our hand and we should feel their fearful pulse... The best defense is an offense... Our military fist should be at the face of every Western politician."

On state TV show *Sunday Evening With Vladimir Solovyov*, lawmaker Oleg Morozov asserted: "The level of relations is so catastrophically low... that the possibility of a local hot conflict in the Ukrainian region is higher than ever. If this conflict takes place, it will break the entire construct of world relations. It will redraw the geographical map of Europe and change its political lines. The result will be what was promised by our president: the end of Ukrainian statehood... It will lead to total sanctions against Russia and the breakdown of all negotiations."

Adding fuel to the fire, host Vladimir Solovyov asked: "Then why should we stop at Ukraine? Why not solve all of our problems at once?"

Solovyov argued that since it's unlikely that the major world powers would resort to nuclear war, Russia can move forward with achieving its objectives undeterred: "If we have to end up behind the Iron Curtain, why not collect some more lands and peoples first?"

The head of the State Duma Committee on Defense, Andrei Kartapolov, suggested on the same show that the Ukrainian problem could be solved militarily in a matter of hours. He said: "If they intend to turn us into a pariah, there is no reason to stop at Ukraine... If they want to make us tremble, we should make them tremble." Morozov chimed in with a sly grin: "Which is what Putin said. Keep them on the edge of their seat."

Russian State TV Drops Deranged Love Letter to Its Darling 'Trumpushka'

Vladimir Putin's recent call with Joe Biden has Moscow's propaganda machine fawning over former U.S. President Donald Trump.

Originally published by *The Daily Beast* on December 08, 2021

Russian state media is, at least on the surface, jubilant about the outcome of the video summit between U.S. President Joe Biden and Russian President Vladimir Putin, which was focused on addressing Russia's potential further incursion into Ukraine.

State media outlet Vesti described the talks as "historic negotiations." State TV host Olga Skabeeva summed up the aftermath of the meeting during Wednesday's broadcast of Russia's *60 Minutes*: "WWIII is canceled—for now."

Suggesting that the delay afforded by the summit is merely temporary, Skabeeva quoted U.S. Undersecretary of State Victoria Nuland, who said that Putin wants not only to create a Soviet Union 2.0, but to control Eastern Europe as a whole. "All I would like to say about that—the sooner, the better," she said. "Russia won the first round," Vladimir Shamanov, who heads Moscow's parliamentary defense committee, added.

The shadow of former President Donald J. Trump hovered over talks between the United States and Russia. On Tuesday, as the summit was about to begin, Skabeeva alleged that Trump's approval ratings were much higher than Biden's.

Kremlin spokesman Dmitry Peskov pointed out that the special channel used for the video exchange between the presidents was created during Trump's tenure: "This is a secure channel. It was created according to decisions that were made by previous administrations. It was inactive but technologically maintained in a working state. Now we have decided to use it for the heads of state.

It creates the effect of a rather personal communication and... makes it possible to discuss very, very secretive topics."

Retired Army Col. Douglas Macgregor, who served as a senior official in the Trump administration's Department of Defense, gave an interview to Russian state media outlet RIA Novosti complaining that Biden "disregarded Russia's interests" and demonstrated his "inability to compromise." This, Macgregor complained, serves as cause for Putin's "surprise and dismay" with the stance of the current American leadership.

Macgregor is apparently comfortable with Kremlin-funded state media, having sat down for multiple interviews on RT over the years. He went on: "Washington has only one interest in the current crisis — to prevent unnecessary war between Ukraine and Russia. But Biden and his friends deliberately ignored this interest because it would involve compromise. As a morally righteous leftist, he is incapable of compromise."

Every time Trump makes a derogatory statement about his successor, Russian state media has showcased and applauded his commentary. The former president's position on Ukraine garnered special attention — and praise, with experts pontificating that under Trump, there would be no need for such a summit.

Two weeks before the talks between Biden and Putin, Trump appeared on Fox News for an interview with Sean Hannity. He said, in part: "I don't want to fight the battle for Ukraine, they've got to fight their own battles."

Trump's words delighted pro-Kremlin propagandists. State TV show *The Evening With Vladimir Solovyov* aired a translated clip of his statements to Hannity, and host Vladimir Solovyov introduced it by pointing out: "Things were so good under Trump... Listen to Trumpushka."

After listening to Trump dismiss the idea of helping Ukraine fight off Russian aggression, Solovyov sighed: "[He is] so sorely missed."

A day earlier, Solovyov had played a clip of Trump's interview with Mark Levin, on Fox News' Life, Liberty and Levin, in which the former U.S. president bashed the Mueller report for undermining U.S. relations with Russia. At the conclusion of Trump's commentary, Solovyov pumped his fist and exclaimed, "He said it well. Thank you, Donald Fredovych!"

Just hours after Biden concluded his video summit with Putin, Trump put out a statement through his Save America PAC, in which he said: "Vladimir Putin looks at our pathetic surrender in Afghanistan... He then looks at Biden. He is not worried!" Russian state media immediately broadcast Trump's comments on the Rossiya-24 TV channel.

Though most Russian experts and pundits had mainly negative expectations for the summit, they acted pleasantly surprised in its aftermath. The most recent version of the National Defense Spending Act (NDAA) for 2022 was released the day of the Biden-Putin talks. Missing from the final legislation was a provision passed by the House that directed Biden to impose sanctions over Nord Stream 2, as well as an amendment that would have banned Americans from purchasing Russian sovereign debt.

Also missing was an amendment to a defense budget bill by Rep. Tom Malinowski (D-NJ), which sought to punish 35 Russian officials, businessmen, and Kremlin propagandists. The list was compiled by the Anti-Corruption Foundation, or FBK, a group linked to jailed Russian opposition politician Alexei Navalny.

During his evening broadcast on Tuesday, state TV host Vladimir Solovyov offered up his hot take on the call. "They [the U.S.] didn't try to project external strength... or to insult the Russian side or President Putin... The news kept coming in: the [potential] sanctions against Nord Stream 2 have been taken out.

The amendment to the Defense Budget pertaining to the sovereign debt of the Russian Federation has been removed. The amendment with the list of 35 personal sanctions has been canceled, where I was named." Solovyov happily grinned and giggled.

Politologist Dmitry Drobnitsky concurred: "We forced them to show all of their cards. They opened up a box of candy, even though it was not their biggest one." Now, Russian state media outlets are forecasting that Trump would likely win over Biden in 2024 should he decide to run—and perhaps anticipating his return with an even bigger box of candy for Putin.

Russian Citizens Are Now Being Prepped for Nuclear War

Russian state TV is increasingly hysterical in its forecasts of an upcoming war, warning domestic audiences that the conflict could even become nuclear.

Originally published by *The Daily Beast* on December 21, 2021

The rhetoric on Kremlin-funded state television is amping up the sense of urgency around Russian President Vladimir Putin's NATO "ultimatum." Olga Skabeeva, the host of state TV show *60 Minutes*, said Tuesday: "The level of anxiety has reached its maximum. We're 20 days away from the expiration of the ultimatum and the stakes are rising, even though it seems they couldn't be any higher."

One day after Moscow submitted a draft of its Russia-U.S. security treaty, containing demands that NATO roll back its military deployments in Europe and deny membership to Ukraine and other post-Soviet countries, Deputy Foreign Minister Sergei Ryabkov threatened that Moscow would raise the stakes if the West didn't treat its demands seriously. On Monday, he told Interfax that Russia needs answers "urgently, because the situation is very difficult."

Pro-Kremlin propagandists and state-media experts filled in the blanks with what kind of escalation should be expected.

On Sunday's edition of News of the Week, state-TV host Dmitry Kiselyov explained: "Russia… prepared and handed over to the Americans its written proposals on strategic stability, or, more simply, on the prevention of nuclear war, since we are already at a critical point, to be honest… It's simple. The U.S. and NATO must roll back from our borders, otherwise we will, figuratively speaking, 'roll up' to their borders and create symmetrical, unacceptable risks… If you put a gun to our head, we will respond in kind… The whole point is that the development of the Ukrainian territory by the [Western] bloc is not only Ukraine's business. This is a complete breakdown of the global balance, which poses an existential threat to Russia. In other words, for Russia it is a matter of life and death... We simply will not allow it, regardless of the cost to us, and regardless of the cost to those responsible for it."

Kiselyov, notorious for his previous assertion that Russia is the only country that can reduce the U.S. to a pile of radioactive ash, revisited his beloved "argument" to explain why the United States will be willing to entertain Putin's unreasonable proposition.

He asserted that Russia is willing to suffer any consequences and go to any lengths to get what it wants: "Never before has anyone published the texts of the proposed treaties. But never before in the 21st century has the situation been so acute, and the risks so great. Non-standard situations require non-standard approaches. Secondly, we're holding very strong cards in our hands. Our hypersonic weapons are guaranteed to produce a response that is so unpleasant for America to hear: being reduced to radioactive ash."

Putin ordered two nuclear-capable long-range bombers to fly into European airspace this weekend, as they were dispatched to patrol Belarus. Just a week ago, Russia warned that it would redeploy intermediate-range nuclear weapons on its Western flank—in striking distance of central Europe—for the first time since they were banned in a 1987 treaty between presidents Ronald Reagan and Mikhail Gorbachev.

There have also been grim signs of things to come from the Russian government. A new national standard for "Urgent burial of corpses in peacetime and wartime" has been introduced by the government in recent months. It will come into force on February 1, 2022, and specifies the burial in mass graves to be dug by bulldozers, disposing of as many as 1,000 bodies in a 24-hour time period.

Bodies are to be placed "in four layers, either in bags, wooden coffins or zinc coffins, prepared in advance... and subsequently covered with dirt. Then the mass graves will be compacted with a bulldozer, filled with "a mineral binder" and equipped with "devices for the absorption and neutralization of radioactive, hazardous chemicals and biological agents formed during the decomposition of corpses."

Russia's government agency responsible for the creation of the new standards did not respond to journalists' inquiries as to the purpose behind this effort. Military expert Alexander Goltz told newspaper Novye Izvestiya: "Those who prepared these standards thought in terms of either a global epidemic or a global war, in which not only the military, but also the civilian population would die. This is only possible with the use of nuclear weapons."

Former military spokesman Viktor Baranets concurred and added: "It may turn out that we will have to send troops not only to Donetsk and the Lugansk regions, but also to the greater Ukraine. We have a flaming fuse in the Black Sea region. There are also dangers in the region of Belarus and concerns in the Kaliningrad region. [NATO] has grandiose plans for the immediate capture of the Kaliningrad region, even with the use of nuclear weapons. And how, then, will we bury? One by one, or what?" He added: "We're getting ready for the major crises."

Chess legend and a highly knowledgeable critic of the Kremlin Garry Kasparov — who was way ahead of his time with his 2016 book "Winter Is Coming: Why Vladimir Putin and the Enemies of the Free World Must Be Stopped" — described the Russian government's creation of the "mass burial" standard as one of "the signposts on the way to apocalypse."

Propagandists on Russia's state-funded television stressed that Moscow is now approaching the West from a position of strength. Discussing the Kremlin's bold and unreasonable ultimatums to the U.S. and its allies, Kiselyov said: "This is a moment of truth in our relations with America, in which we move on to complete reciprocity... From a position of strength, we simply designate a 'cause and effect' relationship. That's how it will be." With brazen arrogance of a seasoned mobster borrowed from The Godfather, Russia's top propagandist concluded: "You, over there in the U.S., NATO and the EU, decide for yourself: Is Russia making an offer that can be refused?"

On Saturday, Russian Deputy Foreign Minister Alexander Grushko discussed Putin's ultimatum to the United States and

NATO with pro-Kremlin propagandist Vladimir Solovyov, who donned a red hoodie emblazoned with a Soviet hammer and sickle emblem. In an episode of Solovyov's show entitled "NATO's Capitulation," Grushko said: "The moment of truth has come. We have reached a red line and our proposals aim to pull us away from this red line and start normal dialogue that will put security interests at the forefront."

He described the Kremlin's hard-nosed demand to the West as "throwing the rock into their swamp" and explained that Western refusal to play by Moscow's rules will lead to "a military or military-technical response," with Russia "creating counter-threats" to the United States and its allies.

On Monday, in response to the question as to whether Russia could deploy nuclear weapons to Belarus, Kremlin spokesman Dmitry Peskov told journalists: "It's no secret that the deployment of various kinds of weapons near our borders, which can pose a danger to us, clearly requires adequate steps to balance the situation. Various options are available."

In past years, Russian lawmakers have been advocating the placement of Russia's advanced weapons systems in Cuba, Central America, and elsewhere "in America's underbelly." Those options likely remain on Moscow's menu. On Tuesday, state-TV host Olga Skabeeva pointed out: "We're contemplating placing our nuclear weapons in Cuba or Venezuela."

Conveying the message that could be summed up as "USSR or bust," Russia's national ice hockey team sparked outrage in Europe by wearing Soviet uniforms in Euro Hockey Tour's Channel One Cup in Moscow on Sunday. The return to Soviet imagery is in total coordination with Putin's ultimatum to the West that seeks a rematch in the Cold War that was lost by the Soviet Union.

On Monday, Skabeeva surmised: "The United States have to sign off on the notion that their hegemony is over." She added: "The declaration about a military response is being made by our Foreign Affairs Ministry... which never happened before. Russia is placing the United States in a no-win situation: either they retreat voluntarily, or we will force them to retreat. At the same time, Russia is not taking any obligations upon itself with respect to the preservation of Ukraine, much less of its sovereignty."

How Tucker Carlson Is Boosting Russia's New Propaganda War

As Putin and Biden talk, Kremlin mouthpieces are rushing to explain the motivations behind Russia's surge in aggression. Fox News is helping them do their work.

Originally published by *The Daily Beast* on December 30, 2021

President Joe Biden and Russian President Vladimir Putin are set to speak on Thursday, in preparation for January 10 talks, convened to address Putin's demand for "security guarantees" that aims to stymie NATO's ability to carry out its functions in Europe. Moscow's elite diplomats and talking heads are openly discussing Russia's goals and strategies. Arguing for America's total capitulation, with the Kremlin allegedly planning to offer no concessions or guarantees, Russian experts propose a plan to make such an outcome acceptable to the general public in the U.S. by waging an aggressive international info-campaign.

Russia's state TV propagandists express their delight in seemingly having the likes of Tucker Carlson in their corner, praising his coverage as the prime example of Russia's successful influence operations abroad. Carlson's talking points often sound identical to those pushed by the Kremlin's propagandists — or by Putin himself.

During one of his broadcasts on Fox News in December, Carlson argued that "NATO exists primarily to torment Vladimir Putin." He worried about the possibility of "a NATO takeover of Ukraine," and described the 2014 Maidan Revolution as a U.S.-organized "coup in Ukraine." He also baselessly accused Joe Biden of fomenting "a hot war with Russia."

The very next day, translated quotes from Tucker Carlson's show were widely broadcast on Russia's state television. After watching Carlson's remarks during the live taping of *60 Minutes*,

Igor Korotchenko, member of the Russian Defense Ministry's Public Council and editor-in-chief of the National Defense magazine said: "Excellent performance, with which we can only express solidarity."

Carlson's claims that the U.S. is pushing the world to the brink of a nuclear war with Russia fit squarely within the Kremlin's current propaganda offensive. During Tuesday's live broadcast of *The Evening With Vladimir Solovyov*, host Vladimir Solovyov expressed his concerns about convincing Americans that the fears of war are real: "Americans change their behavior only when there is an existential threat to their population... Their memory of WWI is much greater than that of WWII, because of the numbers of those who perished and the difficulty of that war. We often think of Americans as the mirror image of ourselves and our concerns. They only look like us. Their mentality is completely, absolutely different."

Political scientist and Professor of Communications Dmitry Evstafiev articulated the fear tactics, meant to convince everyday Americans to surrender U.S. interests in order to avoid war with Russia. He said: "Just look at how much they [the U.S.] started to talk about peace lately. There is only one way to balance that. We need to start talking about war with American and European societies. American and Western societies don't understand what a war with Russia would mean. They think that a war would take place somewhere far off, but we should explain that it will come up close. A war is very comfortable when a drone flies over and kills someone, but no, a bomber plane will come and kill you... A coffin draped with a stars-and-stripes flag should arrive... to an American city. In this context, we should start a very serious conversation with Western societies — not about peace, but about war."

Russian Deputy Foreign Minister Sergey Ryabkov is set to represent Russia during the talks concerning the so-called "security guarantees" sought by Moscow. His comments ahead of the meeting provided a revealing glimpse into the Kremlin's belligerent attitude.

Sitting down with a reporter on Tuesday, Ryabkov threatened the United States: "An abyss between what is desirable and necessary for the collective West — as opposed to what we need — keeps deepening and widening. A bridge could be built upon the platform that we proposed. If that bridge doesn't get built, fortress walls will be built instead, with cannon balls raining down from them and hot tar pouring down onto their heads. People who say that Russia should be placed in the corner, like a misbehaving pupil, underestimate what might happen next. They've lost their grip on reality and common sense. I hope they haven't lost their sense of self-preservation."

Like Ryabkov, Russian Foreign Minister Sergey Lavrov scoffed at the possibility of Russia being punished by additional Western sanctions. During his appearance on Monday's broadcast of Solovyov's online show Solovyov Live, Lavrov dismissed the idea that Russia could be cut off from the world's banking systems or otherwise isolated. He also pointed out that high-ranking members of Russia's military will participate in the upcoming January talks with the United States: "The military will be represented at a high level in our delegation. We asked [the U.S.] to confirm whether we were correct by our understanding that the same would be done on their part." Lavrov added that Russia wasn't planning to offer any concessions, claiming that it has already given up too much over the last decades.

Hosting *60 Minutes* on Wednesday, Evgeny Popov marveled: "It seems to me that our diplomats never spoke to the United States so harshly." Andrei Bezrukov, a Russian spy whose life story served as the inspiration for the hit TV show The Americans, replied: "The balance of power has changed. Twenty years ago we couldn't talk to them this way... Now we can show them something and they understand that. The new balance of power — including military power — is what brought them to the negotiating table."

Vitaly Tretyakov, dean of the Moscow State University's School of Television, concurred: "Nothing in the history of the world ever happens without military force... Pacifists don't determine world politics... Our Foreign Affairs Ministry was so cultured for the past 20 years, now it's hard for Americans and other westerners to fathom that it stopped being so civil. Its formerly cordial demeanor sank into oblivion."

Moscow's approach to the upcoming exchange apparently hinges on the perception of invincibility and the idea of Russia's "military superiority." Offering no concessions, the Kremlin expects to get them from the United States by evoking the threat of World War III as the sword of Damocles that hangs over the world's head. Moscow's elite propagandists are hard at work, gaslighting domestic and foreign audiences.

Appearing on the state TV program *60 Minutes* on Tuesday, military expert Korotchenko predicted: "January is becoming a key month that will determine the course of humanity's modern history... These three summits will determine what will happen next. Whether we will directly move on to WWIII... or the red lines will be acknowledged and we will cement the status quo, where the interests of Moscow and NATO will be balanced. The main thing is, Russia will no longer retreat."

The stream of demands accompanied by nuclear threats continually emanates from Moscow. During last Friday's broadcast of *60 Minutes*, State Duma deputy Mikhail Delyagin asserted: "Nuclear mushroom may rise over Ukraine, but the NATO flag may not."

Trump's Mega-Fans in Moscow Declare They're 'Ready to Elect Him Again'

The U.S. response to Russian aggression in Ukraine has angered the Kremlin's top pundits so much that they're publicly implying they'll help make Donald Trump president again.

Originally published by *The Daily Beast* on January 31, 2022

U.S. lawmakers are preparing to unveil the "mother of all sanctions" against the Kremlin's elite should Russia choose to invade Ukraine, and it's not sitting well with Moscow's top mouthpieces. Faced with growing U.S. resistance, Russia's government-funded state TV has become more brazen than ever in its calls to get former President Donald Trump back in the White House.

"The city on a hill is again being taken over by the Trumpists. Donald already declared that he will become the 47th president of America and will figure things out with Russia and Putin," host Olga Skabeeva said on Monday's segment of the Russian TV show *60 Minutes*. "Donald, we're waiting for you and are ready to elect you again."

In his bombastic tirade at the "Save America" rally in Conroe, Texas two days earlier, Trump claimed that Joe Biden's support for Ukraine and his persistent attempts to deter further Russian aggression do nothing other than "create a very real risk of World War III."

The same idea was discussed by Russian experts, pundits and lawmakers on state television, where they opined that if Americans fear the prospect of a nuclear war, they should agree to look the other way while Russia deals with Ukraine.

After broadcasting some of Trump's translated remarks, in which he bashed U.S. Democrats and boasted about his great relationship with Russian President Vladimir Putin, Skabeeva reiterated some of his offensive commentary, claiming that House Speaker Nancy Pelosi is "crazier than a bed bug." State Duma deputy Mikhail Delyagin chimed in to participate in Trump's trash-talking by claiming those remarks were "insulting to bed bugs." Skabeeva added: "Nancy Pelosi is a bed bug. Could you say he's wrong? You can immediately see that he is our guy. Donald, please come back."

Kremlin-funded state television has been quite brazen about Russian interference in U.S. elections in the past. In 2019, Skabeeva's husband and co-host Evgeny Popov discussed the findings of the Mueller report, defiantly telling *The Daily Beast*: "Soon, we will help you elect Trump once again. Just like the last time. Get ready!"

Earlier this month, Russian state TV reporter Valentin Bogdanov, who is based in New York City, created a new program called "Goodbye America." It focuses on what it describes as the decline and the impending downfall of the United States. The first two episodes predicted Trump will be re-elected in 2024.

Bogdanov also noted Tucker Carlson's contributions in convincing a number of Republicans that the United States should not intervene against Russian aggression on behalf of Ukraine.

In recent interviews, Carlson not only dismissed the idea of helping Ukraine, but made cynical jokes at the expense of the country's bloody fight for its independence. He told The Spectator: "Here, I'm looking at tens of thousands of Russian citizens massed on the Ukrainian border, hoping to get in for a better life. And I'm seeing world leaders say, 'No, you're not allowed to do that—Ukraine is for Ukrainians'! I mean, speaking of ethno-nationalism, why is it if we can import thousands of Haitians illegally, why is it such a lift with the Ukrainians to just let several thousand Russians in?"

Trump's comments encouraging the abandonment of Ukraine were also praised and repeatedly broadcast on Russian state television. His lambasting of NATO appears to fill Kremlin propagandists with nostalgic memories of what might have been.

"Trump was ready to disband NATO," Vladimir Solovyov, the host of state TV show *The Evening With Vladimir Solovyov*, declared this weekend.

Covering Trump's remarks at his recent Texas rally, state media outlet Vesti published a piece entitled "Trump discussed his friendship with Putin and said that Biden ruined everything." Kremlin-controlled talking heads seem to be signaling that Russia sees Trump's potential return as a solution for all of its problems, to the detriment of NATO and the West.

Welcome to the Fantasy World Where Putin Already 'Won This Round'

Celebrations of a great Russian "victory" in the Ukraine crisis are already underway in this media dream land.

Originally published by *The Daily Beast* on February 16, 2022

Russia has not yet launched a full-scale invasion of Ukraine, but pundits on Kremlin-funded state television stress that the delay is only temporary. They openly laugh at the tension and turmoil caused by Vladimir Putin's military build-up near the Ukrainian border. State media host Vladimir Solovyov kicked off his Wednesday's broadcast of Solovyov Live by theatrically yelling, "Good morning Kyiv and Lviv!" apparently attempting to imitate the late Robin Williams in the famed war comedy "Good Morning, Vietnam."

A day earlier, Olga Skabeeva, host of the state TV show *60 Minutes*, theatrically exclaimed, "The war with Ukraine has been temporarily postponed." She opened Wednesday's live broadcast by mockingly announcing, "This is a sad celebration for us, the day of non-invasion of Ukraine."

Through and through, state media propagandists have been hyper-focused on portraying Moscow's every move as a string of strategic victories by Putin.

Appearing on the state TV show *The Evening With Vladimir Solovyov*, political scientist and Professor of Communications Dmitry Evstafiev boasted: "We won this round." The host, Vladimir Solovyov, corrected him: "This was merely our debut, the early stages of our debut."

Evstafiev continued: "We won this debut, it's evident from the way they are taking a step back." The host continued his thought: "They [the West] suddenly started to talk to us. They haven't spoken to us in years. More than that, serious divisions manifested within the European Union. Colossal divisions within NATO."

State media pundits gleefully discussed the statement by Hungary's foreign minister Péter Szijjártó, who asserted that his country will not accept further NATO troops on its soil and criticized sanctions against Russia.

They were also pleased with German chancellor Olaf Scholz, who played down the likelihood of Ukraine joining NATO in the foreseeable future during Monday's press conference in Kyiv. Scholz's refusal to discuss Germany's intent with respect to Nord Stream 2, in the event of Russia's open invasion of Ukraine, also brought glee to Moscow's talking heads. "He publicly buried Ukraine," Solovyov concluded.

Meanwhile, Russian Foreign Minister Lavrov has dubbed recent Western intelligence leaks about Russia's potential invasion of Ukraine as "info-terrorism."

Kremlin media, on the other hand, is continuing to push their pretext-building rhetoric, with Putin himself promoting baseless claims of alleged "genocide" of Russians in Ukraine's Donbas region as state TV hosts air segments packed with gory images of unknown origin.

Kremlin spokesman Dmitry Peskov described the State Duma's request to recognize the self-proclaimed Donetsk and Lugansk People's Republics (DPR, LPR) as "a very clear sign indicating the mood of lawmakers and the nation's prevailing public opinion," but admitted that such a decision would be in contravention with Minsk accords. Nonetheless, having handed out more than 870,000 Russian passports to residents of DPR and LPR, Moscow is not backing down.

Despite Moscow's announcement that having completed exercises, some of its troops are now returning to their bases, information released by Russia's Defense Ministry clarified that Russian units being withdrawn from Crimea are merely going back to their bases located near the Ukrainian border. State media outlet Izvestia reported that the 3rd and 150th motor rifle divisions are based in Boguchar and Valuyki, located in the immediate vicinity of the border with Ukraine. Only the 42nd division is returning back to

Chechnya, which is considerably farther away. NATO's secretary general Jens Stoltenberg told reporters on Wednesday that Russia appeared to be increasing—not reducing—its troop presence along Ukraine's border: "So far we have not seen any de-escalation on the ground. On the contrary, it appears that Russia continues their military buildup."

"The world without Russia would be boring," pontificated Karen Shakhnazarov, CEO of Mosfilm Studio and a prominent fixture on Russian state TV news talk shows on his Tuesday's appearance on *The Evening With Vladimir Solovyov*. He opined that Putin was clearly bluffing and Russia isn't militarily ready for a full-scale invasion of Ukraine, but the strategy of intimidation through Moscow's show of force is working wonders. He surmised: "It's exhausting them, it's exhausting the West and draining its energy."

Margarita Simonyan, editor-in-chief of the state media outlet RT, was pleased with the Kremlin's strategy of ratcheting up tensions. Referring to Putin as "the Boss," she tweeted: "The boss never works according to someone else's schedule. And he doesn't do what he is told to do... We demonstrated everything we wanted to." Simonyan added that the devastating impact of Putin's war games on Ukraine's economy brought her pleasure. Ever the hawkish propagandist and a fervent proponent of an escalation, RT's head added an ominous threat: "Our Defense Ministry's tanks can travel right back, just as fast as they left."

Russian State TV Is So Ridiculous Right Now It Looks Like a Farce

The TV propaganda has taken a farcical turn with Kremlin insiders begging President Biden not to start a vicious war in Ukraine. No mention of the Russian tanks.

Originally published by *The Daily Beast* on February 20, 2022

Anyone watching nothing but Russian state television would never know President Putin has massed his troops on the border of Ukraine, that Kremlin-controlled separatists shelled a kindergarten full of children and Russian forces are in position for an offensive against its beleaguered neighbor.

On Kremlin-funded networks, the vision of events is presented not only upside down, but backwards. Panicked pundits blame the United States and Ukraine for the escalation, claim that Russia doesn't want the war and theatrically ponder: "Why won't somebody stop Biden?"

Chairman of the International Committee of Russia's State Duma, Leonid Slutsky alleged that the president of the United States is painting "an absolutely inverted picture of the situation around Ukraine" and accused Joe Biden of misrepresenting "the alleged readiness of the Russian Federation to invade Ukraine."

Slutsky added that "the American president, talking about the "villain-Russia," the very Russia that today accepts and saves the civilian population of the LPR and DPR, seems like a real character from [Lewis Carroll's topsy-turvy children's book] Through the Looking-Glass."

And yet, it is Russia who has turned white into black, and black into white. If there were not so many lives hanging in the balance, you would describe current Russian state TV as a darkly comic farce.

Events on the ground are unfolding just as the American president had warned, based on the information provided by U.S. intelligence agencies. U.S. Ambassador to the OSCE Michael Carpenter said that according to U.S. assessments, Russia has placed somewhere between 169,000 and 190,000 troops near Ukraine's borders — up from 100,000 at the end of January.

Having massed its troops and armaments on the Ukrainian border, Russia stands ready to invade Ukraine. On Friday, Kremlin-controlled heads of the self-proclaimed "republics" in Eastern Ukraine (LPR and DPR) started unprovoked evacuations of civilians to Russia, followed by suspicious explosions in the region. Russia's state media immediately — and baselessly — blamed the Ukrainian military. State TV channel Rossiya-24 reported: "Let's address the emergency event that took place several minutes ago."

The correspondent present on the scene said, "Everyone is trying to figure out what happened here." The headline read: "The Ukrainian army struck the gas pipeline in Luhansk." What makes this all the more bizarre is that the U.S. had publicly predicted these very tactics.

Just as the U.S. administration had warned, Russian authorities now appear to be readying themselves for the re-invasion of Ukraine under false pretexts.

One of the main pretexts aggressively promoted by the Kremlin and Russia's state media is the unfounded allegation of "genocide" of Russian speakers by the Ukrainian military. Back in December of 2021, Russian President Vladimir Putin claimed: "What is happening in Donbas right how we know and see very well, it's very reminiscent of genocide."

By February, the state media and Russian officials went full bore with their accusations of "genocide" in Ukraine. According to a report by the Wall Street Journal, Russian officials circulated a document at the UN Security Council meeting on Thursday, accusing the Ukrainian government of the "genocide of the Russian-speaking population of Donbas."

Speaking before that UN Security Council meeting, Secretary of State Antony Blinken said that according to the information obtained by the U.S. intelligence agencies, Russia was planning to use a false flag attack in Eastern Ukraine, followed by baseless accusations of "genocide" in the region.

Blinken pointed out: "Russia may describe this event as ethnic cleansing or a genocide, making a mockery of a concept that we in this chamber do not take lightly, nor do I take lightly, based on my family history."

German Chancellor Olaf Scholz's dismissal of Moscow's assertion of "genocide" in the eastern Ukraine's region of Donbas enraged Russian officials. On Saturday, Russian Foreign Ministry scolded Scholz and Germany as a whole: "It is not for German leaders to laugh at the issues of genocide. This is unacceptable, given the historical experience of Germany in matters of massacres against people and the spread of misanthropic ideology." Russian state TV went even further, with the host of *60 Minutes* Olga Skabeeva cynically asserting: "Germans have different ideas about genocide. They'll have to start burning people in ovens, and maybe then they'll concede: 'Yes, it's genocide.'"

Russia's state media is spreading claims of Ukraine allegedly shelling the regions of Donbas and on Saturday alleged that the Ukrainians shelled Russia's Rostov Region, located near the border with Ukraine. The Commander-in-Chief of the Armed Forces of Ukraine, Lieutenant General Valery Zaluzhny, denied all of Russia's accusations, stating in part: "It should be noted that the artillery units of the Joint Forces are located in areas of withdrawal at a distance of more than 21 km from the line of contact, which exceeds the maximum firing range of multiple rocket launchers "Hail" and 122-mm guns in service with the Armed Forces of Ukraine."

Anticipating false accusations from the Kremlin, Ukrainian authorities allowed access to a number of local and international journalists. NBC's Richard Engel noted: "The separatists are claiming Ukrainians are attacking and besieging them. I've walked up and down those trenches for the last several months. Saw no signs of ongoing or impending Ukrainian offensive. None." Meanwhile, streams of state media news reports claim that Ukraine is aggressively shelling Donbas, alleging "the most intensive bombardments by the Ukrainian military in recent months."

In a bizarro world of Russia's state media, America—which has been painstakingly attempting to prevent an escalation—is the true aggressor. Appearing on *60 Minutes* on Friday, lawmaker Oleg Morozov lamented: "I'm hoping there are people next to Biden, next to Scholz, next to the British PM, who will look at the scenarios and say, 'If the big war with Russia's participation were to start, it will cost Europe dearly. Think about that!' That is my last hope, that the fear of this unpredictable situation will stop these hotheads."

Igor Korotchenko, a member of the Russian Defense Ministry's Public Council and editor-in-chief of the National Defense magazine, exclaimed: "The United States want this war. Their main goal is to take over Europe's energy market. Biden could care less about the victims and their suffering, about Europe's losses. He is realizing the plans of the American establishment."

Summarizing the grotesque new theme in the Kremlin's war on truth, Korotchenko theatrically pleaded with European leaders: "Stop Zelensky! Stop Biden!"

Kremlin TV Asks 'Where's the Champagne?' as Ukraine's Kids Are Prepped for War

While Ukrainian mothers share tips on how to make their children's blood types easily identifiable, Putin's most ardent supporters are demanding a little bit of bubbly on live TV.

Originally published by *The Daily Beast* on February 21, 2022

Russian President Vladimir Putin stunned the world on Monday when he unilaterally recognized two Kremlin-backed separatist regions in Ukraine, Luhansk and Donetsk, as independent states and ordered Russian troops to conduct so-called "peacekeeping operations" there. The move has sparked widespread condemnation from global leaders who have accused Putin of violating international law and expressed concerns that the latest escalation may soon morph into a full-scale Russian invasion of its neighbor.

In Ukraine, Putin's decision has only exacerbated the pain and anguish caused by years of bloody conflict, fueled and funded by the Kremlin. Parents across the country have been doing whatever they can to prepare their families for a potential Russian onslaught.

"If you want to know how Ukrainians react to Putin's speech, here's a glimpse: moms on Facebook discuss putting stickers on their children's clothes, when they go to school, indicating their blood type," journalist Olga Tokariuk tweeted on Monday. "Make no mistake: this speech was perceived as a declaration of war on Ukraine."

For some, the new developments have only deepened their resolve to fight back. "With his speech alone Putin consolidated Ukrainians like no-one else here could. My friends are talking about joining the territorial defense," Ukrainian reporter Iryna Matviyishyn wrote. "And currently the Kremlin's madman is the most hated person in Ukraine."

In contrast, there was joy and laughter on Russia's state television.

On Monday, RT's editor-in-chief Margarita Simonyan appeared on *The Evening With Vladimir Solovyov* ready for a major celebration. "First of all, I don't understand why there isn't champagne in the studio," she said. Beaming ear-to-ear, Simonyan described feeling "an overwhelming sense of euphoria" and added: "I've been waiting for 8 years for this... It finally happened. This is true happiness."

Claiming to speak on behalf of the "Donbas' people," Simonyan exclaimed: "Thank you, Mother Russia!" She predicted that the rest of the world will be "overcome by anger to the point of spitting" and that "hard times and more sanctions are coming" for Russia. A day earlier, Simonyan appeared on state TV channel TVC's program The Right To Know and reiterated that she's always been a vocal proponent of Russia "taking Donbas home."

The editor-in-chief acknowledged that such a solution was achievable only by military means. In truly Orwellian fashion, Russian state media was prepping the public for the prospect of war with Ukraine, but attempting to place the blame exclusively on the United States and NATO.

On Sunday's *Vesti Nedeli*, host Dmitry Kiselyov claimed that the United States and NATO want war with Russia. The host praised Russia's nuclear capabilities, for which he thanked Joseph Stalin, Lavrentiy Beria, Julius and Ethel Rosenberg, among others. This attempt to whitewash odious figures of the past corresponded with Putin's obvious desire to turn back time. In his speech to the nation, he rejected the idea of former Soviet republics being allowed to "simply leave" the oppressive union. Kiselyov argued that Russia is "forcibly making the world happy by offering a new global system of equal security... Thanks again to Russian weapons."

On Solovyov's Monday show, prominent pundit Karen Shakhnazarov asserted that Putin's ultimatum to NATO was written for the sole purpose of absolving the Kremlin of its responsibility to peacefully "solve" the issue of Donbas. After Russia sent its proposal to NATO, elite talking heads and military experts on Russia's state television openly stated that it was a mere formality meant to legitimize Russia's forthcoming military actions. In January, RT's Simonyan tweeted that the Kremlin's proposals to "NATO enemies" were never meant to be accepted.

Still seething about German Chancellor Olaf Scholz's refusal to accept the Kremlin's allegations of "genocide" being committed by the Ukrainian government in Donbas, political scientist and professor of communications Dmitry Evstafiev argued that "decent chancellors of Germany" would have shot themselves if they were in his place. He added: "This is a verdict for Germany and its bid for European leadership."

During Solovyov's Monday show, Simonyan seemed particularly excited about one point in Putin's speech, in which he mentioned knowing the names of those Russia wants to "punish." Simonyan interpreted the word "punish" to mean dealing with such people "extrajudicially." These dark proclamations correspond with intelligence warnings about Russia's "kill lists" that would come into play in the event of a military occupation of Ukraine. Appearing on *60 Minutes* last Friday, state TV pundits and experts predicted that in the case of an escalation, many "heads would roll," including that of Ukrainian President Volodymyr Zelensky.

Lawmaker Oleg Morozov asserted: "If the war starts, I wouldn't bet one penny on Mr. Zelensky's life and safety." In another of Solovyov's shows on Sunday, Margarita Simonyan made an ominous prediction. Describing Ukraine as "ungrateful" for all of the "gifts" and benefits it allegedly received from the Soviet Union and Russia, RT's editor-in-chief said: "They became traitors towards us. They're looking to join NATO, our enemy." She concluded: "And what does Russia do to traitors? The answer is obvious."

Putin's Own Minions Are Exposing Him for the Liar He Is

Putin diehards across Moscow have inadvertently revealed the president's web of lies on Ukraine.

Originally published by *The Daily Beast* on February 23, 2022

As Russian President Vladimir Putin painstakingly built up momentum for his recognition of the self-proclaimed "republics" in eastern Ukraine, Russian state media and loose-lipped lawmakers signaled his plans in advance.

Putin's bold-faced demand for "security guarantees'" caught the West off-guard, but the pro-Kremlin mouthpieces were bursting with pride about the leader's "genius" plan. They spilled the beans on state television and even in Russian parliament, boasting about how Putin had intentionally asked for the impossible, only to turn around and use NATO's refusal as an excuse to re-invade Ukraine on a larger scale. In addition to blaming NATO for allegedly threatening Russia with its expansion, Russian state media and the cadre of covert operators in eastern Ukraine worked to ratchet up the tensions. The simmering conflict was set ablaze with a series of alleged attacks against civilians, unexplained explosions and even alleged attempts to shell and penetrate the Russian border.

Eliot Higgins, founder of the open-source investigation team Bellingcat, along with his team, quickly debunked Russia's multiple false-flag videos as sloppy fabrications. Higgins tweeted: "These are genuinely some of the most idiotic efforts at disinformation I've seen. I expected to be lied to, but I didn't expect all those lies to be so blatantly dumb. I'm actually offended at the poor quality of this propaganda..."

The Kremlin's plans were dampened not only by the Biden administration's decision to release key findings of U.S. intelligence agencies. Russian lawmakers and state TV personalities also laid bare the Kremlin's intent to attack Ukraine, a plan they imply was hatched long before the recent false-flag operations were set into motion.

During a recorded speech at the State Duma on December 2021, Vladimir Zhirinovsky, the ultranationalist leader of Russia's Liberal Democratic Party, discussed Putin's sham proposal to NATO. Zhirinovsky told fellow parliamentarians: "I liked one phrase from what the President said yesterday... he said that we won't allow our proposal to result only in futile discussions... They either fulfill it, or we're moving forward with another option... Let it be February 22, 2022 at 4 a.m." Zhirinovsky added: "The year 2022 is the year of the tiger. It's a breakthrough, a jump by the Russian tiger...This won't be a peaceful year, but a year when Russia will become great again and everyone will have to shut up and respect our country."

That wasn't the first time Zhirinovsky had made predictions about the current chaos unfolding in Ukraine. Back in 2018, in an appearance on state TV show *60 Minutes*, Zhirinovsky said: "We don't need a part of Ukraine, we're waiting for it to be primed to take the whole thing. We'll be taking all of Ukraine in its entirety." The audience clapped. Zhirinovsky continued: "Americans [the Trump administration] are ready to accept that Russia will get the southern and eastern regions of Ukraine. But if they get to keep the western parts, they'll be mounting provocations out of there. All of Ukraine will go to Russia. But only when the situation is ripe."

Putin signed a decree ordering troop deployments to eastern Ukraine after announcing his decision to recognize the independence of Ukraine's two breakaway regions on February 21. A day later, Russia's lower house of parliament, the State Duma, unanimously voted to approve friendship treaties with the territories. State TV propagandist Vladimir Solovyov described Zhirinovsky as a "prophet," as he replayed his State Duma predictions on his show *Full Contact*, during a segment entitled "Russian troops enter Donbas... The new world order." But Zhirinovsky's blabbing was hardly a prophecy. It seemed to be part of the plan, known and understood by many in Putin's circle.

Earlier this year, Russian military expert Igor Korotchenko asked on another state TV segment: "Why did we need these talks? I believe, for only one reason: legitimizing Russia's further military and military-technical activities," he said, answering his own question. "We knew in advance how these talks would end... we said, it's time for a new reality, when diplomacy is powerless. It's time for militarily coercive diplomacy on the part of Russia. We will hit carefully, but hard. In this sense, Russia's hands should be—and will be—untied for any actions."

Host Olga Skabeeva responded by saying Putin already made his decision and the talks with Americans and NATO "merely a formality, just to show we tried everything." She went on: "We're talking to them so brashly, it's clear that we've already decided what to do and how to behave." Quoting Putin's infamous expression, Korotchenko added: "If a fight is inevitable, you must strike first." He predicted that Russia's recognition of the self-proclaimed republics in eastern Ukraine would immediately lead to the official integration of their military forces with those of Russia. On the same day, RT's head Margarita Simonyan tweeted that the Kremlin's proposals to "NATO enemies" were never meant to be accepted.

These "prophecies" about the Ukraine crisis on Russian state television go even further back. In November of last year, Kremlin lawmaker Aleksei Zhuravlyov proclaimed: "Ukraine is a problem that I believe will be solved in the near future." When host Olga Skabeeva said she didn't understand what the lawmaker was implying, he cryptically responded: "You will understand, and soon. I'm sure of that." Skabeeva quickly caught on: "The conclusion: Russia has a very secret—and a very smart—plan," she said. Pointing at the Ukrainian panelist in the studio, she sniped: "Stand there and be very afraid."

Fast forward to February 22, as Russian troops were moving into Ukraine's breakaway states, Zhuravlyov was on state TV with some confident ideas about how the next phase of the Russian invasion would play out. Upon entering eastern Ukraine, Russian troops will take the rest of the country "the moment there is a provocation" by the Ukrainian military, Zhuravlyov said. He ominously promised: "And there will be a provocation. I guarantee it."

Sanctioned Russian TV Host Cries About Losing His Italian Villa

It's all fun and games till they seize your Italian villa.

Originally published by *The Daily Beast* on February 26, 2022

The impact of Putin's war is starting to set in, startling even his most ardent state TV propagandists. It's all fun and games till they seize your Italian villa. That's what one of the most prominent Kremlin propagandists found out for himself this week, after Russia's invasion of Ukraine.

In 2019, before he was poisoned and imprisoned, opposition activist Alexei Navalny and his team released a video report that revealed state TV host Vladimir Solovyov owns not one, but two villas in Italy down the road from George Clooney's beloved estate on Lake Como.

His neighbors have protested since he bought the property, even launching a petition in 2019 to try to get the local authorities to make sure he didn't obtain Italian citizenship through his residency. The Kremlin mouthpiece known for constantly condemning Europe and the West for their supposed perversion and decay was thus exposed as an absolute hypocrite. Last Christmas, Navalny's investigative team, FBK, videotaped the state TV host's luxury abodes and left him special gifts—Ukrainian chocolates, since Solovyov is also well-known for his years of anti-Ukrainian propaganda.

The Kremlin's talking head was enraged and complained about what he considered an outrageous privacy violation, but worse was yet to come. Solovyov learned this week that the latest sanctions imposed against the Kremlin's regime and its accomplices would impact him personally. His access to properties in Europe is now being impacted, and perhaps his ownership as well.

During Friday's edition of *The Evening With Vladimir Solovyov*, the host raged: "I was told that Europe is a citadel of rights, that everything is permitted, that's what they said... I know from personal experience about the so-called 'sacred property rights.' With every transaction I was bringing paperwork demonstrating my official salary, income, I did it all. I bought it, paid crazy amount of taxes, I did everything. And suddenly someone makes a decision that this journalist is now on the list of sanctions. And right away it affects your real estate. Wait a minute. But you told us that Europe has sacred property rights!"

Stunned and dismayed, Solovyov griped: "All of a sudden, now they say: 'Are you Russian? Then we will close your bank account, if it's in Europe. And if it's in England, you're allowed to keep no more than a certain amount there. Why? Because you're Russian."

Prominent economist Mikhail Khazin chimed in: "And that's if you have an old account. They won't open a new one."

Solovyov asked: "Is this the Iron Curtain?" Germany-based pundit Alexander Sosnovsky replied: "Yes, absolutely, the Iron Curtain in its worst manifestation, painted in LGBT colors."

This reference again exemplified Russia's intolerance towards human rights and sexual minorities, which nonetheless did nothing to prevent Solovyov and other Kremlin propagandists from acquiring expensive real estate in what they consider to be degenerate, immoral Western countries.

Appearing on NTV's program *Our Own Truth* (Svoya Pravda), RT's editor-in-chief Margarita Simonyan boasted: "I'm not worried about sanctions, isolation, prohibitions or the dollar exchange rate. We used to live without iPhones, we can also do without Paris if need be. It's wild to even contemplate that when the fate of the nation and the future of the world are at stake."

As for those who say "No to war" and are ashamed that they're Russian, Simonyan asserted, "I am ashamed that they are my fellow citizens."

Attempting to deny Russia's intensifying war against Ukraine, Simonyan claimed: "Nobody is fighting against Ukrainians! We're liberating Ukraine!" She followed up with another ludicrous claim: "No one is bombing peaceful Ukrainian cities!"

In her tirade, Simonyan derided those who were caught unprepared or complained that the Kremlin was taking too long to act with respect to Ukraine.

She said, "It's clear that such actions don't get planned willy-nilly and you need to be prepared for them, including in the economic sense. When we listened to the Security Council... [Mikhail] Mishustin [Prime Minister of Russia] uttered important words: we can imagine what kind of sanctions there will be. We anticipated them and we've been getting ready. That also took time."

Simonyan described various preparations undertaken by the Russian authorities for years, directly undermining the talking points that attempted to link the timing of Russia's invasion with the "embarrassing" U.S. withdrawal from Afghanistan.

In fact, experts-in-the-know have been referencing the Kremlin's secret plans for years. For example, in April of 2021, appearing on *Sunday Evening With Vladimir Solovyov*, Andrey Sidorov — deputy dean of world politics at Moscow State University — predicted: "Everything will start in Ukraine. We will be forced to step onto the battlefield in a fight for which they think we're not ready."

The host asked: "A fight against whom?" and Sidorov clarified: "Against the collective West."

In 2022, once Russia's war against Ukraine had fully begun, Sidorov emphasized the importance of choosing the right words during his Friday appearance on Solovyov's show: "Don't call it occupation, call it brotherly help."

While most in the West are too savvy to take Russian propaganda at face value, Moscow's experts are grateful to have the ones who broadcast Kremlin-friendly talking points. Referring to Tucker Carlson as "the most popular host in the United States" during Thursday's segment of *The Evening With Vladimir Solovyov*, the host complained: "They're accusing him of being a Russian spy." Analyst Dmitry Drobnitsky replied: "Well, Tucker is most definitely ours. That's that."

As for Putin's biggest cheerleader, former U.S. President Donald J. Trump, who described the Kremlin's moves in Ukraine as "genius," Putin's men in Moscow anxiously await his return as their sole hope for relief from rapidly accelerating Western sanctions—which will soon include the disconnection of Russia's biggest banks from a global messaging system known as SWIFT.

During his Friday broadcast, amid tense discussions of Western sanctions, Solovyov theatrically looked down at his watch and asked: "Is Trump coming back soon?"

Kremlin TV Tells Ukraine to Listen to Fox News Guest and Kneel to Putin

Russian state media is having a field day with a Fox News guest's recent suggestion that the people of Ukraine should really just lie down and let Putin have his way.

Originally published by *The Daily Beast* on March 02, 2022

Speakers across Kremlin-funded media are voicing their dismay and disappointment with the worldwide condemnation of Russia's invasion of Ukraine. Now more than ever, Fox News — with its endless stream of pro-Russia talking points — seems to be the only bright spot for Kremlin propagandists otherwise under siege by the West.

While guests and pundits on multiple state TV channels expressed frustration with the world's unity in opposition to Putin's aggression, translated clips from Fox News continued to spark joy for them. On Tuesday and Wednesday, multiple state media channels broadcast translated video excerpts from Fox News' Sunday night segment with Trey Gowdy. In these clips, Ret. Col. Doug Macgregor suggested that Ukrainian troops lay down their guns, retreat, and let Russian President Vladimir Putin have his way with Ukraine.

He also complained that Putin is being "demonized" by the United States and opposed any U.S. involvement in helping Ukraine defend itself from Russian aggression.

Macgregor, who previously supported Russia's annexation of Crimea, argued, "What is happening now is the battle in Eastern Ukraine is really almost over, all the Ukrainian troops there have been largely surrounded and cut off... and if they don't surrender in next 24 hours, I suspect the Russians will ultimately annihilate them... The game is over." Russian state media flooded their programs with translated clips of Macgregor's proclamations, using them in support of their own messaging designed to demoralize the Ukrainians.

Predictably, state TV did not include any clips of Fox News national security correspondent Jennifer Griffin's rebuttals that followed Macgregor's appearance, in which she addressed his "distortions" and noted that Macgregor sounded like an "apologist" for Putin.

"Macgregor is expressing his tough position on Ukraine, will he also be sanctioned by the European Union?" asked host Vladimir Solovyov, who recently lost access to two of his Italian villas. Solovyov summed up: "He is de facto justifying Russia's actions."

Host Vladimir Solovyov was especially torn up about RT (formerly known as Russia Today), which was dumped by multiple broadcasters in Europe, Canada, and the United States.

On Tuesday, he brought up RT's editor-in-chief, Margarita Simonyan, saying, "Today is a real tragedy for her. She gave 17 years of her life to create RT, a brilliant company. The way they finished off RT in civilized Europe and in the West, how they are tormenting RT's employees, just destroying it all. It's out of bounds. It's so hard for Rita psychologically, because this was her life's work and now they're destroying it."

Instead of Simonyan's customary appearance on Solovyov's show, her freshly sanctioned husband Tigran Keosayan emerged in the studio. He hypocritically exclaimed, "No one here wants war."

Blaming the West for Russia's invasion of Ukraine, Keosayan opined, "Their biggest fear is that sooner or later they will have to fight against Russia. If they don't stop Russia now, it may later be dissatisfied with something in Latvia, Lithuania, or Estonia. And then everyone in the world will find out that there's no such thing as [NATO's] Article 5, because no one will step in to defend anybody else."

Keosayan followed his wife's lead and demanded silence or praise from all Russian citizens with respect to Putin's war against Ukraine: "Either be quiet or support it. If you have any grievances, we'll talk about it after it's all over... Any anti-war movement while your government is conducting a military operation is anti-government."

The same day, Echo Moskvy, one of Russia's oldest radio stations, was taken off the airwaves after authorities threatened to shut it down over its coverage of Russia's invasion of Ukraine. Russian authorities also threatened to block Dozhd, Russia's independent TV channel. The Prosecutor General's office accused Echo Moskvy and Dozhd of spreading "false information regarding the actions of Russian military personnel as part of a special operation" in Ukraine.

In other words, they dared to tell the truth about Putin's aggression against what he described as Russia's "brotherly nation." This flowery language is now devoid of all meaning to everyday Ukrainians, one of whom tweeted about Russia and Belarus teaming up against Ukraine: "It's good that we have only two brotherly nations."

During Solovyov's show, Keosayan admitted that even pro-Russian voices in Ukraine were stunned by Russian troops invading their country: "Since your program is being watched in Ukraine, I have a sad story to tell. I purposely watched a lot of Ukrainian television for the last several months, and there were some conscientious guys... and now I see their shock and astonishment: 'You attacked my country.' I want to address all of them, since they'll later snap out of it... You were just sitting on your butts, talking... Now Russia is doing for you what you should have done for yourselves!"

Other pundits in the studio were likewise appalled that even pro-Russian Ukrainians weren't more appreciative of Russia's military assault on their country. Nikolai Starikov incredulously complained, "Today I watched one Ukrainian channel and they used a curse word to describe Russian soldiers! The enemy says, "Russian soldiers are here!" They see that as a threat! They hate Russian soldiers!"

In a theme that reverberated on multiple state TV stations, Starikov blamed the West for starting Putin's war against Ukraine: "Our geopolitical adversaries couldn't wage war inside Russia, so they started one near Russia's borders. Now Russia is depriving them of an opportunity to create a bleeding wound next to our borders."

In December 2021, Oleg Voloshin, a former aide to Kostyantyn Gryshchenko, Viktor Yanukovych's 2010-12 foreign minister, predicted that "Russia could destroy Ukraine in less than 10 minutes." Senior military analyst Mikhail Khodaryonok was more generous and claimed that it would take "11 minutes," during the broadcast of *60 Minutes* later the same day. "We're good with that," approvingly said host Olga Skabeeva, who has since been sanctioned for her relentless incitement of war and years of rabid anti-Ukrainian propaganda.

Sobered up by the fierce resistance put up by the Ukrainians during Solovyov's show, Starikov tried to temper expectations.

Instead of "minutes," he predicted that Russia's conquest of Ukraine may take "months, or maybe years." Solovyov compared the situation to Russia's brutal Chechen wars and said the turnaround will take time.

Instead of blaming Putin, Starikov condemned the United States for helping Ukraine defend itself from Russian aggression. He alleged: "Those who send weapons to Ukraine need more destruction and more victims" and threatened: "American protectorate will be publicly destroyed." Having said too much, Starikov snapped back to the approved propaganda line: "It will be liberated. There will be a free Ukraine... U.S. plans have been destroyed for decades ahead."

Host Vladimir Solovyov bitterly added, "They're imposing such sanctions against us, it's a declaration of war. De facto, it's a declaration of war against us. So why should we stop with Ukraine?"

That talking point echoed across multiple government-controlled TV channels. During Friday's broadcast of *60 Minutes*, host Olga Skabeeva said, "Biden announced the goal of our special operation: He said that Putin wants to restore the USSR. As though there's anything wrong with that."

Russian State TV Just Blew Up Putin's 'Nazi Ukraine' BS

Russian lawmakers suddenly blab what Putin actually wants in Ukraine—and it has nothing to do with "Nazis."

Originally published by *The Daily Beast* on March 04, 2022

Confusion reigns on Russia's state TV, as panicked lawmakers and pundits try to explain to the public why their country invaded Ukraine and now faces crushing Western sanctions. And in the process of zealous propagandists striving to justify the unfathomable, they've inadvertently revealed too much.

Kremlin spokesman Dmitry Peskov told state TV on Friday that President Vladimir Putin was directly involved in making command decisions with respect to Russia's military activities in Ukraine.

He urged: "It's time to unite around our president," and encouraged those who understand the Kremlin's aims to "patiently explain" them to anyone who doesn't.

Appearing on the state TV show *The Evening With Vladimir Solovyov* on Friday, lawmaker Andrei Kartapolov, who heads the Russian parliament's defense committee, then set out to justify Putin's military activities in Ukraine.

Starting with the most recent news of a terrifying fire caused by the Russian military's efforts to take control over the Zaporizhzhia nuclear power plant, Kartapolov claimed that Russian troops were ordered to seize Ukraine's nuclear plants to prevent Ukraine's President Volodymyr Zelensky "from building a dirty bomb" with which to attack Russia.

Kartapolov's baseless allegation stemmed solely from Zelensky's statement at the Munich Security Conference on February 19, where he brought up the failure by the signatories to honor the

Budapest memorandum, wherein Ukraine gave up its nuclear arsenal in return for security guarantees. Zelensky requested new security guarantees—or, in the alternative, he stressed that all provisions of the 1994 agreement would be void. This statement contained no threats towards Russia, but was convenient enough to be appropriated as one of Putin's claims as to why Ukraine somehow posed a threat to its larger neighbor.

On Solovyov's show—an Orwellian environment, typical of the Russian state media—the host and every panelist repeatedly denied the obvious, attempting to disprove the notion that Russia is at war with Ukraine. Solovyov asked: "Are we de facto at war with NATO?" Kartapolov concurred: "De facto, we are at war with NATO, because all of Ukraine's military formations are carrying out NATO's tasks... NATO is also solving another problem, getting rid of Europe's excess migrants by sending them to fight in Ukraine." He pompously concluded: "God is not in power, but in truth."

As to the Kremlin's aims in Ukraine, Kartapolov explained them in detail: "Our position is clear and transparent, including during these negotiations. The essence is as follows: Ukraine will recognize Crimea as the Russian Federation, as well as DPR/LPR ['Donetsk People's Republic' and 'Luhansk People's Republic'] within their administrative borders. Ukraine will change its social and state system and become a neutral, demilitarized country. That's it."

Lawmaker Konstantin Zatulin, who is deputy chairman of the Duma commission on relations with the former Soviet Union, seemed unsettled by Kartapolov's revelations and angrily replied: "When a horse has something to say, a saddle shouldn't be the one to talk. This is not the time to tell everything. First of all, we're not the ones who should be saying that, they [Ukrainians] need to be the ones who say that. But that situation has to ripen first. It won't be done during the thunder of cannons. Until our operation has concluded, it won't be clear what 'denazification' will consist of." As for "demilitarization," Zatulin said that even specific kinds of weapons Russia wants to eliminate from Ukraine are being discussed during talks between the Russian and Ukrainian delegations.

The banter revealed Putin's apparent strategy in Ukraine: destroy Ukraine's infrastructure and cause widespread desperation with a brutal military assault, which would then compel the Ukrainian government to concede to Putin's terms and leave their positions or face a violent removal by force.

It's a land grab of Eastern Ukraine, followed by the transformation of the rest of the country into a powerless vassal state, controlled and headed by Putin's puppets. To break Ukraine's resolve, the Kremlin likely intends to replicate the brutality it demonstrated in Syria and Chechnya.

The devastation Putin's military campaign has already caused to its neighboring country was of no concern to the pro-Putin pundits. In a glib and nonchalant manner, Solovyov noted: "Ukraine is sinking into the stone age. Most of its territories are on the verge of a humanitarian catastrophe." Nonetheless, he encouraged the Russian government not to stop their "military operation," known in the rest of the world as brutal, unprovoked war.

Solovyov added: "It should be understood that this is not a war against Ukraine or the Ukrainian people, but a military operation... of denazification and demilitarization of NATO's fist that was directed at us." Zatulin chimed in: "This is a war against the West, a war against NATO." The host agreed: "Of course. This is a battle from the war that started on May 9, 1945, when they — pretending that they're with us — were getting ready to destroy us." Like a mantra, state television talking heads are making references to World War II, invoking the spirit of a fight against Nazism for no other reason but to whitewash Putin's latest land grab in progress.

Lawmakers and pundits essentially debunked Putin's claim that he invaded Ukraine to remove what he said is a "Nazi" government — which is, incidentally, headed by a Jewish man. Instead of demystifying the Kremlin's agenda for the masses, state media demonstrated that in Putin's Russia, anyone who dares to oppose Putin is described as a "Nazi," to the point where the term is devoid of its original meaning.

On Solovyov's show, political scientist and professor of history Elena Ponomareva asserted: "We're fighting not only against NATO, but also against the Nazi European Union."

Two days earlier, on a state TV show *60 Minutes*, journalist Andrei Sidorchik rode the concept all the way down the hill when he exclaimed: "Joe Biden is a Nazi. The U.S. congressmen—Democrat and Republican—are Nazis... German chancellor is a Nazi... EU leaders are Nazis... because their sanctions are attempting to preserve neo-Nazism in Ukraine."

Even Russian State TV Is Pleading With Putin to Stop the War

State propagandists called for Putin to end the "special military operation" before "frightening" sanctions destabilize his regime and risk civil war in Russia.

Originally published by *The Daily Beast* on March 10, 2022

There is a notable mood shift in Russia, as darkness sets over its economy and the invasion of Ukraine hits major problems. While the beginning of President Vladimir Putin's full-scale war against Ukraine was greeted with cheers, clapping, and demands of Champagne in the studio, the reality sobered up even the most pro-Kremlin pundits and experts on Russian state television.

The ugly truth about Russia's invasion of Ukraine is slipping through the cracks, despite the government's authoritarian attempts to control the narrative.

The Kremlin-controlled state media is doing its best to flip the situation upside down, blaming the victims of Russia's aggression for all of the casualties. On Wednesday's edition of the state TV show *The Evening With Vladimir Solovyov*, the host claimed the fallout of Russia's bombing of a maternity hospital this week was "fake" with no one there to be injured, despite photos of pregnant women being carried away from the blast that killed at least one child.

A guest on *60 Minutes* last Saturday even claimed Ukrainians "are firing on each other and blaming us."

On Thursday, Russia's Foreign Minister Sergei Lavrov claimed that Russia never attacked Ukraine and repeated the same lies as Solovyov about the total absence of patients in the maternity ward and children's hospital bombed by Russia.

Putin's most trusted propagandists are becoming ever more desperate to distort or deny the evidence of the atrocities because the truth is finding its way past the roadblocks erected by the Kremlin. Russian citizens are not pleased either with the war, nor with the financial price they have to pay for their leader's ill-conceived military conquests.

Even the infamous show run by Solovyov—who was recently sanctioned as an accomplice of Putin by the European Union—became dominated by predictions of Russian doom and gloom.

Andrey Sidorov, deputy dean of world politics at Moscow State University, cautioned: "For our country, this period won't be easy. It will be very difficult. It might be even more difficult than it was for the Soviet Union from 1945 until the 1960s... We're more integrated into the global economy than the Soviet Union, we're more dependent on imports—and the main part is that the Cold War is the war of the minds, first and foremost. Unfortunately, the Soviet Union had a consolidating idea on which its system was built. Unlike the Soviet Union, Russia has nothing like that to offer."

State TV pundit Karen Shakhnazarov pointed out: "The war in Ukraine paints a frightening picture, it has a very oppressive influence on our society. Ukraine, whichever way you see it, is something with which Russia has thousands of human links. The suffering of one group of innocents does not compensate for the suffering of other innocent people... I don't see the probability of denazification of such an enormous country. We would need to bring in 1.5 million soldiers to control all of it. At the same time, I don't see any political power that would consolidate the Ukrainian society in a pro-Russian direction... Those who talked of their mass attraction to Russia obviously didn't see things the way they are. The most important thing in this scenario is to stop our military action. Others will say that sanctions will remain. Yes, they will remain, but in my opinion discontinuing the active phase of a military operation is very important."

Resorting to the traditional propaganda tropes prevalent in Russian state media, Shakhnazarov accused the United States of starting the war—and trying to prolong it indefinitely. He speculated: "What are they achieving by prolonging the war? First of all, public opinion within Russia is changing. People are shocked by the masses of refugees, the humanitarian catastrophe, people start to imagine themselves in their place. It's starting to affect them. To say that the Nazis are doing that is not quite convincing, strictly speaking... On top of that, economic sanctions will start to affect them, and seriously. There will probably be scarcity. A lot of products we don't produce, even the simplest ones. There'll be unemployment. They really thought through these sanctions, they're hitting us with real continuity. It's a well-planned operation... Yes, this is a war of the United States with Russia... These sanctions are hitting us very precisely."

Shakhnazarov continued, "This threatens the change of public opinion in Russia, the destabilization of our power structures... with the possibility of a full destabilization of the country and a civil war. This apocalyptic scenario is based on the script written by the Americans. They benefit through us dragging out the military operation. We need to end it somehow. If we achieved the demilitarization and freed the Donbas, that is sufficient... I have a hard time imagining taking cities such as Kyiv. I can't imagine how that would look. If this picture starts to transform into an absolute humanitarian disaster, even our close allies like China and India will be forced to distance themselves from us. This public opinion, with which they're saturating the entire world, can play out badly for us... Ending this operation will stabilize things within the country."

The host frowned at the apparent departure from the officially approved line of thinking and deferred to the commander-in-chief. However, the next expert agreed with Shakhnazarov. Semyon Bagdasarov, a Russian Middle East expert, grimly said: "We didn't even feel the impact of the sanctions just yet... We need to be ready for total isolation. I'm not panicking, just calling things by their proper name."

Solovyov angrily sniped: "Gotcha. We should just lay down and die." Bagdasarov continued: "Now about Ukraine. I agree with Karen. We had prior experiences of bringing in our troops, destroying the military infrastructure and leaving. I think that our army fulfilled their task of demilitarization of the country by destroying most of their military installations... To restore their military they will need at least 10 years... Let Ukrainians do this denazification on their own. We can't do it for them... As for their neutrality, yes, we should squeeze it out of them, and that's it. We don't need to stay there longer than necessary... Do we need to get into another Afghanistan, but even worse? There are more people and they're more advanced in their handling of weapons. We don't need that. Enough already... As for the sanctions, the world has never seen such massive sanctions."

Dmitry Abzalov, director of the Center for Strategic Communications, pointed out that even though energy prices will go up for most of the West, it won't do much to ease the pain for the Russians: "We'll still be the ones taking the terminal hit, and an incomparable one, even though other countries will also suffer some losses. We'll all be going to hell together — except for maybe China — but going to hell together with the French or Germans won't make our people feel any better."

Abzalov argued that after taking additional territories in Eastern Ukraine, Russia should get out of Dodge, believing that all Western companies that temporarily paused their operations in Russia would then rush to come back. "It's about toxicity, not just sanctions... It will go away once the situation stabilizes."

Prior to the invasion of Ukraine, state TV experts predicted that Russia could overtake it in a matter of minutes or a few days. Stunned by the fierce resistance on the part of Ukrainians, Solovyov described them as "the army that is second in Europe, after ours, and which has been prepared for eight years and armed with everything you can imagine." Solovyov added: "This is a frightening war that is being waged against us by America."

To lighten the mood in the studio, the host resorted to one of the favorite pastimes of many Kremlin propagandists: playing yet another Fox News clip of Tucker Carlson and his frequent guest Ret. Col. Doug Macgregor. In the translated video, Macgregor predicted Russia's easy military victories over Ukraine and its total invincibility to Western sanctions. Solovyov sighed and smiled: "He's a lot more optimistic than my previous experts in the studio."

Wild Kremlin TV Hosts Threaten the U.S. With Nuclear Strikes Unless Sanctions End and Reparations Are Paid

Russian state media has shut down last week's minor dissent and now demands an end to sanctions and even reparations for affected Russians. Or else.

Originally published by *The Daily Beast* on March 15, 2022

In the surreal world of Russian state television, Russia is about to prevail in its war against Ukraine, which is being presented as a battle against the United States and NATO. According to top Kremlin propagandists, it's only a matter of time before the West admits its defeat and pays reparations to Moscow or risks a devastating nuclear strike.

Pundits who dared to criticize Russia's invasion of Ukraine have not been seen on state-controlled television ever since they spoke out last week. Even though their timid disagreement pales in comparison to the bravery of Marina Ovsyannikova, an editor at Channel One, who has been detained after interrupting live programming with an anti-war sign.

Meanwhile, state TV broadcasts are filled with cheerleaders, who repeatedly insist that the Kremlin's "special operation"—known to the rest of the world as a brutal war—should not stop until all objectives are achieved. They insist that everything is going exactly as planned.

Russian President Vladimir Putin's willingness to negotiate with the President of Ukraine Volodymyr Zelensky is being packaged as a sign of his love and good will, and not the consequence of mounting losses and humiliating defeats faced by the Russian military in Ukraine.

Appearing on a state TV show *Sunday Evening With Vladimir Solovyov*, political scientist and Professor of Communications

Dmitry Evstafiev argued: "Right now, President Vladimir Vladimirovich Putin's third proposal to the Ukrainian leadership is on the table. This, of course, is a demonstration of his greatest respect and—I would even say—of love by our President towards the Ukrainian people."

Multiple state TV shows emphasized the reluctance on the part of the United States and NATO to intervene against Russia's bloody invasion of its neighbor, presenting it as the proof that the Kremlin can go to any lengths to emerge victorious. Olga Skabeeva, the host of a state TV show *60 Minutes*, intentionally distorted the statements of White House press secretary Jen Psaki. On Friday, Skabeeva claimed: "Jennifer Psaki's statement said that no matter what Putin does in Ukraine—whether he uses biological weapons or drops a nuclear bomb—the United States won't get involved."

On Monday, disregarding strong bipartisan support of Ukraine in the United States, Skabeeva claimed that Americans don't care about Ukraine and are concerned only with rising gas prices. She alleged: "To the dismay of the State Department, it turned out that Americans are indifferent towards saving Ukrainian Banderites." Russian state media and government officials have taken to describing any opponents of the Kremlin in Ukraine as or "Banderites," the followers of Stepan Bandera, the ultranationalist political figure who fought for Ukrainian independence before being assassinated by the KGB in 1959. This expression is being used as indiscriminately as branding all opponents the "Nazis."

The show proceeded to broadcast a clip of former U.S. President Donald J. Trump, blaming Biden for his alleged inability to communicate with Putin. Hinting at the upcoming presidential elections, Skabeeva sniped: "Fun times for them are only starting. We're waiting." In the meantime, state media is replete with baseless promises of wide-ranging concessions from the West that Moscow anticipates receiving in the future.

Appearing on *Sunday Evening With Vladimir Solovyov*, Russian parliament member Oleg Matveychev, known as the Kremlin's spin doctor, watched a clip of Fox News' Tucker Carlson—an everyday occurrence in Moscow's tightly-controlled media environment.

Matveychev noted: "There isn't a single country in the world that is as easily manipulated as America."

He argued: "Here's what will be on the table after our victory... After Ukraine's demilitarization is completed... we're going to raise the stakes... For example, the lifting of all sanctions... The dissolution of NATO, because the presence of NATO in some countries is getting in our way. Extradition of all war criminals... like [Anton] Herashchenko [former deputy minister at the Ukrainian Ministry of Internal Affairs], Zelensky, [former President of Ukraine Petro] Poroshenko. Extradition of various oligarchs, like [Mikhail] Khodorkovsky."

In recent days, Russian state television regressed from Orwellian lies to Kafkaesque nightmares, as pundits started to promote the idea of executing Ukrainians resisting Putin's war of aggression by hanging. They noted that the so-called "constitution" of the rogue "republics" created in Ukraine by Russian forces conveniently allows for the death penalty.

Last Thursday on *The Evening With Vladimir Solovyov*, after listening to other pundits and experts endorse the idea of executing Ukrainian citizens by hanging, doctor of political sciences Elena G. Ponomareva argued: "Never let morality prevent you from undertaking correct actions. I understand the importance of a humanitarian component... but morality shouldn't get in the way."

Sunday's *Vesti Nedeli* hosted by Dmitry Kiselyov continued the theme of public hangings, broadcasting the scenes from the public execution of German Nazi soldiers on Kyiv's Independence Square in 1946.

The segment was entitled "Denazification of Ukraine—the new opportunities for growth" and appeared to serve as a tool to desensitize the Russian population for the grotesque war trials and executions the Kremlin is reportedly planning to conduct in Ukraine, perhaps in the same public square captured in the historical video.

Bloomberg previously reported that, according to an unnamed European intelligence official, Russia's intelligence agency, the Federal Security Service, has drafted plans for public executions in Ukraine after cities are captured. Russian state media appears to be laying the groundwork to normalize such an idea, in order to make it seem acceptable to average Russians.

Reciting the list of Russia's future demands during Solovyov's show, Matveychev became even more brazen: "We should be thinking about reparations from the damage that was caused by the sanctions and the war itself, because that too costs money and we should get it back. The return of all Russian properties, those of the Russian empire, the Soviet Union and current Russia, which has been seized in the United States, and so on."

The host chimed in to ask: "Are you including Alaska and Fort Ross?"

Matveychev nodded: "That was my next point. As well as the Antarctic... We discovered it, so it belongs to us... Also, the return of all medals that have been unlawfully taken from our sportsmen during all Olympic games, as well as the extradition of [Grigory] Rodchenkov, along with the extradition of multiple other criminals we'll want. I think we should start voicing all of that, so they understand what will be on the table. You didn't want to talk to us about something small, like Ukraine's neutrality, here's what you get. And that's not even all of it."

Solovyov asked: "Does your list include a tactical nuclear strike, or are we going straight for the strategic one?" Matveychev pompously scoffed, "What for? We can take them down without it."

On Monday, Solovyov revisited the topic of nuclear blackmail, perhaps blinded by rage after the recent seizure of his two Italian villas. He said: "I still think that those who took our money should be told, you have 24 hours to unfreeze our funds, or else we'll send you what you know we've got. Your choice. Tactical or strategic, take a pick. You took our money, you're the thieves, our talk is short with you: a bullet to the head."

Kremlin TV Descends Into Screaming Match Over Putin's War Failures

There's no hiding the cracks that have formed on Russian airwaves over the war in Ukraine any longer.

Originally published by *The Daily Beast* on March 25, 2022

As Russia's war against Ukraine enters its second month, the grim picture of destruction and suffering is breaking through on state-controlled television. Before the invasion, military experts predicted a rapid takeover of Russia's peaceful neighbor in a matter of minutes. Now that the reality is starting to set in, they're grimly surmising that it will take several decades to subdue freedom-loving Ukraine.

State TV's talking heads have tried in vain to paint a rosy picture of the Kremlin's invasion, but the cracks are starting to show. On Thursday, with screens depicting dramatic images of demolished Mariupol flashing behind them, hosts of the state television show *60 Minutes*, Olga Skabeeva and Evgeny Popov, tried to point out the "positives."

They noted that Russia promised to pay compensation to some Ukrainians from the "affected" territories—10,000 rubles each, amounting to a mere $100 dollars.

To make matters worse, Ukrainians forcefully deported to Russia might end up in places like the Russian island of Sakhalin in the Pacific, with freezing cold temperatures and stark landscapes. After discussing news reports about ongoing relocations, Evgeny Popov helpfully pointed out: "But in Sakhalin, the salaries are the highest in the country!"

The chorus of concerned voices in Russian state media blamed their country's information war failures on the fact that the Kremlin's propaganda channels have been banished in Ukraine. State TV pundit Nikolai Starikov proposed: "When we talk about the organizers of the info-war, I'm convinced that their place is on the same bench where Nazi criminals will be tried."

The hosts, who for years agitated for war against Ukraine under false pretenses, nervously looked on without commenting.

State Duma Deputy Gen. Vladimir Shamanov — who is the former commander of the Russian Airborne Troops — accused the President of Ukraine Volodymyr Zelensky of being a "war criminal" for not surrendering to Russia. Shamanov argued: "He has the right to say, "Stop this war," lay down the arms and save all the people." This bizarre upside-down narrative is meant to hide the fact that Russian President Vladimir Putin, seen by the civilized world as a war criminal, is solely responsible for starting and continuing his unprovoked invasion of a neighboring country.

Political analyst Vitaly Tretyakov concluded: "The situation is serious... We have to admit that there was no psychological breakthrough in our operation, where the opposing side would lose their will to resist... The resistance from the Ukrainian side is neither stopping nor weakening." Tretyakov pointed out that despite the Russian media's attempted depictions of Zelensky as a drug addict, he is being perceived by the West as a leader of a country that has been attacked.

He also questioned the wisdom of "liberating" Ukrainians who don't seem to want to be "liberated" and vehemently hate seeing the Russian troops on their territory. Tretyakov noted the unwavering determination of Western leaders to "squeeze" the Russian economy by imposing punishing sanctions.

Host Olga Skabeeva was visibly rattled by the depressing realities brought to the forefront by Tretyakov's comments. She sniped, "So you sprinkled the ashes all over your head, but what do we do now? What's our plan? Everything is bad, nothing is working out?" Skabeeva angrily questioned whether Tretyakov had anything to offer aside from criticism. After he pointed out that societies tend to get tired of any military campaigns rather quickly, Skabeeva argued, "If you're tired, that doesn't mean that everyone else is tired." Visibly angered, she repeatedly shouted at Tretyakov, questioning his support for the Russian military and telling the pundit that his commentary "has a smell of something untoward."

If Skabeeva was counting on other pundits to lighten the mood in the studio, she was sorely mistaken. Military experts proceeded to hammer additional nails into the coffin of popular delusions about the anticipated outcome of Putin's war against Ukraine.

On Thursday, military expert Igor Korotchenko called for any protests to be stopped by military force and any vocal opponents of the Russian armed forces to be "interned." Korotchenko called for all Ukrainian flags and symbols to be destroyed, replaced by Russian and Soviet flags. He also demanded that Ukrainians who fled to NATO countries be denied the possibility of returning to their country.

In January, experts on the same show estimated that Russia could overtake the entire neighboring country in a matter of 11 minutes. Their current predictions have shifted from minutes to decades for the Russian armed forces to achieve Putin's goals in his senseless war against Ukraine.

Korotchenko surmised, "It's obvious that the process of denazification of Ukraine will take the minimum of 15-20 years."

He predicted that the Russian troops would have to remain on Ukrainian territory, with the Russian military in charge of the entire country for the foreseeable future: "Whether this will take 15, 20 years or more, time will tell."

General Shamanov was even more pessimistic, as he grimly anticipated that it would take the "re-education" of at least two generations of Ukrainians before they would welcome or tolerate Russia's dominance.

He also noted that Russia's one-million-man armed forces aren't enough to meet such a challenge, calling for massive increases to the country's military might. Shamanov concluded: "Today, it can be clearly predicted that we will have to remain in Ukraine for 30-40 years."

Putin's Minions Demand Grotesque 'Rewards' for Mass Killers in Ukraine

After a massacre in a Ukrainian city shocked the world, the Kremlin's henchmen are now pushing for pay raises and debt forgiveness for those perpetuating the country's bloodshed.

Originally published by *The Daily Beast* on April 04, 2022

While most of the world gasped at the latest round of atrocities perpetrated by invading Russian troops in Ukraine, Kremlin propagandists and government officials are only doubling down. The shocking footage of the massacre that took place in the Ukrainian city of Bucha was repeatedly broadcast on Russian state television this week with the label "Fake" slapped across the screen.

During Monday's broadcast of state TV show *60 Minutes*, host Olga Skabeeva speculated that the town was chosen for an elaborate fabrication because of its name. "Biden said that Putin is a butcher. Bucha sounds like "butcher." How could they not take advantage of such a town?" She later added: "President Putin described them all as "the Empire of lies," and here is our confirmation."

The so-called "lies" Skabeeva is referring to are the scenes of indescribable horror that were discovered by Ukrainian troops who arrived in Bucha this weekend after the Russian Army withdrew from the city.

Scores of bodies, including those of women and children, were littered on roads and in yards, many of them found with their hands bound behind their backs and signs of rape or torture.

Russian state media churned out ridiculous assertions, claiming in part that the corpses of women and children depicted in the footage from Bucha—some of which were charred beyond recognition—were "moving their arms," "getting their limbs out of the way to avoid the wheels of military vehicles" or even "getting up and walking away."

While scenes from Bucha made headlines around the world, Interfax published a report on a ceremony conducted by the Russian military on April 2, in which several awards were presented to the Airborne Forces (VDV) of the Russian Federation in the Kyiv region. According to state TV outlet Zvezda, that unit had been involved in "holding back the actions of the enemy forces" and "performing the cleaning of settlements" in Bucha.

"In the Kyiv region, in the area where the tasks of the formation of the Airborne Forces were performed, the awarding of Russian paratroopers took place. The commander of the formation presented state awards to servicemen who distinguished themselves in combat missions during this special military operation," the Russian Defense Ministry said in a statement about the awards.

The same day, the media outlet Ria Fan published the names of seven Russian soldiers to its listing of "Z Heroes." The state TV program *Vesti Nedeli*, hosted by Dmitry Kiselyov, showcased the medals awarded to the invading troops: "For Courage", "Suvorov" and "Zhukov."

Immediately, participants of the state TV show *Sunday Evening With Vladimir Solovyov* jumped to heap praise upon the Russian troops and called for various rewards and bonuses, from debt forgiveness to pay raises.

Instead of shaming the killers of Ukrainian civilians, Mikheyev loudly asserted: "We need to support them!" He added: "We need to raise their salaries, because they're risking their lives! Their consumer debts should be written off... During war, we need to support the Russian warrior."

Despite overwhelming evidence of the massacre, the Russian Defense Ministry has claimed that "not a single local in Bucha" suffered any harm while the town was under control of the Russian Armed Forces. During his meeting with UN Deputy Secretary General Martin Griffiths on Monday, Russian Foreign Minister Sergei Lavrov called the extensive evidence of Russia's war crimes "a staged production, organized on the streets," which is being used "for anti-Russian purposes." The same day, Kremlin spokesman

Dmitry Peskov asserted: "From what we have seen, the video materials cannot be trusted in many respects, because our specialists from the Ministry of Defense have identified signs of video fraud and all sorts of fakes."

Russia's Defense Ministry claimed that the videos from Bucha "were fabricated and are a provocation," claiming that Russian troops left Bucha on March 30. Despite Russia's denials, satellite images obtained by The New York Times confirmed that bodies of massacred civilians lay in the streets of Bucha for weeks, while the town was in full control of the Russian troops.

Meanwhile, on his Sunday show, host Vladimir Solovyov angrily yelled that the goal of the West is a total destruction of Russia. He demanded: "Don't get in the way of our Army's work, on all levels! Free their hands!"

Political scientist Sergey Mikheyev then chimed in with his own take on Bucha: "Maybe it's a production, or maybe they brought the corpses from elsewhere. There is no shortage of dead bodies over there. There are no problems with [getting] corpses."

Russia Airs Its Ultimate 'Revenge Plan' for America

Battered and infuriated by sanctions over the war in Ukraine, Putin's henchmen are plotting their master plan for revenge on live television.

Originally published by *The Daily Beast* on April 11, 2022

As Russia's war of aggression continues to ravage its neighbor, the Kremlin's propaganda apparatus has been more blatant than ever in outlining the country's goals for its biggest nemesis: the U.S.

Last week, American intelligence officials reportedly assessed that Russian President Vladimir Putin may use the Biden administration's support for Ukraine as a pretext to order a new campaign to interfere in U.S. elections.

Though AP reported that "it is not yet clear which candidates Russia might try to promote or what methods it might use," Russian state media seem to be in agreement that former U.S. President Donald Trump remains Moscow's candidate of choice.

The time is coming "to again help our partner Trump to become president," state TV host Evgeny Popov recently declared. On Thursday's edition of the state television show *The Evening With Vladimir Solovyov*, Putin's pet pundits offered an update on plans for 2024.

"We're trying to feel our way, figuring out the first steps. What can we do in 2023, 2024?," Russian "Americanist" Malek Dudakov, a political scientist specializing in the U.S., said. He suggested that Russia's interference in the upcoming elections is still in its early stages, and that more will be accomplished after the war is over and frosty relations between the U.S. and Russia start to warm up.

"When things thaw out and the presidential race for 2024 is firmly on the agenda, there'll be moments we can use," he added. "The most banal approach I can think of is to invite Trump — before he announces he's running for President—to some future summit in liberated Mariupol."

Dmitry Drobnitsky, an omnipresent "Americanist" on Solovyov's show, suggested that Tulsi Gabbard should be invited along with Trump. Dudakov agreed: "Tulsi Gabbard would also be great. Maybe Trump will take her as his vice-president?"

Gabbard has recently become a fixture of state television for her pro-Russian talking points, and has even been described as a "Russian agent" by the Kremlin's propaganda machine.

If state television is any indication, the real agenda of the Kremlin's operatives was never limited to boosting any particular candidates, but rather aimed to harm America as a whole.

Dudakov stressed: "With Europe, economic wars should take priority. With America, we should be working to amplify the divisions and—in light of our limited abilities—to deepen the polarization of American society."

He went on: "There is a horrific polarization of society in the United States, very serious conflicts between the Democrats and Republicans that keep expanding. You've already mentioned that America is a dying empire—and most empires weren't conquered, they were destroyed from within. The same fate likely awaits America in the near decade. That's why, when all the processes are thawed, Russia might get the chance to play on that."

Dudakov's Twitter feed, which he maintains despite the service being blocked in Russia, offers a glimpse into his own propaganda efforts. Tweeting as "Duderman67," Dudakov focuses on criticizing U.S. President Joe Biden, Vice President Kamala Harris, and Hillary Clinton—while boosting Trump.

On his Thursday show, host Solovyov argued that Russia wasn't fighting against the United States with full competency just yet, and griped about losing the main weapon behind enemy lines: "the brilliantly working structure of RT," the Kremlin-funded state TV network that was banished from U.S. cable stations last month.

He then offered up his own ideas about how to influence American voters without the help of RT: "I would act through various diasporas. For example, I would work with the Spanish-speaking media—since America is becoming predominantly Spanish-speaking, with the colossal influence of Latin America, I would work through their press, through those narratives, moving in that direction… they aren't allowing us to work with American media directly, but we have many opportunities that we aren't using thus far."

Appearing on Solovyov's show two days earlier, Vitaly Tretyakov, dean of the Moscow State University's School of Television, complained that Russia: "had military hypersonic weapons, but we don't have informational hypersonic weapons… all of our forces need to be dedicated to that. We don't have info-weapons equal in strength to our hypersonic weapons… as opposed to what they have. You can't survive in this world without winning an info-war. That is out of the question."

Pundit Karen Shakhnazarov suggested: "I would find it useful to break diplomatic relations with the United States. I don't see any point in maintaining them. And that would deliver a crushing blow to Biden. There are plenty of people in the U.S. who say that he is bringing us all to the edge of nuclear war. That will be a strong signal."

That wasn't the only talk of nuclear war on Solovyov's show this week. On Thursday, Solovyov confirmed a well-known concept frequently aired on state media when he acknowledged: "De facto, we aren't fighting a campaign against Ukraine, but against the entire West."

A parade of pundits recounted various ways U.S. sanctions are affecting the Russian economy, and the limited avenues for Russian retaliation. Solovyov resorted to pulling out his beloved trump card designed to intimidate the West: the threat of nuclear war. He asked: "Maybe it's time we strike them? Since we're already a pariah state, a war criminal, if everything is so bad."

Short of nuclear holocaust, it is now clear that Russia is focusing its efforts on distracting America from its foreign policy objectives by threatening to meddle in U.S. internal affairs. Speaking about the upcoming midterm elections on Solovyov's show last week, Konstantin Dolgov, the deputy chairman of the Committee on Economic Policy of Russia's Federation Council, predicted that "the results will apparently not be good for the Democrats," because of rising gas prices in the U.S.

But the midterms, he emphasized, are "just a rehearsal. The main elections are further ahead and preparations for those are already underway."

Putin's Stooges: He May Nuke Us All but We Are Ready to Die

Just when you thought Russian airwaves could not get any stranger, Putin's puppets have now surrendered to the idea of nuclear apocalypse, because at least they'll "go to heaven."

Originally published by *The Daily Beast* on April 27, 2022

Russian President Vladimir Putin ominously warned on Wednesday that if any other country intervenes in Ukraine, Russia will respond with "instruments… nobody else can boast of, and we will use them if we have to." In recent days, Russian state media has been hyping up the same rhetoric, bombarding audiences with jarring declarations that World War III is imminent. Every major channel is promoting the idea of an inevitable, never-before-seen escalation over Russia's invasion of Ukraine, which is being portrayed as a war waged against the Kremlin by the collective West.

Patriotic citizens are now being primed for the idea that even the worst outcome is a good thing, because those dying for the motherland will skyrocket to paradise. During Tuesday's broadcast of *60 Minutes*, Vladimir Avatkov of Russia's Diplomatic Academy of the Ministry of Foreign Affairs delivered an Orwellian perspective of current events. "What is happening right now is not about Ukraine, but about the future world order, which has no room for hegemony and where Russia can't be isolated."

Host Olga Skabeeva described a summit hosted by the U.S. in Germany that day to discuss upping Ukraine's defense capabilities as a sign that this is indeed "World War III, no longer just a special operation, with 40 countries against us. They declared a war."

Portraying global opponents of Russian aggression as evil incarnate, political scientist Mikhail Markelov claimed: "The representatives of those 40 different countries are today's collective Hitler."

Later the same day, on *The Evening With Vladimir Solovyov*, host Vladimir Solovyov lamented the West's refusal to heed the Kremlin's warnings. "If they decide to support Ukraine—even though [Russia's Foreign Minister] Sergey Lavrov told them that this could lead to WWIII—nothing will stop them. They've decided to play it big... These are the bastards with no morals."

Head of RT Margarita Simonyan added: "Personally, I think that the most realistic way is the way of World War III, based on knowing us and our leader, Vladimir Vladimirovich Putin, knowing how everything works around here, it's impossible—there is no chance—that we will give up."

In perhaps the most shocking declaration about a nuclear holocaust delivered on Russian television in recent months, Simonyan concluded that the idea "that everything will end with a nuclear strike, to me, is more probable than the other outcome. This is to my horror, on one hand, but on the other hand, with the understanding that it is what it is."

Solovyov chimed in: "But we will go to heaven, while they will simply croak." Simonyan comforted the audiences by adding: "We're all going to die someday."

Once the conversation turned to Western arms deliveries to Ukraine and a series of fires and explosions on Russian territory, Solovyov pondered out loud: "What is preventing us from striking the territory of the United Kingdom, targeting those logistical centers where these arms are being loaded?"

Andrey Sidorov, deputy dean of world politics at Moscow State University, retorted that rather than strike the U.K., Russia should target the real mastermind: America. He specified: "If we decide to strike the U.K., we should rather decide to strike the United States… Final decisions are being made not in London, but in Washington. If we want to hit the real center of the West, then we need to strike Washington."

In a bizarre attempt to soften the blow of Russia's grim predicament, state TV host and media personality Dmitry Kulikov told audiences that war is sometimes "inevitable." "This is a big war.

The West declared it against us. It's being waged through different methods, never seen before, but there's never been as many nuclear weapons in the world either," he said. "That is the only thing that sets this war apart from all others. This is a historical event, something we're used to. Let's be worthy of our predecessors, everyone who lived through that. What made us think that our lives should be better than those of our grandparents? Why should we be free of our historical mission?"

Russian Foreign Ministry spokeswoman Maria Zakharova appeared on the same program and continued with the same hard line. Solovyov asked her: "How far is the West ready to go?" Without hesitation, Zakharova replied: "They'll go as far as they're allowed to. If they aren't stopped, they will go all the way."

Adding his two cents to the nuclear apocalypse sideshow on Wednesday was military expert and retired Colonel Yury Knutov. "I've been observing the American approach from its top levels of leadership towards Russia for several years now," he said on the state TV show *60 Minutes*. "For some reason, they believe that Russia can be choked for as long as it takes, until it surrenders, and Russia will never respond or use its nuclear weapons or its nuclear potential... They themselves are creating the situation when there is a threat to the existence of our nation and our military doctrine prescribes that it gives us the right to use nuclear weapons."

Throughout the program, close-up photographs depicting dead Ukrainian servicemen were repeatedly shown on the screen. Knutov praised the production choice. "We see the Ukrainian land flooded by corpses of Ukrainian soldiers and National Guardsmen... our media needs to be showing more of that."

Putin's Puppets Admit Their Army Has Been a Total Embarrassment

The dismal state of the Russian military in Ukraine is so painfully obvious that even Vladimir Putin's most hardcore loyalists have been forced to address it on television.

Originally published by *The Daily Beast* on May 09, 2022

In his speech preceding the Victory Day celebrations across Russia on Sunday, President Vladimir Putin continued to promote the idea that his troops in Ukraine are fighting "to liberate their native land from the Nazi filth with confidence that, as in 1945, victory will be ours." His portrayal of Ukrainians as Nazis rings so hollow that propagandists on state television have been struggling to justify the so-called "special military operation."

The description itself was meant to portray a nearly painless blitzkrieg, akin to the annexation of Crimea. Instead, it has turned into an ongoing bloody massacre and a slew of crippling sanctions.

Russia was so unprepared for this turn of events, both militarily and economically, that even the most pro-Kremlin propagandists have been forced to acknowledge the grim reality of a pariah state fighting a war of aggression.

During Friday's broadcast of state TV show *The Evening With Vladimir Solovyov*, military analyst Konstantin Sivkov argued that Russia's "current economic market system is unfit to meet the needs of our Armed Forces and of the entire country under these conditions." Instead, he pushed for what he described as "military socialism," a set of wartime rules and regulations that would move all strategic resources–including land and factories–under the direct control of the government to better fund the war.

During the same show, host Vladimir Solovyov griped that Russia couldn't compete with Ukraine's seemingly endless supply of Turkish-made Bayraktar drones, which have been wreaking havoc on Russia's troops and equipment. "They tell us from the frontlines: 'Give us drones!' People are crowdfunding crazy amounts of money. They bought up everything that was available in stores. Why can't that junk be mass-produced in Russia?," Solovyov fumed.

State Duma member Semyon Bagdasarov chimed in: "Everyone is ashamed to talk about this topic. Volunteers, like our mutual acquaintances... are buying it all and transporting it over there. It's a crying shame!" Solovyov proceeded to angrily complain about the restrictions that complicate the delivery of such items to Russian troops in Ukraine, adding: "It's easier to bring it in through the Ukrainian Customs in Lviv. They let in any weapons."

Bagdasarov then resorted to blaming the West for the Kremlin's humiliations, claiming that recent sanctions were designed to provoke a popular uprising, akin to the October revolution of 1917 or the 1991 Soviet coup d'état attempt, also known as the August Coup.

To prevent the potential riots, Bagdasarov suggested the need for "purges" of current "management officials." He claimed that Russia is in sore need for a figure like Lavrentiy Beria—chief of the Soviet secret police who was notorious for his serial rapes and bloody mass executions.

This attempts to whitewash odious figures of the past on Russian airwaves if nothing new., Shortly before Russia's invasion of Ukraine in February, host of *Vesti Nedeli* Dmitry Kiselyov praised the likes of Joseph Stalin, Lavrentiy Beria, Julius and Ethel Rosenberg, among others for Russia's nuclear capabilities.

During Friday's live broadcast of *60 Minutes*, retired Colonel Mikhail Khodaryonok made the stunning confession that even mass mobilization in Russia wouldn't help alter the course of Putin's stalled invasion of Ukraine.

He admitted that Russia would be hard-pressed to replenish its mounting losses in Ukraine, and that sending masses to fight with outdated weapons would be counterproductive because Russia's arsenal does not measure up to NATO's top-notch weaponry.

"Let's imagine the drumroll, the sound of fanfare, and the mobilization is declared. How soon under this mobilization will we get the first fighter aviation regiment? We would get it by New Year's. We don't have the reserves, the pilots, or the planes so the mobilization would be of little help," Khodaryonok said.

"If tonight, we order new ships to be built, how soon will we get the first one? In two years! That's the deal with mobilization. If we set a goal of forming a new tank division, when would it be ready? I would say in at least 90 days. And it wouldn't be equipped with modern weaponry because we don't have modern weapons and equipment in our reserves."

The retired colonel continued: "Sending people armed with weapons of yesteryear into a war of the 21st century to fight against global standard NATO weapons would not be the right thing to do. We need to replenish our losses, of course, but this should be done through industrial enterprises. Mobilization would not solve these issues."

In December of 2021, appearing on *60 Minutes*, Khodaryonok flippantly said that Russia could destroy Ukraine in 11 minutes, but in the beginning of February—when Putin's invasion seemed all but imminent—the colonel was much more clear-eyed. His sobering predictions, published in the newspaper Independent Military Observer, were remarkably accurate.

Khodaryonok contradicted many popular analysts, stating in part that "To assert that no one in Ukraine will defend the regime means, in practice, complete ignorance of the military-political situation and the mood of the broad masses of people in the neighboring state. Moreover, the degree of hatred (which, as you know, is the most effective fuel for armed struggle) in the neighboring republic in relation to Moscow is frankly underestimated. No one will meet the Russian army with bread, salt and flowers in Ukraine."

Khodaryonok correctly predicted long and difficult battles, in addition to the extensive assistance the West would provide to Ukraine, writing in part: "There is no doubt that the United States and the countries of the North Atlantic Alliance will begin a kind of reincarnation of Lend-Lease, modeled after the Second World War."

While open opposition to Putin's war against Ukraine is outlawed, it's clear that the Russian people are resisting in various unconventional ways. A series of fires have erupted at several military enlistment offices in recent days, as rumors of the impending mobilization unsettle potential conscripts.

Putin's propagandists have apparently been enlisted to convince the public that the outcome of Russia's invasion is a matter of life and death for all of its citizens.

State TV pundit Karen Shakhnazarov, who previously pleaded with Putin to end the war as soon as possible, returned to national broadcasts after a temporary absence with a drastically different narrative last week.

During three separate broadcasts of *The Evening With Vladimir Solovyov*, Shakhnazarov claimed that Russians would find "no mercy" from their adversaries should the country lose the war. He threatened opponents of Putin's invasion, predicting they would face a future of "concentration camps, re-education and mandatory sterilization" imposed as a "final solution" for the Russian people sought by Moscow's enemies.

While some Kremlin propagandists begrudgingly admit that Russia can't afford to fight this war, the prevailing narrative force-fed by the state media is that Russia can't afford to lose.

Kremlin TV Betrays Darling Trump in Crazed Defense of Putin's War

Infuriated by an article labeling Russia as a fascist nation, a top Putin loyalist known for his admiration of Donald Trump seems to have turned on the former U.S. president.

Originally published by *The Daily Beast* on May 23, 2022

A New York Times essay by Yale University professor and historian Timothy Snyder entitled "We Should Say It. Russia Is Fascist," has spread through Russian state media like wildfire, producing a bombastic firestorm of outraged reactions from the Kremlin's most prominent mouthpieces.

In his piece published last week, Snyder argued that after being defeated on the battlefields of World War II, fascism has once again raised its ugly head when Putin's Russia unleashed its invasion of Ukraine.

He pointed out the key signs of fascism, indicating that they match up with the current actions and rhetoric of the Russian regime. "If Ukraine does not win, we can expect decades of darkness," Snyder concluded.

In a broadcast of the state TV show *The Evening With Vladimir Solovyov* on Friday, the host of the program and its panel of pundits were breathing fire over the essay.

Solovyov was so desperate to refute the article, in fact, that he resorted to lambasting one of the few Americans beloved by Russian state television: former U.S. President Donald Trump.

"Listen, you bastards," Solovyov fumed in a direct address to Americans. "Let me tell you a secret: first of all, your signs are idiotic in their nature. Secondly, looking at your listed indications, how are they any different from the election campaign of Donald Trump? Down to his slogan, 'Make America Great Again.'"

Solovyov went on to list various signs of Trump's "fascism," without any mention of how those descriptions also applied to Putin. "Strong leader, with large crowds coming out in his support... Discussions of former greatness. Donald Trump promised to make America great again," he said.

Referring to visual symbols as a sign of belonging, Solovyov pointed out "Donald Trump's red hats." To emphasize his point about "mass events to support the leader," the host asked: "Would you like me to put on a video of the dancing Trump?"

Russian propagandists seemed all too comfortable labeling their favorite American president as a fascist, despite the fact that they're counting on Republicans—led by Trump—to gain ground in the U.S. midterm elections and follow an agenda favored by the Kremlin. Meanwhile, Biden's falling popularity ratings have been discussed by state media with gusto on an almost daily basis.

The Biden administration's backing of Ukraine, including the brutal wave of sanctions against Russia over the invasion, has not sat well with Moscow.

"Author, professor of Yale University Snyder, is trying to convince the readers that we are waging a fascist war," Solovyov fumed, referring to the historian as a "pseudo-professor of a pseudo-university. "[They say that] we call Ukrainians Nazis because they refuse to recognize themselves as Russians and dare to resist. Snyder knows nothing and understands nothing. He is simply a liar."

Despite the host's assertions, many pundits on state television—including on Solovyov's own shows—have argued that exact point of view, claiming that Ukrainians are simply Russians who refuse to admit it.

"Those are absolutely Russian people, who speak the Russian language, but who are convinced that they represent anti-Russia and an anti-Russian element," Henry Sardaryan, Dean of Governance and Politics at Russia's MGIMO-University, said on Solovyov's Sunday show. "They are totally convinced that they're in the right. I often hear comments: 'Look at how hard the Ukrainian side is resisting.' But it's not the Ukrainian side, but the Russian side, which was convinced of being Ukrainian."

Appearing on *The Evening With Vladimir Solovyov* last month, political scientist Sergey Mikheyev also falsely alleged that no one in Ukraine speaks the Ukrainian language and claimed that it doesn't even exist.

On Sunday, Mikheyev was back on Solovyov's show, arguing that "the Ukrainian question" must be dealt with once and for all, since future generations of Russians can't be trusted to get the job done.

Equally popular on Russian state television are the talking points promoted by Tucker Carlson of Fox News, which favor abandoning Ukraine and allowing it to be devoured by Russian aggression. As more Republicans start to follow that line, the Kremlin's mouthpieces are hoping that the midterms will shift the balance in their favor.

Though they categorize Trump as someone worthy of a "fascist" designation, it's clear that Russian talking heads also still think of him as a partner and openly hope that the next presidential election will put him back in the White House—and the Kremlin on top of the world.

Kremlin TV Names the Country Putin Will Invade Next

And they don't stop there, suggesting Britain and the U.S. would be targeted in a looming WWIII.

Originally published by *The Daily Beast* on May 31, 2022

While some in the West are pondering what kind of a concessions would allow Russian autocrat Vladimir Putin "to save face" in Ukraine, leading Russian lawmakers and top propagandists are advocating smashing the West, which they say is Russia's ultimate target.

On the state TV show *60 Minutes*, host Olga Skabeeva announced: "I have some unpleasant news... Even though we are methodically destroying the weapons that are being delivered [to Ukraine], but the quantities in which the United States are sending them force us to come up with some global conclusions. Perhaps it's time to acknowledge that maybe Russia's special operation in Ukraine has come to an end, in a sense that a real war had started: WWIII. We're forced to conduct the demilitarization not only of Ukraine, but of the entire NATO alliance."

Vladimir Avatkov, from the Diplomatic Academy of the Ministry of Foreign Affairs, said: "You mentioned WWIII and the way Americans and Poles are acting on the territory of Ukraine—indeed, we need to remember the words of Vladimir Vladimirovich Putin, who said that anyone who tries to interfere in the special military operation will pay a heavy price."

Skabeeva interrupted: "We never forget about these words of Vladimir Vladimirovich Putin, but a great number of people are already standing in line, trying to interfere in Russia's special operation on the territory of Ukraine. Turns out, we have to act—but we're yet to figure out how we can act without conducting a nuclear strike."

Russian parliament member Oleg Matveychev weighed in: "If Poland starts any intervention... its current borders will be worthless." Skabeeva wasn't satisfied: "I wasn't talking just about Poland, but mainly about Great Britain and the United States... they're all lined up." Avatkov chimed in: "No need to rush, there is a line. Everything in its time!"

The first in line is apparently Poland, with Secretary of the Russian Security Council Nikolai Patrushev baselessly claiming on Tuesday that Poland is moving to seize territories in western Ukraine and accusing numerous unnamed countries of "actively working to dismember Ukraine."

Meanwhile, on Russian state TV hosts and pundits routinely refer to Ukraine as "the territory formerly known as Ukraine" and matter-of-factly discuss how many millions of Ukrainians might have to die for Russia to complete its so-called "denazification."

In his recent interview, Russian State Duma Deputy Defense Committee Chairman Vladimir Shamanov, former Commander-in-Chief of the Russian Airborne Troops, admitted that Russia "was built through territorial enlargement" and named Poland as one of Russia's main adversaries.

Appearing on the state TV show *Sunday Evening With Vladimir Solovyov*, Chairman of the State Duma Committee on Defense Andrey Kartapolov expounded on the idea of Russia's crusade against the Western world: "For us, the special military operation is just the first act, an introduction. The war that is going on right now... it's not just an economic war and info-war, this war is about our faith. It's about our right, as the people, to have faith in what we want to believe, to love those we want to love, and to live the way our ancestors would have wanted, on our land and by our birthright."

Kartapolov added: "These wars are not the first wars. In the 19th century—Napoleon, in the 20th century—Adolf Aloisovich Hitler, and every time all of Europe came at us. The same thing is happening now... It's a good thing that a realization is coming, it's time to stop lying. Stop lying to ourselves, stop lying to our leader, stop lying to our own people. It's time to be responsible for our words and deeds and to move forward as one—to the goal that has been set by the commander-in-chief."

The strategy of justifying such a potential attack against additional adversaries is consistent with the Kremlin's previous approach with respect to Ukraine: ludicrous claims that the chosen target was about to go on the offensive against the Motherland. The impending conflict against the West is being framed in terms of an existential battle for Russia's survival.

Kartapolov claimed, "Today, Europe is a de-facto colony of the United States, the new type of a colony. In the '90s, we were the same kind of a colony but managed to break free—thanks to our president and the decisions he made... They put everything in a beautiful wrapper, selling it to us under the guise of democracy, freedom of speech and all sorts of other slogans. Their main goal was to usurp our resources, our natural resources, to split Russia up into many vicious countries fighting with one another."

The alleged desire to "dismember Russia" is also being ascribed to opposition activists, in order to simultaneously target all perceived enemies, both foreign and domestic.

During Monday's broadcast of *The Evening With Vladimir Solovyov*, arguments were made to limit the influence of members of the opposition on Russian society—particularly those who still travel abroad.

Political scientist Vadim Gigin claimed, "People who are planning to return to Russia... are proposing to divide the country."

Host Vladimir Solovyov added, "They have the lists of undesirables... they'll be hanging people. What's scary is that they're coming back."

Shota Gorgadze, a member of the Russian Presidential Human Rights Council proposed that immediately upon their return, opposition activists be criminally charged for their alleged calls to dismember Russia.

Agitated, Solovyov complained, "For months we've been demanding that criminal cases be open against all of [Alexei] Navalny's terrorist sect under article 275 [treason]."

Gorgadze proposed that anyone speaking out "against the interests of the Russian Federation, especially during this difficult time" be stripped of their Russian citizenship. He added, "If the law says this can't be done, I don't see any reason why this law can't be changed."

Urging a more aggressive approach, Solovyov asked, "Are we acting as inert gases, simply taking up only as much room as the West allows? The West is squeezing us and we're accepting it and adapting to it? When things let up, will we exhale and welcome the air of freedom? No, that won't work. It's time to sober up and find our way."

Discussing Russia's confrontation with the collective West during *Sunday Evening With Vladimir Solovyov*, Kartapolov framed it as a crusade: "I'm convinced that this war is about faith. Russia is an Orthodox country, and by "Orthodox" I don't mean just Christianity. Orthodoxy is when on our territory all traditional religions peacefully co-exist: traditional Islam, Buddhism, and Judaism... They're saying, we're destroying the Ukrainian culture. What culture? Look at the devils they pulled out from the basements of Azovstal... It's the face—I can't even call it a face—the snout of the unclean. The holy scripture says, "What has been will be again, what has been done will be done again; there is nothing new under the sun." In the 19th century, we came to Paris, in the 20th century we came to Berlin—we'll come wherever they try to enslave and humiliate us. You won't succeed. Expect us."

Putin's Lap Dog Humiliated by Fed-Up Guest on His Own Show

Russian fearmongering has become so unbearable that even state TV regulars are railing against the mouthpieces committed to pushing Vladimir Putin's destructive propaganda.

Originally published by *The Daily Beast* on June 03, 2022

Determined to quash support for Ukraine in its ongoing self-defense against Russian aggression, the Kremlin has issued a slew of threats against the West, magnified and echoed by the pliant state media. But instead of scaring NATO into backing off, that strategy seems to be causing something of a domestic fallout, with masses of everyday Russians fearing the idea of an imminent nuclear war that has been pushed by propagandists.

It seems that now, even the most dedicated propagandists are becoming alarmed by the side effects of the Kremlin's fear tactics.

Thursday's state TV program, *The Evening With Vladimir Solovyov*, began with familiar rhetoric but was met with some unexpected resistance. The host, Vladimir Solovyov, ranted and threatened the West with gusto: "I'm so sick of them! Constantly reading about whatever they will come up with next, like their new lists of sanctions, and thinking, 'Guys, I'm sick of you!'"

Solovyov, who lost his multimillion-dollar villas in Italy because of Western sanctions, bitterly complained about the increasing cost of Putin's invasion of Ukraine. Instead of suggesting Russian troops pull out from their neighbor's territory, the state TV host followed what appears to be the officially approved line of rhetoric, promoting the idea of unprecedented escalation.

"I don't mind it when inept people try to rule the world, but it irritates me when they're so nervous. If you want war with us, then declare war, so we can start swinging!" he bellowed. Threatening retaliation for the anticipated damage that might be caused to Russian assets by the advanced weapons systems set to be delivered to Ukraine, the host quoted statements by Russian President Vladimir Putin and Security Council Deputy Chairman Dmitry Medvedev.

Solovyov recounted, "Vladimir Vladimirovich [Putin] clearly said and Dmitry Anatolyevich [Medvedev] clearly said, we'll strike the decision-making centers — and those are not in Kyiv."

Solovyov's message was on par with the common theme on Russian state television: nuclear war is imminent, but dying for the Motherland is the best way to go.

But there was one pundit in the studio who was clearly fed up with the fear-mongering — and he made it known. When it was his turn to speak, political scientist Sergey Mikheyev couldn't contain his rage.

"There is a flood of information, including our mainstream media, about how scary and terrible everything is. About 500 times per day, on every channel, every talk show, they're talking about how many more weapons are being sent, how frightening they are," he fumed.

In a rare instance of transparency on Russian state TV, Mikheyev acknowledged that he thinks the changes in public opinion have been destabilizing the entire country.

"Working with public opinion is crucially important, because the stability inside of the country depends on the stability of public opinion. The public opinion, day to night, only hears about the characteristics of foreign weapons, they don't understand what happens next," he said, "They tell us, 'Terrible weapons are arriving over there, they keep coming and coming. They [Ukraine] promised not to utilize them a certain way, but most likely will do it anyway — and that will lead to World War III.' Then we're being told, 'Calm down, comrades, everything will be alright. Don't you worry, there's nothing to worry about.'"

Solovyov had claimed that Russia "could spit" on the weapons provided for Ukraine's self-defense against Russian aggression, boasting about more advanced arms that have been manufactured specifically for a future confrontation with NATO. "We've been anticipating this," Solovyov said.

"Everyone understood that after we destroy all of Ukraine's weapons—which happened long ago, we destroyed all Soviet-made arms—the time would come to demilitarize NATO."

The host flippantly told the audience: "Just calm down. Our guys are doing their job. They're doing it correctly. All the hysteria in the West confirms that we're moving towards our goal. Of course, we'd like it to go faster, but how could we leave our flanks unprotected? We can't expose Kaliningrad or the border with Finland. We understand: our next operation may be war with NATO."

Mikheyev challenged the host on that point, too. Complaining about the messaging employed by many prominent state media mouthpieces, the pundit noted with visible aggravation: "It's rolling in: those will send [weapons] and so will others, on and on; they will most likely try to use them. The common man asks: 'What happens next?' and the answer is, 'Be calm, comrades. Next comes WWIII. Keep on working, don't worry about a thing, keep minding your business. The nuclear war is coming. That's all.'

Staring at Solovyov, Mikheyev asked: "What is that? Is that a normal approach? Is that the way to work with public opinion? I think this is something to think about... People are getting worried. Realistically, we have a huge number of people who are extremely concerned about this."

Unpersuaded, the host immediately dismissed the political scientist's concerns about maintaining some measure of sanity in order to safeguard public opinion. Instead, Solovyov opted to follow the official guidance on messaging to the masses. He defiantly replied: "And after we think about it, then there will be nuclear war."

Team Putin Dishes on the Moment They Could Win It All

And they're betting on America to lock in a path to victory.

Originally published by *The Daily Beast* on June 08, 2022

With Vladimir Putin's bloody war in Ukraine crossing the 100-day mark, the Kremlin seems to be abandoning any pretense of diplomacy. There are several reasons Moscow aborted its initial half-hearted attempts to negotiate with Ukraine, including tangible gains on the battlefront and Western media's waning attention span. But if Russian state TV is any indication, another reason Putin's regime is now rejecting the idea of a diplomatic resolution has to do with the approaching midterm elections in the United States.

During the latest broadcast of state TV show *Sunday Evening With Vladimir Solovyov*, participants discussed the price Russia would ultimately have to pay for its intended conquest of Ukraine. Across various state media outlets, the U.S. midterm elections have been mentioned as a potential saving grace that could halt American support of Ukraine and loosen the screws of sanctions against Russia. During Solovyov's show, Andrey Sidorov, deputy dean of world politics at Moscow State University, asked: "Are we going to count on their electoral issues? Will anything change if Republicans prevail in November in the United States?"

The host, Vladimir Solovyov, responded enthusiastically. "Yes, yes, a lot will change. They will calmly say, 'Why do we need to be involved and send so much of our own money?'" Russian state media has been frequently airing statements showing dissent within the Republican party with respect to U.S. support for Ukraine, often featuring clips from Tucker Carlson's show on Fox News, as well as comments made during public hearings and media appearances by former U.S. President Donald Trump, former Congresswoman Tulsi Gabbard, Senator Rand Paul, Congresswoman Marjorie Taylor Greene, and Congressman Matt Gaetz.

Echoing popular Republican talking points on Ukraine, Solovyov predicted: "Republicans will come and say, why the hell do we need a corrupt, Nazi Ukraine? They will ask: whom are we supporting? Yes, Russia is bad and the sanctions will stay, but why do we need to keep throwing so much money over there? Our schools lack funding, we have plenty of our own problems. Instead of fortifying the border with Mexico, helping our small businesses, we've given that money to corrupt Ukraine and no one knows where it went."

So far, Western appeals for diplomacy seem to have only encouraged Russia to escalate its military offensive, since they're perceived as a sign of desperation. During Sunday's broadcast of Solovyov's show, Sidorov explained: "In my opinion, the talks about negotiations are designed to keep this conflict going.

A ceasefire is needed to secure the transition from Soviet-type weapons of the Ukrainian forces—which they've already run out of—to Western types of arms. They need time. They need corridors through which to move them. Under no circumstances should we agree to negotiate."

Solovyov concurred. "We don't need any kind of negotiations, because time is on our side and the tempo is working in our favor... They're arming [Ukrainians] with NATO systems... if they get some howitzers from here, some howitzers from over there, who is going to repair them?" he said. "If you train artillery specialists, but then you find out that you need not only ammunition, but spare parts and repairmen, you need power supply, you need to maintain the whole system... it's a headache... They need years to deal with this and not just a ceasefire."

On Monday's *The Evening With Vladimir Solovyov*, the host introduced a clip from an old favorite of Russian state media—Tucker Carlson: "Let me show you how Biden is being kicked around by Tucker Carlson of Fox News." In the clip, Carlson ridiculed U.S. President Joe Biden for being unable to destroy the Russian economy, "in retaliation for installing Donald Trump as president."

Solovyov compared Carlson's diatribe to that of the Chinese government officials—a dubious honor for any self-respecting American television host.

Aside from the statement about Trump's election, the rhetoric cited by Solovyov nearly mimicked Carlson's claims about the booming Russian economy, allegedly thriving despite Western sanctions. While the Russian economy is struggling, Kremlin-funded media re-broadcasts useful agitprop from foreign entities to convince the public that everything is going according to plan.

It's clear that western media coverage has played a major role in Moscow's thinking. During Tuesday's broadcast, Solovyov explained: "We're moving as fast as we can, based on the realities of the military circumstances and our intent to minimize our casualties. That's why the mood in the West shifted so drastically. While in recent days they thought it was a done deal, now they want to negotiate and are telling Ukraine to accept the loss of its territories... The mood has certainly changed. This is a long-term war, not in terms of our special operation, but with regard to our war against the West—no doubt about it."

"I'll start by talking about who is losing the war, in terms of our confrontation with the West, although the main battles are only starting... just read the Western press, they're all convinced that they've already lost," Political analyst Dmitry Drobnitsky added. "It's so surprising, I was amazed by this: there's real panic... It's like the floodgates have been opened."

You'll Never Guess the Lie Putin Has Come Up With Now

Not only does he say there's no war in Ukraine, Putin may have told his favorite propagandist that Russia is not even carrying out a so-called "Special Operation."

Originally published by *The Daily Beast* on June 20, 2022

Russia's flagship economic event, the St. Petersburg International Economic Forum (SPIEF, which ended over the weekend), served as another reflection of the country's shifting place in the world. After Russia invaded Ukraine and was largely shunned by the international community, Western investors who had turned up at the event dubbed "the Russian Davos" in droves during previous years were conspicuously absent. Likewise, there would be no foreign moderator. This year's SPIEF was moderated by Margarita Simonyan, editor-in-chief of the controversial media outlet RT (formerly known as Russia Today).

Earlier in June, discussing Simonyan being selected for the role, Putin's spokesman Dmitry Peskov told TASS: "The sanity of many prominent Western reporters is currently raising questions... all of them have simply gone nuts... Margarita [Simonyan] is a world class reporter and media manager. So for us, she leaves journalists in the dust internationally, that's why it's her who will be the moderator."

Fresh from the event, Simonyan appeared on *Sunday Evening With Vladimir Solovyov*, gushing about her recent meetings with Putin and spouting a new fabulist tale about what Russia is supposedly doing in Ukraine.

The host of the program, Vladimir Solovyov, asked Simonyan for details of her meetings with the Russian authoritarian before and after the forum. She grinned and coyly retorted: "Of course, I can't tell all about it publicly, I'll later whisper it into your ear."

Solovyov hinted that Simonyan may have even given Putin some advice herself: "Based on recent observations, the president is open to receiving information that is coming from different levels... Our decision-making centers aren't acting as Olympic Gods. They take information from everywhere: official sources, unofficial sources, war correspondents, people on location, which is very important."

In the best traditions of Soviet and North Korean propagandists, the head of RT started her monologue by praising Putin's great health, indefatigable stamina, unshakable confidence and cheerful disposition. She claimed that the most frequently requested questions average Russians wanted her to ask the Russian president were simple: the first one was a message of implicit support and the second one reflected the everyday citizens' urgent plea to strike the "decision-making centers" as soon as possible.

Angrily clenching her fist, Simonyan exclaimed: "I also want to ask, why don't we strike them? Where are those red lines?" She recounted Putin's response: "I won't say which red lines they are, but they know about them... I won't name them due to the military tactics: why would we show them our cards in advance?"

Simonyan claimed that one of Putin's reasons for not carrying out more intense bombings in major cities was a rather practical one: "He said, 'Would we want to turn those cities into Stalingrad?' Indeed, our people are there! Those are our future cities! It's obvious... This is our land and our people, we'll later have to restore it."

After her secretive meetings with Putin, Simonyan — who for years promoted the idea of Russia's armed intervention in neighboring countries — emerged with a drastically different iteration of the events being witnessed by the rest of the world.

She outright denied that Russia is waging either a war or even a special operation in Ukraine. Instead, Simonyan alleged, there is a civil war and Russia simply took the side of the Russians.

The head of RT did her best to sell an implausible story, laced with genocidal denial of Ukrainians as a people, and an outright dismissal of an idea they could possibly be fighting to defend their Motherland.

Describing one of the videos of a Ukrainian POW she recently watched, Simonyan said: "A surrendered soldier of the Ukrainian Armed Forces was sitting down, his face is absolutely Russian, totally Russian. None of you could tell who he was, he's Russian. Big blue eyes, blonde hair and beard. He said, "I was mobilized under mandatory enlistment." We should understand, not all of them are there of their own free will."

Simonyan, who often claims that the Russian troops are in Ukraine fighting for their Motherland, absurdly denied that such a concept could ever apply to Ukrainians fighting on their own soil.

Recounting the video with a captive POW, Simonyan claimed: "He doesn't even care where to live. He has no military-patriotic feelings that he's defending his Motherland. He understands perfectly well that he isn't defending any Motherland, but somebody else's interests that have nothing to do with his own. He couldn't care less where he ends up living: in Donetsk, Belgorod or his village near Kyiv, where he's from."

As for those fighting against the Russian troops or opposing Russian aggression, Simonyan noted: "There is a significant number of Nazis and indoctrinated people, with whom there isn't much to be done, other than to have them shot under the laws of the DPR [the supposed Donetsk People's Republic]."

In addition to advocating the murder of Ukrainians resisting Russia's invasion, including POWs, Simonyan refused to acknowledge their very existence as a people in any context aside from being either Russian or anti-Russian.

She said, "It's obvious to any person that there is no war between Russia and Ukraine. This isn't even a special operation against the Ukrainian Armed Forces. This is a civil war in Ukraine. Part of Ukrainians, who are Russophobes and are anti-Russian in the same sense fascists were antisemitic—absolutely the same way—is destroying another part of its own people. Russia is simply supporting one side of those warring parties. Why this particular side? That is obvious, because they are Russians. Those are our people. And over there, they are anti-Russians. That's all."

Realizing the impossibility of successfully selling this preposterous explanation to Western audiences, Simonyan speculated that in the event Russian state media abroad continued to operate unabated, Americans and Europeans would believe Russia's alternative portrayal of its aggression and electoral chances of their leaders who support Ukraine "would tumble downward, from 20-30 percent approval rating all the way to zero."

Simonyan surmised, with a sigh: "From their point of view, I understand how smart it was for Europe and America to get rid of RT and Sputnik."

Putin's Lies Have Kremlin TV Flailing and Fighting On-Air

Putin's top propagandists can no longer work out why they started this war as demands for total victory over Ukraine are being shut down by the Kremlin.

Originally published by *The Daily Beast* on July 05, 2022

While Russian troops slowly advance in Eastern Ukraine, questions loom as to how far President Vladimir Putin is planning to take his invasion of Ukraine. During a recent press conference, Putin claimed that nothing has changed and everything is going according to the plan: "I have formulated the overall goal, which is to liberate Donbas, protect its people and create conditions that will guarantee the security of Russia itself. That is all." His deliberately vague responses implied that Russian attacks in other parts of Ukraine were meant "to distract" the Ukrainian leadership.

Some military experts are convinced that fierce Ukrainian resistance may be insurmountable, as long as it continues to be aided by the ongoing Western support. Appearing on the state TV show *The Evening With Vladimir Solovyov* last Friday, Andrey Gurulyov, State Duma deputy and a former deputy commander of Russia's southern military district, stressed that the West will continue to supply Ukraine with every conceivable type of weapons, "up to a nuclear bomb—just not to let us win."

He proposed re-creating the Cuban Missile Crisis, but this time with hypersonic weapons, in order to reach an eventual détente with the United States: "Our hypersonic weapons... should be brought to the near vicinity of the United States, with a flight time of no more than five minutes."

Gurulyov candidly admitted: "That is the only scenario for us to be able to denazify and demilitarize Ukraine. Only a direct threat to the U.S. and the UK... will force all of them to the negotiating table... all of this is part of a greater plan of conducting not only a special operation, but World War III, which is for us the second Great Patriotic War."

He positioned nuclear blackmail as Russia's golden ticket, urging the country's leadership "to seriously think through the plans of how we can painlessly get to the next crisis that will be our ticket to the future."

Host Vladimir Solovyov opined: "Thanks to the idiocy of NATO countries, the world can anticipate hunger and a big war." His constant attempts to deter foreign support for Ukraine through threats of nuclear attacks against Western countries have become so overplayed that even fellow propagandists routinely wince and roll their eyes. Solovyov, who is reportedly purchasing military equipment himself to aid Russia's war against Ukraine, is currently advocating total destruction of the country's critical infrastructure.

His theatrical threats are ringing hollow, but at the same time, they are raising expectations.

On Monday, the Kremlin childishly declined to congratulate the United States on its Independence Day. Military expert Alexey Leonkov appeared on Solovyov's show on July 4 proposing that Russia should declare the U.S. and its allies "state sponsors of terrorism" for helping Ukraine deter Russian aggression.

The host enthusiastically agreed and threatened that Russia would start shooting down American satellites, which would lead to a direct confrontation with the United States. Solovyov added, "I don't know why we haven't already declared them to be terrorists."

While most of the world hopes for a speedy conclusion to Russia's brutal war against its neighbor, the Kremlin's pet propagandists insist that the slaughter must continue — and expand.

On Sunday evening's broadcast of Solovyov's show, one of the program's recurring guests, Yaakov Kedmi, also known as Yasha Kazakov, an Israeli former politician and diplomat, insisted that Russia must take all of Ukraine and that nothing less would do.

"If the results of this operation will be maximally close to the expectations of the Russian people, that will be a victory. If they will be far removed from that, it will constitute a defeat. Semantic somersaults, like claiming, 'We set the liberation and security of the

Donetsk and Lugansk People's Republics as our goal,' will be of no help. It will be regarded by the Russian people as a defeat. It doesn't matter what created that anticipation of the goal, whether it was smart or not, that's what they're waiting for," he said. "If they have such expectations, any deviation from a complete and final victory over Ukraine will be seen as a loss, with consequences for Russia."

Bringing up the remarks of former U.S. Secretary of State Henry Kissinger, Kedmi said, "He noted and others are pointing out an incredible support for Putin as a result of this operation. What is the basis for this support? Unshakable confidence of the Russian people that he will secure total victory. God forbid this trust would be broken or somehow damaged... The people won't accept and won't forgive anything less than a total victory. I'd like to remind you, based on Russia's history, how the people reacted when the government didn't meet their expectations. With the same force they supported [the government], they will stomp it into dirt... Anything less than Novorossiya [a proposed confederation of the self-proclaimed Donetsk People's Republic and the Luhansk People's Republic] and the left bank of Ukraine will be a catastrophe. Not merely a defeat, but a catastrophe."

Solovyov jumped in: "In that case, let's be even more blunt. In reality, the goals were formulated in December of 2021. They are not limited to Ukraine, but demand that NATO's infrastructure be returned to the boundaries of 1997-1998."

Kedmi concurred: "That was another one of Kissinger's mistakes. As I've said before, everything that is happening in Ukraine is a prelude for the main confrontation, the main fight, which will determine the fate of the entire world, the fate of the United States, as well as Russia's fate. This big battle will develop based on the outcome of the actions in Ukraine. Russia has no right to lose this big battle, or the battle in Ukraine, as defeat resembles death." Solovyov concluded: "Defeat is death."

The next guest, Russian Foreign Ministry Spokeswoman Maria Zakharova, seemed to be seething about Kedmi's comments, which may indicate that the Kremlin has indeed settled for a more modest endgame in Ukraine.

She told him to speak to the Israeli government and leadership about the ills of "the Kyiv regime," instead of "fantasizing" about the wishes of the Russian people. She claimed that there is "a total unity" of average Russians with the country's government, with respect to their goals in Ukraine.

Zakharova's angry tirade attempted to cover up the fact that even the top propagandists seem to be unable to figure out the Kremlin's final aims, much less the everyday people.

The latest poll by Russia's Public Opinion Research Center VCIOM shows that 38 percent of Russians believe that the goal of the invasion was to disarm Ukraine, 20 percent think that the aim was to protect Donbas, only 19 percent believe Putin's dubious claim of "denazification" and 8 percent think that Russia's intent is to occupy all of Ukraine and absorb it into Russia.

Instead of helping Putin's regime, the angry bluster by the state media's propagandists only highlights the senselessness of a conflict that even Russia's own population struggles to grasp. The cartoonish promises of taking over the world fail to overshadow the fact that Russia's economy is descending into the abyss. No territorial gains could ever justify the unbearable human toll.

Kremlin TV Says if Putin Ran For U.S. President, He'd Win—and Trump Would Be His Veep

The Kremlin's TV propaganda machine wants Russians to believe that Putin is more popular than ever around the globe, despite widespread opposition to the war in Ukraine.

Originally published by *The Daily Beast* on July 29, 2022

Russia's invasion of Ukraine has led to Moscow's global condemnation and isolation, prompting even the most seasoned propagandists to concede that the Kremlin is losing the information war to the West. Yet, as the conflict grinds on and media coverage of the hostilities starts to wane, Russian propagandists are now trying to convince their population that Moscow has been wildly successful with its info-ops and will be able to win back global public opinion once the "special operation" in Ukraine is over.

Emboldened by the likes of Tucker Carlson, whose show on Fox News is consistently translated and featured on Russian state television, the Kremlin's mouthpieces are assuring everyday Russians that millions of Americans would rather side with Russian President Vladimir Putin than U.S. President Joe Biden.

Back in 2018, Russian state media had a field day with two men at a Trump rally in Ohio, who were photographed wearing shirts that say "I'd rather be a Russian than a Democrat."

During Thursday's broadcast of *The Evening With Vladimir Solovyov*, one of the program's recurring guests, Yaakov Kedmi—also known as Yasha Kazakov—an Israeli former politician and diplomat, bitterly disagreed with those pundits who conceded that the Western media's coverage of the brutal war had battled Moscow at every turn.

He argued: "It was said that [the West] is winning a propaganda war, but I'm not so sure about that. Look at any country in Europe. Look at France: who is more popular—Macron or Putin?" One after another, pundits in the studio said, "Putin!" Kedmi proceeded to opine that the same is true in just about every Western country, including Germany, France, Italy, and the United States.

Talking about American citizens, Kedmi asked, "In who do they trust? If tomorrow Putin announced his candidacy for the president of the United States, who in the U.S. could compete with him in popularity?" Foreign Policy Analyst Alexander Kamkin quickly added, "And Trump would become his Vice President."

During Wednesday's broadcast of the state TV show *60 Minutes*, host Evgeny Popov, who is also a State Duma member, complained that the January 6 Committee was targeting Russia's own Donald J. Trump.

He repeated the propaganda tropes about U.S. elections being "fake, unfair, and falsified" and threatened Americans about the upcoming elections: "The best is yet to come! Wait for it, Americans!"

While it may be tempting to dismiss constant discussions of Russia's ongoing and planned interference in U.S. elections on Kremlin-controlled state television as "trolling," Moscow is indeed funding and controlling these operations.

An indictment unsealed by the Justice Department on Friday in Tampa, Florida, charged Aleksandr Ionov, a Russian national, working on behalf of the Russian government and in conjunction with the Russian Federal Security Service (FSB), with allegedly orchestrating a foreign malign influence campaign that used various U.S. political groups to sow discord, spread pro-Russian propaganda, and interfere in elections within the United States.

Working under the supervision of the FSB and with the Russian government's support, Ionov recruited political groups in Florida, Georgia, and California and directed their activities on behalf of the FSB to further Russian interests in the United States.

He became directly involved in state elections and repeatedly forwarded information to the Russian government, referring to one of the U.S. candidates as the one "whom we supervise."

After the said candidate advanced to the general election, the FSB Officer wrote to Ionov, "Our election campaign is kind of unique," and proudly asked, "are we the first in history?"

Ionov and Russian government officials also involved themselves with a California-based organization whose primary goal was to promote California's secession from the United States. They funded and directed various protests related to the coverage of Russia's war against Ukraine, with the footage and photographs of the said events being later featured in the Russian media, as recently as March 2022.

Ionov's activities in the U.S. closely match the discussions on Russian state television, wherein prominent pundits and decorated propagandists openly plot to harm the United States and other Western countries by stirring up unrest, promoting separatism, and advancing candidates preferred by Moscow.

Head of RT Margarita Simonyan admitted that despite being blocked, her outlet's operations are continuing on a covert basis. Appearing on *The Evening With Vladimir Solovyov* earlier this month, Simonyan said, "When they [Western governments] conducted carpet bombing against us and destroyed everything, denying us any access to disseminating information, we came to our senses and started to penetrate their defenses using partisan trails: under other names, with different people, in new ways. I won't disclose the rest here."

Since the Kremlin is pinning its hopes on the upcoming midterm elections and Russian state media experts anticipate major changes to the U.S. foreign policy if the Republicans were to take control of both the House and the Senate, state media chatter about Russia's planned interference is far from trivial. Some crimes are committed in broad daylight—and openly plotted on live television.

Putin's Pals Furious Younger Russians Don't Want to Die in Ukraine

"If you have to die, you only have to do it once… This is a part of your duty as a citizen, as a soldier, as a warrior, as a Russian man."

Originally published by *The Daily Beast* on August 05, 2022

As Russia's invasion of Ukraine marches on, there is a dark undercurrent of waning public support—and it's coming through even on tightly controlled state television. In the first days of the bloody war, the public was promised a quick victory due to the superiority of Russia's military.

Instead, the Kremlin's offensive has been plagued by heavy losses and equipment deficiencies, to the point that state TV pundits publicly contemplate seeking aid and assistance from other pariah states—including Iran and North Korea.

Russia has reportedly been involved in discussions with Iran to purchase military drones, due to a severe shortage of its own unmanned aerial vehicles. During Thursday's broadcast of the state TV show *60 Minutes*, military expert Igor Korotchenko suggested that North Koreans could help rebuild destroyed Ukrainian regions and join Russia's military ranks.

Conversations about legalizing the participation of foreign fighters alongside Russian forces have been a recurring topic in state media, and for good reason: everyday citizens are less than enthusiastic about the prospect of going to war or dying for Putin. That doesn't sit well with top pro-Kremlin propagandists, such as state TV host Vladimir Solovyov—twice formally recognized by Russian President Vladimir Putin for his services in the benefit of the Fatherland.

During Thursday's broadcast of his show, *The Evening With Vladimir Solovyov*, the host complained: "It irritates me that our society doesn't understand that a watershed moment is currently taking place. We either stand up, build up and end up on another level, or simply cease to exist." His guest, political scientist Alexander Kamkin, concurred and suggested that a "cultural special operation" be conducted in Russia.

The Kremlin's tight control over the information disseminated to the public has failed to curtail access to outside sources, with tensions rising to such a point that on Monday during Solovyov's show, convicted Russian agent Maria Butina suggested jailing parents whose children use a VPN to access foreign media.

The host was likewise disappointed with the younger generation's lackluster involvement in Putin's war, complaining: "People who are planning to join [the military] are mainly of the same age as me, some are a bit younger... That is the generation that was raised on Soviet movies, Soviet literature and values. But the very young people I talk to, they faint if they cut their finger — and they see that as their democratic values... The special military operation is our Rubicon. I get the feeling that many here still can't grasp it."

Writer Zakhar Prilepin, who is wanted by Ukraine's SBU security service on charges of "taking part in the activity of a terrorist organization" for his involvement in Russia's war crimes in Ukraine, added: "We really need volunteers, we aren't hiding that. We need to replenish dislodged personnel. Meanwhile, the topic of death is silenced. The topic of perishing is curtailed. In a society motivated by comfort, you can't talk about death. Everyone is expected to go to war, win and come back alive. Better yet, not to go in the first place. Let me remind you that the Charter of the Imperial Army included in plain language: if you have three adversaries, go to war and advance, kill all three. If you have 10, then defend yourself. If your death has come, then die. It's written very plainly: 'Soldier, death is part of your job. It is part of your duty and your contract with the government.' The same principles were adopted by [Joseph] Stalin, who had an Orthodox Christian education."

Prilepin recited the lyrics of an old Soviet song, entitled "In the woods at the frontline": "If you have to lie in the ground, at least you have to do it only once." He asserted: "The soldier was openly told: go and fight. If you have to die, you only have to do it once...

This is a part of your duty as a citizen, as a soldier, as a warrior, as a Russian man. Today, we're protecting everybody: the government, mothers, conscripts, everyone. We barely forced our governors to put up murals [of the fallen soldiers]... Everyone is afraid to upset society."

Prilepin openly worried that in the event of total mobilization, the younger generation would opt to escape to neighboring countries instead of joining the fight: "The government assumes that in Russia, there is always 1 million men ready to fight. As for the rest of the country, we try not to worry them... We've been discussing difficult topics, which might lead to World War III and the same mobilization we're trying to avoid right now... It's difficult to talk about total mobilization, because I suspect that an excessive flood of people will suddenly pour into Armenia and Georgia. Borders will have to be closed. I'm talking about our younger generation."

Solovyov suggested the rules protecting conscripts from taking part in combat should be changed: "You know what amazes me most of all? That the conscripts in our Army are not supposed to fight... So what are they supposed to do in the Army?" He complained that not many enough volunteers have joined the battle: "We have 150 million people. How many are fighting in Donbas?" The state TV host proposed a massive government-funded propaganda campaign, glorifying the participants of Russia's so-called "special operation" in film and on television, with songs and poetry.

Gone are the days when state TV propagandists were predicting that other countries would flock to Russia's side to join the battle against Ukraine and the West.

During Thursday's broadcast of *The Evening With Vladimir Solovyov*, political scientist Sergey Mikheyev summarized the current mood in Russia: "About these constant discussions as to what we can offer the world, the world can go screw itself... We don't need to offer anything to anybody. We're special, we need to build ourselves up." Solovyov agreed: "We are the Noah's Ark. First and foremost, we need to save ourselves. Ourselves!"

Russia's Panicked Confession: This Is What Scares Us Most

Vladimir Putin's cronies are in a frenzy after admitting that this one move from the U.S. could entirely screw them.

Originally published by *The Daily Beast* on August 16, 2022

In a recent interview with Russian state media outlet TASS, the head of the Russian Foreign Ministry's North American Department, Aleksandr Darichev, said that in the event the U.S. designates Russia a state sponsor of terrorism, it would represent "a point of no return" in relations between the two countries.

Speaking on behalf of the country that ruthlessly invaded its smaller neighbor and is continually being accused of human rights violations and serious war crimes, Darichev shamelessly claimed on Saturday that the West, led by the United States, "has trampled upon international law and absolute taboos in diplomatic practice."

Appearing on the state TV show *Sunday Evening With Vladimir Solovyov* a day later, Foreign Ministry spokeswoman Maria Zakharova raged against the possibility of such a designation, claiming that these plans were caused by failure on the part of the U.S. to isolate Russia from the rest of the world.

Zakharova derided the level of competency of the U.S. officials, questioning whether they even know how to read, since Moscow has repeatedly warned Washington of the "consequences" should the U.S. label Russia a sponsor of terror.

The bipartisan resolution to declare Russia a sponsor of terrorism passed in the Senate at the end of July, after being introduced by Sens. Lindsey Graham (R-SC) and Richard Blumenthal (D-CT). In the House of Representatives, Speaker Nancy Pelosi reportedly warned Secretary of State Antony Blinken that unless he moves ahead with the designation, Congress will pass appropriate legislation of its own accord.

Last week, the parliament of Latvia declared Russia a "state sponsor of terrorism" for attacks on civilians during the war in Ukraine, urging other countries to follow suit. Rihards Kols, who chairs the parliament's foreign affairs committee, asserted: "Russia has for many years supported and financed terrorist regimes and organizations in various ways, directly and indirectly."

To illustrate that point, Kols brought up Russia's involvement in Syria, its downing of the MH-17 flight over eastern Ukraine in 2014, and the 2018 poisoning of Sergei Skripal in the U.K.

Lithuania adopted a similar resolution in May and Estonia may soon do so as well. The prospect of this initiative gaining global traction terrified prominent talking heads on Russian state television.

The measure would add Russia to the list of such pariah states as North Korea, Iran, Syria, and Cuba, allowing global governments to expand the list of measures and sanctions to exert further pressure against Putin's regime, including a ban on defense exports and additional financial restrictions. Prominent pundits and experts on Russian state TV clarified that the potential designation bothers Moscow the most not because of the damage to what is left of Russia's reputation, but for legal and financial reasons.

Two weeks ago, Andrey Sidorov, deputy dean of world politics at Moscow State University, explained why Moscow is so apoplectic about being labeled the sponsor of terrorism: "Regarding the declaration of Russia as a sponsor of terrorism — they will most likely pass this legislation. Unquestionably, all the sanctions they can impose against us are already in place. That's not the scary part. What's going to hurt is that the families harmed by the country that is a sponsor of terrorism have the right to file claims in American courts. Masses of Ukrainian citizens will be able to file suits. Where will the resources come from to pay out these claims?"

Referring to $300 billion out of the $640 billion that Russia had in its gold and forex reserves, which have been frozen by Western sanctions, host Vladimir Solovyov opined: "They're looking for the way to grab our $300 billion." Sidorov agreed: "They'll take that $300 billion pursuant to court orders."

Russian experts openly cherish the idea of taking Ukraine's vast mineral and energy resources, which they predict will boost Russia's failing economy. In addition to stealing Ukraine's riches, pro-Putin propagandists have been openly hoping to get their seized funds and properties back—even threatening nuclear strikes in order to secure their release. The prospect of losing these billions for good is infinitely more worrisome than any label Putin's regime so richly deserves.

Solovyov, twice honored by President Vladimir Putin for his services to the Fatherland, proposed a solution: forcefully turning all Ukrainians into Russian citizens after taking over Ukraine in its entirety.

While Russia's genocidal objectives with respect to the neighboring country were obvious from the start, Moscow's mouthpieces are now attempting to blame the West for their destruction of Ukraine.

Speaking of Ukrainian victims of Russian aggression, Solovyov said: "These families should not have the opportunity to file lawsuits in a court of law. They should become Russian citizens and the nation of Ukraine should completely disappear."

Earlier in August, appearing on the state TV show *60 Minutes*, military expert Igor Korotchenko conceded that Russia wants to erase Ukraine off the map, because "it never really existed in the first place," is perceived to be "anti-Russia" and therefore has no right to exist.

Regardless of the final outcome of Russia's war against Ukraine, Moscow's prospects as a global power are bleak. Appearing on the program *Solovyov Live* on Monday, Yevgeny Satanovsky, president of the Institute of the Middle East, noted with grim resignation, "With respect to the West as a whole, particularly where America, Europe or international organizations are concerned, Russia has nothing to hope for."

Kremlin TV Desperately Wants You to Move to Russia Right Now

Vladimir Putin's war has made the dire population crisis in Russia even worse, forcing Moscow's mouthpieces to scramble for solutions on live television.

Originally published by *The Daily Beast* on August 26, 2022

Vladimir Putin's invasion of Ukraine was meant to bring Russia millions of new citizens, as well as the country's fertile land, flush with mineral and energy resources. Instead, the war has caused monumental losses on the battlefield, and the exodus of the best and the brightest from Russia.

Now, dwindling human resources are causing the Kremlin and its pliant mouthpieces to brainstorm about replenishing the gaping holes in Russia's general population, workforce, and military.

Appearing on the state TV show *Who's Against?* on Tuesday, Anna Revyakina, deputy chairwoman of the Public Chamber of the so-called Donetsk People's Republic in occupied Ukraine, voiced her ideas about attracting potential immigrants to Russia. She suggested that instead of worrying about the wave of European visa bans on Russians who want to travel abroad, Moscow should do more to attract foreigners to Russia.

"All of us Russians and our government should create maximally attractive conditions for the citizens of other countries to come to us, augmenting our population," she said. "We have an enormous territory, a huge country, maybe not even fully developed, 140 million people—of course, we need more. Vladimir Vladimirovich [Putin] is concerned about this, with various programs for families with many children."

Revyakina urged Russian-speakers living in the Baltics to move to Russia, adding that such potential immigrants should be "loyal, in love with Russia, and speaking the language." Moscow has long looked with hopeful anticipation at Russian-speakers in the Baltic states, with state TV propagandists highlighting their protests against the removal of Soviet-era monuments and urging them to come to Russia.

The exodus of young Russian professionals at the onset of the war has some Russian companies forcing employees to work overtime, during weekends, holidays, or their usual days off, as needed. Even that is not enough, and propagandists have gone so far as to urge authorities to employ prisoners with necessary qualifications.

"There's nothing better than receiving a ready-made specialist, who already has an education and work experience," Revyakina emphasized in her Tuesday TV appearance. Host Dmitry Kulikov cautiously added that the country desperately needed real programs that would allow for such a resettlement of foreigners.

It's not the first time Russian state TV has brainstormed ideas to reverse its negative demographic trends by fishing for new immigrants even on the other side of the pond. Appearing on *The Evening With Vladimir Solovyov* last year, Maria Zakharova, the spokeswoman for Russia's Ministry of Foreign Affairs, claimed that she had received a flood of inquiries from Trump supporters in the United States, disillusioned with the outcome of the storming of the Capitol on Jan 6. According to Zakharova, they urgently sought information about obtaining Russian citizenship, allegedly fearing "repressions."

There was no follow-up as to whether any of those inquiries later materialized into tangible attempts to immigrate to Russia and the lone runaway Capitol rioter, Evan Neumann, went to Belarus instead.

The Kremlin's talking heads are quite open about American immigrants they find particularly attractive, with the likes of Steven Seagal and Ronald Reagan's former adviser Suzanne Massie often showcased as top-shelf newcomers and brand-new pro-Kremlin patriots who received Russian citizenship.

The state media's persuasion playbook usually consists of stoking discontent in other countries, presenting Moscow as a paragon of religious propriety and freedom, and hoping that disgruntled foreigners will flow into Russia's welcoming arms.

Westerners are being lured with the promise of "conservative" values and Russian-speakers who live outside of the Motherland are being told that it's time to come home to avoid persecution and discrimination by the "Russophobic" West.

While Russia is concealing and underreporting its losses in Ukraine, the constant search for volunteers — those willing to risk their life and limb to serve the expansionist ambitions of the largest country in the world — speaks volumes.

Top propagandists on state television have been laser-focused on encouraging people of all ages to enlist. Back in May, state TV host Vladimir Solovyov complained about Russia's "demographic gap," and praised a bill crafted to increase the upper age limit for military eligibility. It was approved in the State Duma the same month, allowing 65-year-olds to serve in the Russian army, including any foreign nationals wishing to enlist.

Solovyov has also been openly soliciting an infusion of foreigners to stand in the gap: Last week, on his radio show *Full Contact*, he wished out loud that 100,000 North Koreans could join the Russian Armed Forces on the front lines in Ukraine.

Russia's younger generation has made it clear they are in no rush to die in a mindless attack on Ukraine, but that doesn't seem to faze Vladimir Putin. On Thursday, he signed a decree increasing the number of Russian military personnel by 137,000 to 1.15 million troops, the biggest expansion in a decade.

Putin Cronies Threaten 'Hundreds' of American Coffins on Live TV

Moscow's mouthpieces are now resorting to direct threats of terrorism against Americans as a way to "force" the U.S. to rethink its position on Vladimir Putin's war.

Originally published by *The Daily Beast* on August 31, 2022

On Russian state television, the initial bravado about conquering Ukraine in days has been replaced with poorly concealed desperation—and outright terrorist threats against the United States. Experts on state-controlled television are now pondering whether American support for Ukraine would only change if "dozens or hundreds" of caskets draped in U.S. flags started arriving from all over the world.

During Tuesday's broadcast of the television show *The Meeting Place*, hosts and panelists discussed Ukraine's planned counteroffensive. While the Ukrainian will to defend their homeland is undeniable, the Kremlin's mouthpieces are firmly convinced that it could be overcome—if only Americans would get out of the way. With former U.S. President Donald Trump no longer in office, convincing Washington to see things Russia's way is not an option. As a result, Russian propagandists are now suggesting persuasion through violence.

Dmitry Drozdenko, deputy editor of the Russian military publication Arsenal of the Fatherland, declared that subversive activities are a part of any war. Since Ukraine is starting to bring war back to Russia, Drozdenko suggested the revival of SMERSH—a counterintelligence agency, named after a contraction of the phrase, "Death to spies."

Host Andrey Norkin asked the experts whether Russia should resort to extraterritorial actions that extend beyond Ukraine. He mentioned Pavel Sudoplatov—a historical figure who was involved in planning and carrying out assassinations and sabotage actions in Western countries—as the kind of actor the nation could really use right now. Sudoplatov was involved in the assassination of Leon Trotsky in Mexico, Ukrainian political and military leader Yevhen Konovalets in Rotterdam, and ran networks of "illegals" in NATO countries.

There was no need to look that far back into the past, given recent allegations against Russia of state-sanctioned attacks and murders abroad, including but not limited to the poisoning of Alexander Litvinenko in England, the killing of Zelimkhan Khangoshvili in Germany and an attempted poisoning of Sergei Skripal in England. Indeed, pundits brought up the names of Ruslan Boshirov and Alexander Petrov—believed to have carried out Skripal's attempted poisoning—as the ones who might carry out the killing of Natalia Vovk, whom the Russians are accusing of blowing up Darya Dugina's vehicle.

Viktor Olevich, a lead expert with the policy group The Center for Actual Politics, noted, "Subversive actions are already taking place within the Russian Federation, in Moscow. We already have casualties. There is no doubt that we may witness certain events on the territory of third countries, not just Ukraine. Definitely."

Co-host Ivan Trushkin decided to take it further: "Pardon my fantasy, but what if some Pentagon official, who was responsible for handling Ukraine, chokes on a cherry pit? Would that help to stop subversive activities on our territory?" Olevich cautiously replied: "They most likely won't stop, but with time, tit-for-tat actions could change the situation. I just wouldn't count on it having an immediate effect."

Fanning himself with a green folder, Norkin surmised, "Everyone is carefully dropping hints over here... but last Saturday's CNN report said that all the processes happening in Ukraine are being crafted and directed only by Washington—not that anyone ever doubted it."

Trushkin pondered which measures would make "the American handlers" understand that they have to stop their activities in Ukraine. He surmised, "As long as there are powers outside of

Ukraine, willing to send people, give them weapons, fill their heads with radical information, it seems to me that we will be unable to attain a total victory."

State Duma member Alexander Kazakov said, "Within the next two weeks, if five SBU (Security Service of Ukraine) colonels and one CIA colonel were to perish by any means—ran over by a car, fell out of a window, got shot, died in an explosion—in America, Europe or elsewhere, will that change anything in terms of the terror directed at us? Nothing... Of course, it would be cool to see the five SBU Colonels die, but how effective would that be?"

Another expert vehemently disagreed. Igor Shishkin, Director of the CIS Countries Institute, argued, "It has to come back to bite them and doesn't have to be limited to some Colonel falling out of the window. Americans have plenty of agencies and bases, located in hot spots, where something could fly over to that base and cause several dozen or hundreds of coffins to go back to the United States. If they start getting caskets, draped in stars and stripes flags, after every terrorist act they've authorized, it will finally force them to think."

Even as Russia vehemently objects to being designated a state sponsor of terrorism, the terrorist mentality projected on state television is undeniable. Last Tuesday, the host of a popular state TV program *The Evening With Vladimir Solovyov*, Vladimir Solovyov, openly identified himself as a terrorist, as he described his ideas about destroying Ukrainian cities along with civilians, as needed.

The terrorist mindset seems to be prevalent not only on state-controlled television but also among Russian lawmakers. During Tuesday's broadcast of Solovyov's program, retaliation against enemies of the Motherland was a hot topic of conversation. Panelists condemned the statements about Darya Dugina's demise that were made by Ilya Ponomarev, a former member of Russia's Duma who currently lives in Kyiv. The Sudoplatov name was again fondly invoked.

Military expert Alexander Artamonov, who also serves as editor-in-chief of Radio Sputnik in France, said of Ponomarev: "I don't know whether Ilya could be put into a sack and brought here, but if not—he should be liquidated on the spot. If you read the works of classics, upon which Sudoplatov was taught, you respond to the white terror with red terror."

State Duma Deputy Andrey Gurulyov articulated the fate that should befall Ponomarev and any other perceived enemies of Russia: "As Iosif Vissarionovich [Stalin] said, "No man, no problem. Enemies of the Motherland have to be destroyed."

Team Putin Admits Their Worst Case Scenario Is Coming True

In the face of major new setbacks in the war, Vladimir Putin's cronies are now confessing that "mistakes" were made—and they're getting "worried."

Originally published by *The Daily Beast* on September 09, 2022

In the beginning of Russia's invasion of Ukraine, the Kremlin's top propagandists predicted a swift victory and derided the Ukrainian military as an unwilling bunch of incompetents. As the war dragged on, they continued to claim that Volodymyr Zelensky's government was about to fall. Faced with Ukraine's mounting counteroffensive, which is rapidly achieving impressive gains, Russian propagandists are now describing an enormous horde, armed with the best Western weaponry and swimming in foreign specialists.

With state TV studios full of doom and gloom, prominent pundits and experts seem to be preparing Russian audiences for future losses of occupied Ukrainian lands, which are being painstakingly reclaimed by the Ukrainian military.

During Wednesday's broadcast of the state TV show *60 Minutes*, host Evgeny Popov said: "We wish courage to our warriors, who are indeed doing very important work, they are resisting an enormous horde that has been trained in the West."

Evgeny Buzhinsky, a retired Lieutenant-General of the Russian Armed Forces, claimed that the Ukrainian military is overflowing with American participants: "There are not only advisers, but specialists. I think that there are thousands of American advisers and specialists on the ground in Ukraine, they're probably present in every unit."

During his Wednesday's radio show, *Full Contact*, top Kremlin propagandist Vladimir Solovyov—with a noticeably bruised face—

surmised: "I'm worried. Naturally, we want for our guys to crush [the other side] and only to advance, but life doesn't work that way." Solovyov refused to address the source of his injuries, but in light of Ukrainian military gains, his bruised ego was likewise on full display.

By the time his nightly program *The Evening With Vladimir Solovyov* started, the host's facial abrasions had been covered with makeup. Speaking to State Duma deputy Andrey Gurulyov, who is a former deputy commander of Russia's southern military district, Solovyov attempted to downplay his initial reaction to Russia's recent losses. "Comrade Lieutenant General, you always speak so beautifully and convincingly. Calm people down, because there are all sorts of rumors. I can only imagine what would happen if Telegram existed in 1942-1943," he said. Gurulyov grimly replied: "Today, I believe there is a difficult situation on one of our fronts. Yes, Ukrainians concentrated their assault troops there and started to advance."

Hemming and hawing, Gurulyov added: "We'll need some time to bring things back to order. Yes, the situation isn't easy. Were mistakes made? Yes, probably so. You can't avoid mistakes in life or in war."

Solovyov warned that no matter what, there would be no peace deal with Ukraine: "There won't be a Minsk-3... The frontline can breathe, there can be local failures, there could be excited screams coming from Kharkiv and Kyiv. That won't change our general hard line... we'll suffocate this serpent. There are no other options... We'll bury as many of them as we need to."

Appearing on Solovyov's show, military expert Mikhail Onufrienko threw aside the term "special military operation" and complained: "This is a difficult war, it's a big war, the world hasn't seen wars of this magnitude since WWII, at least after Vietnam... The panic is being stoked not by the Ukrainian side, not by the Kyiv regime or Western sources, but by our own patriotic [social media] channels... Nonetheless, objectively speaking, this is the most successful advance of the junta since February 24... We clearly don't have enough troops to contain them... but they couldn't take Balakliya."

Pro-Kremlin propagandists have lost that bit of joy as well, given that as of Thursday, Ukraine has retaken Balakliya—a strategically important city.

During a briefing in Kyiv, Ukrainian Brigadier General Oleksiy Gromov said that Ukraine had retaken about 700 square kilometers of territory in both the east and south of the country.

During Thursday's airing of *60 Minutes*, Apti Alaudinov, the commander of Ramzan Kadyrov's Chechen detachment "Akhmat," revisited his routine portrayal of Russia's war as a battle against the Antichrist. "Let me assure everyone who thinks that we lost something or were defeated somewhere, let me remind you of an old proverb: being defeated in a battle doesn't mean losing the war," he said. "Don't you worry about a thing, everything is fine."

Host Olga Skabeeva tried to comfort the audiences by claiming that everything is going according to the plan: "If social media and 'couch-experts' existed during WWII, Stalin would have surely lost his mind. We won't succumb to panic," Skabeeva's pep talk notwithstanding, the long faces in the studio spoke louder than words.

Team Putin Threatens Maniacal Response to Bitter War Losses

Vladimir Putin's mouthpieces are threatening to unleash "real hell" after a slew of staggering failures in the war.

Originally published by *The Daily Beast* on September 15, 2022

The humiliating defeats of Russia's Armed Forces in Ukraine are prompting the Kremlin's mouthpieces to propose increasingly violent tactics.

Lobbying for a "scorched earth" policy on state television, Russian pundits and expert guests have been openly comparing the Ukrainian battleground to Chechnya, Syria, and even the infamous Beslan school massacre, where Russian special forces killed many hostages along with their terrorist captors.

Appearing on Wednesday's broadcast of the state TV show *60 Minutes*, military expert Igor Korotchenko said: "This is a new reality, which is why we should be acting quickly, harshly and uncompromisingly. First of all, we need to scale up our strikes against critical infrastructure in such a way that one region after the next, one district after another, Ukraine is plunged into darkness... By December, 20 million residents of Ukraine should flee to the West, to the European Union. This is our goal and the task we should accomplish."

Korotchenko proposed: "Perhaps we should openly declare: 'Leave. Zelensky is turning this territory into a real hell. No one knows what will happen here next. Twenty million, go to Europe.' After that, we sink region after region into darkness. This is our enemy nation, the modern Third Reich, and we should act accordingly."

Similar proposals permeated Russian airwaves, with experts arguing that the rules of the civilized world prohibiting war crimes are merely recommendations, compliance with which is optional. On Monday, appearing on *The Evening With Vladimir Solovyov*, Andrey Sidorov, deputy dean of world politics at the Moscow State University, explained why those international conventions are irrelevant: "The rules of war, according to international conventions, are of an advisory nature: not to strike [certain objects], if possible. But it's no longer possible."

Appearing on the show *The Meeting Place* on Monday, Bogdan Bezpalko, member of the Council for Interethnic Relations under the President of the Russian Federation, argued: "As far as what needs to be done, as I previously said, we need to strike the infrastructure—which can't be separated into military and civilian. If all of Ukraine is plunged into cold and darkness, if they have no fuel, reserve armies won't help them and no one will be able to deliver equipment or ammunition... These strikes should go on for two, three, five or six months in a row, leaving not one gas station intact."

Konstantin Zatulin, deputy chairman of the committee of the State Duma for the CIS, said on *60 Minutes*: "This military operation—or this war—is entering another phase... The idea that we could achieve a victory with little blood or one massive strike is now in the past... Last week, there was a widespread message—everywhere, except for our television—that this is no time to celebrate, while we're experiencing difficulties and failures at the battlefront, while we're retreating... We are pondering what they will do. We need to overcome that... because victory is our only option."

Host Olga Skabeeva cautioned: "Don't scare our people prematurely, as I understand you're talking about the possibility of mobilization." Even the most gung-ho propagandists admit that the Russian society would be deeply unsettled at the thought of total military mobilization, and that the country's economy is not currently equipped for such a step. The only alternative proposed by the state TV's talking heads is inflicting utter devastation upon Ukraine.

Professor Alexei Fenenko, leading research fellow at the Institute of International Security Studies, attempted to lay the blame for Russia's increasing brutality upon the United States. With images of the city of Mosul in ruins playing on the screen, Fenenko claimed: "After February 24, they waited for us to do this to key cities in Ukraine. Then they would have said, 'Yes, those guys are strong.'" Without a hint of self-awareness, Skabeeva noted that the bodies of the dead were left on the streets of Mosul, to decay in plain sight. Fenenko noted that this gesture was meant as a message to other enemies.

Neither Skabeeva nor Fenenko made any mention of the horrific scenes in Ukraine that unfolded in recent months, when the retreating Russian troops left multiple corpses of Ukrainian civilians on the streets of Bucha, and scores of massacred civilians in other towns and cities.

Fenenko argued that in order to be respected by the United States, Russia has to reduce much of Ukraine to rubble. He said that America respects only those who can inflict devastating damage upon their adversaries: "Either you can do this to your enemies, or else you're a nobody. If you can't do it, you're a coward and a loser."

Putin Crony Belts Out Song in Cringey Push for More Russian Troops

The Kremlin's mouthpieces are desperate for more cannon fodder in Ukraine, and it's leading to some terrifying—and awkward—TV moments.

Originally published by *The Daily Beast* on September 16, 2022

Russia's military campaign in Ukraine is faltering, and so are their efforts to recruit volunteers. A man resembling Yevgeny Prigozhin, the Kremlin-linked businessman who is believed to be in charge of the infamous Wagner Group, was recently filmed recruiting prisoners to fight in Ukraine.

Top Russian propagandist, Vladimir Solovyov, often offers to publicize contact information that would drive more volunteers to sign up. Military experts on state TV openly admit that Russia's presence on the frontline is sorely lacking, but government officials insist that total mobilization is not being considered.

Writer Zakhar Prilepin, who is wanted by Ukraine's SBU security service on charges of "taking part in the activity of a terrorist organization" for his ongoing involvement in Russia's war crimes in Ukraine, often talks about his travels to the frontline and boasts of extensive first-hand knowledge about the war.

Appearing on Friday's broadcast of *60 Minutes*, Prilepin raged: "We really don't have enough men fighting over there. When people say we have 150k, 100k, 200k, I want to tell them: we don't have that many people there! It can't go on this way... We have a very small contingent. For a country of our size, it's no good."

With all current recruitment efforts falling short, head of RT Margarita Simonyan decided to throw her hat into the ring, trying to scare everyday Russians into volunteering.

Appearing on the state TV show *The Evening With Vladimir Solovyov* Thursday evening, Simonyan performed one of her cringiest routines thus far. She opened the conversation by preempting any attempts to discuss the state of Russia's ongoing invasion of Ukraine: "I guess, something needs to be said about the current state of war—whether it was or wasn't declared against us by NATO, NATO troops and Ukraine; about the "special military operation," as we call it. I won't talk about it right now, because this is not the time for uplifting statements."

Solovyov suggested pundit Yaakov Kedmi should help Simonyan look at the "bright side of life", even though his prognosis of how Russia's war against Ukraine would progress turned out to be completely off the mark. Instead of pitching in, Kedmi let out a long cough and refused the opportunity to lighten up the moment. Head of RT claimed that "her conscience and her knowledge about what's going on" would not allow her to comment any further.

After noting that the situation is very difficult, Simonyan decided to sing verses from an old Soviet song, "The March of the Red Cavalry." Other panelists awkwardly looked down, as she sang and then reiterated the lyrics about moving forward and never backing down.

Simonyan went on: "If we back down, what awaits us—and I don't mean it as hyperbole or metaphorically speaking—is everything that is described in [Adolf] Hitler's table conversations, written down by his aides and secretaries. With a lot of gusto, he described in great detail how he saw our place on earth. It was a plan to turn us into yahoos—from "Gulliver's Travels"—abominable creatures, resembling human beings. They look just like us, but in reality, they're nothing like us. They can't read or write, they can barely talk—that was written in Hitler's table conversations. He even wanted us to lose our language, communicating with the use of signs and gestures."

Simonyan recounted Hitler's plans to turn Russians into a mass of people, denied basic rights, from vaccination to education. To keep them in a good mood, the enslaved masses would be entertained with happy tunes, constantly being played for their enjoyment. Simonyan argued: "If you think that sounds wild, let's remember that it isn't. Let's remember the 90s when this is exactly what happened. There was fun and music everywhere, but nothing to eat." Head of RT alleged, in all seriousness: "This is exactly what awaits us in the future if we back down. Are we ready to live that way?"

She added: "Let's not think that this is just some local conflict... For us, this is a question of continuing to exist in our current state." Simonyan described the civilized West as "hypocrites, armed with Hitler's fascist rhetoric, plans and methods."

While the host and his guests enthusiastically claim to condemn Nazism, Solovyov's show often serves as a platform for genocidal anti-Ukrainian rhetoric. During Monday's broadcast, political analyst Dmitry Drobnitsky claimed that the Ukrainian people do not exist, prompting an unusual rebuke from another pundit, Alexander Sosnovsky, who described Drobnitsky's statements as "clear-cut nationalism." Despite frequent denials of the Ukrainian identity and Russia's blatantly genocidal invasion of Ukraine, the culprits and their mouthpieces describe everyone who opposes their bloody war of aggression as "Nazis."

During Wednesday's broadcast of *60 Minutes*, political analyst Andrei Sidorchik exclaimed: "Not only the representatives of certain power structures in Ukraine are Nazis, but the head of the government of the United States Joe Biden is a Nazi. [Chancellor of Germany] Olaf Scholz is a Nazi. [President of the European Commission] Ursula von der Leyen is a Nazi... When we hear them say that Russia and the Russian people should be defeated and learn their lessons, this is their war not only against our nation, but against our people. Therefore, this is clear-cut Nazism."

Simonyan called on the Russian people to push forward until the bitter end, squeezing out "nerus," a disparaging term, used to describe anyone who is not Russian, along with "vyrus," the word used to describe those who are Russian, but refuse to self-identify as such.

Concluding her bizarre performance on Solovyov's show, Simonyan said: "People ask when, where and how our special operation will end. It will end when all the 'nerus,' all the 'vyrus,' everyone who wants to turn us into yahoos, everyone who directs them, everyone who brainwashes them, will suffer infamy and shame. It may take 3 months, 3 years or 30 years, so be it. What other choice do we have?" Solovyov replied: "Our other choice? Reduce the whole world to dust. Just not yet." Smiling, Simonyan replied, "And we will go to heaven."

Team Putin Begs Rich Russians to Help Save His Failing War

The Kremlin's cronies are now demanding that Russians "who are fattened up" help fuel Vladimir Putin's disastrous war.

Originally published by *The Daily Beast* on September 22, 2022

Russian President Vladimir Putin's speech announcing partial mobilization has prompted heated reactions across Russia. Prominent lawmakers and pundits expressed their enthusiastic support on state television, but tangible concerns have been brewing behind the bluster.

Even the most dedicated pro-Kremlin propagandists haven't been able to hide their apprehension about the obvious shortcomings of the Russian economy and its military-industrial complex. In Wednesday's broadcast of state television show *60 Minutes*, even the studio seemed to be in disarray, with a large puddle of water clearly visible near one of the podiums.

Senior military analyst Mikhail Khodaryonok poured yet more water on Putin's declaration when he noted during the show that: "Mobilization is the face of the nation." That face seems to be lacking some teeth, with glaring issues pertaining to the lack of military equipment and technologies bemoaned even by the most rabid propagandists.

Khodaryonok pointed out: "An issue that is no less important than others is how well these people will be armed and equipped... They should receive modern uniforms, modern gear, rations, medical kits, items having to do with support and logistics, modern weapons... It's just inappropriate."

Those fortunate enough not to face mobilization should contribute in other ways, declared military expert Igor Korotchenko during his appearance on the show.

"It's extremely important that our new military divisions that are being formed today receive necessary equipment and weapons," he stressed. "Since we're talking about the future of our nation, there has to be the consolidation of all available resources. We should create a fund of support for the special military operation. Our socially responsible prominent oligarchy should share their profits, so that our fighters on the front lines can be properly armed and equipped."

Korotchenko went on: "Everyone should play their part. We can't have it that some will luxuriate in Rublyovka [a prestigious residential area in the western suburbs of Moscow], while others are defending the Motherland. Those who are fattened up in the economic sense need to share their resources so that we can supply our troops with everything that is needed."

It appears that the Russian elite however—including many top pro-Kremlin propagandists—would much rather cheer from the sidelines than join Russia's brutal and bloody imperial endeavor.

Host of *60 Minutes* Evgeny Popov pondered on-air whether he was subject to mobilization, with an expression devoid of any signs he was feeling particularly lucky.

Dmitry Nizovtsev, host of Popular Politics, a YouTube channel operated by supporters of the opposition leader Alexei Navalny, prank-called the sons of the Russian president's press secretary Dmitry Peskov and Prime Minister of Russia Mikhail Mishustin.

Neither Nikolai Peskov nor Alexey Mishustin expressed any desire to fight on the front lines, and both of them rushed to end the call. As luck would have it, the rich and the well-connected in Russia won't have to risk their life and limb to serve the Motherland.

Still, that hasn't stopped many of these talking heads from vehemently expressing their verbal support for the Kremlin's new decisions to millions across the country.

In another broadcast of *60 Minutes*, State Duma Defense Committee's head Andrey Kartapolov tried to persuade the sour-faced panelists how lucky they are "to live in such wonderful times," with Russia "becoming the axis of a new world order."

Apparently not feeling lucky, Dmitry Abzalov, director of the Center for Strategic Communications, questioned the preparedness of the Russian economy for what's to come.

In the hours preceding Putin's announcement, another State Duma member, Andrey Gurulyov, was brimming with excitement. "It's clear to me that today's decision is the beginning of the end of Ukraine. That's it, that nation no longer exists," he said on a broadcast of *The Evening With Vladimir Solovyov*. "Ukraine's history is ending and perhaps it's a good thing."

In the weeks preceding the announcement, the Kremlin's state TV mouthpieces appear to have been laying the groundwork for the mobilization. State TV show *60 Minutes*, which spent many months deriding Ukrainian troops and scoffing at Western weapons, suddenly changed its course, with host Olga Skabeeva unexpectedly admitting that the Ukrainian army was a "powerful" force and NATO's weapons were "highly effective."

Appearing on Wednesday's broadcast of *The Evening With Vladimir Solovyov*, head of RT Margarita Simonyan admitted that Putin's mobilization is a forced measure, prompted by the military defeats of the Russian Armed Forces in Ukraine: "Am I glad we declared partial mobilization? No, I'm not glad... Obviously, partial mobilization was declared because we can't achieve our aims without it."

Russia Desperately Tries to Sell Its Ukraine War Draft as Citizens Flee

The Kremlin's talking heads tried to remain upbeat about calling up citizens to fight amid reports that men were being sent to the front after only one day of military training.

Originally published by *The Daily Beast* on September 25, 2022

Russia's recently announced "partial mobilization" of men for the Ukraine war brought turmoil to the home front, where everyday citizens were suddenly greeted by a conflict many perceived as another country's problem. Hundreds have been detained in anti-mobilization protests across the country, including Dagestan and the Sakha Republic, which are among the regions that have been heavily targeted for mass recruitment.

Most state TV programs are promoting the idea that the mobilization is a necessary measure, unconvincingly claiming that it's welcomed by the Russians at large. However, cracks are forming just beneath the surface, since even the most enthusiastic pro-Kremlin cheerleaders are unwittingly revealing too much to the alarmed Russian population.

On Thursday, one day after Russian President Vladimir Putin announced the partial mobilization, Colonel Rustem Klupov, a retired military intelligence agent, appeared on the show *Full Contact*, hosted by Russia's top propagandist Vladimir Solovyov.

The host immediately asked Klupov whether he was ready for the mobilization and he enthusiastically confirmed: "Yes, I took out my uniform and ironed it, got it all squared away, got my rapid deployment knapsack ready and bought two cans of Spam."

While his Colonels were buying Spam, Putin reportedly went off to rest up at his secret palace near Gelendzhik—providing yet another reminder about Russia's resources being siphoned off by its leadership, which might explain why the country's military is experiencing a lack of equipment and supplies during the Kremlin's war of imperial conquest against the neighboring nation.

Klupov told Solovyov that Ukraine's fierce resistance to the occupying force was not the real reason for the mobilization. Instead, he claimed that NATO's extensive involvement was to blame, baselessly alleging that "30 percent of the Ukrainian Army's personnel" is comprised of NATO officers. Klupov also had an explanation as to why Putin decided to mobilize specifically 300,000 people: "One of the reasons for this mobilization is that, subsequent to the Madrid Summit this summer, an announcement was made about the enlargement of NATO forces by 300,000 in the eastern part of Europe."

He also praised the idea of sending prisoners to fight in Ukraine, predicting that many of them would be reformed in the process, returning to Russia as model citizens. This only underscores the well-known shortage of troops Russia sent to Ukraine, since Putin initially anticipated—and his state media mouthpieces publicly predicted—a fast and easy invasion with minimal resistance.

Klupov contradicted the promises made about the new recruits by Russia's Defense Ministry and government officials, who vowed on state television that the newly mobilized soldiers would not be sent into combat zones, but instead be stationed in Ukrainian territories currently under Russia's control. Klupov told Solovyov that the new arrivals with prior military experience would be immediately sent to the frontlines, whereas others would first receive between one and two months of training: "They won't be immediately thrown into the furnace of war." And yet, a recent report published by the independent Russian media outlet Mediazona revealed that some of the freshly-mobilized men are being sent directly to the frontlines after a whopping one day of "training."

The wife of a man mobilized from Lipetsk, Tatyana Dotsenko, told the publication that her 45-year-old husband Andrei Kozyrev received his call-up notice on September 22. He was sent to the Belgorod region on a bus, was issued a bulletproof vest and a helmet, underwent one day of military exercises and then was told he is going to the frontline, having been assigned to the 237th tank regiment. She added: "There were 1,000 of them, and no medical examination."

Even prominent pro-Kremlin propagandists are openly expressing their concerns with the mobilization. On Friday, Roman Babayan, the host of the TV program *Our Own Truth* on the channel NTV, said that he was worried about military enlistment offices grabbing people without much thought for their usefulness on the battlefront.

Babayan also reiterated the well-known problem with Russia's troops relying on public support to secure various supplies for the military: "I hope that we will train these people well and equip these people well. I simply insist on that, because all of us know — and no one is hiding this information — that all of us are helping, sending money, there is crowdfunding, various foundations are working."

Babayan's monologue again highlighted that partial mobilization was meant to counteract Russia's military failures in Ukraine and not the phantom threat of NATO's expansion throughout Europe. He asserted: "I hope that these people will not lack anything. Only then can we count on some changes in the situation on the battlefield, that it won't be dragged out indefinitely, and that it won't lead to us being forced to use tactical nuclear weapons, with the possibility of exchanging nuclear strikes."

While the escalating nuclear talk is meant to dissuade NATO countries from continuing to help Ukraine resist Russia's invasion, even Russian analysts are getting tired of this loathsome strategy. Instead of scaring the opponents, they acknowledged that it reveals Russia's weakness and highlights its inability to defeat Ukraine by conventional means. Appearing on the state TV show *60 Minutes* on Friday, Dmitry Abzalov, Director of the Center for Strategic Communications, replied to the tirades about the possibility of using nuclear weapons by stating: "I hope that we have enough strength and resources to solve these issues without nuclear war. Nuclear war is the very last resort... it would mean that everything else has failed." Abzalov added: "Nuclear war won't start, because I hope we won't start it."

Putin Crony Says He Drafted Russian 'Kill List' of Western Officials

"Those who are with us will be fine, and the rest we will kill," said one of Vladimir Putin's most prominent mouthpieces while promoting his idea on Russian state television.

Originally published by *The Daily Beast* on October 05, 2022

Russia's ill-fated invasion of Ukraine is coming apart at the seams, and top Kremlin propagandists are unraveling right along with it. In the absence of good news from the front, Putin's regime is promoting other ideas on how to deal with the self-inflicted disaster.

Prominent experts routinely featured on Kremlin-controlled state television roundly reject the mere idea of negotiations, and none of them dare suggest Russia's withdrawal from Ukraine in order to end the war. Instead, they're doubling down—and proposing to kill leading Westerners in charge of helping Ukraine defend itself from the Russian invasion.

Appearing on the state TV show *The Evening With Vladimir Solovyov* Tuesday night, Yevgeny Satanovsky—one of Russia's most prominent pro-Putin propagandists—proposed a deadly solution. Solovyov cut to the chase, asking Satanovsky: "How do we win? How should we react to the Americans? What should Russia do?"

Satanovsky, who serves as the president of Russia's Institute of the Middle East after heading the Russian Jewish Congress, replied, "Russia is what it is, in terms of a nation. We'll continue to be the way we are. Those who are with us will be fine, and the rest we will kill... Acting against us is a relatively small group that is in charge of this camp—they are menacing and fear nothing. Since Gorbachev's time, once we started to play by their rules, they stopped fearing us. This is the main factor."

Solovyov questioned whether he meant that the approximately 1.5 billion NATO-affiliated people of the world should be massacred. Satanovsky elaborated: "There aren't 1.5 billion people directing the process from the other side, but about one to two hundred. They should realize that if push comes to shove, that means the end of them, personally... You're aware that I know these people. I know all of them. I've seen them all. Only the understanding that they're personally facing the end... only that will have an effect on those people."

Satanovsky confirmed having drafted a list of such names, and Solovyov promptly dubbed it "The Satanovsky List." The pundit surmised: "In the Book of Life, we also create entries for ourselves. 'The Satanovsky List'? Perhaps. We should be doing these sorts of things, because any attempt to negotiate with [Volodymyr] Zelensky or Biden would be like making a deal with your killer."

Satanovsky said he gets enraged when people suggest that peace is better than war. "No, peace is not better. There will be no peace. The goal of these people is for our country not to exist, for the people who live here not to exist and even for the language we speak to be gone—or even a memory that any of that ever existed," he said. "They want to make an entry in an encyclopedia: 'There used to be Russians, there used to be Russia—but now it's gone.'"

Andrey Sidorov, deputy dean of world politics at Moscow State University, wholeheartedly agreed, noting that in light of Russia's recent annexations, the war is now happening on what they consider to be a territory of the Russian Federation. Sidorov stressed: "Now these are our defeats, we're fighting on our land. Why should we show any mercy to those who are directing this war?"

Humiliating failures on the battlefield are indeed at the core of Russia's desperate attempts to redirect rage at NATO for helping Ukraine fight the invasion.

Appearing on the state TV program *60 Minutes* on Tuesday, war correspondent Alexandr Sladkov nonchalantly admitted that Ukrainians have been able to retake 17 settlements—and counting. Sladkov also told a stunned host Olga Skabeeva that Russian forces are at least two months away from even attempting to advance, due to lack of manpower and the time it will take to train newly-mobilized reinforcements.

Devastated by the failing conquest in Ukraine, state TV host Vladimir Solovyov admitted he was in a foul mood and advocated the restoration of the death penalty, in order to execute those who dare to retreat, surrender, or desert.

In Wednesday's broadcast of Solovyov's show *Full Contact*, his sidekick Roman Golovanov interviewed war correspondent Alexander Kots, who stood on the ruins of Svatove and reported, "The problem right now is that we don't have enough people on the frontlines in order to contain such a large front... We simply don't have physical forces, which is the reason for those failures we're currently observing. Quite a difficult period of military actions is underway right now. In the near future, there won't be any good news out of the Kherson region. On the Lugansk front, everything is not that great either."

Appearing on the same show, TV host Boris Korchevnikov broke down in tears, accusing those who don't want to die in Russia's war of being "a zero, decay, and garbage." While the despondent propagandist wept live on-air, urging others to join the battle, he didn't express any desire to do so himself.

Team Putin Wakes Up
We Never Should've Laughed at Ukraine

"A war should be waged for real or not at all. Now we don't have any other options," Russian state TV host Sergey Mardan said following a series of losses.

Originally published by *The Daily Beast* on October 08, 2022

Russia experienced a number of embarrassing setbacks on the battlefield in Ukraine, but none of them were as humiliating as an explosion that rocked the Crimean Bridge, also known as Kerch Strait Bridge or Kerch Bridge, early Saturday morning.

During his Saturday broadcast on Solovyov Live, Russian state TV host Sergey Mardan opened his show with heavy sighs. He noted, "All day long we'll be talking about how this happened and what will come of it. I can tell you right now that nothing good will come of it, that's for sure." Mardan grimly concluded: "They've achieved an enormous propagandistic effect."

Repeatedly referring to Ukrainians with an often-used slur, Mardan complained that Russia apparently underestimated not only them, but also the Americans. Chauvinistic disregard for the Ukrainians as Russia's "lesser" opponents manifests in the way Russian propagandists tend to blame the West for any painful blows inflicted in the course of Russia's ill-fated invasion.

Mardan noted: "There was no shock that they would try to attack the Crimean bridge, but there was an initial shock that they managed to pull it off, especially in the early morning hours."

He explained that—as usual—the West is to blame: "Many competent people explain that this was a complicated task—not just journalists or commentators, but specialists. There is a high level of certainty that an operation of this magnitude could have been staged only by Western intelligence agencies."

Mardan urged the Russians to stop underestimating the Ukrainian Armed Forces, bristling even at the comparisons to ISIS. He asserted: "Comparing Ukraine to ISIS is insulting to the Russian Army, which has been fighting them on an enormous front for seven months... ISIS are tribespeople in sandals made out of tires. They have no cities, power plants, railways or factories. Ukraine has it all. Ukraine is a cruel, motivated, well-prepared enemy. This is an enemy nation that has been waging a full-fledged war against us for at least seven and a half months. We keep calling it a special military operation, but they are waging war... Good Lord, I can't keep listening to this thick and sticky rhetoric, it's time to stop talking about the peace process and the collective West. This rhetoric doesn't look good—in fact, it's harmful. Since the mobilization has been announced, we're talking about war, a people's war."

Mardan predicted an escalation, quoted Vladimir Lenin and urged a harsh response: "We stand on the precipice of another escalation. It's unavoidable... A war should be waged for real or not at all. Now we don't have any other options... No one will allow us to retreat, even though some would like that—and actually want that to happen. We should have no illusions about that."

He somberly revisited fantasies harbored by many Russians in the very beginning of the invasion, stoked by top propagandists on state television, who predicted that a war against Ukraine would be fast, pain-free and nearly bloodless.

That dream rapidly evaporated and reality hit hard, affecting even the staunch supporters of Putin's war. Mardan reminisced: "During the first week, we had a naive expectation of another "Crimean miracle," like it happened in 2014. There we were, at Kyiv's door, having solved all problems... That hope was gone 1-2 weeks later."

Mardan grumbled about the problems Russia continues to have with supplying its existing forces, especially in light of the recently announced partial mobilization. He outlined the well-known shortages of uniforms, drones and basic gear, which have been replenished through donations and crowdfunding.

The host noted that at this point, every grandma in Russia knows what a quadcopter is, having had to contribute funds to supply the Army.

Now the citizens are being prepared to skip New Year's celebrations, to do without Christmas trees or fancy lights adorning city centers — with that money to be sent to the front, securing winter uniforms for the troops. Mardan sternly noted: "This is no time to celebrate."

He also revealed that not everyone is as receptive to the idea of an indefinite war against Ukraine as Russian public polls alleged. Behind the scenes, many are anxious for the armed conflict to be over. In light of this rapidly growing trend, state TV propagandists have been tasked with convincing the public that unless Russia wins, its citizens would be locked "in concentration camps," enslaved by the West or killed.

Mardan said, "After the mobilization, I noticed the growth of pacifist inclinations in my circles, among the people of my generation or older. Very cautiously, they're starting to come out and say how nice it would be if everything came to an end, since we're not pulling through."

The host proposed that the best strategy to shut down those inclinations was to vividly paint what the future of Russia would look like if it's defeated in this war. He suggested, "We should be painting the image of defeat with the same colors we used to describe the impending victory back in March, when we were planning a parade on Khreshchatyk [the main street of Kyiv]. I was dreaming about those scenes, as well as some of my colleagues."

Mardan invited his guest, political commentator Evgeny Norin, to specify what Russia's defeat would look like. Norin ushered in the historical memories of Russia's distant past. He opined: "Russia's defeat would resemble the Mongol yoke, with a modern technological twist... Crimea, Donbas and other contested regions would be taken away, just to put us in our place. From the standpoint of national humiliation, we would be forced to give up Sevastopol. Remember the fate of Serbia and Yugoslavia, who had to give up all of their military and political elites. Of course, many people here would say, 'So they'll cut off their heads, no big deal.' Our soft pacifists say exactly that... Naturally, we'd also be forced to pay an enormous amount of reparations, huge amounts would be taken."

Mardan and Norin concurred that Russian oligarchs and major companies would find a way not to pay and the cost of reparations would land on everyday citizens. Norin mused that Russia would not be allowed to manufacture anything that is more sophisticated than a foot stool and Western companies would lure away all of the specialists—much as they're already doing. He predicted: "After the capitulation, we would be unable to offer them anything aside from the joy of standing by your Motherland."

Norin darkly predicted that Russia's capitulation "would be like Yugoslavia on steroids," with decolonization as "a cherry on top." He said Russia would be forced to break up into at least 10 separate parts, with Sharia law being instituted in at least some of them.

During the same show, State Duma member Alexander Kazakov offered a cheerful imperialistic prediction of what will happen if Russia perseveres and prevails: "If we win, we'll take back what's ours and whatever is theirs as well."

Kremlin TV Exposes the Real Goal of Putin's 'Revenge-Bombs'

Putin's top cheerleaders have unwittingly revealed that the latest Russian atrocities were not just about vengeance after all.

Originally published by *The Daily Beast* on October 11, 2022

Russia escalated its reign of terror against its neighbor this week, raining missiles on the people of Ukraine and civilian infrastructure in what appeared to be a series of indiscriminate strikes. While the attacks seemed to be devoid of any military meaning—changing nothing on the battlefield, where Russia continues to lose—the rationale behind them was revealed on Russian state media, where the ugly truth is systematically breaking through state-erected barriers.

An explosion that rocked the Crimean bridge last week was an attack against one of the symbols of "Russia's pride," said State Duma Defense Committee's head Andrey Kartapolov during the latest broadcast of *Sunday Evening With Vladimir Solovyov*. According to Kartapolov, another such symbol was the sunken warship Moskva—and now, the only symbol that remains is Russian President Vladimir Putin. Kartapolov urged Russians to unite behind Putin, and his desperate plea spotlighted the true reason behind Moscow's barrage of missiles: to curb waning public support for Putin's mindless war.

Aggravated by the excitement in Kyiv that followed the explosion of the Crimean bridge last week, Konstantin Dolgov, the former Russian commissioner for human rights, said during Monday's broadcast of state tv show *60 Minutes* that the retaliatory strikes were justified, and that all of Ukraine's infrastructure should be considered military targets that are fair game for destruction.

Dolgov yearned for pained reactions from Ukrainians affected by the strikes, asking: "Are they whining yet? Are they howling yet?"

Appearing on *60 Minutes*, member of Russia's State Duma Andrey Isayev noted that the strikes served as a mood booster for Russian audiences: "It's absolutely clear that the citizens support the decisive actions of the president and the mood of many has improved."

Anton Krasovsky, director of broadcasting for the state-funded RT channel, said that he was beyond happy and posted a video of himself dancing on his balcony in his pajamas on Telegram, while the strikes were taking place on Monday.

Konstantin Zatulin, first deputy chairman of the committee of the State Duma for the CIS and relations with Russian nationals abroad, said that seeing the aftermath of Russia's missile strikes against Ukraine brought a "feeling of satisfaction." He stated that Russia's short-term goal is "to reclaim the initiative we used to have, which was unfortunately depleted during the summer, which resulted in considerable losses of the territories we previously controlled."

Political scientist Sergey Mikheyev argued that the destruction of Ukraine's civilian infrastructure should have been the priority from the get-go. He opined that the best way Russia can exhibit compassion in Ukraine would be best compared to cutting a dog's tail off: the faster, the better.

Mikheyev advocated leaving all of Ukraine without gas, electricity, running water or sewers. He explained that unless Ukrainians are forced to freeze, they won't understand what a war truly is. Mikheyev added, "Five to ten million of them should head to Europe."

The same view was previously voiced last week, when Andrey Sidorov, Deputy Dean of world politics at the Moscow State University, urged Russia to cause a massive refugee crisis in Europe, exacerbating economic and political tensions by prompting a massive influx of Ukrainian refugees.

Solovyov wholeheartedly agreed that the Ukrainian infrastructure should be demolished with a constant barrage of missile strikes: "They already consider us villains anyway. It's better to be feared than to be laughed at." Sidorov concurred and said that the latest strikes were important for "psychological reasons" and should continue.

Mikheyev stressed that propaganda was a far more effective weapon than HIMARS. He argued that Russia "legitimized" the Ukrainian government and described the President of Ukraine Volodymyr Zelensky as a "roach," who was turned by Russia into a figure of global stature.

Excitedly talking over each other, Mikheyev and Solovyov asserted that Zelensky and the rest of the Ukrainian government should be considered top military targets for the Russian military. Mikheyev added: "Symbolic strikes are very important — we live in the information age."

Karen Shakhnazarov said he was disturbed by the escalation that he described as a potential Armageddon, but immediately tried to excuse Putin's strikes against Ukrainian civilians by comparing the Crimean bridge incident to the September 11 attacks in the U.S.

"It is a terrorist action. More than that, in its magnitude, it's comparable to September 11th in the United States. For Russia, the Crimean bridge is of an even larger importance. The skyscrapers are symbols, but they had no importance to the infrastructure," Shakhnazarov said. "The Crimean bridge is of enormous importance in linking Crimea to Russia... The United States immediately declared those whom they believed responsible for the destruction of those towers to be outside the law."

Top Putin Lackey Urges Russians to Choose Violent Death Over War Defeat

Kremlin's most prominent mouthpieces are now promoting martyrdom on Russian airwaves as the country prepares for a possible nuclear holocaust.

Originally published by *The Daily Beast* on November 01, 2022

In his latest speech last week, Vladimir Putin was desperate to convince foreign audiences that a so-called "new world order" was on the horizon. In his remarks, given at the 19th Annual Meeting of the Valdai Discussion Club, the Russian president dropped some key messages to those who dared to question his vision of the Kremlin's new place on the global stage—both with what he said out loud, and what he didn't.

Fyodor Lukyanov, editor-in-chief of Russia in Global Affairs, chairman of the Presidium of the Council on Foreign and Defense Policy, asked Putin about comments he made four years ago on the potential use of nuclear weapons. "You said that we would all go to heaven, but we're in no hurry to get there, right?"

In response, Putin held a long theatrical pause. He wouldn't answer the question. Lukyanov noted: "You've stopped to think. That's disconcerting."

In a response that seemed to spotlight the descent of Russian foreign policy to nuclear terror tactics, Putin scoffed: "I did it on purpose to make you worry a little. Mission accomplished."

Putin's answer stumped his own media mouthpieces. So much so that Margarita Simonyan, head of state news agency RT, decided to take the non-response as an opportunity to reaffirm her readiness for martyrdom for the sake of the Russian president.

During the latest broadcast of *Sunday Evening With Vladimir Solovyov* on state television, where Simonyan is always the first guest to deliver her monologue and the only queen bee who is allowed to sit down in the studio, she gushed over Putin's remarks in Valdai.

"A transformation of the world is underway and that is the source of hope. When you sit in that auditorium, you experience hope," Simonyan said. "For me, it was a session of psychotherapy, as meetings with Putin customarily tend to be. A correct psychotherapy session."

By "correct" kind of psychotherapy, Simonyan explained, she meant that Putin's ideas are worth dying for. "The world is at a dead-end—first and foremost, in terms of values. If the Western world continues to develop in the same way and proceeds along the same insane trajectory, then it's headed towards the destruction of mankind—even without any kind of a war," she said.

"Another fifty to a hundred years and no one will give birth anymore. No one will be able to give birth. With all the hormonal therapies, with their pharmaceutical lobbies, with brainwashing the mentality of their own nation and others, their own people and their own empires."

She went on: "I don't want to live in this kind of a world. It's better to go to heaven right away, as Putin said: We'll go to heaven and they'll just croak."

The panelists admitted that they "all shuddered" after the pause Putin made when confronted with Fyodor's question. Nonetheless, they emphasized that they would rather die than live in a world where people can deal with their own sexuality according to their own free will.

Simonyan proclaimed her unwillingness "to live in the world where I'd be prohibited to put dresses on my daughters and to explain to my son that he is a boy." She concluded: "This is already happening in many countries. For me, it's unbearable. For me, this is worse than war. Indeed, it's worse than war."

Simonyan proceeded to describe the beauty of war, as opposed to societal freedoms. "War has goals. Along with tragedies, pain and other understandable things, war has pride, the happiness of victory, and certain personal growth. There are changes in personality that lead to deeper self-awareness as a part of your nation, as a part of certain values and ideals," she said.

"What does that ultra-liberal fascist trash have? I don't know. It spreads as an uncontrollable tumor, against which the chemotherapy is ineffective. If you allow it anywhere near your borders, before you know it, you'll be living in a country that is dictating that you must live a certain way. With our mentality, to live this way is unbearable."

She added that returning to everyday matters after this "psychotherapy session" with Putin is "scary" and questioned: "Will we win? Do we have enough strength? Do we have enough weapons? We're not talking about a victory over Ukraine... right now, it's abundantly clear that we're dealing with the origin of that tumor I just mentioned, with the monstrous organism that is known as the collective Western world. It's powerful, successful, well-armed and at the same time, utterly screwed-up, hotheaded and totally uneducated."

Russia's terror tactics against the Ukrainian civilians, which generated some pushback even on the tightly controlled state television, suggest that Putin would be perfectly willing to harm countless civilians of other nations, as well as his own. Nonetheless, some state media experts attempted to interpret Putin's silence in a way that doesn't involve drinking nuclear Kool-Aid.

Evgeny Buzhinsky, a retired lieutenant-general of the Russian Armed Forces, tried to discuss the possibility of negotiations with the West, only to be shut down by both Simonyan and Solovyov.

The host asked Buzhinsky: "What is the source of your optimism? What makes you think that by the year 2026 there'll be anyone left to talk to?" Simonyan chimed in: "The one who is positively minded is ill-informed."

Buzhinsky sheepishly noted: "I'd like to think about good things and not about all of us being gone, even though I understand that it's nice to be in heaven... but the president didn't give a clear answer as to whether we're in a rush to get there."

During Solovyov's show on Monday, the host and guests continued their attempts to convince fellow Russians that dying would be a better option as opposed to being defeated.

Professor Dmitry Evstafiev offered up a hypothesis that if they lose, Russians would be exhibited in American zoos along with animals. He said, "Western people like colonialism... They want to have us in their zoos. They will come and see—over there is an elephant and over here is a Russian... Don't come close and don't try to feed him through the cage."

Putin's Top TV Puppet Threatens 7 Countries With Air Strikes After Poland Blast

Russian state TV star Vladimir Solovyov delivered a menacing tirade on Wednesday, claiming certain countries should think twice if they believed "the war wouldn't come to them."

Originally published by *The Daily Beast* on November 16, 2022

The deadly blast that killed two people in Poland sent shockwaves across the globe this week, fueling fear that Russia's invasion of Ukraine might escalate into a world war with the direct participation of NATO. While many are relieved that the incident was likely an attempt by Ukraine to intercept a Russian missile—on a day when Moscow launched about 100 strikes on Ukraine—Russian propagandists were seething with anger and irritation.

After all, that reaction undermined Russian state media's notion that NATO is already fighting against Moscow, itching to get directly involved in the bloody conflict. State TV host Vladimir Solovyov took that opportunity to spew more threats against the West, while describing Ukrainian territories recently taken back from Russia's invading troops as Russian territory occupied by Ukraine.

During his show *Full Contact*, Solovyov exclaimed: "This is war... you thought you could fight against us and the war wouldn't come to you? You want to wage war against Russia! But you want to do it on the territory of Ukraine or on the Russian lands Ukraine just occupied."

Solovyov baselessly alleged: "The language being heard on the frontline is mainly Polish and English. Are you bastards thinking that sooner or later this war won't come to you?" He threatened: "If we dealt with you bastards, you would feel differently... I have a question: where is the Polish air defense?"

The host slid right into his go-to tactics, asserting that anyone who believes Russia might be running low on conventional missiles should remember the "6,000 nuclear warheads" it also possesses. He asked: "Do you have air defense systems? Europeans, are you certain that all is well with you? You've been delivering everything to Ukraine... Germans, you are naked right now! N-a-k-e-d! You've given up your IRIS-T [high-tech air-defense missile systems]."

One by one, Solovyov threatened Poland, Germany, the Czech Republic, Slovakia and the Baltic nations, saying that "Yesterday it finally became clear what and how we should do." He opined that NATO's measured response gave away its hesitation to escalate, claiming that the alliance lives in fear of the great and mighty Russia. He called upon NATO to carefully weigh every word in its final resolution, so that it does not become a damning "verdict."

The rest of Solovyov's rant revealed the fear that lies beneath the surface of Vladimir Putin's bravado and bluster: growing domestic discontent within Russia.

Solovyov yelled about how Russia needs to promptly produce everything that is needed by faltering troops in Ukraine. "If anybody didn't understand it, this is war. War! This is a war against NATO," he raged.

Pundits and experts on other state media shows expressed similar frustration. During Monday's broadcast of *The Meeting Place* on NTV, an expert at the Strategic Development Council, Igor Shatrov, complained that "We weren't ready for the war that we started!"

During last Thursday's broadcast of *The Evening With Vladimir Solovyov*, the head of the State Duma Defense Committee, Andrey Kartapolov, delivered a pompous speech, urging citizens not to panic and claiming that Russia finally has a historic chance to do away with the West.

He boasted that Russia is far ahead of the West, having already conducted a mobilization, while NATO countries "haven't even started."

Other participants promptly rained upon Kartapolov's parade, worrying out loud that unless things improve, Russia might be headed for a revolution.

Tigran Keosayan, husband of RT boss Margarita Simonyan, complained that Russia's defeats in Ukraine were caused by a series of internal problems, such as corruption, intentionally false reporting and the withholding of information from people who are expected to fight and potentially perish in this war.

Keosayan opined that the average Russian might be more inclined to accept defeats in Ukraine, including the recent retreat from Kherson, if the government comes clean and admits its mistakes. Responding to Kartapolov, he sniped: "Comrade Colonel-General said that he fears panic. What are you talking about? There is no panic. There is something much worse: irritation."

Kremlin TV Stars Combust as Russians Admit War Is Aimless

Putin's media darlings are promptly melting down as more Russians realize they "don't understand what they're doing" in Ukraine.

Originally published by *The Daily Beast* on December 16, 2022

Russia's invasion of Ukraine continues to stall—along with the Kremlin propaganda blitz meant to convince the Russians that supporting the war is their sacred duty. Pro-Kremlin propagandists unanimously agree that Vladimir Putin's war is here for the long haul, but bristle at the fact that no one seems to know the end goal of the so-called "special operation."

During Wednesday's broadcast of NTV's show Meeting Place, hosts Andrey Norkin and Ivan Trushkin spearheaded a discussion about the effectiveness of homegrown propaganda, complaining about the lack of views and comments on "patriotic" promo reels urging the youth to rush for the front lines.

One guest, Russian rapper Ptakha, whose real name is David Nuriev, didn't beat around the bush. "As far as the youth is concerned, honestly speaking, I communicate with a lot of them and very few understand what we're doing there, because they [Ukrainians] didn't cross our borders. Very few understand," he said. "Trying to ride the wave of the Soviet ideology, claiming that we're fighting Germans, is also very questionable."

Trushkin asked: "Can you produce a clip explaining what we're doing there, in a language that's easy to understand?" Ptakha replied: "I don't quite understand it myself." Norkin angrily retorted: "I categorically reject what you're saying right now, young man. Let's stop butting heads over here."

Undeterred, Ptakha continued to speak and said the Wagner Group of mercenaries are at war solely "to make money," and that the rest of Russian troops don't understand Moscow's aims.

As the guests piled on, loudly arguing with the inconvenient assessment, Norkin shut Ptakha down: "I don't want to offend you or insult you, but you are very certain that you're right, despite your lack of basis. You want us to explain all of this to you, but we aren't going to do that. This is not the point of today's program."

During Monday's airing of *The Evening With Vladimir Solovyov*, the eponymous propagandist complained about the "generation gap," stating that mainly men of his own age are fighting in Ukraine, while younger Russians aren't eager to march into battle.

In Solovyov's Wednesday broadcast, the topics of propaganda and the widespread lack of understanding as to Russia's long-ranging goals was likewise front and center.

Andrey Sidorov, deputy dean of world politics at the Moscow State University, predicted that the West will intensify its information offensive against Russia during the spring of 2024—targeting the presidential election. "Russia's destruction is the main goal of the West, they openly admit that," he said.

With notable irritation, Sidorov pointed out: "When the government does not identify clear goals, it's very difficult to fulfill your oath... so what is our goal?" He complained about the lack of clarity on how much of Ukraine Russia intends to occupy, expressing his hope that the final aim includes all of the Ukrainian territory.

During Tuesday's broadcast of the show Time Will Tell, State Duma member Alexander Kazakov likewise argued that Russia should take all of Ukraine: "We need all of it—everything!"

State media's desperation to control the narrative of the war is palpable, with propagandists seemingly competing for the most outrageous theory on what would happen if Russia loses the war.

Head of RT Margarita Simonyan previously alleged that the Russians would end up in Western concentration camps or be turned into mindless "yahoos," while Professor Dmitry Evstafiev predicted that they would be caged and displayed alongside animals at the zoo.

"What will happen if the West is allowed to build the kind of a world it wants to create? What kind of world will it be? Can a normal person live in this world?," political scientist Sergey Mikheyev lamented on Solovyov's show. "Humans will turn into non-humans... humanity as a whole will be eradicated... What is ahead of us is the forced replacement of people with robots and robotization of the people... If we don't confront the West, utter horror will follow, it will be a catastrophe."

In an apparent effort to strengthen Russia's ideological standing and eliminate foreign influence, Vitaly Tretyakov, dean of Moscow State University's School of Television, pushed for Russia's liberals to be forced into publicly denouncing their written criticism of the Soviet Union. He called for the Russian Academy of Sciences to arrange for these public denouncements and threw in another proposal: "Maybe we should burn these books!"

Mikheyev eagerly chimed in: "Right along with their authors!"

Putin's Cronies Turn on Russian Elite in Paranoid War Frenzy

Vladimir Putin's top cheerleaders are panicking about Russian "sellouts" in their midst.

Originally published by *The Daily Beast* on December 19, 2022

Poorly concealed panic has permeated Russian airwaves this week, with pro-Kremlin pundits arguing not against the war—but against any possibility of a negotiated peace. Western proposals are being treated with the utmost suspicion, and the same goes for any Russians in positions of power who might be willing to consider them.

Appearing on the state TV program *Sunday Evening With Vladimir Solovyov*, Professor Dmitry Evstafiev brought up a recent article by former Secretary of State Henry Kissinger, in which he laid out his suggestions for a potential peace process.

In Moscow, Kissinger's proposals were treated as a hostile trap to ensnare Russia's elite, while state tv pundits attempted to distance themselves from their own elite status.

"The problem with Kissinger's article is not that he's luring us into some kind of a trap, but that some are walking into it—which means that they want to do it," Evstafiev argued.

"It should be openly said that within our elites—and perhaps within the government—there is a considerable number of people rooting for Russia's defeat. Yes, a shy, partial defeat, but let's call things by their proper names."

Evstafiev described peace-seeking articles in the Western press as "acts of manipulation" and predicted that their number will keep on growing. Resorting to conspiratorial tone about shadowy Western power brokers, Evstafiev alleged that Kissinger didn't even read the piece, much less author it.

Evstafiev described the willingness of Russian troops to fight until the end and shrieked: "Will our elites fight until the end, or will they be shown a carrot and run after it? What percentage of our elites are ready to sell out?"

Andrei Bezrukov, a Russian spy whose life story served as the inspiration for the TV show "The Americans," likewise asserted that Kissinger and other Westerners are basing their proposals on the belief that the Russian elite are always ready to betray their country.

He proposed that the Yeltsin Center, named after Russia's former president Boris Yeltsin, be renamed into "Traitors Center," warning those who are willing to cooperate with the West that they too would be considered traitors to the Motherland.

Host Vladimir Solovyov argued that the West is proposing negotiations solely because Russia's strategic nuclear arms surpass their own, urging Russian leadership to use the full arsenal of weapons at its disposal. He asserted that the superiority of NATO's conventional arms is reason enough for Russia to turn to nuclear strikes as the way to victory.

Andrey Sidorov, Deputy Dean of world politics at the Moscow State University, incredulously asked the host: "Would we like to experience a retaliatory strike?" With bizarre enthusiasm, Solovyov responded: "Yes! Victory starts with not fearing the consequences of your own actions!"

Sidorov cautiously asked: "Are you ready for a war with NATO, for real?" The host preached that the fear of nuclear strikes is the only thing that may stop NATO from continuing to deliver weapons and equipment to help Ukraine defend itself from Russian aggression. Deriding the elite who might consider peace proposals as the traitors to the Motherland, Solovyov extolled the troops he visited on the frontlines.

He tearfully recounted: "When you talk to them, they have no questions about whom they're fighting and what they're fighting for... We'll march all the way to the big puddle and maybe we'll have to take Washington as well... Until we drive them into the swamp, until only their hand is sticking out of it as they plead: 'Help me, help me!' Then we'll decide what to do with them."

State media's nuclear bravado and threats against anyone who might be willing to peacefully negotiate with the West might be used to conceal a very real fear that propagandists — along with military and government officials — would be forced to answer for their war crimes, including public incitement of these actions on state television.

In recent days, multiple state TV programs have warned that Russia's defeat in this war would lead to war crimes tribunals at the Hague or elsewhere, arguing that the only way of escaping that fate is ensuring Russia's victory, by any means necessary. During Friday's broadcast of NTV's program *Our Own Truth*, host Roman Babayan led panelists into discussions about the need for Russia's own war crimes tribunals, which should be set in motion in anticipation of an impending victory over Ukraine.

Russian state media's push for nuclear attacks continued on Monday's NTV's show Meeting Place. Hosts Andrey Norkin and Ivan Trushkin played a clip from a recently released song "Sarmatushka," celebrating the Russian ballistic missile Sarmat.

Former head of Russia's space agency, Dmitry Rogozin, took the credit for the deranged lyrics of the song, glorifying the missile's ability to destroy the United States and NATO. After writer Valery Pecheykin dared to say he wasn't inspired by the murderous tune, Norkin and Trushkin pounced on him, repeatedly asking whether he was proud of Sarmat. Instead, Pecheykin said: "It's alleged that our superpower is that we can die better than anybody else... but when will we learn how to live?"

Russians Fear They'll Soon Be Starving 'Like North Koreans'

The brutal economic reality of a long war is beginning to dawn on even the most ardent pro-Putin propagandists, as Russia prepares for misery at home.

Originally published by *The Daily Beast* on January 10, 2023

Russia rang in the new year with gaudy excess, patriotic fervor and echoes of a Soviet past. In studios filled with visiting servicemen, brought in from the front lines to film the New Year's extravaganza, hosts and performers toasted victory and mocked the West for the side effects of Russian sanctions.

Comedian Yevgeny Petrosyan cheered for the troops, assuring them that the entire country was behind them. He taunted Ukraine and its Western allies: "Like it or not, Russia is enlarging!"

Noisy bravado couldn't hide the fact that no one was drinking from the champagne glasses seemingly filled with sparkling water, or the blank stares on the faces of the visiting troops.

One of the hosts, sports commentator Dmitry Guberniev, compared life to a biathlon—a grueling cross-country ski race with rifle shooting—and surmised: "If you're having a hard time, then the finish line is near and victory is close!"

Holiday cheer notwithstanding, even Russian propagandists realize that hard times are only starting and attempts to summon a ghost of the Soviet past are directly related to a starkly different way of life that awaits the average Russian. On Wednesday, Sergey Mardan, who hosts a show on channel Solovyov Live, struggled to contain his feelings about "the grinning and glee on the federal channels," which continued even after the news of a HIMARS strike that killed dozens of Russian troops in Makiivka.

Mardan raged: "What happened in Makiivka is a tragedy! A real tragedy! There didn't have to be a phone call from the top for them to figure out that TV programming should be changed to something that is more fitting. Instead of vulgar anecdotes, put on any old Soviet movie."

The Soviet grooming that is being implemented by many Russian propagandists is meant to condition the people to the rapid decline in the standards of living to which many of them have become accustomed. The expectations are so dire, Mardan posed a startling question to his economic expert, Denis Raksha: "What are our chances? Do we even have them or not? Will we have to live like South Korea in the 1950s-1960s? Will we end up having to eat fire ants?"

Raksha explained that if Russia intends to drastically rebuild its economy in order to be self-sustaining everyday life will become quite difficult, even if Russians won't have to resort to eating ants.

He added: "Currently, the industrialization reminiscent of that of the 19th century or the 1920s-1930s is practically impossible. In that case, we'd have to live not like South Koreans, but like North Koreans."

Workers remove debris of a destroyed building used as temporary accommodation for Russian soldiers, 63 of whom were killed in a Ukrainian missile strike as stated the previous day by Russia's Defense Ministry in Makiivka, Russian-controlled Ukraine, January 3, 2023.

Another kind of hunger is also concerning Russian experts: a looming lack of ammunition. On January 2, Victor Murakhovsky, editor-in-chief of the Arsenal of the Fatherland magazine, raised an alarm on his Telegram channel, where he wrote: "In 1914, miscalculations of the General Staff as to the rate of accumulation of shells (900 shots) led to an acute shortage of shells for the army in the field. Urgent measures were required to save the army from a complete shell starvation. The military industry was not ready to solve this problem... the "ammo hunger" was fully eliminated only in 1916."

Murakhovsky went on to explain his calculations for the same problem that is raising its head now: "In the early 1990s, the Russian army inherited from the Soviet army about 15 million tons of missiles and ammunition... As of January 1, 2013, the Armed Forces of the Russian Federation had 3.7 million tons of ammunition, of which 1.1 million tons are unusable. This means that 2.6 million tons of ammunition are usable.

In 2020, almost 300 thousand pieces of ammunition were repaired and more than 20 thousand shells for multiple launch rocket systems were collected. The realistic need for ammunition is MILLIONS of pieces per year."

During his program, Mardan described the predictions of the upcoming ammunition shortages as "apocalyptic writings" and pondered out loud whether Russian industry would be able to solve this problem. His guest, military expert Vladislav Shurygin, cautiously replied: "I read that post. It should be acknowledged that it was written by one of our best military professionals... but his calculations didn't include the rate at which the ammo is currently being produced."

He argued that imposing strict usage norms on the battlefield was the way to keep the issue under control. Meanwhile, Russia is reportedly continuing to court other pariah states to source weapons and ammo to replenish its dwindling stocks.

An ammunition depot of the Russian military, which was destroyed by Ukrainian servicemen in the city of Izyum, Kharkiv region on December 13, 2022. Military equipment of the Russian forces and ammunition of various calibers, including non-detonated ones, were destroyed all around.

The simple solution of abandoning Russia's failing invasion of Ukraine never seems to occur to the pro-Kremlin propagandists.

Mardan raged: "The enemy has to be destroyed down to the root! It has to be exterminated! Russian history of the last 1,000 years shows that the deed has to be brought to its final conclusion... If Stalin had deported [the people of] Western Ukraine — to me, it's still a mystery why he didn't do it — perhaps none of this would be happening."

To sweeten the pot, the host rejoiced over millions of Ukrainian refugees who ended up in Russia, while Moscow struggles to alleviate a severe demographic crisis: "Look at how much the Motherland is spending to solve the demographic problem... We got these people [Ukrainians] for free, for nothing — approximately five million of them! Five million souls!"

Concluding the program, Mardan grimly noted: "To everyone who says that Russia should get up off its knees — myself included — my friends, I'm afraid that our former way of life is a thing of the past... It's practically unavoidable... perhaps we'll be reflecting upon the past year as our last fat year. On the other hand, a great victory is ahead of us!"

Putin's Henchmen Threaten 'Tens of Thousands' of Dead U.S. Troops

Some of Putin's top propaganda merchants realize nuclear threats are starting to ring hollow so they recommend slaughtering American servicemen in vast numbers instead.

Originally published by *The Daily Beast* on January 20, 2023

Patriarch Kirill, the head of the Russian Orthodox Church, delivered a sermon marking Orthodox Epiphany in Moscow this week. He spoke to those who wish "to defeat Russia," using the occasion to deliver a threat to the West: "We pray that the Lord admonish those madmen and help them to understand that any desire to destroy Russia will mean the end of the world."

Russia's top propagandists, from former President of Russia Dmitry Medvedev to state TV host Vladimir Solovyov, have been spreading the same not-so subtle nuclear threat far and wide—and yet, Putin's mouthpieces are now worried that the "boy who cried wolf" routine is no longer being taken seriously by their target audience in the West.

The dilemma manifested during a live broadcast of *The Evening With Vladimir Solovyov*. After the lineup of talking heads took turns reiterating that Russia's defeat would mean the end of the world, their agitprop was suddenly deflated by Yevgeny Satanovsky, President of the Institute of the Middle East.

"First of all, our main enemy is certainly the United States. What does the U.S. react to? They react to two things: the threat of physical annihilation and the liquidation of a certain number of military personnel. What we know based on wars in Vietnam and Korea is that several tens of thousands of annihilated American servicemen will cause the public opinion in the U.S. to be severely strained. I will repeat: not several thousand, like in Afghanistan or

Iraq, but a certain number of tens of thousands. Who will liquidate them, where they will be liquidated and in what way is completely irrelevant, but this is one of the objectives if we want to influence the American leadership. We have absolutely nothing to lose."

Head of RT Margarita Simonyan described the mood in the country: "In every home, in every kitchen and living room, in every courtyard all conversations are only about what will happen next, how it will all end... I don't see any possible course of events except for the following: first of all, they will not stop. I'm not talking about Ukraine or Zelensky [She is talking about the West]... They will keep raising the stakes to the point that it will cause us pain. Safety of the territory of the Russian Federation will be at issue, not just the newly added territories. I don't doubt that they will do all that they can so that we have to be concerned about the safety of Moscow, or at least seriously thinking about it... This will certainly happen!"

Simonyan concluded: "This can only end with an immediate threat that is voiced and presented, a threat of a nuclear confrontation." She argued that the failure of the West to acquiesce to the list of demands presented by Russian President Vladimir Putin in December of 2021 led to the invasion of Ukraine. Simonyan said that after Putin's ultimatum was made public, she told her friends: "Guys, there will be a big war, for sure. By the end of winter, something very big will happen!"

She claimed that this time, the refusal of the West to back out of its support of Ukraine would lead to even bigger consequences: "It's true that no one will win in a nuclear war, but who needs the world if Russia isn't in it? It was voiced out loud, it was said by Vladimir Vladimirovich Putin!" The head of RT concluded: "I don't see any other outcome... It will be a wrecking ball! It will be all-in! It will be like two planes, flying head-on into one another. Someone will have to back down and something tells me that it won't be us."

Andrey Kartapolov, the head of the Russian State Duma Defense Committee, followed up Simonyan's diatribe by boasting of the Motherland's nuclear might and absurdly claiming that Russia defeated the West in World War II, causing NATO to be "afraid of WWIII." Resorting to grotesque threats, Kartapolov addressed the

West with a line from an old Soviet movie: "Don't worry, it won't hurt when we cut your throat. We'll slice just once and you're in heaven... Our victory will take place wherever the Russian soldier will stop—and wherever he stops, from there he will never leave."

Not everyone in the studio went along with the notion that only bringing the planet to the brink of a nuclear catastrophe would solve Russia's quagmire in Ukraine. Political scientist Sergey Mikheyev took exception to Simonyan's scenario of a head-to-head confrontation, arguing that the art of diplomacy should not be reduced to that deplorable state. He argued for asymmetric measures to achieve Russia's goals. Solovyov chimed in to soften the blow, telling Mikheyev: "Sergey Alexandrovich, we're just irresponsible journalists. We can afford to do that." Mikheyev retorted under his breath: "We aren't even journalists."

Americanist Dmitry Drobnitsky likewise derided Simonyan's idea of a "head-to-head" confrontation accompanied by nuclear threats, arguing that this strategy would repulse Russia's current sympathizers like India or China.

Even Satanovsky dismissed the simplistic thinking behind Simonyan's narrative, telling her: "If the stakes are that we'll stop existing, we can't limit ourselves by thinking they've read what the president said and believed it—no, Margarita, they don't believe it." He argued that his idea of killing thousands of U.S. troops to avoid destroying all of America was much more doable. Not one pundit in the studio argued against Satanovsky's macabre proposal.

Drobnitsky had only one exception: "In our country, we embraced one American we wouldn't want to kill: that would be Tucker Carlson."

Putin's No. 1 Cheerleader Rips into Russia's War Failures

Putin's favorite propagandist lost it on his latest TV show, blasting the failed tactics and strategy that's left Russia losing in Ukraine and facing worse to come.

Originally published by *The Daily Beast* on January 27, 2023

Top Russian propagandist Vladimir Solovyov has been spending his weekends on the frontlines in order to support and promote Russia's stuttering invasion of Ukraine. Unfortunately for the Kremlin, all that time being confronted by the grim reality is teaching Solovyov just how badly this war is going. And he's not happy about it.

In a wild rant on Thursday, Solovyov attacked the overall strategy, claimed the Russian Army was failing miserably to suppress their enemies, and said he had first-hand evidence of foolish tactical errors on the frontline.

During his show *Full Contact*, Solovyov was raging about the recent announcement that Ukraine would soon be getting Abrams and Leopard-2 tanks from NATO countries. The host started his monologue with a deep sigh, asking, "So, we lived long enough to see this?"

He urged the audience not to trust the numbers of the tanks slated for the upcoming deliveries, predicting they will send even more: "They will deliver everything. I've been saying it for a while, these bastards will also rehabilitate Hitler in our lifetime… this is where everything is going… WWIII is underway and the West has returned to its Nazi roots. Germany got tired of concealing its Nazi nature and America finally openly acknowledged its own Nazi ways."

Calling Americans "conniving liars," Solovyov said that their arrogance is Russia's own fault: "We aren't creating any threats against them. We aren't conducting strikes against New York, we aren't banging Washington, we aren't threatening Miami, we aren't doing anything to endanger Americans. They blew up our pipelines, we just wiped our face off. They're delivering heavy tanks, we're wiping our face off. Stop talking about red lines! It's a totally empty phrase that doesn't mean a thing!"

Enraged, Solovyov screamed: "Berlin, Paris, Madrid, London, Washington should be on fire! The capitals of Nazi countries who made a decision to go to war with Russia... Why wasn't Kyiv wiped off the face of the earth after the Nazi nation of Ukraine conducted a strike against our strategic aviation base? Stop resorting to empty, worthless words!"

The host went on to claim: "Strikes are being carried out against our cities! Against our land! Russian soldiers are perishing! Russian people are dying! Nazis are rejoicing! How are we planning to respond? By howling that avoiding nuclear war is the most important thing? Then why the heck do we have a stockpile of tactical and strategic nuclear weapons? To be afraid to use it? So that big decorated generals would gasp, "Do you want a nuclear war?" Do you want the destruction of Russia with conventional weapons, of which NATO countries have 3 and a half times more than we do?"

Solovyov yelled that destroying Ukraine's infrastructure was insufficient. He demanded to know: "Why do Odesa, Kharkiv, Dnipropetrovsk [Dnipro] still exist?" He angrily shouted: "We are no longer stationed near Kyiv! Was it a damn goodwill gesture? A goodwill gesture? And Kharkiv was a goodwill gesture? No one was executed by shooting for [surrendering] Kharkiv! No one was sent into retirement, at least not publicly. The society didn't get any answers to its questions. I'm asking you, why did you move the frontline closer to Belgorod? We still didn't get back to those positions! In response—silence. Silence."

Solovyov demanded that enemies be destroyed "on their land": "Citizens of NATO countries should not feel at peace, while the Russian man is suffering... Citizens! A war has been declared against us. Wake up! Wake up."

Solovyov's guest, military correspondent Alexander Kots, revealed one of the reasons for the host's helpless rage: glaring incompetence and mismanagement of the invading forces by their military leadership.

Discussing new items slated for delivery to Ukraine by NATO countries, Kots said: "While we have this list, only on paper for now, we should start thinking about what we will do when or if all of it gets to the frontlines. Somehow, we have to counter their artillery systems and tanks. For the last month, throughout the holidays, as a member of the presidential Human Rights Council, I was receiving outraged and concerned messages from the relatives [of soldiers]."

He continued, "We have trained—I won't say how many, but a decent quantity of the artillery battalions, but all of them were sent to the infantry. This is a huge number of people, we've been training them for three months, spending ammo, spending money to house them, great instructors from our military universities—including the Mikhailovskaya Artillery Military Academy—had given their time and knowledge to train them. With respect to our artillery, it's a very sad story... we don't have any artillery schools left! We used to have eleven and now only Mikhailovskaya remains."

Solovyov remarked that he was aware of this problem because of his frontline visits. Kots added that the same issue is happening with the anti-tank divisions, describing them as "the very units that should have been the ones meeting this tank Armada, burning up those Abrams and Leopard tanks. Instead, for some reason, they're also being transferred to the infantry. I can't understand why this is happening... We professionally trained up specialists, trained them well, but they sit without being given appropriate tasks... While we're facing a threat of these deliveries from the West to the frontlines by Spring, it's very wasteful on our part."

Solovyov chimed in: "I understand that you don't fight tanks with tanks, you use other means. Our anti-tank fist should be ready."

Kots hit him over the head with more bad news: "The first line of defense that will be meeting these tanks will often be comprised of mobilized men. Our mobilized soldiers on the frontlines are armed solely with Kalashnikovs. Unfortunately, there are no anti-tank weapons on many stretches of the frontline."

Solovyov reverted to his favorite topic, claiming that it's only a matter of time before NATO gives the Ukrainians tactical nuclear weapons. He said, "I believe that the use of tactical nuclear weapons is unavoidable. The question is who will do it first: us or them." Playing along, Kots pointed out: "The tanks that are being delivered contain depleted uranium."

After Solovyov noted that depleted uranium is not radioactive, Kots suggested: "It could still be used as the pretext, in order to use our tactical nuclear weapons."

But even his trademark shtick of threatening Russia's adversaries with nuclear mayhem failed to bring the bitter propagandist even a modicum of customary satisfaction. Introducing his next guest, Solovyov bitterly complained: "I'm sad. All of this is very sad."

Gloom Envelops Putin's TV Propagandists

There is an appreciable change of tone among Kremlin mouthpieces.

Originally published by *The Center for European Policy Analysis* (CEPA) on March 9, 2023

There was a time, not very long ago, when Russia's most prominent TV talk show host, Vladimir Solovyov, delighted in warning of a nuclear apocalypse that would hit the US or Britain (but not Russia.) So compelling were these arguments, they once attracted the on-air support of his show's weather forecaster.

How things change. The first anniversary of Russia's bloody, all-out invasion seemed to blanket Russian TV sets with doom and gloom. By the end of February 2023, reality crashed the set, joining the once-jolly pundits who used to predict that Ukraine was about to fall and the West would soon back down, in fear of nuclear-armed Russia.

The idea that Russia's victory was far from inevitable and that Russian defeat is a possibility had finally entered the once-impenetrable studios of state media. Appearing on *The Evening With Vladimir Solovyov* on February 28, 2023, movie director Karen Shakhnazarov noted: "This situation brings us a danger of very heavy consequences, if we lose. We have to consider the possibility of losing. I disagree with those who say, 'No need [to consider that], we will win!' I don't know about that."

Solovyov, who once read out lists of the many Western publications mentioning his nuclear threats, suddenly changed his tune on March 6. For the first time in months, discussions about the potential course of Vladimir Putin's war steered clear of bombastic predictions that London or Washington would soon be wiped off the face of the earth.

Solovyov's tone was dark, prompting his guests to hang their heads. He asked: "Can our army, in its current state, with its current numbers of people and with our military-industrial complex, fulfill its goals — which are not about the war against Ukraine, which does not exist — but against NATO?"

Vitaly Tretyakov, dean of the Moscow State University's Higher School of Television, failed to read the room. Russia must not agree to any ceasefire or commit to peace talks, since that would "rob Russia's servicemen of their victories."

Tretyakov then listed various Ukrainian regions, Russifying their names at will and declaring them part of the Russian Federation. He demanded that Russian officials make corresponding proclamations as to the fate of each region. Solovyov's tone was cold: "Who is supposed to declare it?" Tretyakov replied: "The victors!" The host cut him down: "Seriously? How are they going to attain this victory?"

State Duma deputy Andrey Gurulyov, a former deputy commander of Russia's southern military district, has likewise frequently appeared on state TV and likewise proposed the use of nuclear weaponry against NATO countries. Now he, too, has changed his tune.

Replying to Solovyov's questions, Gurulyov grimly surmised: "All of us understand very well that we are fighting against NATO, we've discussed it on many occasions. I am asked: 'Can we defeat NATO?' If you use math and calculate the correlation of forces and means, in the best-case scenario, we can merely defend ourselves."

It's hard to be sure how much of the tone change is attributable directly to the talk shows' Kremlin masters, but we do know that senior media staff receive directions on coverage from the regime, and that these guides are sometimes cut and pasted into media articles.

The Kremlin guides also suggest content, as in March 2022 when media were told it was "essential" to quote the Fox News host and Ukrainian war skeptic, Tucker Carlson. We also know that Russian has suffered at least 200,000 casualties and that as a result, ordinary Russians are aware that the conflict is proving extremely difficult, at best. Reality denial is getting harder.

A lot has changed since the first days of Vladimir Putin's war. In April 2021, long before Putin launched the all-out invasion of his neighbor, state TV hosts, experts, and State Duma members repeatedly stressed that Russia intended to invade Ukraine and warned average Russians about an upcoming war against the collective West.

In September 2021, a new national standard for "Urgent burial of corpses in peacetime and wartime" was introduced by the Russian government, set to come into force on February 1, 2022 — the month that the full-scale invasion began. An escalating drumbeat on state TV warned of an upcoming clash, and that it might become nuclear.

After February 22, 2022, state TV's talking heads continued to cultivate the soil of public opinion, claiming that Russia's victory was imminent and the West — terrified of its nuclear might — would not only back down, but offer significant concessions. Once it was clear the invasion was stalling, multiple military experts on state TV argued that Russia must now destroy all of Ukraine's critical infrastructure — long before these strikes commenced in September.

Yet, while the tone has changed, the willingness of state-funded writers and speakers to advocate a continuing war has not altered. While begrudgingly admitting that Russia is not ready to fight NATO and quietly setting aside their nuclear threats, state TV pundits still emphasize the importance of crushing not only Ukrainians — described by Tretyakov as "animals" — but also Russia's internal opposition, while tirelessly developing various methods of attacking the West in the future.

Russia's propaganda methods might be shifting, but its rage against those opposing Putin's bloody pursuit of his imperial ambitions is unsatiated.

'Morality Shouldn't Get in the Way' — Russia's Genocidal State Media

It occasionally occurs to Putin's mouthpieces that they may one day face charges in a war crimes tribunal. The case for the prosecution is in their own words.

Originally published by *The Center for European Policy Analysis* (CEPA) on March 13, 2023

When Russia invaded Ukraine, Vladimir Putin's elite propagandists wanted to drink champagne in the studio to properly celebrate the moment. Head of state propaganda agency, RT, Margarita Simonyan, expressed "an overwhelming sense of euphoria" and added: "I've been waiting eight years for this... it finally happened. This is true happiness."

With the bloody all-out invasion now in its second year, the euphoria has been replaced by a lingering sense of dread, with Putin's mouthpieces routinely fretting about the possibility of war crimes tribunals. The issue is playing on their minds.

Appearing on the state TV show, *The Evening With Vladimir Solovyov* in November, Simonyan said: "Let me tell you that if we manage to lose, the Hague—whether real or hypothetical—will even come for the street cleaner sweeping the cobblestones behind the Kremlin."

The same month, Olga Skabeeva, the host of the state TV show *60 Minutes*, likewise predicted that if Russia loses its war against Ukraine, every Russian will be considered guilty. She argued that a resounding victory was the only way "to avoid tribunals at the Hague, criminal cases, and having to pay reparations."

As the months go by, these concerns have not subsided. During Solovyov's show on March 6, Vitaly Tretyakov, dean of Moscow State University's Higher School of Television, worried out loud about the statements from "significant" Western figures expressing the demand that Putin and other Russians face war crimes tribunals.

The Kremlin's propagandists have plenty of reasons to be concerned; street sweepers and other average citizens rather less so. The agitation for war crimes against Ukrainians (described as animals and worse), the descriptions of them as Nazis, and the delight at the attacks on their homes and civilian energy grid have, after all, not been broadcast by people on the street.

From the lowliest pawns on Putin's chess board to the queens of propaganda like Simonyan and Skabeeva, the state-controlled media has played a central part in prompting, encouraging, rationalizing, and normalizing the Kremlin's massacre of its next-door neighbors.

It may be tempting to interpret such lurid language as silliness designed for a domestic audience.

But the outpourings of the propaganda machine have often foreshadowed or justified serious acts of state violence against Ukraine, including the mass murder of civilians, the mass kidnapping of Ukrainian citizens, the weaponization of migrant flows, and the evisceration of the Ukrainian polity.

Examples of such talk are easy to find. They proliferate nightly on live TV. Before the full-fledged invasion, Russian state media favored the description of pro-independence Ukrainians as "pigs," with corresponding cartoons featured on state television, where Ukraine's language, food, and traditions were routinely mocked.

Since February 2022, the descriptions have descended into the realm of open dehumanization. During his show in July, Solovyov said: "When a doctor is deworming a cat—for the doctor, it's a special operation, for the worms, it's a war, and for the cat, it's a cleansing."

In October, RT's director of broadcasting, Anton Krasovsky, suggested drowning Ukrainian children, setting Ukrainian homes on fire—with the inhabitants inside—and alleged that Ukrainian grandmothers would gladly pay to be raped by Russian soldiers.

He insisted that Ukraine should end in its current form, with its only surviving sliver zoned for pig rearing. Krasovsky felt the need to clarify that when he said "pigs," he did not mean Ukrainian women.

In October, Pavel Gubarev, a Russian political figure who proclaimed himself the "People's Governor" of the Donetsk Region in 2014 and later as leader of the Donbas People's Militia, explained that Ukrainians were, "Russian people, possessed by the devil," and that Russia's aim was to "convince them" that they are not Ukrainian. He added: "But if you don't want us to change your minds, then we will kill you. We will kill as many of you as we have to. We will kill 1 million or 5 million, we can exterminate all of you."

Months earlier, in May, State Duma deputy Aleksey Zhuravlyov appeared on *60 Minutes* to outline his calculations about the number of Ukrainians to be reeducated by "re-installing their brains," as opposed to the millions who would refuse to abandon their Ukrainian identity and who must therefore be killed "A maximum of 5% are incurable. Simply put, 2 million people . . . These 2 million people should have left Ukraine, or must be denazified, which means to be destroyed."

There is a widespread consensus in the state-controlled media that this so-called "denazification" means mass murder. In April, again on *60 Minutes*, Zhuravlyov and Skabeeva concurred that this process is "accomplished by shooting, or ripping heads off."

Nor was there any question in the minds of Russian officials that the invasion's aim was to oppress, not to "liberate" its population.

In his RT interview in December, Dmitry Rogozin, Russia's former ambassador to NATO and former Deputy PM for Defense and Space Industry, acknowledged that Ukrainians did not welcome their Russian invaders and that a huge effort would be needed to change their outlook "Many years will pass even after our victory before we will be able to secure total loyalty of this population." Turning this "extensive territory" into Russia will require plenty of manpower, time, and effort, he said.

The theme of a long occupation is common. State Duma Deputy, General Vladimir Shamanov, Russia's former airborne commander, estimated that it would take the "re-education" of at least two generations of Ukrainians before they would tolerate Russia's dominance. Appearing on *60 Minutes* in March, Shamanov concluded: "Today, it can be clearly predicted that we will have to remain in Ukraine for 30-40 years."

During the same show, military expert Igor Korotchenko surmised, "It's obvious that the process of the denazification of Ukraine will take a minimum of 15-20 years." He predicted that Russian troops would have to remain on Ukrainian territory, with a substantial Russian presence for the foreseeable future.

On March 6, Tretyakov, of the Higher School of Television, emphasized that Russian military bases should be established throughout Ukraine, "in order to control the mentality of this territory." He claimed that Ukrainians have "turned into animals" and Russia must plan its actions accordingly.

It is easy enough to understand the link between talking points that routinely compare the Ukrainians to animals, bugs, or worms with atrocities like Bucha, the torture and murder of Ukrainian prisoners of war, attempts to freeze and starve civilians to death by destroying critical infrastructure and forcibly deporting Ukrainians — including children — to Russia.

Russian academics are happy to explain the logic of Kremlin-directed violence and to provide an intellectual gloss. It is explained that attacks to deprive Ukrainians of electricity, running water, and food are part of a bigger plan. So the forced movement of millions to Russia is to compensate for its severe demographic shortcomings, while 8 million more have been pushed westwards to overwhelm Europe and undermine its economy by creating a refugee crisis.

In October, speaking on Solovyov's show, Andrey Sidorov, Deputy Dean of world politics at Moscow State University, acknowledged that Ukraine's destruction had a secondary benefit: "We should wait for the right moment and cause a migration crisis for Europe with a new influx of Ukrainians," he said.

And in January, the host of channel Solovyov Live, Sergey Mardan, rejoiced at the souls forced to leave their homes and enter Putin's Russia: "Look at how much the Motherland is spending to solve the demographic problem... We got these people [Ukrainians] for free, for nothing — approximately five million of them! Five million souls!"

In the world of Russian state TV, everyone has a soul, but not everyone has a right to live out their life. Some things are just more important, as Professor Elena Ponomareva of the Moscow State Institute of International Relations explained on Solovyov's show in March: "Never let morality prevent you from doing the right thing. I understand the importance of a humanitarian component... but morality shouldn't get in the way."

It is not hard to imagine those words echoing in a courtroom, as the prosecution lays out its case against Professor Ponomareva and her co-defendants.

Team Putin Melts Down Over International Arrest Warrant

The Kremlin's propagandists say Vladimir Putin is being mistreated by the legal system just like Donald Trump.

Originally published by *The Daily Beast* on March 20, 2023

The announcement by the International Criminal Court that an arrest warrant was issued for Russian President Vladimir Putin caused shockwaves in Moscow. Even before the announcement, the pro-regime propagandists expressed their concerns about the possibility of being charged with war crimes by the Hague tribunal.

Nonetheless, many were taken completely off-guard when the charges were announced, since they apparently believed that this turn of events was possible only if Russia lost the war in Ukraine.

Radio host Sergey Mardan said it was "strange" that the ICC had decided to charge Putin for the illegal deportation of children and unlawful transfer of citizens from Ukraine to Russia, which are war crimes: "It seems to me like all of us were bewildered. I had the feeling that our entire system did not anticipate that they would make such a crazy and irreversible move," he said.

His guest, Henry Sardaryan, Dean at the Moscow State Institute of International Relations complained that the news of the ICC's charges dominated the Russian social media since the announcement became public. Sardaryan proposed for Russia to retaliate in a symmetrical fashion, by initiating charges against U.S. President Joe Biden. He said, "To accuse us as a country of war crimes is laughable... Why don't we take the initiative and make a move that would force the entire American society to discuss for several days straight whether Joseph Biden will be arrested, whether he will end up in an electric chair or spend the rest of his days in faraway places?"

Sardaryan said: "The only path that is left is bringing the special military operation to its logical conclusion and achieving all the goals set forth by the president. After that, they will be forced to negotiate with us and the ICC, as an integral part of the globalist world order, will recall the order and close the case very quickly." He threw in an obligatory reference to Putin's statement that has by now become a propaganda cliché: "There is nothing more important in the world than our country. If our country doesn't exist, then nobody needs this world—first and foremost, we don't need it."

Head of RT Margarita Simonyan responded to the ICC announcement by implying that any country that arrests Putin would face nuclear destruction, even though this would technically mean that "the boss," as Simonyan calls him, would go up in flames along with the offending country. She had long reported widespread concerns about the potential charges for war crimes within the top echelons of Russian officials.

Appearing on *Sunday Evening With Vladimir Solovyov*, Simonyan said she was appalled by the ICC's charges, because Russia merely "took the children no one else wanted."

Simonyan added: "the Hague is shit" and said that the era of civility is over. She proceeded to wish the best of luck to Donald Trump with respect to the potential charges he is anticipating.

Vladimir Solovyov called for arrest warrants to be immediately issued for all ICC judges, describing them as "bastards" and "degenerates" who should be hunted down and arrested by Russia's intelligence services abroad. He demanded nuclear strikes against any country that might try to arrest Putin and added, "They should fear us!"

Former president Dmitry Medvedev picked up the theme on Telegram on Monday morning, threatening the ICC with a hypersonic missile strike.

Alexander Bastrykin, who heads Russia's Investigative Committee, proposed that Moscow creates its own "international court"—the same idea multiple propagandists have been test-driving on state TV. Senator Andrei Klishas also called for an immediate arrest warrant for all the judges of the International Criminal Court.

On Monday, Russia's Investigative Committee opened a criminal case against the prosecutor and judges of the ICC.

Deputy Chairman of the State Duma of the Russian Federation Irina Yarovaya said that the decision taken by the ICC constitutes an act of international terrorism directed against Russia and proposed introducing new legislation that would classify "Russophobia" as a dangerous crime.

Appearing on the channel Solovyov Live, political commentator Andrey Perla noted: "This is an extremely serious move. This is a declaration of intent to enslave Russia. In practice, of course, Russia can't be enslaved, because we will win this war. Since these demands will continue to be voiced, they will prompt the creation not merely of an iron curtain, but of a titanium wall between Europe and Russia — between the world that is ruled by Anglo-Saxons and the world where free people live. Russia and China will be the leaders of the free world, as well as all independent nations that will collaborate with us — like Iran."

Appearing on *Full Contact*, economist Mikhail Khazin expressed his outrage with the ICC's decision and said that heads of state can't be charged with crimes, unless they stand accused of genocide. Even though multiple talking heads on Russian state TV share this opinion, host Vladimir Solovyov previously threatened the Chancellor of Germany Olaf Scholz with inevitably having to face "another Nuremberg tribunal."

Political commentator Yevgeny Satanovsky said: "I think that the order for President Putin's arrest, issued by the ICC in the Hague, has been initiated by Americans. I always understood that current Western bosses and their entire team have gone completely mad, but not to this degree!"

He erupted into threats: "We have made it all the way to Berlin and Paris before. I understand that Hague would be on our way to Paris. If things keep going this way, we might visit Washington as well. President Biden fervently approved of the arrest warrant for President Putin, issued by the ICC in the Hague."

Bewilderment at the ICC's charges didn't prevent Putin's propagandists from bemoaning the current — not hypothetical — legal jeopardy that Donald Trump might soon face in the court of law.

Trump's Russian biographer Kirill Benediktov told host Sergey Mardan that Trump's and Putin's circumstances are similar, since both of them are not being accused of the most serious crimes. For example, instead of being charged with genocide, Putin is being accused of "sending children to a resort."

Benediktov noted: "It's possible that our Donald Fredovych Trump might end up in the slammer for the same kind of a crime for which people used to get released without a bond. Of course, it's shocking." Citing Elon Musk's Tweet, the host and his guest agreed that "our redheaded Donald Fredovych" might politically benefit from his impending arrest in the long run.

God's Propagandists

Kremlin mouthpieces have invoked a range of deities in aid of Russia's war of aggression.

Originally published by *The Center for European Policy Analysis* (CEPA) on March 22, 2023

Before Russia unleashed its full-scale invasion of Ukraine, the topic of religion was rarely discussed by the most prominent state media performers. The war was supposed to be quick and painless, and the motivation for stealing its neighbor's land did not need God's endorsement.

On December 31, 2021, Oleg Voloshin, a former aide to the pro-Russian government of Viktor Yanukovych, predicted that "Russia could destroy Ukraine in less than 10 minutes." During the broadcast of the state TV show *60 Minutes* later the same day, senior military analyst Mikhail Khodaryonok claimed that it would take all of 11 minutes.

After the rude awakening delivered by Ukraine's military, the Kremlin needed a better explanation for its decision to invade—and a stronger incentive for the masses to join the bloody endeavor. By April, state media and lawmakers started to portray Putin's war of aggression as a holy crusade.

Appearing on Channel One, Deputy of the State Duma Vyacheslav Nikonov (a grandson of Stalin's foreign minister, Vyacheslav Molotov) claimed: "In the modern world, we are the embodiment of the forces of good. This is a metaphysical clash between the forces of good and evil... This is truly a holy war we're waging and we must win."

By July, this premise was expanded to include Islam along with Christian Orthodoxy. Appearing on *60 Minutes*, Apti Alaudinov, commander of Ramzan Kadyrov's Chechen Akhmat militia, asserted that Russian forces in Ukraine are fighting a "holy war" against the Antichrist, who he explained was supported by gay people and other sexual minorities.

The notorious state TV host Vladimir Solovyov used similar language in October, publicly describing Russia's war as a jihad. During his program *Full Contact*, the host declared: "This is jihad. This is a jihad, this is a holy war!" By January, Solovyov — who claims to be an observant Jew — was chanting "Allahu Akbar" on state television.

Promoting Putin's full-scale invasion as a religious crusade is not the result of a religious revelation among Kremlin propagandists. It is crafted to appeal to two distinct target groups. The first is the domestic audience, and the second is the religious right in the US. It is the role, after all, of Russian official mouthpieces to exploit any potential division in the West, especially, the US, as Ukraine's main military and financial backer.

Every Tweet or comment by notable US figures opposed to President Biden's Ukraine policy is endlessly promoted on state television, with the underlying message that it is only a matter of time before anti-war Republicans cut Ukraine's lifelines and leave Russia the victor.

Most Russians are not overly religious, with church attendance sparse (only 6% attend church regularly.) Most propagandists, many of them raised in the atheist Soviet state, are not only irreligious, they openly admit this, while at the same time peddling the idea of a holy war against Ukraine and the West.

Sometimes the hypocrisy is too much to take, even for the most seasoned Kremlin mouthpieces. Appearing on *Sunday Evening With Vladimir Solovyov* in March, Pavel Astakhov, Russia's former Children's Rights Commissioner, asserted: "There should be no godless people in the places where governmental decisions are made, no agnostics, the undecided, the doubting ones. Friends! The enemy understands where to hit us. It was no accident that Congressman [Jamie] Raskin said that first, Orthodoxy should be destroyed, since this is the foundation of Russia."

In reality, Representative Raskin made no such comment, the attribution originating on Tucker Carlson's Fox News show.

Replying to Astakhov, Solovyov objected: "After 30 years of attempting to restore Orthodoxy, preceded by 80 years of total godlessness, we're trying to find a group of highly professional people for whom we are supposed to check their degree of Christianity?" He argued that qualifications are much more important than beliefs.

Solovyov said: "We believe in the triumph of our weapons." Panelist Vladimir Kornilov chimed in: "This means I'm surrounded by believers. Now I know."

When Astakhov proposed a ban on abortions, Solovyov said that was going too far: "If we use the methods of evil and say that we want to implement harsh measures, then how are we different from them?" Astakhov argued: "We're different because we're on the side of good."

The host replied with a surprisingly lucid argument, apparently without realizing that his words also apply to Russia's genocidal war in Ukraine: "If we're using evil methods, what makes us think that we're still on the side of good?" He added: "This is what the Inquisition was based on: they believed they were on the side of good, but they've committed such horrible evil. In all the Crusades, they believed they were on the side of good, but look at what they've done!"

Russia Laments the Loss of Tucker Carlson

The Kremlin's talking heads were appalled by the loss of a valued voice from the airwaves, but soon made the most of it.

Originally published by *The Center for European Policy Analysis* (CEPA) on April 26, 2023

The April 24 departure of Fox News host Tucker Carlson from his job sent ripples all the way to Moscow. The decision seemed so important to the Kremlin that Foreign Minister Sergey Lavrov publicly questioned it and RT, Russia's most prominent propaganda network, immediately offered Carlson a slot.

The RT offer, unavailable in the many countries where it is banned, was spelled out to Newsweek in a statement. "We already had the pleasure of working with the greats like [the imprisoned] Julian Assange and the late Larry King and had extended an invitation to President Trump in 2020, and we continue to welcome outspoken, diverse personalities on our network," it said.

Not to be outdone, the Russian television host Vladimir Solovyov used his Telegram channel to make another offer. "Tucker, come and join us. You don't have to be afraid of taking the p*** out of Biden here," he said.

Official Russia's affection for Carlson seems genuine and profound. Even before Russia's all-out invasion of Ukraine 14 months ago, Carlson's clips were a mainstay on Russia's tightly controlled state-funded television. The American television host is a household name in Moscow, along with domestic TV figures like Solovyov, Margarita Simonyan, Dmitry Kiselyov, and other spokespeople for the war. Carlson has never outright endorsed the full-scale invasion, but has repeatedly questioned US support and asked, "Why is it disloyal to side with Russia but loyal to side with Ukraine?"

Solovyov's show returned to Carlson-related events on April 25. While Solovyov Live has previously boasted the participation of Scott Ritter — a former US marine who attributes the Russian army's Bucha massacres to Ukraine — guests said dreaming of a Tucker hiring was a bridge too far. Israeli ex-diplomat and politician Yaakov Kedmi taunted Solovyov on his own show when he said: "You offered Tucker Carlson to join you. Volodya, you don't have that much money!" Solovyov retorted: "I will find it! We will sell two soccer players and buy one Tucker Carlson!" Kedmi raised his voice: "He doesn't need you!"

On the other hand, Moscow still needs Carlson and dreams of his triumphant return. Russia's political scientists and prominent talking heads are already brainstorming about what he might do next.

Andrey Sidorov, Deputy Dean of World Politics at the Moscow State University, suggested that Carlson should run for President. Addressing Solovyov, Sidorov noted: "At some point, you suggested that he should announce his candidacy for the Presidency of the United States. I don't see why not. His 3.5 million nightly viewers would translate into 3.5 million voters, which means he has support. His position is a lot more clear than Trump's stance, which is veering every which way."

For Russian commentators, the bloom is off the rose where Trump's candidacy is concerned. Their disdain now seems to match Carlson's (private and leaked) description of the former US president as a disaster whose administration had been "a s*** show."

Most say Trump would be the easiest candidate for President Joe Biden to defeat. More creatively, they suggested that Trump might serve as a vehicle for Carlson by becoming his running mate. Solovyov noted: "If he [Trump] takes Tucker as his vice president, that would be truly excellent!" Sidorov questioned this logic, doubting that Trump would cherish the notion of being outshone: "He [Trump] won't take Tucker. He certainly won't take him. He will choose someone like Pence, a bland nobody, somebody faceless."

Whether or not Carlson has ever aimed for such an influential fan club in Moscow, his segments have been much valued in

Vladimir Putin's Russia. Carlson had a huge US audience and his themes chime with state propaganda by demonstrating that it is not just pro-Kremlin voices who argue that US foreign policy is built on a hidden agenda concealed to ordinary people. That echoes the long-running campaign by RT and others to describe US democracy as itself a sham.

With guests such as his Russia expert, Clint Ehrlich—a former researcher at Russia's Foreign Affairs Ministry's MGIMO university—Carlson's show emphasized doubt and the risks of open war with Russia. Another frequent participant, Col. Doug Macgregor (rtd.), former advisor to the Secretary of Defense in the Trump administration, expressed the view that Ukraine would soon be overrun by superior Russian forces.

Carlson's departure is in this sense a loss to the Kremlin's information war. But it can also be used to underline the Kremlin message that all countries behave cynically, that hidden forces determine the real outcome, and that resistance to any government is a hopeless undertaking. Russia is once again stating that the US does not enjoy freedom of speech or freedom of the press. That in turn helps to justify the jailing of Wall Street Journal reporter Evan Gershkovich and open acts of repression like the 25-year sentence handed to Vladimir Kara-Murza.

While Maria Zakharova, of Russia's Foreign Affairs Ministry, says she cannot remember Gershkovich's name, none of Russia's government officials and talking heads seem to experience the same memory lapse with Tucker Carlson—for reasons that are all too apparent.

Married Putin Stooge Accused of Hiding Kids With Secret American Lover

A bombshell investigation has tied Moscow's most prominent mouthpiece to a second family of U.S. citizens.

Originally published by *The Daily Beast* on May 22, 2023

Vladimir Solovyov is one of Russia's top-tier propagandists, omnipresent on the airwaves of the state media and twice decorated by Russian President Vladimir Putin for his service to the Kremlin. He often derides the West as "satanic," and refers to Russia's invasion of Ukraine as a "holy war." Scarcely a broadcast goes by without Solovyov calling for nuclear strikes against the United States and its allies.

As it turns out, the 59-year-old TV host might be hiding an explosive secret himself.

A bombshell report from Alexei Navalny's FBK team on Monday, called "Vladimir Solovyov's American secret," claims that Solovyov—who is married with eight children—is suspiciously linked to another family. While investigating properties in Russia with obscure ownership records, the Navalny group reportedly tied Solovyov to a villa in Sochi and an apartment in Moscow reportedly owned by 42-year-old Svetlana Abrosimova, a retired basketball player and U.S. citizen.

Records obtained by the team allegedly show that Abrosimova traveled to the U.S. with the Russian propagandist in 2016. Abrosimova reportedly stayed in the U.S. through 2017, during which she gave birth to twin girls. According to the investigation, Solovyov made almost monthly visits to the U.S. until Abrosimova and her newborn twins moved back to Russia in June 2017.

The details of the trips were reportedly gleaned from paperwork filed for a coronavirus test the pair took in November 2021, which listed them as sharing the same address. The document reportedly featured Solovyov's passport details, including travel information. The Navalny team also concluded that the pair share a driver and have made several doctor's visits together, including one where they filed paperwork for the coronavirus test.

Photos of the pair—including one where they are standing side by side and another where they appeared to be chatting to each other while seated at a sport's game—were also published in the documentary investigation.

In the report, the Navalny team alleges that multiple anonymous sources close to the couple have confirmed that Solovyov is the father of Abrosimova's two children. The twins reportedly share the middle name "Vladimirovna," in what appears to be a derivation of the propagandist's first name. Solovyov's daughter, Yekaterina, is likewise a citizen of the U.S.

Solovyov did not immediately respond to a comment request from *The Daily Beast* about the allegations. Neither did Abrosimova.

During his shows, Solovyov often bemoans the loss of his Italian villas, but gleefully points out that he is yet to be sanctioned by the United States.

Given his patriotic fervor and theatrical desire for the destruction of the West, news that Vladimir Solovyov may be secretly nurturing an American dream of his own has many Kremlin critics blasting him as a hypocrite on social media.

The Navalny team investigation has also uncovered luxury homes in the same Sochi neighborhood where Ambrosimova reportedly lives, allegedly owned by General Sergey Surovikin and Andrei Patrushev, the son of Nikolai Patrushev, who serves as Secretary of the Security Council of the Russian Federation.

Team Putin Spars Over Baffling Russian 'Victory Plan' in War

The Kremlin's communication problems are triggering awkward moments and fiery clashes between Russian state television's biggest stars.

Originally published by *The Daily Beast* on May 31, 2023

It appears that even the most ardent pro-Kremlin propagandists are still struggling to explain Vladimir Putin's murky goal of "demilitarizing and denazifying Ukraine" more than a year into the invasion.

With Russian war efforts stalling and faltering on the ground, Putin's talking heads are struggling to get on the same page about what a "Russian victory" actually looks like, leaving state television brimming with clashes and contradictions.

In Monday's broadcast of the popular talk show *The Meeting Place*, none of the panelists appeared to have a clear understanding of Moscow's end-goals in the war—much less how they may be achieved.

"During the last year and two months since the start of the special operation, I've traveled dozens of times throughout the country... Every time I am asked: 'Why is it taking so long, why isn't it more decisive? To put it harshly, why aren't we destroying them like rats?," host Andrey Norkin said.

It did not take very long for that comment to blow up in Norkin's face.

"You know, when you say that your audience, your viewers are asking you why we aren't being more harsh, why aren't we destroying all of them like rats, I would answer them with a question," political analyst Viktor Olevich said, addressing the host. "'Are you ready for all of your children to die, to be pulverized in the trenches? Do you want for all of them to end up there?'"

A seemingly frazzled Norkin snapped back: "They are asking this question because they don't want that... who was saying to bomb, to bomb and to bomb them some more?" referring to past comments made by Olevich.

The expert, in turn, simply concluded that his prior remarks about bombing Ukraine to hell were "no longer relevant, because Russia currently lacks resources to establish control over Ukraine and won't get these resources in the near future." That wasn't the only point of contention on the broadcast.

In a truly Orwellian display of doublespeak, State Duma member Alexander Kazakov declared that the war should end only in a complete Russian victory. "I am for peace, I am anti-war. I am for peace after our victory," he said. When asked what his exact definition of victory was, he delved into fantasy. "We get to the borders of NATO, either through our military or diplomatic efforts, Ukraine disappears from the political map," said Kazakov.

"As a result of that, the United States gets out of Eurasia and along with China, India and other leading countries on this continent, we will set our own rules."

Bogdan Bezpalko—a member of the Kremlin's Council for Interethnic Relations, which acts as an advisory committee to Putin—had a much more straightforward definition of Russian victory. He described it simply as "the destruction of Ukraine's nationhood." Co-host Ivan Trushkin flatly dismissed his guests' answers, deriding them as "a call to surrender," before offering up his own, painfully vague idea of when Moscow can officially claim triumph.

A Kremlin win, he said, would be the "elimination of a threat... Whatever that looks like, whether reaching certain borders or signing some kind of an agreement, we should stop feeling the existential threat to our nation. This would constitute victory."

Similar conversations are taking place across all state-funded "news" networks in Russian. Earlier this month, state Duma member Andrey Gurulyov berated expert Dmitry Abzalov for admitting his unwillingness to perish in a nuclear war and pushing for Russia's "operation" to conclude as soon as possible.

The Monday broadcast, too, featured a rare moment of brutal honesty on Russian state television, with one panelist offering up a particularly grim prophecy about Putin's end game.

"What would victory look like? We can see it by looking at Bakhmut, the city where 70,000 people used to live, with children and kindergartens. It was simply wiped off the face of the earth. Everyone who could escape from there did just that," former state Duma deputy Boris Nadezhdin said, appearing exasperated.

"If victory means conquering ruins without the people, I don't know who needs this kind of victory... In some Russian cities, they are running out of men," he added. "The sooner this horror comes to an end, the better it will be for Ukrainians and Russians alike."

Russian State TV Anchors Aghast That Putin Didn't Kill Prigozhin

The Kremlin's propagandists praised Putin but were dumbfounded that he allowed the Wagner boss and his mercenaries to escape punishment.

Originally published by *The Daily Beast* on June 25, 2023

In the aftermath of Yevgeny Prigozhin's mini-mutiny, prominent Russian state TV propagandists were left grasping at straws—desperately trying to temper their outrage at what had happened in order to justify the Kremlin's decision to allow the Wagner boss and his mercenaries to escape accountability.

Prigozhin's intended march on Moscow was signaled as early as May, when he hinted at the inevitable uprising during his media blitz, which seamlessly combined self-aggrandizement with endless grievances against Russia's military leadership. Despite the writing on the wall, the short-lived uprising by the Wagner Group—officially known as PMC Wagner—caught everyone by surprise.

Decorated state TV host Vladimir Solovyov was shocked and dismayed at the dismal state of the country's preparedness that allowed Prigozhin's forces to roll through the land unimpeded. Solovyov seemed caught between a rock and a hard place, having to justify Russian President Vladimir Putin's decision to let Prigozhin and Wagner walk free, despite having advocated for the death penalty for less grievous offenses.

During the first post-mutiny broadcast of *Sunday Evening With Vladimir Solovyov*, propagandists focused on praising Putin's infinite wisdom for ending the revolt in a speedy manner. The head of RT, Margarita Simonyan, asserted: "There is nothing more frightening in the world than civil war." This outlook unwittingly highlighted frequent discussions on Russian state media hoping for a civil war in other countries — namely the United States.

Simonyan expressed her relief at the quick resolution of the ordeal and added: "There are many discussions right now: how can this be? They opened a criminal case and then let them go! [Prigozhin] left for Belarus. This is a mockery of legal norms! Let me remind you that legal provisions are not like Christ's commandments or the law of Moses. Legal norms are written by people to protect the order and stability in a country. There can be extraordinary, critical circumstances when legal norms stop to function... then these legal norms are set aside. They were written without accounting for the possibility of this kind of a situation."

Simonyan surmised: "It was a choice between the terrible and the horrendous... There is nothing more frightening than civil strife, which is incomparably more significant than a violation of some legal norms." Setting aside his daily demands for nuclear strikes and executions, Solovyov pompously added: "On this day, we found out a lot about our own country. We turned out to be much wiser than anyone might have thought... Yesterday, our leadership demonstrated strength and wisdom. Most importantly, it demonstrated strength without a bloodlust."

But State Duma member Andrey Gurulyov, retired deputy Commander of the 58th Combined Arms Army of the Southern Military District, was too flabbergasted about Prigozhin's exploits to go along with the propaganda narrative. After letting out a long, exasperated sigh, Gurulyov said: "I am firmly convinced that during wartime, traitors have to be destroyed! Today, no matter who says what, whatever fairy tales they are telling, a bullet to the forehead is the sole salvation for Prigozhin and [Dmitry] Utkin. They know me! They know that I stand behind my every word. There is no other option!" (Utkin is alleged to be the co-founder of the Wagner group.)

Aside from blasting the decision that provided immunity for the organizers and the participants of the intended coup, Gurulyov expressed his outrage that it was fomented and carried out without being detected beforehand and prevented. He said, "I totally don't understand why it even happened, where are those agencies that should have known about this in advance? It should have been prevented, it should have been stopped when it was underway!"

Outraged that the Wagner Group was better equipped than Russia's Armed Forces or its National Guard, Gurulyov exclaimed: "How much longer are we going to crowdfund every loaf of bread, every quadcopter and all the rest? It's enough already! When society came together to do this, it allowed us to survive at that point in time, because we had nothing! Now things are different."

Contradicting Putin's decision, Gurulyov reiterated: "Treason cannot be forgiven under any circumstances! It simply can't be forgiven, regardless of any past achievements! I will repeat it once again: the only way out for these friends is to kill themselves before [a] bullet finds them! There are no other options for traitors."

Lieutenant-General Evgeny Buzhinsky added: "For me, what happened yesterday was completely surreal." Like Gurulyov, he was bothered by the promise of impunity. Referring to reports that Wagner fighters shot down several military helicopters and a plane, Buzhinsky stressed: "Someone has to be held accountable for the deaths of pilots who have perished."

Instead of showcasing the strength and wisdom of Putin's regime, Solovyov and his fellow propagandists highlighted its fatal shortcomings and the discontent that is brewing not only within their ranks, but in society at large. A concern that currently permeates the tightly-controlled state media is that their country, which is waging a genocidal war of conquest against its neighbor, is woefully unprepared to withstand an internal rebellion or an invasion from abroad—and no amount of propaganda can cover that up.

The Kremlin Has a Batshit New PR Position: There Was No Armed Mutiny

Russian propagandists are rapidly changing their narrative. They say the insurrection was only ever a minor inconvenience and President Putin saved the day.

Originally published by *The Daily Beast* on June 28, 2023

The failed coup by Yevgeny Prigozhin and his private army, known as the Wagner Group, shocked the nation, with even the most dedicated Kremlin propagandists criticizing the deal that allowed the plotters to walk free and admitting that it made Russia look weak. Belarusian President Aleksander Lukashenko added to the national humiliation, by portraying himself as a hero who single-handedly negotiated an end to the mutiny, while Kremlin officials couldn't even get Prigozhin to pick up the telephone.

Days after the failed insurrection, Putin's propagandists are contorting themselves into pretzels with a new narrative that is drastically different from their first reaction. Decorated state TV host Vladimir Solovyov, who is personally protected by the Russian National Guard as a national treasure, admitted being in contact with members of the administration of Russian President Vladimir Putin.

He is now guiding participants of his show, *The Evening With Vladimir Solovyov*, into downplaying not only Lukashenko's contribution, but the significance of the failed rebellion itself.

Appearing on Solovyov's show on Monday, political scientist Yevgeny Satanovsky said: "Regarding the situation that some are calling a putsch or a mutiny. What putsch? What mutiny?" He explained that the armed uprising was merely an ordinary internal turbulence, using the Russian word "smuta," which translates as strife or turmoil.

"There is nothing exceptional about that," Satanovsky asserted. "This is merely a usual dust-up among the boyars [members of the ruling nobility in medieval times] that is traditional in Russia—and no more than that!" Satanovsky and Solovyov waxed metaphorical, comparing armed stand-off to a casual disagreement about turnips.

Satanovsky shrugged off the meaning of the events that were initially described by other state TV propagandists as historic: "This sort of thing has happened hundreds of times." Solovyov chimed in: "Note that it's always about turnips and not about love for the Motherland! It's always about some business fund and not defending your Fatherland." By referring to turnips and business funds, the talking heads intimated financial interests, which Putin stressed were at the heart of Prigozhin's gripe with authorities.

During a televised appearance at a military gathering, Putin alleged that the Wagner Group was paid more than 86 billion rubles (over $1 billion) by the Russian government and Prigozhin's Concord Group earned 80 billion rubles ($941 million) from a contract for supplying food items to the military. Setting the stage for an investigation, Putin added: "I hope they didn't steal anything. Rather, I hope they didn't steal too much."

Russian authorities and talking heads fully realize the danger of Prigozhin's mass appeal, with his pre-mutiny media blitz that underscored the disparity between the way Russian elites protect their own safety and a lavish lifestyle, as opposed to the sacrifices that are demanded from everyday citizens. His statements that described Putin's motives for launching the invasion as "lies" were equally significant—and dangerous for the Russian regime.

Prigozhin's expletive-laden diatribes resonated with average Russians and Wagner Group fighters were welcomed by locals in the Russian city of Rostov-on-Don. Putin's propagandists desperately tried to flip the narrative, by claiming that the residents of Rostov didn't cheer the Wagnerites, but merely celebrated their departure from the city.

During Solovyov's show, political scientist Vladimir Kornilov dismissed Western reporting on the matter as "fake news" and alleged that all of it was simply made up.

He comically claimed, "Almost all Western media came out with front-page photos of the Rostov residents hugging and kissing the Wagnerites, claiming that it means they supported them. Of course, no one noted that they were merely seeing them off, celebrating that the Wagner Group was leaving Rostov!"

Lukashenko's involvement, which was initially cheered as wise and crucial, is likewise being downplayed, since it came too close to outshining Putin—a cardinal sin that is not allowed by the state media. Appearing on *The Evening With Vladimir Solovyov*, State Duma member Mikhail Delyagin said: "President of Belarus Lukashenko saved Russia in its current state. Period." This statement was met with dirty looks from fellow panelists.

Andrey Sidorov, Deputy Dean of world politics at the Moscow State University, incredulously asked: "Saved?" Delyagin got the message and corrected himself: "OK, he made a significant contribution to resolving the crisis."

Ivan Starodubtsev, an expert on Russian-Turkish relations, further cleaned it up: "I disagree that Lukashenko was the savior, I believe Putin was!"

Kremlin News Stars Unravel in Post-Mutiny Television Fiasco

The chaotic Putin vs. Prigozhin showdown appears to have broken the Russian propaganda machine.

Originally published by *The Daily Beast* on July 12, 2023

In the aftermath of a short-lived mutiny by Yevgeny Prigozhin and his private Wagner Group army, Russian state media has been struggling to control the narrative. The initial outrage about Prigozhin's treasonous deed going unpunished was replaced by claims there was no armed mutiny.

Now, the propaganda machine is overridden by two contrasting images of the Wagner boss—one as a patriotic hero, and the other as a shadowy criminal.

Even the most seasoned Kremlin propagandists had a hard time with the dizzying descent: from glorifying the "heroic deeds" of Prigozhin's brutal fighters and his role in Russia's invasion of Ukraine to portraying the Wagnerites and their leader as a bunch of convicts and unsavory characters.

That disarray was palpable on a recent broadcast of the state TV show *60 Minutes*, when Eduard Petrov, who heads the network's Legal Programs Production Service, asserted that criminal investigations against Prigozhin were far from over.

Instead of joining in, the host, Evgeny Popov, repeatedly mentioned how successful the Wagner group had been in Ukraine. Other panelists contributed mainly by rolling their eyes and grimacing. When offered a chance to speak, they immediately changed the topic, leading Petrov to question whether they were too afraid to talk about Prigozhin.

Sunday's *Vesti Nedeli* followed suit, attempting to undo the efforts of Prigozhin's media empire, describing it as "an army of bloggers and so-called journalists" that was portraying him as a Robin

Hood of sorts. The program set out to prove that the "wannabe Robin Hood" was actually "robbing the hood," with hosts recalling Prigozhin's criminal record—down to candy bowls and napkin holders he stole 43 years ago—as well as his alleged attempts to take over the city of St. Petersburg, mafia style.

Even the most prominent state-sponsored propagandists are floundering to produce a consistent narrative about the mercenary boss, arguably because Prigozhin's exploits are directly tied to his decades-long relationship with Vladimir Putin.

One of Prigozhin's main cheerleaders, host Vladimir Solovyov, went from praising the Wagnerites and participating in the filming of their commercials, to complaining that it took them over 200 days to take Bakhmut. He snapped back at his viewers for defending Prigozhin and angrily claimed that he could take Kyiv in three days.

While condemning Prigozhin, Solovyov repeatedly urged the Wagnerites to officially join Russia's dwindling armed forces.

After the Kremlin's revelation that President Putin met with Prigozhin just days after the failed mutiny, Solovyov again changed course at breakneck speed. During Monday's broadcast of *The Evening With Vladimir Solovyov*, the host alleged that the group's undisclosed location—(most of them are not eager to sign up for regular military service)—is all a part of Putin's ingenious plan.

"According to what [Putin spokesman] Dmitry Peskov says, it turns out that on June 29th, there was a meeting of the mutineers—and let me remind you, Vladimir Vladimirovich Putin clearly defined it as a mutiny. These people came and it turns out, they are ready to go and carry out any task that is set by the Supreme Commander," Solovyov said. "Now, this is an equation with many unknowns! Tens of thousands of well-trained, well-equipped men can pop up on any stretch of the front line, because now we know that they are not against Putin! They say they are Putin's soldiers!"

Solovyov added: "Vilnius is nearby... so is Kyiv, so is Kharkiv, or Mykolaiv and Odesa! Twenty thousand storm troopers is a major headache! When they're assembled into a fist, they can cause major problems!"

Top Putin Crony Curses Audience and Berates Colleague On-Air

Moscow's most famous mouthpiece resorted to calling members of his audience "idiots" and "cretins" when challenged about his position on the latest war scandal to rock the Kremlin.

Originally published by *The Daily Beast* on July 13, 2023

Yevgeny Prigozhin's armed mutiny has exposed unprecedented cracks in the regime of Vladimir Putin—and the divide keeps widening. On Thursday, decorated Kremlin propagandist Vladimir Solovyov attempted to squash the latest controversy coming out of Moscow, only to see his efforts backfire dramatically.

On his radio show, The *Full Contact*, Solovyov weighed in on news that Major General Ivan Popov, who commanded Russian military units in southern Ukraine, was allegedly dismissed from his position for informing military leadership about the grim realities of Russian forces on the frontlines. In an audio message published by Russian lawmaker Andrey Gurulyov—an ever-present fixture on Solovyov's shows—Popov complained about the deaths of Russian soldiers and the lack of Russian counter-artillery systems and reconnaissance.

Addressing the scandal, Solovyov compared Popov to Prigozhin and criticized his friend Gurulyov for disseminating the recording. "I think that publicizing his statement is a brave and phenomenally incorrect step.

Popov is a respected general who had every opportunity to carry his point of view across, since he knows many people in the presidential administration very well. He could have picked up the phone and gotten his message and his point of view to the Supreme Commander, with whom he met, as I understand it."

Solovyov went on: "For him to make it public was an emotional step which was wrong, in my opinion. Now the Ukrainian media is happily rehashing it. Publicizing this does not make us stronger.... As a combat general, he unfortunately was excessively emotional. He recorded a strong statement, I understand him. But it shouldn't have been made public."

Viewers immediately barraged Solovyov with a bevy of messages — and to the host's dismay, most of them supported Popov's stance.

One viewer wrote: "Perhaps his leadership shouldn't have allowed things to get that far and then remove him." Solovyov fired back: "After something like this, you could not avoid removing him!"

He added: "Every time you move on to the way of ultimatums, you are making a colossal mistake. You can't do this! Every general understands this very well. It no longer matters who's in the right! These methods of uncovering the truth are unacceptable in times of war... Otherwise, a comparison to Prigozhin is unavoidable!"

He hinted at cracking down against those who refuse to sugarcoat the problems, referring to "the Great Purge" by Joseph Stalin: "Do you want 1937 that preceded 1945? Is this where everything is going?"

"For me, it's extremely sad that [Popov] succumbed to his emotions and decided to act in this manner. His questionable methods overshadow his goals. It is a big mistake! And it was a big mistake for my friend, Lt. Gen. Andrey Gurulyov, to publicize it... The country is at war! You have to be able to control your emotions!"

Apparently failing to follow his own advice, Solovyov angrily snapped back at one listener after another for supporting Popov. "Some cretin says we never declared war. Some cretin is trying to lecture me. Listen, you, cretin, get out of here! I'm responding to some idiot by the name of Andrey... I don't care at all whether we officially declared war," he said.

Another audience member, identifying herself as Yulia, complained that military commanders are not being allowed to tell the truth. Solovyov fired back: "Who isn't being allowed to do it? How can you not allow a combat general to tell the truth? Why are you pouring out this nonsense? You have to shoot people at the front for lying! That's for sure!" Solovyov proceeded to complain about the widespread media coverage of Popov's statement: "Now it's everywhere! In the enemy media and everywhere else, everyone is writing about this!"

Another listener, Irina, wrote that Popov did not violate any rules by recording his message. Solovyov promptly shut her down: "Yes, he did. If you don't understand what you're talking about, that is your problem!" He then yelled at another commentator, without specifying what he said or asked: "Andrey, you are a pathetic nobody, a cretin! Get out of here, Ukrainian swine!"

Afterwards, the host—notorious for his neurotic behavior and frequent emotional outbursts—demanded: "I call on everyone to stop and think before making any emotional statements... Anything else leads to anarchy and death!"

The host bitterly complained about the Wagnerites who are "resting," instead of participating in the conflict alongside Russian troops, despite recently claiming that Prigozhin's mercenary army consists of "Putin's soldiers," ready to carry out his every command.

Referring to another Russian general who has not appeared publicly since the coup, another commentator asked the host: "Where is Surovikin?"

"I would also like to know the answer to that question," Solovyov responded ominously. "When the time is right, we will find out."

Kremlin Flacks Tease Next 'Global' Targets of Putin's Wrath

Russian lawmakers and pro-Kremlin news stars have taken to live television to bet on the next international crisis Putin is eyeing after Ukraine.

Originally published by *The Daily Beast* on August 22, 2023

Wagner Group chief Yevgeny Prigozhin, whose short-lived mutiny against the Kremlin made global headlines in June, reappeared in Africa on Monday with a brief video message. In it, he claimed that Wagner is "making Russia even greater on all continents, and making Africa even more free. We bring justice and happiness to the African people."

The mercenary boss' return coincided with the emergence of a new campaign on Russian state media programs, where pro-Kremlin pundits and lawmakers have been pushing for Russian President Vladimir Putin to "go global" with his "special military operation" in Ukraine.

During his Monday appearance on *60 Minutes*, State Duma member Andrey Gurulyov declared that "Today, the whole world is a special military operation!" Throughout the segment, the lawmaker and other panelists claimed that Russia is not interested in peace accords—a view that is frequently echoed on many pro-government TV and radio programs.

Referring to recent comments by General Mark Milley—the U.S.'s highest-ranking military officer, who recently suggested that a peace deal might be one of the ways of ending Russia's invasion of Ukraine—Korotchenko stressed: "General Milley included diplomacy as one of the options, meaning the signing of a peace deal on conditions that are not acceptable to Russia: return to the borders of 1991 and reparations that will have to be paid by generations of Russians to the Kyiv regime. Would this option suit us? I think not."

Instead, according to the Putin loyalists, the Kremlin intends to expand its horizons far beyond Ukraine, undermining and confronting the West at every turn. Gurulyov laid out what he sees as the Kremlin's potential course of action—not just in Ukraine, but across the world.

"I would like to turn our attention to the Asia-Pacific region. The issue of Taiwan is there, it isn't going to disappear. Americans said they will first contain China and then North Korea, but now they're in a situation where they have to contain both!" he said.

Gurulyov added, "Based on the statements made by North Koreans, including the ones they made here, nuclear war is inevitable—it's only a matter of who and where will start it! It's crystal clear that if a conflict starts, the United States will get involved... This will 100 percent include the sinking of the US Navy in the Pacific Ocean. There is no other way! This is an achievable goal, even if China acts alone."

For the Russian politician, there was no question about which side Russia would take in the impending global crises. "Of course, North Korea's goal is the unification with South Korea and the disappearance of the border that separates one people. People ask, 'What if they lose? What is our part in this situation?' For us, it's not acceptable for the North Koreans to lose. Otherwise, NATO forces will be stationed across from our Vladivostok!" he said. "For us, there is no other option but to get prepared for the challenges that are happening in the Asia-Pacific region. These challenges are already happening, we should be preparing today, right now and figuring out how to solve this problem!"

During his appearance, the lawmaker claimed that Russia's Pacific Fleet is "actively preparing" for such a conflict—and predicted that the "the first strike will be against the oldest enemy of Koreans, Japan, accompanied by supportive hooting from South Korea."

"We're with those who fight against colonialism," he said, emphasizing that Russia's special military operation is global and not limited to Ukraine. "Here you have all of the elements of World

War III that are currently emerging. I'm not even mentioning the Persian problem, the threats in the Arctic and Afghanistan. We should be ready to deal with all of these challenges."

On Tuesday, Marina Kim, one of the hosts of Russia's Channel 1, appeared on Vladimir Solovyov's show *Full Contact*, where she talked about her role in the soon to be released TV project, The New World.

Kim said it would be aimed at forecasting what the new world order will look like in the coming decades, considering Russia' efforts to undermine the U.S. dollar as a currency and Western influence as a whole.

Arguing that Russian experts are so highly intellectual that they know more about China than the Chinese, Kim noted that even those superb intellectuals are not sure what the map of the world will look like in 2073.

Solovyov, who frequently threatens the West with nuclear strikes, asked an uncharacteristically sobering question: "Will Russia even exist in the future?" Kim cheerfully assured him that Russia's destiny is to keep leading the world — but acknowledged that it can do so only in concert with China.

Putin Stooge Loses It When Confronted About Prigozhin's Death

Moscow's most famous mouthpiece descended into a blind rage after his narrative about the death of Wagner Boss Yevgeny Prigozhin was publicly questioned.

Originally published by *The Daily Beast* on August 24, 2023

Russian state media appears to have one goal in the aftermath of the plane crash that reportedly killed the head of Wagner Group, Yevgeny Prigozhin, the group's founder Dmitry Utkin, and their associates on Wednesday: to deflect any blame away from Russian President Vladimir Putin.

On Thursday, state media network Rossiya-24 referenced a criminal investigation that was opened by the Investigative Committee of the Russian Federation, citing "potential violations of air transportation safety and operation rules" that may have caused the crash.

The most popular star of Russian state television, Vladimir Solovyov, likewise did his best to divert the focus from the most likely beneficiary of the incident—even going so far as to claim that Putin had nothing to gain from Prigozhin's demise.

During his show *Full Contact* Thursday morning, Solovyov complained about the Western media's coverage that described the incident as "Putin's revenge."

"Prigozhin and Wagner did not present any threat to the Kremlin! None at all… They presented a colossal threat for the European countries! I'm trying to figure out who might have benefited from it. The very last person it would benefit is Putin!" he said. "Putin gave a word, he forgave all of them… Putin was never known not to keep his word! He is a man of his reputation… all about the laws," he insisted.

Although he conceded that Prigozhin's "march on Moscow" was indeed a "stab in the back" of the Russian president, the host brushed off any possibility of a revenge killing, asserting, "We're not a gang! We are not the mafia! This is not Mario Puzo's book The Godfather. We are a nation of laws!"

Solovyov ticked off other "suspects" he claimed could be behind the incident. He alleged that NATO countries benefit from Prigozhin's demise "to a colossal degree," because they want to undermine Russia's military capabilities in Africa.

The next alleged beneficiary named by Solovyov was, of course, Ukraine: "For Ukraine, this is a major celebration! Yesterday, the Ukrainian segment of the internet exploded in total happiness!" The host pointed out that if any remnants of an explosive device on board the plane are found in the future, Ukraine would likely acknowledge its involvement.

"For them, Prigozhin is target number one!" he said, suggesting that Ukrainians blew up Prigozhin to mark their Independence Day on Thursday.

When a female audience member challenged his conspiracy theory by stating that an operation of this magnitude was too complex to have been organized by the Ukrainians, Solovyov exploded in rage, spewing insults and vulgarities at her. Describing the commentator as a "fantastic fool," Solovyov asked, "How hard is it to sneak a bomb on board? It is the simplest thing there is… I'm so sick of fools writing to me! I hate cretins! I just hate them!" He referred to multiple other viewers writing into the show as "degenerates" and refused to address their commentary.

Solovyov then accused Western media outlets of attempting to shift the blame from the real perpetrators responsible for the crash, just to screw over Putin. "The Anglo-Saxons are undoubtedly behind this crime!" he fumed. Solovyov went on to name France, Poland, the Baltic states, and NATO countries in general as other likely beneficiaries of the incident. "This does not benefit Russia at all!" he reiterated.

Just one day before the fatal crash, Solovyov had been complaining that Russia's main weakness is its failure to retaliate against those who cause it harm: "We aren't retaliating for anything!" One of the grievances he brought up specifically pertained to Prigozhin: "Fifteen pilots have perished during a mutiny! So? Who answered for them? No one!" he said.

In the aftermath of the short-lived mutiny back in June, Solovyov and his guests on *The Evening With Vladimir Solovyov* were aghast that the Wagner chief was allowed to live after his march on Moscow. State Duma member Andrey Gurulyov, retired deputy Commander of the 58th Combined Arms Army of the Southern Military District, said that "traitors have to be destroyed" and urged Prigozhin and Utkin to commit suicide before a bullet finds them. "There are no other options for traitors," he stressed.

In July, Eduard Petrov, who heads the Legal Programs Production Service, insisted that criminal investigations against Prigozhin were far from over, while various state media outlets portrayed Prigozhin and the Wagnerites as a bunch of unsavory characters, convicted of a plethora of shameful crimes.

Despite that earlier stance, Solovyov claimed there was no coordinated media campaign to besmirch Prigozhin, referring to him as "Hero of Russia." He called on Wagner fighters to take Kyiv "in honor of Prigozhin," and urged viewers to consider who benefits from Prigozhin's death, naming the French, Americans, and Ukrainians as the most likely culprits. The weatherman, Evgeny Tishkovets, then chimed in with his own theory about the plane crash. He blamed the weather.

Who Assassinated Prigozhin?
Duh, the English

Russia's belief in the cunning of UK spies and saboteurs is a go-to explanation when things go wrong for the Kremlin.

Originally published by *The Center for European Policy Analysis* (CEPA) on August 31, 2023

In the ethereal world of Russian state media, Vladimir Putin is never to blame for anything bad. Russia's almost-emperor is above rebuke — an unwritten rule his otherwise cynical and snarling propagandists obediently follow.

Conveniently, however, there is a long-established lineup of the usual suspects, presented to domestic and international audiences whenever blame has to be assigned. The United States is prominent in this list, but what really gets the Kremlin's mouthpieces agitated is the diabolical work of the United Kingdom, invariably referred to as England.

The latest case in point is the untimely demise of Yevgeny Prigozhin, the Wagner Group's head mercenary, who had led the organization on a bloody but lucrative global rampage funded by the Kremlin. The ex-convict enjoyed easy access to Vladimir Putin even as the Russian government constantly refused to admit that the group even existed.

From Ukraine and Syria and the interference in US elections, Prigozhin enjoyed the status of Putin's untouchable shadow warrior — until his poorly judged mini-mutiny in June put an end to his sledgehammer-wielding reign of terror. Once the short-lived uprising was over, the Kremlin's mouthpieces on state television were furious.

Despite Putin's public assurances that all was forgiven, official propagandists revealingly insisted that Prigozhin was a traitor and should die, along with his right-hand man, the founder of Wagner, Dmitry Utkin. Prigozhin must have realized that this did not augur well.

During the first post-mutiny broadcast of the TV show, *Sunday Evening With Vladimir Solovyov*, State Duma member, General Andrey Gurulyov, retired deputy commander of the 58th Combined Arms Army, said: "I am firmly convinced that during wartime, traitors have to be destroyed! Today, no matter who says what, whatever fairy tales they are telling, a bullet to the forehead is the sole salvation for Prigozhin and [Dmitry] Utkin. They know me! They know that I stand behind my every word. There is no other option!"

Gurulyov suggested Prigozhin and Utkin be given the option of committing suicide, or else being executed for their actions, as he reiterated: "Treason cannot be forgiven under any circumstances! It simply can't be forgiven, regardless of any past achievements! I will repeat it once again: the only way out for these friends is to kill themselves before a bullet finds them! There are no other options for traitors."

Just as Gurulyov had predicted, Prigozhin and Utkin perished in a fiery plane crash on August 23, two months to the day after their mutiny began. Many noted they had been meeting with unnamed Kremlin officials just before the fatal flight—providing a convenient way for anyone interested to track their whereabouts thereafter.

The smoking remnants of the warlord's personal jet had barely cooled before the propaganda narrative took a bizarre twist. The same propagandists who insisted that Prigozhin must die now dismissed the possibility that the Kremlin had heeded their demands, and focused on deflecting the blame from Putin.

Leading Russian propagandist Vladimir Solovyov immediately pointed the finger at the regime's default enemy: "The Anglo-Saxons are undoubtedly behind this crime!" This despite his call one day before the crash for someone had to be held accountable for the deaths of as many as 15 Russian Air Force pilots shot down by Wagner during the course of the mutiny.

So great is Russia's habit of framing the proverbial "Anglo-Saxons" as the perennial suspects, that they are being blamed not only for past offenses but also for future crimes. After forensic testing reportedly confirmed Prigozhin's death, former politician Igor Markov appeared on *Sunday Evening With Vladimir Solovyov*, to blame the British, to predict that General Sergey Surovikin—a top Russian general sacked but not seen since the failed insurrection— might be next.

Discussing Prigozhin's demise, Markov feverishly stated: "I think, special services of only two countries were capable of this: the US and Britain... I have no doubt this is the handiwork of the British!" He added, "All that's missing for a complete picture is for Surovikin to die of a heart attack! I'm not joking, he should be very careful, they will be doing this! In order for them to complete all of their puzzles, this is all that is missing."

This statement caused some alarm among those in the Kremlin overseeing state propagandists, who immediately cut this portion of Markov's diatribe from the broadcast. The show's rerun was missing any mention of Surovikin, as did the archived recording on its official website. That portion of the program, which formerly started at 02:22:07, was neatly removed.

This is unusual since even the most outlandish statements on state TV shows are usually left intact. Perhaps Surovikin truly is in danger, due to his alleged prior knowledge of Prigozhin's mutiny. And blaming the British would be a lot harder if this retribution had previously been predicted on Kremlin-controlled state television.

Regardless of what happens next, Russia always includes the British on the list of its top suspects. This is not a coincidence, but a well-established tradition. The phrase *Anglichanka gadit*, which means, "The English are causing us problems," is a well-known expression that is used to describe everything from sanctions to assassinations. Its first utterance is ascribed, albeit without proof, to the legendary Russian General Alexander Suvorov in the 18th century.

It has remained in circulation ever since, having been immortalized in poetry during the reign of the last Emperor of Russia, Nicholas II, and repeatedly used in literary works ever since. A slightly modified version of the expression was even included in the Explanatory Dictionary of the Russian Language in 1935, underlining its deep roots among Soviet communists who had fought a fierce shadow war with Britain's MI6. This concept remains heavily entrenched in Russia's popular culture and psyche.

The Kremlin's 2006 assassination of Alexander Litvinenko and the 2018 poisoning of Sergei Skripal on British soil made for convenient occasions to use this catchall phrase. The evergreen expression usually accompanies calls from top Kremlin propagandists to turn Great Britain into a radioactive wasteland using Russia's nuclear weapons.

That however would be a waste. Without Britain, who could be blamed for dastardly acts?

'Woe to My Enemies'
Rages Russia's Mouthpiece-in-Chief

If there was ever a perfect example of the way Russian propaganda operates and the degree of brazen arrogance exhibited by Vladimir Putin's pet propagandists, the September 6 edition of *Full Contact* with Vladimir Solovyov was it.

Originally published by *The Center for European Policy Analysis* (CEPA) on September 9, 2023

There was fakery and pomposity, but mostly outrage, when the Kremlin's No. 1 mouthpiece responded to a public attack made by critics within Russia. There was a wonderment in Vladimir Solovyov's eyes and voice that ideas like this could be stated in public. And then a promise to root out those responsible for such lese-majesty. "You know how this country works," he told his enemies in what can only have been intended as a threat.

The drama developed on September 5 after a poignant essay by Valery Garbuzov, who was at the time the director of the US and Canada Studies Institute (ISKRAN) at Russia's Academy of Sciences. ISKRAN is one of Russia's leading think tanks.

Garbuzov decided, heroically, to tell the truth in a public space rammed with lies. He must have known what was coming.

In a piece entitled "On the lost illusions of a bygone era," published in Nezavisimaya Gazeta, the longtime think tank leader (he had worked at ISKRAN for 23 years) argued that Russia is in the throes of a post-imperial crisis and has returned to expansionism under Putin's administration, even though Russia's "menacing character" was kept under wraps for more than 30 years. Garbuzov explained that Russia's ruling elites perpetuate anti-Western mythology to remain in power, resurrecting long-outdated narratives about the ever-present "Anglo-Saxons."

He explained how the Russian government is using state-controlled media to further this agenda, stating, "These myths are being spread day and night by a new generation of well-paid professional political manipulators and numerous panelists on television talk shows."

Garbuzov noted: "The purpose of all this is quite obvious — plunging one's own society into a world of illusions and accompanied by great-power and patriotic rhetoric, undisguised and deliberate indefinite retention of power at any cost, preservation of property and a political regime by the current ruling elite and the oligarchy integrated with it."

Taking an obvious swipe at Putin and his pet propagandists, Garbuzov wrote: "The current domestic minions of authoritarianism (like the satraps of ancient Eastern despotisms that have sunk into oblivion), apparently completely devoid of any historical consciousness, without hesitation, with touching tenderness, sincerely identify the head of state with the state itself, the temporary ruler of the country with a great national and historical constant."

The satraps were predictably upset. Very upset. In Putin's increasingly dictatorial Russia, no one speaks in this way about his trusted spokespeople. Solovyov appeared soon afterward, visibly furious and threatening legal action as well as less detailed promises of revenge. Shortly thereafter, Garbuzov was fired.

His former colleagues at the ISKRAN then penned a message of support, identifying Solovyov's program as the heart of the witch hunt and comparing him to Hitler's propaganda chief, Joseph Goebbels. Predictably, the show of solidarity was short-lived. The fear of further retribution likely motivated Konstantin Remchukov, Editor-in-Chief and CEO of Nezavisimaya Gazeta, to quickly remove the post from the website.

It wasn't enough to calm Solovyov. He began his show, "My name is Vladimir Solovyov, and woe to my enemies!" and threatened to eviscerate his opponents using Russia's mock justice system. That made Solovyov very certain of a positive outcome, as he threatened his critics, "I will fuck you up!"

The accusation of spreading "primitive lies" and being compared to Goebbels got under Solovyov's skin (even though, as a broadcaster, he may have greater similarities to Axis Sally and Lord Haw-Haw than to the true heads of Russian propaganda, men like Kremlin string-puller Alexey Gromov.)

After concluding his diatribe, Solovyov gave a shameless demonstration of precisely the factual distortion his critics accuse him of. He showcased the trailer for Hulu's new documentary series, "Drugs. Power. Chaos," announcing that the film focused on Volodymyr Zelenskyy and examined the impact his supposed drug use had on the latest events in Ukraine.

The host, who routinely demands more censorship in his own country, bemoaned the alleged interference by the US government in blocking the docu-series premiere. Solovyov accused American democracy of being "sick" and theatrically sighed.

The trouble is that the supposed documentary is imaginary. It does not exist. A phony trailer was posted on a Telegram account clearly marked as a "parody." It was then shared on an obscure blog. Anyone who cared about fact-checking could have discovered this within seconds with a website search.

Much later in the show, Solovyov was informed that the documentary was a complete fake. There followed a rare moment when viewers could observe a master propagandist presented with one of his lies, live on air. What would he do? Without blinking an eye, Solovyov remarked: "They say it's fake! I don't know about that. Every frame of it is true! Every phrase and every answer is true! So what's fake about it?"

Russia Lauds North Korea's 'Square-Headed Dude' and His Pauper Legions

While Russia claims to have escaped the grip of Western sanctions, everyday Russians are struggling. The Kremlin's mouthpieces responded with admiration for penniless North Koreans.

Originally published by *The Center for European Policy Analysis* (CEPA) on September 22, 2023

The week-long visit of Kim Jong Un to Russia couldn't have come at a more perfect time, allowing Putin's mouthpieces to gush over Russia's newfound affinity for North Korea, to express admiration for the hermit kingdom, and conclude that viewers should reject "savage capitalism."

During last week's broadcast of *The Evening With Vladimir Solovyov*, political scientist Sergey Mikheyev praised Kim Jong Un as a "dude with a square head," who is keeping the West on tenterhooks. He marveled at the way the people of North Korea were able to withstand Western pressure because they aren't sensitive to the absence of modern luxuries and are therefore inured to sanctions.

"What can you forbid to North Koreans?" Mikheyev said. "To drink Coca-Cola? They don't have it anyway! To watch Hollywood movies? They don't have them anyway! You'll turn off their Internet? They don't have it anyway! You won't import iPhones? They don't have them anyway! You will forbid them to travel to Europe and America? They aren't traveling anyway! There is no way to get to them."

The irony of this celebration of hopeless poverty seemed lost upon the host, Vladimir Solovyov, who uses the latest version of the iPhone, had his $9m Italian properties on Lake Como seized by the authorities and complained about the sanctions-related inability to service foreign-made cars.

Presenters on Solovyov's own channel, Solovyov Live, took the austere line of reasoning even further. The host of *"Day Z"*, Yulia Vityazeva, played video clips of a Russian military choir giving a concert in Pyongyang, claiming that the appearance of "clean and smiling" people in the audience disproved Western narratives about the scarcity of food. She said that on closer inspection, all the stereotypes are shattered "into a million pieces," while admitting that Russians have habitually ignored North Korea, and acknowledged she's never visited.

On Karnaukhov's Labyrinth, host Sergey Karnaukhov called upon Russia to reject "savage capitalism" and usher in a North Korean-style asceticism, for the sake of the state. He scolded wealthy Russians for becoming accustomed to living in the lap of luxury and added: "Turns out, there are different values and a different lifestyle. North Korea preserved them and even increased them. It means we can rely on them! We can go there, look at their life, and see that what we've considered to be valuable in our country isn't valuable at all."

Karnaukhov added: "North Korea is offering its system of values! We've been chuckling at Juche [North Korea's state ideology], but turns out it isn't funny. Turns out we should laugh at ourselves! We've dissolved our identity in hedonism and leisure. Russia no longer exists! That's what we have achieved. But now is our chance and all will be well."

Even as Russia's tightly controlled state media has been perpetuating the myth of an unscathed, booming economy, the cracks are showing. Prominent propagandists now regularly acknowledge that things are difficult and prices are on the rise. Videos of everyday Russians periodically posted on social media recognize that price increases and high-interest rates leave them unable to afford much more than the bare necessities.

In one of the street interviews posted on Telegram by a popular user @slvn_pomet, an unidentified woman advised all poor Russians to simply "eat less and then everything will be alright."

However, at least one leading propagandist saw the problem with this thinking. On September 18, Sergey Mardan, the host of

"Mardan" on the Solovyov Live channel, attempted to raise the alarm over a potential repeat of what happened in the Soviet Union.

The host asserted that Russia can be destroyed by its internal problems: "What can fuel this discontent? Economic problems, poverty, hunger, currency depreciation, inflation." Mardan recalled the 1980s when the Soviet people suffered chronic food shortages. He added: "The problems with food existed all the way until the dissolution of the Soviet Union. They varied from region to region, but always existed."

He concluded that this failure to meet even the most basic needs created a widespread feeling of discomfort and said: "I think this contributed to the end of the Soviet Union more than the CIA, Mossad, BND, MI6, and the rest of the global intelligence services put together."

And yet the Kremlin is unable to contain the worsening situation and is tightening its grip, determined to contain the blowback.

The media's celebration of North Korea paints a grotesque portrait of the future that might lie ahead for the average citizen. Of course, this dreary vision would certainly exclude Putin and his clique of oligarchs and cronies, including the propagandists. For the common people, the future looks rather less cheery.

Putin's Pals Brag: Elon Musk 'Really Is Our Agent!'

Kremlin propagandists are rejoicing after Congress omitted aid to Ukraine from its most recent government funding bill.

Originally published by *The Daily Beast* on October 02, 2023

Russian experts have long predicted that it's only a matter of time before U.S. aid to Ukraine is jeopardized by war fatigue and domestic issues. The MAGA branch of the Republican Party is currently delivering in spades, as a stopgap funding bill that was passed by Congress to avert a shutdown excluded much-needed funding for Ukraine.

As a special bonus for supporters of the Russian war effort, Elon Musk over the weekend mocked Ukrainian President Volodymyr Zelensky on X (formerly Twitter) for seeking international support to help his country repel a genocidal aggressor.

Predictably, Musk's cruelty brought joy to Putin's mouthpieces. During Monday's broadcast of *60 Minutes,* state TV host Olga Skabeeva noted, "It's impossible not to notice that the West is getting sick not only of Zelensky but Ukraine as a whole, as a circumstance that is constantly siphoning away their money. Elon Musk is magnificent, he is wonderful and perhaps he really is our agent! He published a meme about a beggar that recently became popular, using Zelensky's face instead of that person. It says, 'When it's been five minutes and you haven't asked for a billion dollars in aid.'"

Skabeeva mentioned the congressional bill that specifically omitted aid to Ukraine and cheerfully noted, "Only recently, it was impossible to even imagine anything like this!" She also surmised, "Unless something changes in the next 45 days, the United States will certainly stop helping Ukraine!" Skabeeva described Ukraine as "a walking corpse" and opined that the West is ready to write it off as a loss.

Thrilled with Musk's contribution to the Russian trove of anti-Ukrainian propaganda, Skabeeva praised his wealth, his commentary, and the "exquisite hat" he recently donned during a visit to the southern U.S. border.

State Duma deputy Andrey Isayev concurred, saying, "The strategy of our president turned out to be quite wise. Just a short while ago, the West seemed to be a consolidated and united front that was fighting against us. This consolidation keeps on fading."

Isayev pointed out, "We remember that when Zelensky went to the United States one year ago, he received a standing ovation in their parliament." He noted that this year, the president of Ukraine wasn't even allowed to speak before Congress and later, both the Republicans and the Democrats voted for a bill that cut out funding for Ukraine. Isayev concluded, "We have arrived!"

Political scientist Vladimir Kornilov added that the draft law of the Lend-Lease Act, which authorized the Biden administration to lend or lease military equipment to Ukraine and other Eastern European countries, quietly expired September 30 without being extended.

He concluded that the program represented the faith of the West in Ukraine's eventual victory and the failure to renew it signifies that U.S. faith and commitment to the war effort expired along with the law.

Dmitry Abzalov, Director of Russia's Center for Strategic Communications, said that the changes Russia is observing in the United States would be unthinkable just one year earlier. He surmised that the diminishing U.S. support will bear fruit in the theater of military operations in the near future, leading to the decline in Western support overall and the corresponding deterioration of Ukraine's defense capabilities.

Some of the most prominent Kremlin mouthpieces repeatedly reiterated that Putin's invasion is nothing more than a land grab and a gambit to restore the Russian empire, with an unabashedly genocidal agenda towards Ukraine. Nonetheless, the moral clarity on this issue is taking the back seat to domestic power struggles in the United States.

During the evening broadcast of *60 Minutes,* Skabeeva was still praising Musk for his anti-Ukrainian stance. She proudly noted that "the wealthiest person in the world" is now known as "Elon Moskal," meaning "Elon the Muscovite."

'Only Good News Today' — Russia's Propagandists Delight as Israelis Die

Russia reacts to events in Israel with schadenfreude and mockery.

Originally published by *The Center for European Policy Analysis* (CEPA) on October 8, 2023

While the Western world reacted with horror to the heart-breaking scenes of Hamas gunmen preying on Israeli civilians on October 7, the reaction in Russia was markedly different.

Kremlin-endorsed propagandists celebrated the fighting as a distraction to tear the West's eyes from Ukraine, produced new conspiracy theories to explain the news, and delighted in the discomfort and fear of Russian Jews who have emigrated to Israel.

There's yet no evidence that Russia knew of the impending attack, although it has fostered ties with Hamas. In March, Hamas reportedly sent a high-level delegation to Russia and held talks with Russian Foreign Minister Sergey Lavrov, warning the Kremlin that the group's "patience" with Israel was "running out." Senior Hamas figures also visited Russia in May and September 2022. The group has said its attack was supported by Iran and other countries but did not name them.

But while the Kremlin may not have been directly involved, many of its citizens are openly antisemitic, as are senior officials. Military correspondent Dmitry Steshin, known for his overtly genocidal statements about Ukrainians, posted on his Telegram channel Russky Tarantas that there should be "not a drop of pity or sympathy" for Israelis, including former Russian citizens. Steshin complained about people who left Russia for Israel, describing them as "relocants."

He wrote: "We stayed here and are still standing knee-deep in blood. Let the ones responsible for our tears do that as well! Or let them run, to refresh their historical memory. Greetings to the relocants!"

Sergey Mardan, one of Russia's best-known propagandists and host of the eponymous show on the state channel Solovyov Live, wrote on his Telegram channel that he was happy for the Russians who moved to Israel because they didn't want to live in a country that is at war with its neighbors.

He added, "This mess is beneficial for Russia, because the globalist toad will be distracted from Ukraine and will get busy trying to put out the eternal Middle Eastern fire." Mardan explained, "Iran is our real military ally. Israel is an ally of the United States. Therefore, choosing a side is easy!"

During his show, Mardan, the host made a bizarre comparison between Palestine and Russia, claiming that Russia "has been occupied since 1991" and is only now seeking to correct the situation.

Russian propagandists frequently claim that Ukraine is "occupying" Russian lands, which Russia is fighting to reclaim.

Head of RT, Margarita Simonyan, wrote on her X/Twitter account, "The country that is not at war with its neighbors is again at war with its neighbors. We await the exodus of Russian pacifists. Then again, we won't hold our breath."

Host of the show *Morning Z* on Solovyov Live, Boris Yakemenko, blamed the violence on gender issues (presumably a reference to LGBT+ debates in the West), stating, "What is happening today in different corners of the world shows that the world has come to a dangerous point, beyond which lies the new world. Crossing into it will be preceded by horrendous casualties, because of a feeling of total injustice, insanity, a total lack of understanding of what is happening, with all of these genders, with all of these strange phenomena!"

Yakemenko read caustic messages from members of his audience, pondering which citizenship Russian relocants would choose this time. He addressed former Russian compatriots, telling them to "Go ahead and run, or hide in bomb shelters."

During his show on October 7, Vladimir Solovyov, described the Hamas attack as a "loud slap" to Israel and its intelligence services, assigning all fault to America as a "guarantor of peace in the region" and baselessly blaming Ukraine for providing arms to Hamas. (Hamas' main arms supplier is actually Iran).

Such accusations were repeated across Russian state media, despite its military illogic, clear Ukrainian support for Israel, and the enormous difficulties of shipping arms to Gaza.

Military correspondent Alexander Kots discussed this preposterous talking point with Komsomolskaya Pravda and made it clear that he isn't rooting either for Israel or for the Palestinians. Kots then went on to say: "In the event of a conflict, it's anticipated that we must be on someone's side. I don't want to take either side. One helps Kyiv arm itself and fight against Russian troops, while the other side takes civilians hostage and abuses their corpses. And, judging by the footage that comes from there, they also rape female soldiers of the Israeli army. A plague on both your houses!"

Putin's former advisor, Sergey Markov, added a supernatural claim by blaming Russian émigrés for bringing war to Israel by "jinxing" any country they run to. He said: "Russia is calling for peace, but understands that war is inevitable.

"The Soviet Union has been helping Palestinians for many years. The main ally of Israel is the United States, which is also Russia's main enemy right now. Russia's ally, Iran, is an ally of Hamas. Russia will benefit from the rising oil prices as a consequence of this war... Any conflicts on which the US and the EU have to expend resources are beneficial for Russia because this lessens the resources sent to the Russophobic regime in Ukraine."

Marat Bulatov, who hosts Day Z on Solovyov Live, decided to start the show with more important news, congratulating Russian President Vladimir Putin on his 71st birthday. Bulatov proceeded to describe Putin as "our boss, our Commander-in-Chief, our president, and our sovereign."

He told the audience, "We have to be with our president, with our country, or else we could experience something like what is happening in Israel." Bulatov absurdly alleged that Prime Minister of Israel Benjamin Netanyahu "is calling for jihad" against Palestine and later read a message from a viewer that said, "We are calling on Palestine to keep it up!"

Nina from St. Petersburg sent a message that Bulatov read out loud: "It's not like last year, when the Crimean bridge was destroyed for Putin's birthday. We only have good news today!" The host replied, "Yes, I completely agree!"

Russians Divide Over Terrorist Attack on Israel

There is confusion and contradiction in Russia on how to respond to the terror attacks on Israel.

Originally published by *The Center for European Policy Analysis* (CEPA) on October 11, 2023

The response of Russian state propagandists to the butchery of Israelis by terrorists has been morbidly jubilant; a reflection of the Kremlin's cozy relations with groups including Hamas and Hezbollah, and countries like Iran and Syria.

Nonetheless, state media coverage is now starting to reflect a growing split within Russian society—with many supporting Hamas, even as others recoil in disgust over the carnage and in particular acts of butchery against Israeli civilians, including women, children, and the elderly.

The issue is perhaps starkest for the Kremlin's most influential propagandist, Vladimir Solovyov, who has struggled to align his Jewish heritage with the outspoken, and sometimes gleeful, support of Hamas among his peers in the Russian media.

During the October 9 broadcast of his state TV program, *The Evening With Vladimir Solovyov*, the host complained: "This is hard for me. One of my acquaintances sent me a text message, saying 'Long live the intifada!' and talking about how great all of it is. I told him that while I know the history of this issue, and I can understand different points of view, I could never justify the people who do these kinds of things to women, children, and civilians."

It was certainly a curious statement. Solovyov has been one of the fieriest advocates of hardline action against Ukraine and its people, up to and including the use of nuclear weapons both there and elsewhere in Europe.

Solovyov was keen to stress that despite his Jewish roots, his only loyalty was to Russia. And he has a point—his programs and guests have repeatedly highlighted the beneficial side effects that events in Israel might have for Moscow's war against Ukraine.

Solovyov is not the only one struggling to maintain consistency as a result of events in the Middle East. Pro-Hamas commentators condemn Israel's blockade of Gaza, while omitting any mention of Russia's propagandists and military experts who have urged the total destruction of Ukraine's energy infrastructure, in mid-winter, and advocate for Russia to cut off supplies of food and water, and to flood the streets of the Ukrainian cities with raw sewage.

Perhaps the contradictions are to be expected when the government is also visibly struggling. The Kremlin has declared its neutrality, with calls for both sides to cease the hostilities.

Foreign Minister Sergey Lavrov said on October 9: "We cannot agree with those who say that security should be ensured exclusively by the fight against extremism and terrorism." Which seems wholly at odds with innumerable official Russian statements since its full-fledged invasion of Ukraine began almost 20 months ago.

Many Russian propagandists have simply decided that the best course is to openly side with Hamas. Igor Molotov, RT's Special Editor, penned a piece for a Belarusian state paper, Minskaya Prauda, rejoicing about the attack on Israel. The article was eventually removed, but an archived version is still accessible.

Molotov took credit for the idea that was recently promoted by the head of RT, Margarita Simonyan, suggesting that a thermonuclear bomb should be set off over Siberia. He wrote, "My name is Igor Molotov. It was I who advised detonating a thermonuclear bomb over Siberia. I apologize. It should explode over Israel."

He recounted speaking with the Palestinian ambassador in Moscow, who reportedly told Molotov, "Igor, brother, this is our common victory." Molotov said: "The victory of Palestine in the occupied territories is a victory for Moscow and Minsk. Even if the Palestinian resistance does not win the deadly battle with Tel Aviv now, Palestinian flags will fly over the Al-Aqsa Mosque in Jerusalem. We have already won. Hamas and Fatah are marching along the same road to victory... Today, we are all Palestinians. Today, all of us are winning."

During Monday's broadcast of *The Meeting Place* on NTV, political scientist Maxim Yusin mentioned that it's (allegedly) forbidden on Russian state television to describe Hamas as terrorists but asserted that he intended to do so anyway because they kidnap and murder women and children. Hosts Andrey Norkin and Ivan Trushkin then made the point for him, shouting down the panelist and repeatedly asserting that at the official level, Hamas is not considered a terrorist organization.

Yusin mentioned a growing divide in Russian society, estimating that roughly half the population supports Hamas and the other half favors Israel. State media employees veered off in various eccentric directions with a series of assertions on social media, including the statement that Israel's inclusion of female soldiers explained the country's lack of preparedness.

The host of *60 Minutes*, Olga Skabeeva, mocked the female soldiers for their social media posts preceding the invasion, because they were depicted dancing in their free time. Skabeeva posted the clips with a notation: "Here is how the Israeli army was getting ready for war."

That at least fits with the Kremlin ideology. The number of women in the Russian military is tiny and has halved to fewer than 5% during Putin's rule.

Putin Flack Claims 'Ethnic Cleansing' of Jews on Kremlin TV

The Israel-Gaza war has kicked off a profanity-laced firestorm among the Kremlin's star propagandists.

Originally published by *The Daily Beast* on October 25, 2023

The Israel-Hamas war has activated fault lines all over the world, including in Moscow, where the Kremlin's most influential propagandist, Vladimir Solovyov, has found himself in the middle of a media firestorm spurred by the conflict.

First, Solovyov—who previously vowed that as a Jew, he would fight for Israel if it was ever involved in a war—went back on his promise. He claimed that his duty is to be with Russia as it fights in Ukraine, although Solovyov has no plans to risk his life or limb in that war either.

And now, there is a growing rift within his media empire. A wave of public figures in Russia are attacking his channel, Solovyov Live, suggesting it employs too many Jewish staffers in comments Solovyov says amount to an attempted "ethnic cleansing."

The scandal appears to have started because not everyone at the network was willing to abandon their affinity towards Israel in favor of Hamas, Hezbollah, and the countries that sponsor their endeavors.

Last week, Yevgeny Satanovsky—a prominent fixture on Solovyov's state TV programs and a host on his channel—was interviewed by an Israeli YouTuber, Alexander Waldman, and did not hold back.

Criticizing Russia's approach towards the Israeli-Palestinian conflict, Satanovsky described Russia's deputy foreign minister, Mikhail Bogdanov, as a hopeless drunk and an old man who might be looking for a golden parachute in the form of a hefty payout.

Bogdanov, who is Russia's former ambassador to Israel and Egypt, had urged "a peace process" and a ceasefire between Israel and Hamas and said that Russian officials have been in touch with all parties involved in the conflict, including unspecified Arab countries.

Satanovsky also unloaded on Maria Zakharova, the spokeswoman for Russia's Foreign Affairs Ministry, describing her as "a heavy-drinking skank, who does not like the Jews and can't stand Israel." He referred to the significant presence of antisemites among Russian government officials, saying that they've "livened up" after Hamas attacked Israel and claiming that Kremlin leadership is trying to keep them in check.

The pundit said that he doesn't have a problem with Vladimir Putin's government, because he realizes that the main goal of global leaders is to pass down their riches that are sometimes stolen, sometimes earned, to their descendants. He described coming to terms with this realization and learning to accept Russia just the way it is.

"The country where I'm living right now, with its antisemites, thieves, scumbags and bandits, is no better and no worse than others," he said. "There is nowhere to run."

He went on: "Putin is not eternal, he is getting older. It's customary for strong leaders to choose weak ones to follow them. Putin is very strong from the standpoint of retaining power... he will pick some puny, weak shit to take his spot. [Dmitry] Medvedev was an example of that."

Solovyov promptly fired Satanovsky on Saturday and apologized to Russia's Foreign Affairs Ministry. Satanovsky initially replied that he regrets nothing, but by Monday, he had posted a vague apology on his Telegram channel. But the scandal is only growing. During his program on Tuesday, *Full Contact*, Solovyov was exploding with rage, because his channel is now under attack for being "ethnically askew."

Speaking of the controversy, Putin confidant Alexander Dugin told Eurasia Daily: "This was inevitable. The divide between the Jews who are loyal to Putin and the special military operation after the escalation in the Gaza Strip was inevitable. Satanovsky and [Yaakov] Kedmi chose Israel. Solovyov, despite his fiery Judaism, chose Russia... Solovyov diffused tensions, but this is just the tip of the iceberg. Nothing is over, it barely even started... This is very serious, because the Jews play an enormous part in Russian politics." Dugin surmised, "Satanovsky's motherland is Israel... It's time for Armageddonych [Satanovsky's nickname] to go home."

Sergey Markov, who is often reported to be Putin's former close adviser, told the same publication, "This won't be the last conflict in Solovyov's pool. As many have noted, there is an enormous ethnic imbalance. Mainly the representatives of two diasporas [Jewish and Armenian] are discussing what the policies of great Russia should be. This is laughable and improper... This isn't normal. There will be more scandals, because Russia's relations with Israel and Armenia are getting worse. Many of Solovyov's experts can't find balance between Russia and their ethnic identity. Satanovsky lost it. He won't be the last."

In response, Solovyov called Markov "a total lowlife" and expressed his amazement that "this scumbag somehow made it to the State Duma at one point in time." The host added: "This man used to be a trustee of the president of the Russian Federation and now he is calling for ethnic cleansing... This creature is opening his mouth to criticize the hosts of a channel, where he is constantly appearing, as though it was his job!"

Solovyov called on Olga Skabeeva and Evgeny Popov, his colleagues from the program *60 Minutes*, to take note of Markov's commentary, implying they should stop inviting him to participate in their program. Solovyov questioned what differentiates Dugin, Markov and other commentators on this issue from Hitler.

He cautioned, "The old ghost of antisemitism is rising once again. The ghost of the Fourth Reich."

Israel Conflict Rekindles Russian Antisemitism

Putin's Russia is suffering aftershocks from the Hamas terrorist attack against Israel.

Originally published by *The Center for European Policy Analysis* (CEPA) on November 1, 2023

Vladimir Solovyov, the Kremlin's top propagandist, has been forced to fire one of his hosts, Yevgeny Satanovsky. He had trashed Russia's pro-Hamas approach towards the Israeli-Palestinian conflict and described Russia's deputy foreign minister, Mikhail Bogdanov, as a hopeless drunk.

In an interview with an Israeli YouTuber, Satanovsky also alleged that Maria Zakharova, the spokeswoman for Russia's Foreign Affairs Ministry, is "a heavy-drinking skank, who doesn't like the Jews and can't stand Israel." He said that antisemites permeated the Russian government and have significantly "livened up" after Hamas attacked Israel.

The host's frank description of high-level antisemitism and corruption in the Russian regime (his best defense was that every other national elite was as crooked as the Kremlin) could not have come at a worse time for Solovyov, who is Jewish and under sustained attack from leading racists.

The heavily bearded far-right ideologist Alexander Dugin waded into the debate, telling Eurasia Daily: "The divide between the Jews who are loyal to Putin and the special military operation after the escalation in the Gaza Strip was inevitable... This is very serious because the Jews play an enormous part in Russian politics."

Sergey Markov, who is frequently described as a former senior adviser to Putin, said: "This won't be the last conflict in Solovyov's pool. As many have noted, there is an enormous ethnic imbalance. Mainly the representatives of two diasporas [Jewish and Armenian] are discussing what the policies of great Russia should be. This is laughable and improper... This isn't normal."

Solovyov is not a man who takes insults lying down and swiftly trains the guns of his Solovyov Live channel onto both men. One of his hosts, Boris Jakemenko called for Dugin to be investigated for his fascist teachings, or perhaps detained in a medical health facility. Markov is now being mentioned by Solovyov almost daily, with a barrage of unflattering epithets and calls for the authorities to investigate him for various statements.

While this may merely look to be a succession of squabbles among Russia's propagandists, they represent a much deeper ailment in Russian society. Satanovsky wasn't wrong in noting that antisemitism was bubbling just beneath the surface.

Last week, the journalist Yury Dud interviewed the famous singer, Vika Tsyganova, and her husband Vadim. In their startling interview, the couple blamed the breakdown in the early negotiations between Russia and Ukraine on the ethnicity of the negotiators, claiming that Russian Jews ought never to have been sent to negotiate with a regime of Ukrainian Jews.

Tsyganova intimated that they were the reason for the country's troubles, adding, "And look at where Ukraine is now!" (As always in Russian propaganda, the Kremlin's allegation that Ukraine is a Nazi state went unmentioned during the antisemitic attacks.)

The Tsyganovs claimed that the Jews had actually engineered Putin's invasion of Ukraine. They shared the conspiracy theory that "the world government" provoked Russia to invade Ukraine to "cleanse" that area of people and communities. The couple alleged that Israel was running out of space and once a part of Ukraine was "mowed down" for their benefit, Israel's 9 million citizens would move there.

Antisemitic sentiments in Russia aren't limited to crackpots, propagandists, and government officials. They are also manifested in violence.

On October 28, hundreds reportedly gathered in the city of Khasavyurt, in the mainly Muslim region of Dagestan, outside the Flamingo and Kyiv hotels, claiming that the buildings were "full of

Jews." The mob carried Palestinian flags and demanded that hotel guests come to the windows and show themselves. When the guests did not obey, the group pummeled the walls of the hotel with rocks. Fearing further attacks, the Flamingo put up a sign that Jews from Israel are not allowed to enter the building.

The same day, a large group of individuals gathered in Cherkessk, demanding that ethnic Jews be expelled from the area. In video footage posted online, an unidentified woman asserted, "We don't want to live next to Jews!"

According to the Interior Ministry, 34 protesters were charged with participating in unauthorized rallies. The following day, unidentified arsonists set fire to a construction site of a Jewish cultural center in Nalchik. The perpetrators wrote "death to Jews" on the wall.

A co-owner of an agency renting homes and apartments in 47 building complexes, who identified herself simply as Leila, recorded a video asserting that her company does not rent to Jews. She promised to regularly check surveillance footage, to ensure that "Jews from Israel" are not sneaking into her properties.

Later, an anti-Israeli mob stormed Makhachkala International Airport in Dagestan, violently searching for Jews and Israelis who were said to be on a flight that arrived from Tel Aviv.

The disturbances have clearly rattled the Kremlin and its regional administrators, who may fear that anti-Jewish protests could swiftly turn against the government. As of October 31, 15 of the airport rioters had been charged with disorderly conduct and will be imprisoned for terms varying between three and eight days.

A representative of Russia's Chief Rabbinate in Dagestan, Ovadia Isakov, said, "People from the [Jewish] community are afraid, they're calling, and I don't know what advice to give them." Nor could he reassure the estimated 300-400 Jewish families in the region regarding a place of safety. He added: "Russia isn't a refuge: Russia has also had pogroms. It isn't clear where to run to."

State TV networks, like Solovyov's, have been instrumental in causing tensions to boil over onto the streets. Given Russia's embrace of Hamas, the country's media followed suit and took the terrorist group's side in its faceoff with Israel.

Day after day, week after week, state television condemned "barbaric" attacks by Israel and matter-of-factly showcased meetings with Hamas officials. State TV's hosts and experts repeatedly emphasized that in Russia, Hamas is not considered a terrorist organization and shouldn't be referred to as such.

As for Russia's residual Jewish population of perhaps 80,000 (it has sharply declined since 2010), they face an uncertain future caused by officially endorsed propaganda. The worst might be yet to come.

Women Enter the Putin Regime's Crosshairs

The Russian regime had hoped that its full-scale invasion of Ukraine would solve a plethora of issues, including the country's severe demographic crisis. In fact, it made the situation much worse.

Originally published by *The Center for European Policy Analysis* (CEPA) on November 16, 2023

Between October 2020 and September 2021, the population of Russia experienced its largest peacetime decline since records began, shrinking by 997,000 people.

That would be bad news for any government, but for Putin, it is a disaster. In 2019, he admitted that the thought of a shrinking population "haunts" him. As a result, his haunted regime is now looking for shortcuts to population increases — the targets are Russian women and Ukrainian children.

The link between Putin's current and potential wars and looming restrictions on abortion is far from subtle. Russian billboards feature the photo of a fetus on one side and the picture of a small boy in a military uniform on the right, with the text stating, "Defend me today, so I may defend you tomorrow."

The Kremlin is also attempting to replenish its shrinking population with Ukrainian refugees, some of whom were forcibly moved to Russia, as well as stolen Ukrainian children — a war crime, for which the International Criminal Court (ICC) issued warrants against Putin and Commissioner for Children's Rights in the Office of the President of the Russian Federation, Maria Lvova-Belova. Russia says it has taken at least 700,000 children.

In January 2023, the host of Solovyov Live, Sergey Mardan, rejoiced over these tactics, stating: "Look at how much the motherland is spending to solve the demographic problem... We got these people [Ukrainians] for free, for nothing — approximately five million of them! Five million souls!"

Panelists on state TV shows argue that just as Chechens now fight on Russia's side — despite the brutality of the two Chechen wars — at some point in the future, Ukrainians will do likewise in support of Putin's imperial expansionism and the anticipated invasions of other countries.

This year, the drive to produce additional battalions of future soldiers has reached a fever pitch, with propagandists and government officials urging women to give birth to more children. In May, Akhmat Battalion Commander Apti Alaudinov insisted that women should have at least five children each to achieve a geometric increase in population.

During the plenary session of the Russian Orthodox Church congress, Patriarch Kirill said: "There truly is a population problem in Russia. It's an enormous country, but it definitely lacks a sufficient population... Indeed, we need more people, this is obvious, everyone recognizes it," he said. "If we solve this problem, if we learn how to talk women out of getting abortions, statistics will immediately increase."

State Duma deputy Dmitry Vyatkin suggested that women start giving birth at 20 years of age, so they can have multiple children. He noted, "I have three children. It's not enough." And Natalya Moskvitina, founder of "Women For Life," complained at a religious conference: "What is an abortion? It is a culture of death! We have a culture of death in our country. We approve of it, we allow it . . . You're either on the side of good or evil."

But this flood of anti-abortion arguments has not been universally acclaimed. After airing the Moskvitina clip on the TV show *The Meeting Place*, host Ivan Trushkin caustically noted: "Ms. Moskvitina appeared on our program many times. I didn't always get the impression she was on the side of good."

The hosts played another clip, featuring Margarita Pavlova, a member of the Federation Council Committee on Defense and Security. During the Russian Economic Forum in Chelyabinsk, Pavlova said, "Girls are being told they should first get an education, build a career, buy an apartment, and only then get married and have children. As a result, we have a generation of 40-year-old unhappy women... We should stop encouraging young women to seek higher education." Trushkin added, "It should be noted that Ms. Pavlova herself has a higher education."

Political scientist Aleksandr Sytin said: "I am a consistent homophobe but a total proponent of abortions. I also believe they should be totally free and 100% covered by insurance." And pundit Gevorg Mirzayan chimed in to say, "Straight to the point, every normal person will always be in favor of abortion."

Russia's most prominent propagandist, Vladimir Solovyov has also entered the fray, attacking a call from Pavel Astakhov, a former Children's Rights Commissioner, for a ban on abortions. Solovyov said: "If we use the methods of evil and say that we want to implement harsh measures, then how are we different from [the Americans]?"

Typically, state media figures operate as obedient weathervanes, amending their stance whenever it is required. However, even some of the most pliant talking heads have a problem with their country's current direction. Putin's propagandists eagerly anticipated that the discourse over abortion-related issues would shatter America, but Putin's disastrous policies brought these divisions home.

Meanwhile, anti-abortion measures are taking effect. Efforts to force pregnant women to use government clinics subject them to numerous delaying tactics where they are forced to see psychologists and priests or to have extensive and unnecessary testing to prolong the process beyond the legal limit of 12-22 weeks. Private clinics in the Kursk and Chelyabinsk regions, in the Republic of Tatarstan, and in occupied Crimea, have already halted abortions, while others are imposing fines for the "promotion" of the procedure.

Give the Kremlin an Inch and it Will Take Half of Europe

Signs of Western hesitation over support for Ukraine encourage Russian propagandists to speculate on which country might be the next victim.

Originally published by *The Center for European Policy Analysis* (CEPA) on December 1, 2023

With more than 300,000 Russian servicemen dead and wounded in Vladimir Putin's war of aggression against Ukraine, you might think his propagandists would exhibit some humility when discussing the utility of war as a policy tool. You'd be wrong.

Instead, the Kremlin's mouthpieces have interpreted signals of Western hesitation in the funding of their Ukrainian ally as a weakness. Putin's people have seized on hints that the West is pressing Ukraine to consider negotiations to formalize its division as a green light to go much further. Why not grab even more, they ask?

And if these sound like the typical statements of over-heated spokespeople, bear in mind that they broadly accord with Russia's December 2021 demands that the US effectively abandon NATO's newer members, like the Baltic states and Poland. It is also worth remembering that Russia's invasion of Ukraine was likewise discussed and openly plotted for years on state-run media, after which it actually happened.

Appearing on the show *Our Own Truth* on NTV last Friday, writer Dmitry Lekuh said that Poland is "the next candidate to be thrown under Russian tanks." He asserted that "dividing Poland between Russia and Germany is our national pastime."

Lekuh bemoaned the fact that Germany is "no longer the same," a reference to Nazi Germany's alliance with the Soviet Union in 1939 in the Molotov-Ribbentrop pact. As so often with

Kremlin propagandists, the logic was blurry—Russia pining for its Nazi German allies hardly accords with its stated pretext for aggression against Ukraine; that it was clearing the country of supposed Nazis.

Appearing on state television, pundits and lawmakers alike insisted that Russia is not interested in negotiations and simply cannot allow Ukraine's sovereign existence to continue.

Convinced that Europe had emptied its arsenals to help Ukraine, and were thus vulnerable, the Kremlin's talking heads asserted that other European countries should also be removed from the map.

During his morning show *Full Contact* on Wednesday, Russia's leading propagandist, the state TV host Vladimir Solovyov, asked: "Should the Ukrainian nation continue to exist? My response is, in its current state, it should not. No! A nation whose ideology poses a danger to us cannot exist next to us."

He added, "I believe we have entered a period of colossal geopolitical change. Many accidental formations, incapable of their own statehood, may not survive this era. By that, I mean the Baltic states and all of Europe. I don't think that the European borders in their current configuration will continue to exist much longer. I don't see any reason why they would."

Moscow mouthpieces do not limit themselves to the redrawing of European maps. Another favored theme has been the need to punish Russian exiles and so-called enemies of the state through assassination.

And as with their ruminations on future wars, their demands often become real. On November 28, Ukraine's intelligence service reported that a number of people, including SBU head Kyrylo Budanov's wife, Marianna Budanova, had been hospitalized due to suspected heavy metals poisoning.

This is an old and familiar path for Russia. As far back as the 1930s and 1940s, Stalin's henchmen led by the legendary spymaster Pavel Sudoplatov, plotted and carried out assassinations of individuals including Leon Trotsky. In more recent years, Russian assassins have used radioactive and nerve agents in the UK and in Russia itself.

It is a campaign that has been warmly embraced. The idea has been promulgated in the state media since at least 2022, with one pundit suggesting that the US needed "hundreds" of coffins draped in the Stars and Stripes as a wake-up call.

Guests on Solovyov's show advocated either kidnapping Russia's enemies in Ukraine or killing them on the spot. State Duma Deputy Andrey Gurulyov articulated the fate that should befall Russia's enemies: "As Iosif Vissarionovich [Stalin] said, "No man, no problem. Enemies of the Motherland have to be destroyed."

In February, appearing on *The Evening With Vladimir Solovyov*, Yevgeny Satanovsky, president of the Institute of the Middle East, asserted: "If Europe is a garden, parasites in the garden should be exterminated." Making sure that the metaphor wasn't lost on the viewers, Solovyov quickly added, "I think this is the anniversary of Mercader," a reference to Ramon Mercader, the NKVD agent who used an ice pick to assassinate Trotsky in Mexico City in 1940.

Professor Alexander Kamkin, member of the Russian Academy of Sciences, echoed Satanovsky and stressed, "Parasites in the garden can be chemically exterminated or you can use a good hoe or an ice pick and destroy them selectively."

In May 2023, the head of RT Margarita Simonyan openly called for the assassination of the Republican Senator Lindsey Graham, again invoking Sudoplatov's name.

So it's hardly surprising that the fate of Marianna Budanova prompted lukewarm denials, accompanied by sly smirks and knowing glances.

State TV show *60 Minutes* invited none other than the notorious State Duma Deputy Andrey Lugovoy—identified by a British judge as one of Alexander Litvinenko's 2006 assassins in London—to discuss Budanova's poisoning. Lugovoy was all smiles, right along with the hosts Olga Skabeeva and Evgeny Popov, who smirkingly and half-heartedly denied that Russia would resort to such "old-fashioned" methods as poisoning, and insisting instead that it would take out Budanov and others using some unnamed "high-tech" means.

The bottom line is that none of Putin's propagandists are talking for the sake of talking. These figures articulate the ideas contemplated by the regime they serve, with whom they socialize, and from whom they take orders.

Appealing to the morality or humanity of the Kremlin is an exercise in futility. Putin's Russia is not constrained by high ideals but only by its capabilities. Western discussions about the possibility of abandoning Ukraine and forcing it into a peace deal with Russia encourage Moscow to expand its offensive, by military or non-military means.

Those who hope to appease it are making a profound mistake; give ground to the regime, and it will only demand more.

Reality Check for Putin as Russians Get Damn Tired of War

Kremlin propagandists are pushing the idea that the West is tired of this war. That may be true but it's clear Russians are even more sick of it.

Originally published by *The Daily Beast* on December 04, 2023

Russia's relentless TV propaganda has entered a heavily depressed new era. The trend began last month when audio from a duo of Russian pranksters apparently tricking the Italian prime minister into making an unguarded remark surfaced.

In the clip, which was recorded in September, Vladimir Kuznetsov and Alexei Stolyarov (known as Vovan and Lexus) are posing as African diplomats and a voice that sounds like Meloni candidly admits that fatigue has set in with respect to Russia's invasion of Ukraine: "There is a lot of tiredness on all sides."

For weeks afterwards, the Russian state media has publicized the call, in continuation of the latest propaganda narrative that the West is tired of Ukraine and wants to negotiate a deal with the Kremlin. Russian talking heads proudly assert that Moscow is not interested in any deals and pontificate about invading other countries to continue the expansion of the Russian empire.

This preposterous propaganda is designed to obscure a crucial detail: that the Russians are also sick and tired of an invasion conceived by their perennial leader, with no end in sight.

In recent months, Sergey Mardan, one of the hosts on Vladimir Solovyov's channel, Solovyov Live, started to wonder out loud why his boss's relentless coverage of the war and its "heroes" isn't gaining traction on social media or being picked up by other state TV channels. Solovyov himself noticed the waning public attention and mentioned it last week on his morning show, The *Full Contact*. He complained that "people are psychologically tired of this topic" and asked his viewers to let him know what they're actually interested in.

Tired or not, any dreams of a potential reprieve were extinguished when Russian President Vladimir Putin signed a decree boosting Russia's troop numbers by 15 percent or some 170,000 people. This will bring the overall number of Russian military personnel to about 2.2 million, including 1.32 million troops. The Russian Defense Ministry blamed NATO for the required increase and claimed that it would be achieved solely through the recruitment of volunteers and not through conscription or mobilization.

The wives of those who were mobilized in the beginning of the invasion have recently started to express their outrage—not with the evils of a genocidal war against the neighboring nation, but with the fact that their husbands are yet to be relieved through rotation.

The women authored a petition and disseminated stickers that said, "Bring my husband back. I'm fucking tired of this." This movement is currently being strangled, with participating military wives being taken in for questioning and threatened with being potentially charged for "discrediting the army."

Putin's decree wasn't meant to address these complaints but merely to fill the gaps created by Russia's massive casualties, while the true extent of the losses remains taboo within the country. During his Saturday show on Solovyov Live, Mardan did his best to dispel the notion that the new infusion of manpower was meant to replenish the 300,000 dead—a number he also denied.

Mardan's guest, State Duma member Andrey Gurulyov claimed that the decree was designed to address the threats Russia is allegedly facing all over the world: from unnamed Western foes in the Arctic; because of the expansion of the Taiwan crisis; an escalation between North and South Korea, Finland and possibly Sweden joining NATO; the war in the Middle East and issues in the Caucasus.

Gurulyov complained about the militarization of the Baltics, Poland and other countries and added that he couldn't rule out another mobilization. Instead of acknowledging that multiple countries are preparing to defend themselves from Russian aggression,

Gurulyov portrayed them as the potential aggressors, encircling Russia and plotting to attack it. He asserted, "Today, our army should be ready for WWIII."

Beyond the shrinking cadre of soldiers available to bolster Putin's wars, Russia's workforce is also being depleted. Last Tuesday, during the broadcast of the state TV show *60 Minutes*, Dmitry Abzalov, Director of the Center for Strategic Communications, noted: "Our main problem, the limiting factor, is the absence of the workforce. Next year, our GDP may decrease because we are short-handed." Abzalov hinted that the workers were sent to the frontlines or moved to work in the factories producing weapons, equipment and ammunition for the military.

Host Evgeny Popov pointed out that one of Putin's recent decrees was meant to address this problem, by simplifying the process of repatriation of Russians currently living in other countries. He added, "This is being done because we don't have enough people." State Duma member Leonid Kalashnikov proposed importing workers from North Korea.

Head of RT Margarita Simonyan had an even better idea. Last Sunday, Simonyan appeared on *Sunday Evening With Vladimir Solovyov* and predicted that Russia's demographic crisis would be resolved in the not-so-distant future, when desperate Americans will flock to Russia to take up the jobs the locals don't want. Russia's self-imposed turmoil is so unrelenting that Putin's mouthpieces are having to resort to increasingly ridiculous suggestions and predictions — but even they find it challenging to obscure the grim reality with a cheerful demeanor.

Last Thursday, the host of *60 Minutes* Olga Skabeeva said, "It seems like lately, every day is significant in some way." Dmitry Abzalov replied: "Things were so good in the past that now, every day seems to have a special meaning."

Putin's Pals Think the GOP Just Won Them the War in Ukraine

"Well done, Republicans!" Kremlin propagandists celebrate the Republican move to block funding and predict President Trump will totally cut off Ukraine and Israel.

Originally published by *The Daily Beast* on December 07, 2023

Republicans voted to block a $110.5 billion emergency spending bill to aid Ukraine and Israel Wednesday night, sparking celebrations in Moscow where they believe the U.S. will withdraw support for Kyiv allowing them to win the war.

A classified briefing with administration officials reportedly devolved into a meltdown on Tuesday afternoon, making it clear that the measure would fail. "We are about to abandon Ukraine," Senator Christopher S. Murphy told the press as he left the briefing. "When Vladimir Putin marches into a NATO country, they will rue the day they decided to play politics with the future of Ukraine's security."

These developments prompted jubilation in Moscow. During Wednesday's broadcast of a state TV program *60 Minutes*, Evgeny Popov said Ukraine was now in "agony" and it was "difficult to imagine a bigger humiliation."

During his morning show *Full Contact* on Wednesday, top pro-Kremlin propagandist Vladimir Solovyov joyfully noted: "[Janet] Yellen screamed, "Don't you dare!" [Joe] Biden screamed, "Don't you dare!" but Republicans said, "Go to hell! We won't give your khokhols [slur for "Ukrainians"] any money." The segment was entitled, "No one needs Ukraine anymore—especially the United States."

Appearing on his program, America analyst Dmitry Drobnitsky noted, "The downfall of Ukraine means the downfall of Biden! Two birds with one stone!"

During his appearance on *60 Minutes*, Dmitry Abzalov, president of the Center for Strategic Communications, predicted that the fiasco with the funding for Ukraine will spell the political demise of Biden. Host Olga Skabeeva added, "We'll have no pity for him! To the contrary, we're ready to hammer those final nails right in!" With a happy grin, Skabeeva said, "Well done, Republicans! They're standing firm! That's good for us."

Roman Golovanov, the host of Golovanov's Time on Vladimir Solovyov's channel Solovyov Live, pointed out, "This will be a great revelation to other countries. It is even more dangerous to be a friend of the United States than its enemy. In the end, they will abandon you, leaving nothing but the scorched earth on your territory."

The turmoil comes at a critical point in time, with Russia facing internal issues, while its invasion failed to proceed at the rate anticipated by the experts.

The population is tired of the war but is predictably hesitant to express that for fear of being arrested or otherwise persecuted. Instead, many show their displeasure by tuning out the relentless war coverage.

On Wednesday, Solovyov noted, "We lived in peace for too long and now we have to get used to living through war... With great interest, I'm observing the negative growth on my Telegram channel, meaning that the number of followers is sharply declining. Oh well, that's life." Solovyov previously complained that every day Russians are losing interest in Putin's war.

The GOP's willingness to jeopardize Ukraine's ability to defend itself provided a sudden boost to the faltering Russian propagandists—a crucial element of Putin's war effort that is used to motivate the masses. In recent months, their rhetoric devolved from "When we win" to "If we win," reflecting realities on the ground. Winter's arrival added another layer of concern. The Republicans brought back the joy for Putin's gloomy propagandists, reviving their musings as to how they will "punish" Ukrainians once Russia wins.

The only news that dampened the celebration in Moscow was the revelation that Taylor Swift—and not Vladimir Putin—was named TIME Magazine's Person of the Year. The host of *The Meeting Place* Andrey Norkin angrily complained, "Taylor Swift! No one knows who that broad is, but Americans worship her."

While the Russians are pleased with Republicans, they believe that Donald Trump could do even better. The Kremlin's mouthpieces make no secret of their desire to see Trump return to the White House and now they have yet another incentive.

Appearing on *The Evening With Vladimir Solovyov* Tuesday night, Dmitry Drobnitsky predicted that if Trump wins the presidency, he will ditch not only Ukraine but also Israel.

He explained that he no longer has to demonstrate being a pro-Israel president to his evangelical base. Drobnitsky said, "Trump already gave them all that he could: the Golan Heights, Jerusalem, and everything else. He already paid them in full. Now, after the empire of Sheldon Adelson has turned away from him, he owes them nothing."

Drobnitsky explained that Putin is meeting with the leaders of the Arab countries to get ready for a time when the region will be freed of American influence.

Vladimir Solovyov predicted that the U.S. will be forced to focus on its internal affairs as opposed to its former foreign interests. Implying there will be a civil war in the United States, Solovyov exclaimed, "The main war will unfold in Washington!" Drobnitsky concurred and added, "It's impossible to resolve their current situation without repressions and without armed clashes."

'Shocking' Reality of Ukraine Blowback Hammers Putin at Home

Even the Kremlin's propagandists can no longer cover up the brutal impact on ordinary Russians caused by Vladimir Putin's war in Ukraine.

Originally published by *The Daily Beast* on January 08, 2024

For years, Russian government officials and state media propagandists have been claiming that Western sanctions don't cause any real harm to their economy and to the contrary, actually help it develop. But the main industry that seems to be thriving despite the sanctions is the country's military-industrial complex. As for everyday people, their lives are progressively getting worse.

During Russia's New Year's show *The Little Blue Light* 12 months ago, one of its hosts, Dmitry Guberniev assured the viewers that victory in Ukraine was near. He said, "Life is like a biathlon or ski racing. If you're having a hard time, then the finish line is near." During the same program, comedian Yevgeny Petrosyan claimed that the West had tried to destroy Russia but instead was forced to freeze and suffer without Russian gas supplies. He boasted: "Like it or not, Russia is enlarging!"

The mood was markedly different during this year's festivities. Instead of laughing at the West, Petrosyan wished fellow Russians to have "barns and cellars that are fully stocked and regularly replenished with patience and optimism."

This tempering of expectations is not coincidental. Russian President Vladimir Putin—who is running for re-election in March—and a bevy of state-funded propagandists insist that the invasion of Ukraine will not stop until Moscow's goals are achieved. This also means there will be no relief from the impact of sanctions within Russia itself.

The relative stability of the Russian economy is ensured by injections of trillions of rubles from the budget, secured through the National Welfare Fund (NWF). Since the beginning of the invasion, half of this stash has already been spent. Analysts say that the remaining liquid part of the National Wealth Fund, $52 billion, wouldn't be enough to handle another crisis.

The Russian ruble showed its strongest decline since 2015 and became one of the three weakest currencies of developing countries tracked by Bloomberg. This comes at the same time as a "demographic catastrophe" bemoaned by Russian experts and commentators, which has seen migration exacerbate a natural population decline in almost half of the regions. Migrants from the CIS nations are also less inclined to work and live in Russia, due in part to a weakening ruble and also because police raids, rounding up migrants for military mobilization, have become so frequent.

In 2023, therapists reported an increase in complaints about permanent stress and financial worries. The poorest Russians, including pensioners, suffer the most.

Just in time for the holidays, the price of eggs in Russia shot up by 40 percent or more and their availability greatly diminished. Some regions started to limit the number of eggs an individual could buy, with some stores even selling them individually. This was an especially sensitive issue, since a traditional New Year's salad, the Olivier, requires eggs as one of its main ingredients. During his annual televised event, Direct Line, Putin had to apologize for the rising egg prices—a fact that even state TV propagandists described as "shocking."

Experts on TV show *The Meeting Place* blamed the sanctions and economist Alexey Zubets suggested that people can switch from eggs to "better sources of protein, like beef." Even hosts, Ivan Trushkin and Andrey Norkin, seemed shocked by his callous attitude, which resembled Marie Antoinette's legendary "Let them eat cake."

Egg shortages prompted Russia to step up imports from other countries, including Turkey and Azerbaijan Chicken is also disappearing from grocery store shelves.

Russian State Duma Deputy Speaker Vladislav Davankov, who filed his paperwork to the Central Election Commission to take part in the 2024 presidential campaign, accused the Federal State Statistics Service of fudging the numbers "to make it seem that all is well with the prices." He said that prices on many items, including rice, grains, and butter, are rising 10-30 percent faster than officials claim. "When statistics diverge from reality, it is impossible to make effective decisions to curb prices," Davankov added.

According to official statistics, basic food products sharply rose in price: eggs by 59 percent, tomatoes by 52 percent, bananas by 46.5 percent, cabbage by 29 percent, poultry by 27.7 percent, and apples by 20.7 percent. Polls reveal that two-thirds of Russians complain about the prices rising at a faster pace—and that Russians in general are tired of war, with over 50 percent of participants hoping for the end of the so-called "special military operation" as their biggest wish for 2024. Witnessing Western hesitation to continue aid to Ukraine, Putin is unlikely to grant the wish of his own citizens anytime soon.

Russian lawmakers and other state TV propagandists promise an expanded agenda, with all of Ukraine on the menu. Encouraged by the disarray in the U.S., they hope for a civil war in America that will permanently distract the country from helping Moscow's intended victims.

With Putin's unrelenting grip on power, the suffering of his own people seems inconsequential, as opposed to the illusory "greatness" of conquering other nations. The escalating brutality with which the Kremlin welcomed the New Year in 2024 shows that many challenges lie ahead for Ukraine and its global allies, but Russia is certainly not escaping the economic and demographic consequences of its own actions.

Putin's Sham Election Rivals Can't Even Keep a Straight Face

When asked if he thought he could win, one of the notional challengers said: "Of course not! Do I look like an idiot?"

Originally published by *The Daily Beast* on January 10, 2024

For years, Russian propagandists and government officials did their best to portray the U.S. elections as deeply flawed and unreliable. They openly rejoiced when former President Donald J. Trump and media personalities like Tucker Carlson helped their argument by claiming that elections in America can be easily faked or stolen.

Aside from discrediting the United States, the subterfuge of criticizing Western democracies provides a veil of legitimacy for Russia's own elections, which are more of a show than a real democratic process, considering Vladimir Putin's unrelenting grip on power.

In light of a predetermined outcome, the spectacle is so irrelevant that the leader of the Chechen Republic, Ramzan Kadyrov, suggested canceling the upcoming presidential election while the invasion of Ukraine is still underway, or holding elections with Putin as the sole candidate.

Top Russian propagandists like Vladimir Solovyov, State Duma member Andrey Gurulyov, film director Karen Shakhnazarov and many others repeatedly pointed out that Putin is essentially the only candidate and faces no real opposition. This is a feature, not a bug, since every strong opposition figure is either dead, in exile, or languishing in prison after unsuccessful poisoning attempts, like Vladimir Kara-Murza and Alexei Navalny.

Those allowed to participate in the charade that is the Russian presidential election are well aware of their token position and the precarious way in which they must operate: both pretending to run for president and skillfully avoiding any pretense of opposing Putin — or actually winning.

So far, only three candidates were officially approved to participate in the election to be held from March 15 to March 17: Liberal Democratic Party candidate Leonid Slutsky, who currently serves as head of the state Duma's Foreign Affairs Committee, Nikolay Kharitonov, of the Communist Party, and the New People Party candidate Vladislav Davankov.

During a recent press conference, an unidentified reporter asked Davankov, "Are you planning to win?" The candidate looked away and laughed. He said, "It depends on what you consider to be a victory."

A reporter asked State Duma member Nikolay Kharitonov, "Do you think you can win?" He cautiously replied, "I can't talk this way, to win or not to win."

A slew of other contenders are trying to throw their hats into the ring, but they harbor no illusions as to their chances in the process.

Andrei Bogdanov, chairman of the Russian Party of Freedom and Justice, was quite forthcoming when he was asked, "Are you planning to win?" Bogdanov replied, "Of course not! Do I look like an idiot?"

State Duma member Sergey Baburin said that he "plans to do everything to consolidate Russian society." When he was asked whether he plans to win the presidential election, Baburin replied, "You should always dare to dream." The reporter insisted, "But are you planning to win?" Baburin hesitated for a moment and then replied, "You know, only Lord God can plan."

Igor Girkin, also known by the alias Igor Strelkov, who is in custody awaiting trial for inciting extremism, wanted to run for president, even though he acknowledged that the upcoming election would be a mere imitation and its "winner" is predetermined in advance.

Girkin is a former Federal Security Service (FSB) officer who took part in Russia's annexation of Crimea and its initial invasion of Eastern Ukraine. In November 2022, a Dutch court found Girkin and two of his collaborators guilty of the murder of 298 people onboard flight MH17, which was shot down by a Russian surface-to-air missile when it was flying over Eastern Ukraine in 2014.

Girkin and his followers were unable to successfully file the paperwork for his attempted presidential candidacy, since their signatures had to be notarized and multiple notaries refused to cooperate with them in the process.

Former regional legislator Yekaterina Duntsova's nomination was rejected by Russia's Central Election Commission, which claimed to have found over 100 mistakes in her paperwork, including alleged spelling errors. Russia's Supreme Court rejected Duntsova's appeal against the commission's decision. Duntsova is calling for peace and urged her supporters to help former State Duma member Boris Nadezhdin, who vocally urged the Kremlin to cease the hostilities and to negotiate with Ukraine.

When he was asked by a reporter whether he plans to win, Nadezhdin replied with chilling realism and sincerity. He said, "You know, I just hope that at the conclusion of this electoral campaign I will stay alive, remain free, and won't be declared a foreign agent."

Kremlin Cronies: Putin-Tucker Interview Will 'Blow Up' U.S. Election

Russia's state TV stooges believe a Tucker Carlson-Putin interview will boost Putin at home and help restore Trump to the White House.

Originally published by *The Daily Beast* on February 06, 2024

Tucker Carlson's trip to Russia came as a shock to many, except for the Russian propagandists who have been lobbying for the fulfillment of his long-standing wish to interview Russian President Vladimir Putin. In recent years, the head of RT Margarita Simonyan pleaded with the Kremlin to make appropriate arrangements, and state TV host Vladimir Solovyov offered Carlson a job on his channel, Solovyov Live. Like many Putin propagandists, Simonyan realized that Carlson's softball sit-down with Putin would be even more of a propaganda boon than his pro-Russian, anti-Ukrainian, and borderline anti-American rhetoric over the years.

While Solovyov had to settle for Scott Ritter, it seems like Simonyan may have finally got her wish. State media reported that Carlson's minivan, full of TV equipment, had left his hotel and traveled to the presidential administration Monday evening. During the same timeframe, Putin's motorcade reportedly traveled towards the Kremlin.

On Tuesday, Alexei Venediktov, former editor of Ekho Moskvy radio station, hinted in a post on X (formerly Twitter), "As I understand, Tucker Carlson got what he wanted."

The timing was quite obviously chosen to coincide with Russia's upcoming presidential election. This event is merely one of the performances in the Kremlin's Kabuki theater of democracy, where even Putin's rivals acknowledge they have no hope of actually winning, and merely hope to stay alive and remain out of prison. However, being able to show that a well-known American figure is willing to bend the knee to an international pariah is a great opportunity for Putin to re-assert his dominance and standing.

There is still no confirmation of an interview between Carlson and Putin, but a Russian government official anonymously told The Moscow Times, "The boss [Putin] will win the election without Tucker's help, but access to an American audience through Carlson during the heated struggle between Biden and Trump is again an opportunity to exert that proverbial influence on the U.S. election, given Carlson's huge audience." He also noted, "our propaganda will blast Carlson's words criticizing the Democrats, which means he will confirm our hawks' line up to the tiniest detail."

A source close to the presidential administration told The Moscow Times, "Tucker has been expected here for a long time. He is welcome here."

Carlson's arrival in Moscow threw Russian state TV media into a frenzy of detailed coverage, showcasing Carlson's visit to the ballet, his luncheon, visiting a Kamchatka stand at the Exhibition of Achievements of National Economy, and going for a ride on a subway. During Monday's broadcast of the state TV show *60 Minutes*, host Evgeny Popov gleefully declared that during his exploration of Moscow, Carlson "charged his smartphone via a USB port and connected to a fast and free WiFi internet." Popov proudly added, "American citizens can't even dream about such wonders of civilization!"

To underscore the depth of Carlson's commitment to the Russian cause, state media programs pointed out that in America, he is called out as a traitor and his trip is being compared to Jane Fonda's visit to Vietnam in 1972. During Sunday's broadcast of a show At Dawn on channel Solovyov Live, former New York Times correspondent John Varoli feverishly exclaimed that Carlson could be "liquidated" at any moment, describing him as "Joe Biden's enemy number one."

In Russia, where the killings or imprisonments of journalists and dissidents are quite routine, an absurd assertion that the Biden administration is trying to hunt down Tucker Carlson might sound believable.

During Monday's broadcast of *The Evening With Vladimir Solovyov*, the host claimed, "The main problem in America right now is what to do with Tucker Carlson!"

Solovyov alleged that previous interviews American journalists conducted with Putin were "chopped up," re-edited, and used "out of context."

He fumed, "In our journalism, this sort of thing is unacceptable by definition... it's taboo!" Solovyov assumed that this wouldn't happen with Carlson and Putin's potential interview which he thought would be showcased in its entirety.

Earlier on Monday, recognizing the fired host of Fox News as one of their own, the Russian Union of Journalists offered Tucker Carlson to join the organization, pay the dues, and abide by its rules.

During *The Evening With Vladimir Solovyov*, political scientist Sergey Mikheyev noted, "A few words about Tucker Carlson, since he is a popular figure. Lately, when I see him, I think there is something wrong with his psyche, because everyone is pressuring him. His eyebrows are raised, he constantly looks worried. He used to look better than this."

Mikheyev said, "If Tucker dares to broadcast this interview in the United States, first and foremost, this will blow up their informational blockade from within." Mikheyev predicted that Putin's interview would be more interesting than anything that is uttered by American politicians, claiming that both the Democratic and the Republican elites are "uninteresting and stupid."

Mikheyev said he was shocked to discover how many Americans believe that Michelle Obama was born a man. He intimated that if they were gullible enough to believe something like that, Tucker's interview with Putin is bound to have some "interesting" consequences.

Solovyov chimed in to add, "It will blow them up into pieces!" During a discussion about the United States, Mikheyev wistfully noted, "God willing, there will be a civil war!"

Putin Nearly Bores Tucker Carlson to Death With Two-Hour History Lesson

The longtime Putin defender is the first Western "journalist" to sit down with the authoritarian leader since Russia invaded Ukraine.

Originally published by *The Daily Beast* on February 08, 2024

The long-anticipated interview between former Fox News star Tucker Carlson and Russian President Vladimir Putin finally dropped on Thursday on X, making the longtime Putin defender the first Western "journalist" to sit down with the authoritarian leader since Russia invaded Ukraine.

Carlson began the more than two-hour long video with a brief monologue about his impressions following the interview, complaining that the two-hour conversation was longer than expected while adding that he emerged convinced that Putin's long-stated belief in Russia's historic claim to Ukrainian territory was sincere.

"Putin went on for a very long time, probably half an hour, about the history of Russia going back to the eighth century," Carlson said. "We thought this was a filibustering technique and found it annoying and interrupted him several times, and he responded. He was annoyed by the interruption."

"Vladimir Putin believes that Russia has a historic claim to parts of western Ukraine," Carlson added. "So our opinion would be to view it in that light, as a sincere expression of what he thinks."

When Carlson seemed to be unfamiliar with basic details preceding Russia's invasion of Ukraine, Putin snapped at the former Fox News host: "Are we having a talk show or a serious conversation?"

A long, drawn-out and thoroughly twisted history lesson would follow, which is one of Putin's favored tactics. Apparently tuckered out by Putin's spiel, Carlson pointed out, "I'm not sure why it's relevant to what happened two years ago."

After the modified history lesson was over, Tucker asked an astonishing question, "But may I ask, you're making the case that Ukraine, certainly parts of Ukraine, eastern Ukraine is in effect Russia — has been for hundreds of years. Why wouldn't you just take it when you became president 24 years ago? You have nuclear weapons. They don't. It's actually your land. Why did you wait so long?"

Instead of responding, Putin delved into another history lesson, going back all the way to 1654 and prompting Carlson to ask, "Do you believe Hungary has a right to take its land back from Ukraine, and that other nations have a right to go back to their 1654 borders?"

When Putin demurred, Carlson persisted, "Have you told Viktor Orbán that he can have part of Ukraine?" Putin replied, "Never. I have never told him. Not a single time."

In the course of the interview, Putin revisited old grievances about Russia offering to join NATO and being rejected. He blamed the U.S. for helping Ukraine to get rid of its formerly pro-Russian presidents, to which Putin was accustomed. He recalled successfully pressuring Yanukovych into not signing an association agreement with the EU.

Putin blamed Ukraine's Revolution of Dignity on the CIA, noting, "the organization you wanted to join back in the day, as I understand. We should thank God they didn't let you in."

With zero pushback from Carlson, Putin claimed that "they" (presumably, still talking about the CIA or Americans in general) "launched a large-scale military operation. Then another one. When they failed, they started to prepare the next one."

Putin brazenly claimed, "Our goal is to stop this war. And we did not start this war in 2022. This is an attempt to stop it." With no pushback whatsoever, Tucker asked, "Do you think you've stopped it now? I mean, have you achieved your aims?" Putin answered this rhetorical question by stating that so-called "de-Nazification" of Ukraine is yet to be completed.

In a comical exchange during the meandering interview, Tucker asked Putin: "Who blew up Nord Stream?" Putin replied, "You for sure."

Carlson parried: "I was busy that day. I did not blow up Nord Stream. Thank you though." Once again, Putin blamed the CIA, but refused to elaborate as to whether Russia has any evidence to prove that.

One of the leading questions Carlson asked attempted to blame NATO for Russia's invasion of Ukraine: "Right before you sent troops into Ukraine, the vice president of the United States, went to the Munich Security Conference and encouraged the president of Ukraine to join NATO. Do you think that was an effort to provoke you into military action?"

Putin broke out in another long speech, complaining, "No one listens to us."

Jumping from topic to topic, Putin assured Carlson he has no intention to invade Europe, claimed that Christianity does not stand in the way of the war Russia is waging in Ukraine and even threw in a comment about the owner of X (formerly Twitter): "I think there's no stopping Elon Musk."

To his credit, Carlson asked Putin to release the Wall Street Journal reporter Evan Gershkovich as a goodwill gesture. Putin harshly replied, "We have done so many gestures of goodwill out of decency that I think we have run out of them." He added that this matter could be solved through appropriate channels.

Despite Ukraine's heroic resistance and passionate commitment to its own Ukrainian identity, Putin claimed that even Ukrainian soldiers on the battlefield "still identify themselves as Russian" and described the bloody invasion as "an element of a civil war."

He dramatically proclaimed that Ukrainians and Russians would be "reunited" in the end: "No one will be able to separate the soul." The proclamation concluded Putin's two-hour history lesson, which included little if any pushback to the Russian leader's perspective.

Tucker Carlson has been desperately seeking to interview Russian President Vladimir Putin even before he was formally recognized as a wanted war criminal, sought by the International

Criminal Court (ICC). The designation did not repel the fired Fox News host and instead led him straight to Moscow, to shake hands with the man who spearheaded a bloody invasion of a neighboring nation, in his apparent quest to restore the Russian Empire.

Carlson revealed the slant of his inquiry even before the interview was released, portraying it as his noble attempt to inform clueless English-speaking audiences. He alleged this was necessary because "their media outlets are corrupt, they lie to their readers and viewers." Carlson asserted, "It is government propaganda, propaganda of the ugliest kind, the kind that kills people." This declaration sounded especially preposterous, since it was uttered from Moscow — the capital of government propaganda that kills people.

Government-controlled propagandists have long been cheering for Carlson to get this opportunity.

The spot where he stood to record the introduction spoke louder than words. Russian journalist, and political scientist Yevgenia Albats noted that for security reasons, this location is off-limits for most journalists: "The Ritz Carlton Hotel in Moscow stands right across from Red Square. Its roof is controlled by one of the KGB's successors, the Federal Security Service."

Carlson claimed, "Most Americans have no idea why Putin invaded Ukraine or what his goals are now. They've never heard his voice." To the contrary, the coverage of this invasion, along with the Kremlin's alleged rationale for doing so, has been extensively covered by Western media — including Putin's own on-camera statements, immediately prior to the invasion and thereafter.

Nonetheless, Tucker Carlson promised to deliver something the English-speaking world hasn't heard before — Putin's perspective, undiluted and uncut.

Despite state media personalities, along with the Kremlin's spokesman Dmitry Peskov, denying their foreknowledge of this interview, they've announced that it would be released in its entirety and without cuts or editing — days before Tucker did.

While many are questioning Carlson's motivation for pursuing this interview, Putin's most likely rationale for sitting down with an unaffiliated vlogger was articulated by Henry Sardaryan, Dean of the School of Governance and Politics at the Moscow State

Institute of International Relations, during Wednesday's broadcast of *The Evening With Vladimir Solovyov*.

He explained, "They [Americans] were so afraid of election interference by the Russian Federation, so worried that Russia is influencing them! I don't doubt that this interview alone, if it does not play a pivotal role, at the very least it will influence the outcome of these elections to an extraordinary degree."

Appearing on *60 Minutes* on Wednesday, political scientist Sergey Luzyanin said that Putin is "hammering this nail straight into the Western mainstream media" and described his interview with Carlson as "a slowly burning fuse, leading to the tinderbox known as American elections 2024." Luzyanin surmised that Americans will be opened up to the infusion of Putin's undiluted talking points. He noted, "It will be just like Columbus discovering America!"

Thursday morning, state TV host Vladimir Solovyov described Carlson's interview as Russia "beating the West with its own weapons."

Tucker Carlson Misses the Bullseye

The US polemicist's much-anticipated interview with Russian President Vladimir Putin landed with a thud of missed opportunities.

Originally published by *The Center for European Policy Analysis* (CEPA) on April 26, 2023

Prior to the sit-down, state TV propagandists had predicted that it would convince ordinary Americans that Russia is a land of "traditional values," fighting against "Satanism" in Ukraine and all over the world, having invaded the neighboring country mainly to destroy dangerous American biolabs.

Instead, Vladimir Putin rambled on for nearly two hours, delivering an utterly perverted version of history, obsessing about Yaroslav the Wise (who died in 1054, apparently) and failing to articulate why he decided to invade Ukraine.

Carlson, for his part, never asked about the massive death toll of Putin's needless military adventure, nor did he utter a peep about war crimes or asked about thousands of kidnapped Ukrainian children. The former Fox News host (fired last year for his role in a $787.5m defamation defeat) did ask about journalist Evan Gershkovich, who is wrongfully imprisoned in Russia, but nonetheless tacitly justified his arrest by conceding that he may have broken some Russian laws.

Head of RT Margarita Simonyan couldn't conceal that her first reaction was disappointment. She wrote on X (formerly Twitter), "It's a shame that Tucker didn't bring up conservative values. This is his strong point—as well as the strong point of the Boss [Putin], first and foremost."

Carlson did attempt to skew the conversation in a way that would allow Putin to showcase himself as a savior of Christianity and the defender of conservative values.

He asked, "You are a Christian leader by your own description. So, what effect does that have on you?" Instead of delivering a spiel that could potentially appeal to MAGA Americans, Putin went back to the year 988 and then proceeded to explain that Russia "absorbed" various nations that practiced Islam, Buddhism, and Judaism and these religions continue to be practiced in modern-day Russia.

Carlson tried it again, asking Putin, "So do you see the supernatural at work as you look out across what's happening in the world now? Do you see God at work? Do you ever think to yourself, these are forces that are not human?" Somehow, Putin again missed the cue and let his true Soviet feelings shine through. He replied, "No, to be honest. I don't think so."

Despite her initial disappointment, Simonyan bounced back and a few days later was praising the sit-down on Vladimir Solovyov's show, *Sunday Evening With Vladimir Solovyov*.

After all, she was admittedly instrumental in making sure that this interview took place, having been pestered by Tucker Carlson to make it happen since 2021.

Voicing no criticism whatsoever this time, Simonyan's only complaint was that the interview didn't happen sooner, since she believes it would imperil US aid to Ukraine even more than it currently is. Filmmaker Karen Shakhnazarov noted, "Information is the most powerful weapon!"

Simonyan declared, "This was the most successful, the most significant, and a truly historic media event in journalism in the history of humanity!"

Margarita praised Putin's intellect and claimed that the breadth of his knowledge "stunned" uneducated Americans, who don't read, typically don't own any books, and whose homes don't have any bookcases or bookshelves. Simonyan predicted that the interview would impact the US elections because Carlson's agenda was "to kick Biden as hard as he could."

The RT head and her husband, Tigran Keosayan, reportedly broke into tears listening to Putin, when he described the bloody and brutal invasion of Ukraine as "a civil war." Simonyan compared the fighting to the two Chechen wars (1994-1996 and 1999-

2000), rejoicing that despite prior bad blood, Chechens now fight alongside Russians in Ukraine—and essentially doing to Ukrainians what Russia did to them.

This is a popular theme that has been frequently showcased by the Russian media—a belief that once Russia defeats Ukraine, Ukrainians will cheerily join the ranks of the Russian armed forces and fight alongside them against Europe and America.

Last year, during his appearance on *The Meeting Place*, violinist Petr Lundstrem said: "What we need is the repeat of what happened 20 years ago in Chechnya. The people who are fighting against us now, should be fighting for us in the future."

In January of this year, Daniil Bezsonov, Deputy Minister of Information of the Kremlin's puppet government, the Donetsk People's Republic, described Ukrainians as Russia's "mobilization resource in a future war with NATO."

Last Tuesday, appearing on *Full Contact* with Vladimir Solovyov, Maj. Gen. Apti Alaudinov, Chechen commander of Akhmat special forces and deputy commander of the 2nd Army Corps, promoted the same notion.

He predicted, "I think that the final outcome of all this will be that the Ukrainian people will join our ranks and will jointly fight with us to defeat the Hydra that is in power there and the Hydra that is confronting them from abroad, in America and Europe."

Alaudinov said he anticipates that these battles will continue until approximately 2030.

Putin Says He Was Not Impressed by Tucker Carlson

"Sincerely speaking, I didn't fully enjoy this interview," the Russian leader said this week.

Originally published by *The Daily Beast* on February 14, 2024

Tucker Carlson did all that he could to impress the Russian authoritarian Vladimir Putin: he asserted that Russia is not an expansionist power, claimed that Moscow is better than any American city, posed in a Buryat costume, and lobbied against continued U.S. aid to Ukraine.

Nevertheless, Putin was not impressed. He told interviewer Pavel Zarubin this week, "Sincerely speaking, I didn't fully enjoy this interview."

"Frankly, I thought he would behave aggressively and ask tough questions. I wasn't just prepared for this, I wanted it!" Putin insisted.

The Russian president complained that Carlson's failure to ask pointed questions "didn't give him an opportunity to do what he was prepared to do" and therefore, this interview didn't turn out to be as engaging or substantive as it could have been.

When Zarubin queried the Russian president as to what he thought about negative reactions of Western leaders, Putin evasively replied that it's a good thing they're watching and listening.

He added, "If today, due to their own reasons, we are unable to conduct direct dialogue, then we should be grateful to Mr. Carlson for the fact that we can do this through him as an intermediary."

For years leading up to Tucker Carlson's interview with Putin, he was a darling of the Russian state media. Top Russian propagandists gushed about him, featured translated clips of his Fox News segments and even described Carlson as "the only American they wouldn't want to kill."

Head of RT Margarita Simonyan recounted that Carlson repeatedly contacted her since 2021, pleading for an interview with Putin—and his attempts intensified after Russia invaded Ukraine. Simonyan said that she went "from office to office, begging for what we [RT] believe is important for the country." State media's talking heads predicted that the interview would blow up the U.S. elections and stun gullible Americans.

Instead, the sit-down was more of a monologue than a conversation, with Putin droning on about ancient and modern history, deliberately twisted to justify Russia's revanchist aspirations with respect to Ukraine. The outcome was clearly underwhelming.

Carlson's softball endeavor was not only ridiculed in the West, but also rejected by Russian audiences. The interview, showcased two times during primetime hours on Channel One, received dismal ratings. It ranked 19th in the nationwide lineup and 11th in Moscow, against the lineup of the most popular television programs for that week, barely beating out a competition of psychics.

Even Simonyan, who was so instrumental in laying the groundwork for this fiasco, couldn't conceal her initial disappointment. She wrote on X (formerly Twitter), "It's a shame that Tucker didn't bring up conservative values. This is his strong point—as well as the strong point of the Boss [Putin], first and foremost."

Russian propagandists anticipated questions about Satanism, LGBT issues and American biolabs. The closest they got was when Carlson asked Putin, "So do you see the supernatural at work as you look out across what's happening in the world now? Do you see God at work? Do you ever think to yourself, these are forces that are not human?"

Putin failed to take advantage of the leading question and delivered a very Soviet-minded response: "No, to be honest. I don't think so."

Despite her initial frustration about wasted propaganda opportunities, Simonyan quickly bounced back and was soon praising the interview on Vladimir Solovyov's show, *Sunday Evening With Vladimir Solovyov*. With fervor rivaling the infamous North Korean "woman in pink," Simonyan declared, "This was the most successful, the most significant and a truly historic media event in journalism in the history of humanity!"

To spice things up, Simonyan claimed that herself and her husband Tigran Keosayan were so moved that they wept while watching the interview.

Now that Putin has revealed his disappointment with the outcome of her pet endeavor, Simonyan may be crying for other reasons — or quickly changing her rhetoric to match that of "the Boss."

Putin's Pals Link Death of Alexei Navalny to Tucker Carlson Interview

Kremlin propagandists promoted all sorts of lurid fantasies soon after it was announced that Vladimir Putin's nemesis was dead.

Originally published by *The Daily Beast* on February 16, 2024

Alexei Navalny, the most formidable critic of Russian President Vladimir Putin and his corrupt circles, who survived a poisoning and endured brutal persecution for years, died in the "Polar Wolf" Arctic penal colony. The Federal Penitentiary Service of the Yamalo-Nenets Autonomous District claimed that Navalny "felt unwell" after he went on a walk and "almost immediately lost consciousness." Prison officials said that a resuscitation was unsuccessfully attempted.

Navalny has long been a thorn in Putin's side and was relentlessly smeared by the Kremlin's cheerleaders. Even after his demise, Russian propagandists couldn't feign any dignity or humanity. Head of RT Margarita Simonyan posted on X (formerly Twitter) that the so-called "victims" of Navalny's corruption investigations keep calling her, wishing for him not to rest in peace. She hypocritically claimed she couldn't join them in those wishes, but only because she is observing an Armenian Lent.

In 2021, Simonyan described Navalny as "a traitor of the Motherland" and argued that like any traitor, he deserves to die. Referring to the Skripals and Litvinenko, Simonyan asserted that any method is acceptable when it comes to the people she deemed to be "traitors."

NATO Secretary-General Jens Stoltenberg said that "Russia needs to answer all the serious questions about the circumstances of his death." Simonyan sniped back, "Russia owes nothing to no one, let's start with that."

Since in Russia "death of natural causes" can mean many different things, especially with respect to the opposition leaders and journalists, Simonyan immediately started to stir up rumors of foul play—not by Putin, but his enemies. She wrote, "Everyone has long forgotten him, there was no point in killing him, especially before the elections, it would be beneficial to completely opposite forces."

Simonyan shared a post from a Telegram channel "BP Online" that said, "This is the retaliation for the interview. Thankfully, it wasn't [Tucker] Carlson." Despite Putin's displeasure with the way Carlson's interview with him had unfolded, the former Fox News host is a darling of the Russian state media, where he is described as the only American they wouldn't want to kill.

This feeling is clearly mutual.

On Monday, while he was at the World Government Summit in Dubai, Carlson was asked by Egyptian journalist Emad El Din Adeeb why he never pressed Putin about the freedom of speech in Russia and why he "did not talk about Navalny, about assassinations, about restrictions on opposition in the coming elections."

Carlson coldly replied, in part, "Every leader kills people. Some kill more than others. Leadership requires killing people." He openly endorsed the elimination of inconvenient opposition figures and journalists, falsely alleging that this kind of a domestic policy is common everywhere.

Other Russian propagandists also pushed the idea that Navalny's death was somehow beneficial to the West, implying that foul play was involved. Writer Nikolai Starikov posted on Telegram, "Navalny departed from life at a very convenient time for the Western puppeteers" and argued that this may have been done to undermine the PR effect of Carlson's interview and to prompt the U.S. Congress to approve the aid to Ukraine. Starikov claimed that Navalny's wife Yulia is at the Munich Security Conference on the same day, which is "part of the plan."

Despicably, Starikov claimed that Navalny's widow "is barely holding back her smile." His revolting post was boosted by Vladimir Solovyov, a notorious state TV host who for years maligned Navalny as a "traitor," smeared his followers as "Satanists" and proclaimed that he deserved the death penalty.

Now, in light of an untimely death of Russia's most prominent opposition leader, Russian propagandists are both enjoying it and pretending that anyone but Putin is to blame.

Putin Plants 'Info-Bombs'

The Russian leader was openly disappointed about his widely mocked interview with Tucker Carlson. He took to the air again days later to answer the questions he hadn't been asked.

Originally published by *The Center for European Policy Analysis* (CEPA) on February 16, 2023

Vladimir Putin always likes to behave like the tough guy. In a February 14 interview, he sounded like a boxer disappointed that his sparring partner had been such a poor match.

"I honestly thought he would be aggressive and ask so-called sharp questions," he told state television's Pavel Zarubin. "And I wasn't just ready for that, I wanted it, because it would have given me the opportunity to respond sharply in kind... But he [Carlson] chose a different tactic."

The sense of Kremlin disappointment was clear. And this was no doubt echoed by Putin's senior staff in their regular behind-the-scenes meetings where propagandists are given their lines to repeat.

The days before the big interview on February 8 (it clocked in at more than two hours) were a time of gleeful anticipation for the leader's information machine.

The big-name pro-Kremlin propagandists predicted that it would have an immediate impact, disrupting the upcoming US presidential elections and changing public opinion in the West. Their excitement was all too apparent, with RT head Margarita Simonovna taking credit for organizing the meeting and later revealing that it had made her cry.

Understandably perhaps. The softball sit-down was lambasted the world over as an exercise in futility and for offering a bored planet an unwanted lecture in Putin's brand of twisted history.

It's fair to say that more people have now heard of Prince Ryurik and Yaroslav the Wise because of Putin's initial, rambling 32-minute answer, but perhaps not in the way the Kremlin had hoped.

The Kremlin likes to say that Russia is a great power standing apart (and often above) the West, and yet it has a near-obsession with the contours of debate in the free world's media. Putin openly acknowledged that he had followed the West's post-interview debate when he arranged the Valentine's Day discussion with Zarubin.

The broadcast was perhaps a version of how Putin would like the interview to have gone and was (with tedious predictability) applauded by his propaganda staffers. But if he thought this second bite of the cherry would create the headlines that Carlson had failed to generate, he was wrong.

The Russian leader agreed with former US President Donald Trump's views about NATO, stating, "I personally believe that there is absolutely no point in NATO.

Its only purpose is to serve as a tool of US foreign policy. If the United States considers this tool no longer necessary, that is their decision."

At the same time, Putin blamed the Biden administration for allegedly "pursuing what amounts to a harmful and erroneous policy."

These comments made Putin's stance on this year's US Presidential vote as clear as day, and it was in perfect alignment with his loyal state TV propagandists and experts. They have repeatedly pined for the return of Trump, as "the destroyer of America," and their best hope that the US will retreat from the world stage and focus in on itself, thereby giving the Kremlin a free hand.

In all likelihood, Carlson didn't ask whether Putin prefers Trump because the answer was too obvious. And yet, as Putin's follow-up interview demonstrated, that was a question that he did want to answer — for nefarious reasons.

Putin, the former KGB agent, does have some grasp of the world he inhabits, and his disinformation is pitched accordingly.

After starting the biggest land war in Europe since World War II, Russia has become so toxic that Putin's praise inevitably taints its recipient.

So when Putin told Zarubin that Biden would be better for Russia than Trump, it might have seemed to be a subtle piece of manipulation. Except that minutes before, he had been condemning his policies.

Even the most credulous propaganda consumer could hear the sound of screeching tires as Putin executed his 180-degree turn.

The unsubtlety continued. His propagandists immediately gave the game away by extolling this move as a top-notch disinformation gambit and sycophantically praised the boss's unsurpassed tradecraft.

When some media outlets said that Putin was merely "trolling" when he claimed to prefer Biden, Russia's No. 1 Kremlin mouthpiece, Vladimir Solovyov, used his TV show, *The Evening With Vladimir Solovyov*, to argue.

"This was the first time the president of the Russian Federation said whom we prefer [as the US president]. They say it's trolling. No, this is not trolling. It's a precise calculation."

Political scientist Dmitry Kulikov noted: "I like how [Putin] is working them. Yesterday, it gave me pleasure watching his interview with Pavel Zarubin. The president said he wasn't pleased about his conversation with Tucker Carlson, but I was pleased with this one."

Kulikov suggested the second interview was designed to supplement the Carlson flop, since the fired Fox News fanboy was simply overwhelmed by the presence of the great man: "It included topics not covered by Tucker—or questions he couldn't figure out how to ask, because he was in such a state of shock."

During Solovyov's February 14 morning show, he described Putin's comments about Biden and Trump as "a large number of carefully placed info-bombs and mines."

Professor Dmitry Evstafiev added: "Russia is often being criticized for its inability to wage information wars. Often, this criticism is quite justified. We have lost in many political and information-related situations. But let me tell you, we are learning!"

Evstafiev pointed out that after Putin saw the reactions and read the comments about the Carlson interview, he arranged for the "after-party" with Zarubin and filled in the blanks. He proudly added, "This will be in the textbooks as a perfectly executed action, with respect to its place, its timing, and style."

Discussing Putin's commentary on Trump and Biden on Thursday, host of *60 Minutes* Olga Skabeeva surmised, "Putin said one thing, but everyone understood that he meant something else entirely."

Russia Issues Chilling Warnings to Navalny's Widow

The name of Alexey Navalny was taboo across Russian state media for years preceding his death. No longer.

Originally published by *The Center for European Policy Analysis* (CEPA) on February 21, 2024

Following Russian President Vladimir Putin's lead, state TV hosts referred to the opposition leader as "that man," "that citizen," or "the Berlin patient"—a mocking reference to his recovery period after being poisoned with Novichok by suspected agents of the Russian state.

After Navalny died in the prison north of the Arctic Circle to which he had recently relocated, prominent propagandists started to drop his name with ease. Once his widow, Yulia Navalnaya, said on February 19 that she was "going to continue the work" of her late husband, she entered their crosshairs as well.

Some of the language and accompanying hints of a dark future for Navalnaya left the discerning viewer with an ominous impression of Kremlin rage that the widow had shown impudence to step into her husband's shoes.

During his February 20 show, *Full Contact*, the host Vladimir Solovyov targeted Navalnaya in one of his infamous rants.

Implying Navalny's death was linked to Western security services and his attorneys and timed to coincide February 16-18 Munich Security Conference, he said: "It's all clear with the death of this Berlin patient on the opening day of the Munich Conference, two days after his attorneys paid him a visit at the colony."

Solovyov wondered whether Navalny should even be afforded a burial place, baselessly accusing him of being a "terrorist." He brought up opposition leader Boris Nemtsov, who was assassinated in cold blood just yards from the Kremlin (by suspected state agents in 2015), warning those who seek to honor his memory: "You are enemies of my country!"

Solovyov's diatribe, already menacing, then took an even wilder turn as he returned to the subject of Navalnaya.

The Kremlin-decorated state TV host warned that Navalny's widow will suffer the same extreme persecution as her late husband. Solovyov exclaimed, "The same fate awaits Navalnaya! If she comes to Russia, she will go to prison."

Some elements of Russian propaganda are better understood inside the country than in the West. Solovyov was not unsubtle enough to state that Navalnaya is now an enemy of the state and subject to the same targeting by the security services, but he didn't need to. After all, we now know what happens to those who "go to prison."

By detailing Navalny's supposed crimes, he made a typical Putinist defense of state murder while seeking to shift the responsibility elsewhere. "The West is the only beneficiary of his death! Here, he wasn't interesting to anyone, unwanted and forgotten— totally gone. They had to revive interest, shake things up, and disrupt the fantastic effect from the interview of our country's leader with Tucker Carlson. There was the opening of the Munich Conference, his wife is there... and here is a gift for them!"

Solovyov recalled a long-standing Russian tradition of not speaking ill about the dead but immediately maligned Navalny, calling him "a Nazi" and the creator of a "totalitarian cult" that is sending donations to the Ukrainian Armed Forces. He claimed that Navalny's followers "will send Navalnaya back to Russia so she can be imprisoned." He surmised, "She already said and did enough to end up in prison."

Solovyov continued, "As Navalny's own experience demonstrates, no amount of pressure would change anything."

As always, other propagandists joined the Navalny denunciation with supporting content (unsurprising given that TV network executives regularly hold meetings with top Kremlin officials, who decide their lines of attack.)

Host Roman Golovanov started his February 20 broadcast of *Golovanov's Time* on Solovyov Live by stating, "I would like to say a couple of words about Navalny... He was under constant surveillance by the British and American intelligence services... despite everything that happened, I am certain that prison was the safest place for Navalny. There was no safer place for him! If he was somewhere in Berlin or roaming free someplace here, all of this would have happened a lot faster and a lot sooner."

Golovanov then contradicted himself, speculating that Navalny most likely died of natural causes. "There is no need to even talk to anyone who says that the Kremlin gave an order to kill Navalny... It's clear for whom all of this was beneficial. First and foremost, the British!" he said.

This follows a long-established Kremlin obsession where Putin's Russia—like the Soviet Union before it—looks to blame the British for most suspicious deaths that actually benefit the Kremlin.

Golovanov added: "The fact that Yulia Navalnaya immediately appeared—within seconds—she stepped out at the Munich [Security] Conference and started to speak, with a beautiful manicure."

Head of RT Margarita Simonyan did the same, as she falsely accused Navalnaya of smiling and enjoying her time in the spotlight, baselessly claiming that she never truly loved her husband. In the same breath, Simonyan praised Putin for working as hard "as a galley slave" and urged everyone to thank him, just in time for next month's "presidential election"—where he has no real opponents.

Putin Inc. Fears Navalny Even Beyond the Grave

During Alexey Navalny's life, you would rarely hear his name being uttered on Kremlin-controlled state TV or by the Russian President Vladimir Putin.

Originally published by *The Center for European Policy Analysis* (CEPA) on February 29, 2024

The ban on the opposition leader's name perished with the 47-year-old's untimely death at the hands of the Russian state on February 16. Now, Russia's No. 1 propagandist and state TV host, Vladimir Solovyov, can't stop talking about the opposition leader, as he seeks to besmirch him even in death and settle some personal scores in the process.

Solovyov exemplifies the motivation for the flaming hatred of Russia's ruling elites toward Navalny. In fact, he openly spells it out. Navalny and the organization he founded, the Anti-Corruption Foundation, known as the FBK, published explosive, extensively researched, and well-documented investigations into corruption by high-ranking Russian government officials, propagandists, and other stooges serving Putin's regime.

As the leading state TV host, cherished and decorated by Putin and the Kremlin, Solovyov is handsomely compensated for spreading propaganda to the masses. According to recent leaks attributed to Russia's presidential administration, in 2023, Solovyov's company received 1.5 billion rubles (roughly $16 million) from the Russian state budget. The same documents showed that in 2024, Solovyov's propaganda operation will receive $32 million.

Instead of spending his handsome earnings in his own country, as might be expected from a self-proclaimed ultra-patriot, Solovyov has been investing abroad—purchasing Italian villas, sending one of his sons to live and study in London, and constantly flying to the United States, where it was alleged that he had a secret family. The allegation resulted from investigative work by The Insider, Navalny's anti-corruption publication.

The opposition leader's work exposed and embarrassed not just Solovyov, but Putin himself and many others in his circle. At a time when so many Russians are struggling to make ends meet and are being sent to die for Putin's imperial dream, these revelations continue to be especially damaging.

Head of RT Margarita Simonyan stated that the "victims" of Navalny's corruption investigations keep calling her, wishing for him not to rest in peace.

During one of his infamous tirades on the February 27 broadcast of *Full Contact* on the Solovyov Live channel, which is broadcast on TV and on radio, the host raged about his feelings for the deceased opposition leader and laid out a series of untruthful statements designed to blacken his name.

"Politely speaking, I didn't like Navalny... Navalny did what is completely unconscionable and improper, he released information about my minor children during his Italian investigation," Solovyov said. "It was totally vile on his part."

He went on, "I considered him a lowlife! Once, I saw him in person. He was with his family, so I decided not to beat him up. What a creature he was, I don't even want to talk about it."

Solovyov complained that after the beginning of Putin's full-scale invasion, some of his friends became ashamed of him and were instead in awe of Navalny. He baselessly described his FBK, as "a network of spies," and once again insisted that Yulia Navalnaya should be criminally charged for comments made after her husband's untimely death.

Solovyov alleged that Navalnaya was "happy" that her husband died and stated untruthfully that she never visited him in prison — although she certainly did when such visits were allowed.

Addressing criticism from listeners that he had broken one of Russia's silent codes — that the dead should not be maligned — Solovyov responded: "Who started it? Alburov! Alburov started it! Who likes to dig around? The FBK!"

Georgy Alburov, an FBK investigator, presented a video entitled "The American Secret of Vladimir Solovyov."

Despite all of Russia witnessing the debacle with the government's refusal to release Navalny's body to his family in a timely manner, Solovyov shamelessly and falsely accused the wife and mother of the deceased of abusing his remains.

During a February 29 broadcast on the Solovyov Live channel, the host Roman Golovanov urged authorities to identify and arrest any attendees at Navalny's March 1 funeral, unless they can prove to be relatives. The detained would include Yulia Navalnaya, whom they also want to see arrested and imprisoned (although she does not live in Russia.) It was later reported that funeral agencies are refusing to take Navalny's body to the church for the funeral service, citing "anonymous threats."

Solovyov also has a role as the regime's chief explainer. No doubt understanding that many in Russia have witnessed the Putin administration's repellent treatment of Navalny's remains, with officials refusing for days to hand it over to his mother, and demanding there should not be a public funeral, the broadcaster suggested all blame lay with Navalny's relatives.

"Can you imagine what is happening to the corpse you have been keeping in a warm room for 10 days?" He went on to say: "You are abusing the corpse! Can you imagine the level of decomposition? What are they trying to conceal?"

Solovyov complained that the family failed to bury Navalny "according to Christian customs," within three days of his death when in reality they were still fighting to get his body from the authorities.

Georgy Volkov, the head of Moscow's Public Monitoring Commission (ONK), appeared on Solovyov's program to share the supposed charmed existence Navalny had enjoyed in prison.

Volkov asserted that Navalny was in great physical shape and had no health problems, aside from periodic back pain. He surmised that the photos in which he appeared to be emaciated were either faked or taken from bad angles.

Volkov said, "[Navalny] spent most of his time with his attorneys, who visited him every day. They spent practically all daytime hours with him, while he was supposed to be serving his time in prison." He repeatedly reiterated the improbable claim that Navalny's attorneys visited him every single day at the Arctic prison some 1,200 miles northeast of Moscow, where he spent all his waking hours in their company.

Volkov alleged that Navalny and the imprisoned Wall Street Journal reporter, Evan Gershkovich, whom he also visited in prison, exhibited more self-control than an average inmate, baselessly speculating that both had received special training that prepared them for their eventual jailing. The unsubtle hint was that both men were undercover spies.

Solovyov aired a clip of Kyrylo Budanov, the chief of the Main Directorate of Intelligence of Ukraine's Ministry of Defense, who claimed Navalny died of natural causes — before any official conclusion as to the cause of his death has been released by Russian authorities. If Budanov's comment was a clever trap for his country's invaders, Solovyov swallowed the bait — hook, line, and sinker.

Solovyov argued that the opposition leader likely did not die of natural causes. He accused the CIA and Ukrainians of being instrumental in "the perfect timing" of Navalny's death, which he alleged was designed to undermine the PR effect from Tucker Carlson's interview with Putin and the capture of Avdiivka in Eastern Ukraine, while also designed to coincide with the opening of the Munich Security Conference.

It's extremely doubtful that Solovyov believes what he says, and certain that he really does loathe the late Alexey Navalny. Whether the rest of Russia swallows the first and shares the second is open to doubt.

Trump is 'Unhinged' But We Love Him, Say Kremlin Mouthpieces

The controversial journey of Hungary's leader to the US resulted in ominous tidings for Ukraine and delight in Moscow.

Originally published by *The Center for European Policy Analysis* (CEPA) on March 12, 2024

After meeting with Donald Trump in Florida, Hungarian Prime Minister Viktor Orbán decided on March 10 to detail what he said were the former US president's plan to end the war in Ukraine in 24 hours.

Just as Russian experts and pundits had long suspected, the plan is merely an intention to terminate US aid to Ukraine, in hopes that the conflict between the empowered invader and his intended victim would eventually fizzle out.

Orbán said: "[Trump] will not give a penny in the Ukraine-Russia war. That is why the war will end." He added, "If the Americans don't give money and weapons, along with the Europeans, then the war is over. And if the Americans don't give money, the Europeans alone are unable to finance this war. And then the war is over."

The Hungarian leader, still bristling from being brushed aside at the February 1 European Union (EU) summit that agreed to provide $54bn in Ukraine aid, suggested Trump's actions would bring a truce. Leaving Ukraine without Western aid would eventually force it to capitulate. While the further dismemberment of Ukraine was not mentioned, the Kremlin has made clear it has greater ambitions beyond the lands it already seized.

The horrors of Russia's occupation and the avowedly genocidal intent of its state-funded mouthpieces towards Ukrainians got no mention at all.

It is highly unusual for a visiting foreign head of government to meet with a former president, and to completely bypass the US administration.

Even Trump's Russian admirers found the arrangement quite brazen. During the evening broadcast of a state TV show *60 Minutes* on March 11, State Duma member Leonid Kalashnikov marveled at Trump's devil-may-care attitude.

Describing Trump as "unhinged," the Russian lawmaker said that the former US president is "behaving as a Russian," citing Orbán's recent visit as an example.

Kalashnikov stated: "I am a fan of Trump, based on the interests of my country." He expressed gratitude for the four-year reprieve he said Trump's presidency provided for Russia, allowing the country to prepare for its expanded invasion of Ukraine. This is not unusual — lawmakers and foreign policy experts frequently gush about their affinity for Trump as "the destroyer of America."

During the morning broadcast of *60 Minutes* on March 11, host Olga Skabeeva smirked and gloated about Orbán divulging Trump's "secret plan."

Set to a jolly tune, the report remarked that Make America Great Again (MAGA) Republicans in the US Congress are already helping Trump in his plan, blocking American aid to the fledgling democracy.

Skabeeva said: "If Trump wins the election, he won't give a penny to Ukraine." She cited Orbán's words that after America ends aid to Ukraine, Europeans would follow suit and the conflict will resolve itself. Skabeeva noted: "This scheme suits us well."

After mentioning Trump's alleged intent to restructure any potential aid to Ukraine as a debt that would have to be repaid, Skabeeva flashed a lopsided grin and let out an uncontrolled giggle. Even the former president's cheerleaders in Moscow suspect that this is not a serious suggestion, but merely a fig leaf to conceal his indifference to Ukraine's future and a delaying tactic towards a country at war, where delays translate into more death and suffering.

Recent overtures about negotiations by Pope Francis have garnered nothing but scorn from Russia's most prominent propagandist, state TV host Vladimir Solovyov (despite the Pope's suggestion that Ukraine "show the courage of the white flag.")

He was more inclined to fawn over Orbán's assurances that Trump simply plans to abandon Ukraine, allowing it to be erased by the Kremlin. Readying for an authoritarian new world where the democratic norms are obsolete, Solovyov suggested that Russia abandon language suggesting it's a democracy, or even stop using the related terms.

During the March 11 broadcast of *The Evening With Vladimir Solovyov*, political scientist Sergey Mikheyev hypothesized that during Trump's potential second term, Orbán might become an official intermediary between Trump and Putin. Mikheyev said that Hungary would thereby gain an invaluable position of global influence.

Surmising that Trump's return to the White House would mean the inevitable fall of Ukraine, Solovyov added that Hungary would also expand its borders by being gifted the Ukrainian Carpathians — courtesy of both Trump and Putin.

Pundits in the studio laughed out loud, but Solovyov shook his head and emphasized, "I am not joking whatsoever."

Putin's Friends Celebrate Re-Election With Photos of Mass Hanging

Images of Russian "traitors" being executed were shown on state TV in a chilling warning about the next six years of the "Supreme Commander."

Originally published by *The Daily Beast* on March 18, 2024

Russian President Vladimir Putin continued to maintain his unrelenting grip on power through the latest sham election, in which none of the other contenders had any hopes, plans or even dreams of winning. The only peace candidate, Boris Nadezhdin, was threatened by top pro-Kremlin propagandist Vladimir Solovyov and prevented from participating in the election. Some of his supporters are now being arrested and their homes are being searched by law enforcement. The main opposition leader, Alexei Navalny, died suddenly in prison, just in time for Putin's big show.

Leonid Slutsky of the Liberal Democratic Party of Russia (LDPR), who ended up in the last place, hammered home the obvious, as he said during a TASS press conference, "In these elections, the main point is not victory but participation." Slutsky added, "This percentage—the difference between the three candidates—does not matter in the slightest. It matters that we participated in the historic campaign for the Russian presidential election, which once again confirmed the authority of the leader of the nation."

State media's coverage consisted of jubilant proclamations, juxtaposed with violent threats to any opponents of Putin's regime—foreign and domestic. Appearing on Monday's broadcast of a state TV show *60 Minutes*, State Duma member Oleg Matveychev proclaimed, "These elections were truly unprecedented and, by the way, legitimate." He added, "The result is unprecedented and historic! People came, first and foremost, to support our guys that are now fighting on the frontlines. Everyone saw their vote as a shot towards the enemy."

During Saturday's broadcast on TV channel Solovyov Live, while the electoral kabuki performance was underway, host Marat Bulatov described the process as a mere "ritual," designed to support Putin. Commentator Vitaly Serukhanov added, "Everyone understands, Russia is currently in a certain historic stage. It would be incorrect, not to say criminal, not to support the Supreme Commander."

Serukhanov asserted that Putin's re-election had global implications, stating, "You can see that tectonic shifts are happening all over the world. The North American hegemon is falling." Host Marat Bulatov added, "These are historic times! We are becoming the center — even if not the center of creation, then at least the center of global changes."

Referring to the enemies of Putin's regime as "Vlasovites," Bulatov said that a picture is worth a 1,000 words and put up a photograph of what happened to Andrey Vlasov, a controversial figure in Russian history. Showcasing a graphic picture of a mass hanging, Bulatov said, "Here they are! This is how they ended up. There is no other way. Enough with half-measures. Traitors have to be dealt with in a radical way." Serukhanov chimed in, "This is it, this is the only way."

During his jubilant appearance at his campaign headquarters on Sunday, Putin made a similar reference: "During the Great Patriotic War, there was a formation created by the traitor Vlasov — the Vlasovites. They also fought against their homeland with weapons in their hands. How they ended up is well known."

It should be noted that Russian propaganda uses broad strokes in describing not only armed resistance, but Putin's opposition leaders as "Vlasovites." For years, Putin's top propagandists referred to Alexei Navalny as a "traitor" and argued that he deserved to die.

Gruesome imagery and threatening messaging were accompanied by extreme excitement about Putin's re-election, reminiscent of North Korea's theatrical celebrations. State TV host Marina Kim and actor Vyacheslav Manucharov seemed to be beside themselves during Monday's broadcast for Solovyov Live straight from the Red Square, celebrating the 10th anniversary of the annexation of Crimea and Putin's re-election.

A group of grim-faced men in folk outfits silently stood behind them. Manucharov turned to the extras and urged them to join him in yelling "Hurrah!" Kim excitedly announced, "I feel like a child! I want to simultaneously cry and explode! It's a feeling of total happiness!" She added, "I spent practically all night at Putin's campaign headquarters, all of us are celebrating the electoral victory of Vladimir Putin! We won't forget this victory!"

Manucharov excitedly exclaimed, "This is an extraordinary number! Absolute trust and love of the people! Total happiness! We're glad we can finally voice it on-air and congratulate our Supreme Commander with his stunning victory! Hurrah! Hurrah! Hurrah!"

During his Monday's appearance on the program At Dawn, weatherman Evgeny Tishkovets went even further and claimed that even nature is celebrating Putin's re-election. He pompously asserted, "Our fifth ocean, the sky, is rejoicing over the victory of our president!"

Moscow Terror Attack: A Lie Too Good to Waste

The glib, truth-twisting narratives of Putin's mouthpieces serve the regime but dishonor the dead.

Originally published by *The Center for European Policy Analysis* (CEPA) on March 24, 2024

The March 22 terrorist attack at Crocus City Hall, on the outskirts of Moscow, was still unfolding, and the fire was engulfing the upper levels of the seven-story concert hall when the Kremlin's television outlets got to grips with the unfolding tragedy.

Russian law enforcement had launched a huge (if belated) manhunt to apprehend suspects who had managed to shoot dead at least 133 concert-goers attending the event by the band, Picnic. The bloodshed lasted about 20 minutes, without any apparent intervention by the security forces.

The four suspected terrorists then managed to flee the scene, although their exact number and identities were unknown at that point in time.

And yet, in the absence of almost all the key facts, Russian government officials and propagandists immediately started to blame Ukraine. (All evidence so far suggests the mass murders were, in fact, organized and executed by a branch of the so-called Islamic State terrorist group, ISIS, based in Pakistan and Afghanistan.)

Sergey Karnaukhov, host of Solovyov Live, claimed that the terrorist attack was unprecedented and had no global equivalent — seemingly forgetting the numerous, mostly Islamist terrorist attacks of the Putin era. These included the 2002 Dubrovka theater attack, which killed 130, the 2004 Beslan school siege, which left 330 dead, and several others.

More recently, the October 7 Hamas pogrom in Israel resulted in at least 1,200 deaths—an event that Russian propagandists branded as "good news," while mocking the Israelis for their lack of preparedness.

Earlier this month, the US had publicly warned of a potential attack targeting large gatherings in Moscow. Just three days before the massacre, President Vladimir Putin dismissed these warnings and said they resembled "outright blackmail and an intention to intimidate and destabilize [Russian] society."

Following the attack, these warnings were cited as evidence that the West had foreknowledge of the planned assaults.

Karnaukhov said: "All of you remember, embassies of the United States and Great Britain called on their citizens to leave Russia due to the impending terrorist attacks. What did you mean? You knew this?"

He added: "We know that Ukraine is the link between British and American intelligence services... Ukraine is a proxy force of American and British military and intelligence services. Does anyone have any doubt as to who did this?" Karnaukhov confidently asserted, "I'm sure that Ukraine did this!" The US-British motive was apparently to "delegitimize" Putin as a leader by depicting him as unable to protect his people despite a prior warning.

Karnaukhov remarked that the evacuation of survivors was currently underway, and law enforcement was in the process of storming Crocus City Hall. Even at that early stage, he urged Russians to reject any claim linking the attack with terrorist cells or groups, insisting that Ukraine and the West were certainly to blame. "Without a doubt, the main organizers of this act are sitting in London, Washington, and Kyiv," he told Russians grappling with the terrible news.

The TV host then played a deepfake clip of Ukraine's top security official Oleksiy Danilov, which was designed to show that Ukraine—and not ISIS—had actually accepted responsibility. Shortly thereafter, Karnaukhov admitted it might have been an old clip, but insisted that it "doesn't change anything."

The show then wheeled in another senior propagandist, Armen Gasparyan, who likewise blamed the West and Ukraine and predicted that Moscow "would drive a wooden stake" through the chest of the perpetrators, drawing parallels with Russia's brutal tactics previously used in Chechnya—along with the physical liquidation of the Ukrainian government.

Dmitry Medvedev, Deputy Chairman of Russia's Security Council, posted on his Telegram account: "If it is established that these are terrorists of the Kyiv regime, it is impossible to deal with them and their ideological masterminds in any other way [than by executions and repression.] All of them must be found and mercilessly destroyed as terrorists—including government officials of a nation that committed such an atrocity. A death for a death."

When ISIS did claim responsibility, some hours after the event, it was dismissed by senior figures in the propaganda hierarchy. The head of RT, Margarita Simonyan, wrote on X (Twitter): "ISIS! ISIS??? About ISIS, that's fake." She repeatedly blamed the Ukrainians, using slurs, calling them "dogs," and describing the West as their "trainers."

The early narrative did not alter, even as information emerged to support Islamist responsibility. After the alleged attackers were captured and revealed to be from Tajikistan, Simonyan claimed that the West knew the identities of terrorists in advance, though she offered no evidence.

Meanwhile, it appeared the Russian security forces were using tested torture techniques to find more about the alleged gunmen. In a graphic video posted on Telegram, one of the detained had his ear cut off and was then forced to eat it by one of his interrogators.

Despite the evidence of what had transpired being readily available, Karnaukhov preposterously claimed that the suspect's ear "was ripped off by a tree branch, as he ran through the forest."

The man was identified as Radzhab Alizade. Karnaukhov played a clip of his interrogation, during which a voice off-camera sternly reminded the suspect: "I'm right here! You only have one ear left." Alizade struggled to answer questions and was barely able to speak Russian. Another suspect was provided with an interpreter to communicate with his interrogators.

Russian authorities routinely resort to violence and torture to obtain a desired confession. The problem is that suspects may say what the interrogator demands to avoid further abuse rather than tell the truth. It's equally clear they will be forced to claim links to Ukraine—even though ISIS-K reportedly posted a video pre-recorded on Alizade's phone and claimed responsibility.

In his speech to the nation the following day, March 23, Putin made no mention of ISIS and instead alleged that attackers were captured "while fleeing to Ukraine." The Bryansk Region, where the suspects are said to have been apprehended, borders both Belarus and Ukraine.

From a wholly cynical Kremlin perspective, the terror attack was too good an opportunity to waste.

Known to the world as a state that uses terrorist methods against its own people and against its neighbors (see the endless stream of war crimes in Ukraine), Russia's rulers jumped at the chance to tar Ukraine's government with the same brush.

The Islamist threat to Russia is established and decades-old, but it serves no useful propaganda purpose.

Alleged ties to Ukraine, on the other hand, are deemed useful to undermine global support for Ukraine's ongoing fight against the Russian invasion.

The attack can also be used as a justification for even more brutal measures against Ukrainians and the tightening of screws on the domestic opposition.

It's clear why the claims of so-called Ukrainian ties suit the Kremlin, and why—as so often—the truth does not.

Kremlin Glee as US Dithers on Lifesaving Ukraine Aid

Russian propagandists believe some US politicians are seeking to weaken Ukraine's hand in its war for national survival.

Originally published by *The Center for European Policy Analysis* (CEPA) on April 14, 2024

House Speaker Mike Johnson visited ex-President Donald Trump at his Mar-a-Lago resort in Florida on April 12, purportedly to present a new Republican "election integrity" bill. But pundits and experts on Russian state television watched Johnson's pilgrimage with very different expectations. Appearing on that night's broadcast of the flagship state TV show *60 Minutes*, Dmitry Abzalov, Director of the Center for Strategic Communications, described it as "the most important day."

He explained that Johnson's trip would decide the future of US aid for Ukraine. A $95bn supplemental aid package, mostly for Kyiv, is stalled in the House of Representatives because Johnson has so far refused to allow a vote, seemingly at Trump's behest. Its passage would be a serious setback for Russia.

Russia's top propagandists have argued Russia has a friend in Johnson since his election as Speaker in October. At the time, *60 Minutes* host Olga Skabeeva was thrilled.

She stated: "Johnson is not only an extreme-right Trump supporter, [he] always voted against aid to Ukraine and made corresponding statements that were considered to be anti-Ukrainian... Where Ukraine is concerned, it's sufficient to look at Johnson's ratings with respect to his support of Ukraine. His rating is very poor! This means that all of this suits us well."

Skabeeva proceeded to make a prediction as to what Johnson would do: "With a Trump fanatic as speaker, the bill... that was proposed by Biden definitely will not pass. Johnson will simply not put it up for a vote!"

Apparently pleased with Johnson, Skabeeva described him as "our Johnson" — not to be confused with Boris Johnson, the former British Prime Minister. This description was reminiscent of the way Trump is routinely described on state television as "our Trump" or Trumpushka.

The problem for the Kremlin's mouthpieces is that their reading of US domestic politics is driven by hope. While Skabeeva was right to identify Johnson's largely anti-Ukraine voting record, his current thinking is elusive. Some on the far-right accuse him of changing his mind on Ukraine, and he has been saying there will be a vote on the aid package.

Even so, many in the US pro-Ukraine camp are deeply skeptical of his intentions and furious that his actions to date have benefitted the Kremlin. The military situation is already deteriorating — Ukraine will be outgunned 10-1 in the coming weeks without an influx of arms, according to the most senior US general in Europe.

Russia's military likely assesses delays to US aid, or its termination, mean: "Ukrainian forces will be unable to defend against current and future Russian offensive operations," according to the Institute for the Study of War on April 13.

Although propagandists are poor predictors of international events, they can offer insights into their regime's thinking. Of course, they spread untruths and distortions, but they also have a license to truthfully explain what's in the Kremlin's heart. And they know of what they speak — senior government officials regularly meet state-funded journalists and issue "lines to take" on current events.

This use of mouthpieces to signal the regime's true feelings was visible when Putin said in a February 14 interview he hoped Joe Biden would win re-election. This attempt to feign a preference for the current president was met with open smirks by his state media talking heads. Multiple experts explained on state television that this was merely a jab designed to hurt Biden.

American aid to Ukraine is in doubt, and excited Russian propagandists cherish the prospect of Trump's return to office.

Some even predict that the US will be ruled by a Trump dynasty for decades to come.

Russia's preference for the Trump-controlled Republicans has been made abundantly clear, and efforts to infect Republican leaders and voters with Russian propaganda were openly discussed on state television in 2021 before Putin's full-fledged invasion of Ukraine.

Russian state media remains an extremely good predictor of what the Kremlin really intends. Even as many in the West and in Ukraine doubted intelligence warnings of the February 2022 all-out invasion, Moscow's mouthpieces were happily predicting it. The tactic of destroying Ukraine's infrastructure to "plunge Ukraine into darkness" and drive 20 million Ukrainian refugees to Europe was likewise openly discussed and continues to unfold. Likewise, the mass murder of Ukrainians was openly promoted and is being carried out.

Russia's tactic is not unlike the Zodiac killer's letters to the police—a desire to boast about its own crimes while at the same time concealing its true nature and identity. A clearly imperialist Moscow poses as a fighter against Western imperialism, while Putin's oppressive regime tells gullible Westerners that they are the ones being oppressed at home—and that opposing US aid to Ukraine is an assertion of their liberty.

The Kremlin's propagandists routinely explain that the best way to destroy the West is from within, by undermining its principles and compromising its vital alliances. And, they explain, there is more to come. As Putin's mouthpieces routinely say: "Ukraine is just the beginning."

Whiplash as Russia Toasts Derided Marjorie Taylor Greene as Their Top New Hero

Speaker Mike Johnson is no longer Russia's No.1 favorite, he's been replaced by a congresswoman who was once roundly mocked on Russian TV.

Originally published by *The Daily Beast* on April 19, 2024

In recent years, clips from Tucker Carlson's shows were prominently featured on many Russian state TV shows, with hosts and guests clinging to his every word and even surmising he might be the only American they don't want to kill.

After Carlson's flat-footed interview with Russian President Vladimir Putin, followed by caustic comments from both the host and the subject, the bloom was off the rose.

Similarly, Mike Johnson's arrival as the 56th Speaker of the House was cheered on state TV with the anticipation that—at Trump's request—he would block U.S. aid to Ukraine. For months, Johnson did just that, prompting state TV host Olga Skabeeva to describe him as "our Johnson." His recent reversal of this stance prompted Russian propagandists to debate whether he was "bought" or simply "bent over" by the Democrats.

Now, Russia's former favorites have been edged out by Congresswoman Marjorie Taylor Greene—the new darling of the Kremlin-controlled state television. In the past, Greene was routinely mocked for her uneducated statements and used as a prime example of how stupid all Americans are, which is a popular refrain in Russian media. After laughing at Greene for confusing gazpacho with the Nazi Gestapo and claiming that California wildfires have been caused by "Jewish space lasers," leading propagandists described her antics as evidence of the "mental debilitation" of Western politicians.

But the mood changed once Greene started to say things that the Russian propaganda apparatus found extremely useful. Her Tweets that labeled NATO as a useless organization and demanded the U.S. withdraw from the alliance it is currently leading were featured on state TV and described as "sensational." Greene's rhetoric has been interpreted by state TV host Evgeny Popov to mean that "She believes that Americans should help Putin win. Yes, you heard that right. To help him win in Ukraine."

Greene's baseless claims that the U.S. is "supporting Nazis in Ukraine" were likewise lauded by state TV propagandists and showcased on multiple channels. Previous mockery did not deter the state-controlled media from gladly using Greene's misleading statements to their advantage. The U.S. congresswoman was starting to become a long-distance darling for the Moscow crowd, prominently featured on state television and adored to the point that the Kremlin's favorite propagandist Vladimir Solovyov proclaimed, "Thank goodness she exists."

The importance of influential Westerners repeating the Russian talking points is constantly underscored by the head of RT, Margarita Simonyan—who admits that her state-controlled network is running covert operations in the United States and other countries. She described RT's efforts as the "empire of covert projects that is working with public opinion."

Greene is now routinely showcased on the most popular programs as a prime example that the cracks in the GOP support for Ukraine are "good signals from Washington." Solovyov and the guests on his show even touted Marjorie as a possible replacement for Russia's perennial favorite, Donald Trump, as the next U.S. president—while acknowledging that the congresswoman is "somewhat funny."

Greene's latest hijinks have firmly cemented her status as one of Moscow's most useful tools. Leading propagandists lauded her efforts to threaten Mike Johnson's speakership for his belated decision to allow a vote on the life-saving U.S. aid to Ukraine. They similarly rejoiced over a flurry of amendments to the Ukraine aid bill Greene filed with the House Rules Committee, including one to require any member who votes in favor of the package "to conscript in the Ukrainian military."

Greene filed more than 20 amendments to the bill and most of them sound as though they have been handcrafted by Russia's Foreign Affairs Ministry. Some of them demand that Ukraine close all its bio-laboratories, to prove that "Christian churches in Ukraine are able to operate free from government interference" and bar funding until "restrictions on Hungarians in Transcarpathia" and other minorities are lifted.

In light of Greene's own prior statements, one might imagine that the plight of Hungarians in Transcarpathia is not something she would organically discover or take any interest in. Perhaps coincidentally, the same narratives are being actively promoted by the Russian media.

During Thursday's broadcast of *The Evening With Vladimir Solovyov*, expert on America Dmitry Drobnitsky urged everyone to stop focusing on Mike Johnson and instead pay attention to Greene. He said, "The issue is not with Johnson. Speaker Johnson is not the one who is running Congress. Marjorie Taylor Greene is running Congress! It's all about those to whom she is willing to give the money. Everyone is afraid of her! She is everywhere, on every Committee, involved in all impeachments... This is a curious phenomenon in the camp of our real enemy. These are the kinds of people they have working in their Congress."

Florida Democratic Rep. Jared Moskowitz offered his own amendment that would appoint Greene "as Vladimir Putin's Special Envoy to the United States Congress." The Russians seem to agree.

Putin's Propagandists Rage Against the Republican 'Betrayal'

Kremlin mouthpieces are having a hard time explaining why a supposedly sympathetic US Congress has just passed a huge military aid package for Ukraine.

Originally published by *The Center for European Policy Analysis* (CEPA) on April 22, 2024

It seems like only yesterday Russia's propagandists were rejoicing over the successful interruption of the US aid to Ukraine, reportedly at the behest of former US President Donald Trump.

The delay has undoubtedly cost countless lives and imperiled Ukraine's critical infrastructure, left wide open due to diminished air defenses. Russian state TV had delighted in the destruction of the Trypilska Thermal Power Plant, the largest supplier of electricity to Kyiv, Cherkasy, and Zhytomyr regions, remarking that it will take years to rebuild it.

Celebrating the decline in Ukraine's capabilities without American help, prominent propagandists started to refer to Speaker of the House Mike Johnson as "our Johnson," in a similar vein to claiming Trump as their own, calling him "our Trump" or affectionately referring to him as Trumpushka.

When Speaker Johnson finally advanced the long-stalled aid package and the House approved $61bn of desperately needed foreign aid for Ukraine—including a measure to allow the sale of frozen Russian sovereign assets to help Ukraine's war effort—the disappointment in Moscow was palpable.

During Sunday's broadcast of *Sunday Evening With Vladimir Solovyov*, Russia's No. 1 propagandist Vladimir Solovyov took comfort by repeating his go-to nuclear schtick, describing himself as "a member of a small group of nuclear maniacs, the proponents of nuclear Armageddon." He vowed that Russia would keep fighting and that the war or wars would continue for a long time. He surmised, "I believe that a war with NATO is unavoidable."

Solovyov noted: "We are dealing with a cunning, systematic, and extremely brutal enemy. It's not about negotiations. It's either us or them." He added: "What is interesting is how Biden totally broke Trump and his supporters. He utterly destroyed them! This is Biden's unequivocal, brutal victory because, in return, he did not give anything to Republicans."

Solovyov yelled, "Biden achieved everything! He apparently used backstage methods to lure to his side the man whom the Republicans chose to represent the House [Speaker Johnson.] He betrayed them! He totally betrayed them! Not us, we have no friends there... This is all you need to know about American politics. They're traitors!"

Solovyov immediately contradicted himself by lauding one congressional representative who has stuck with the anti-Ukraine campaign. He approvingly played a clip of the extreme right-wing Congresswoman Marjorie Taylor Greene and one of her tirades against US aid for the embattled country. She was followed by the head of RT, Margarita Simonyan, a frequent guest on Solovyov's programs who always gets the first word after the host.

Simonyan praised Greene, describing her as "a real beauty," for her blonde hair, white coats, and fur collars. Later in the show, the RT head clarified that it doesn't take much in America to be considered beautiful or to win a beauty contest. In case viewers wondered about her expertise on the issue, Simonyan revealed that she had once worked as a waitress in Maine.

Having implied that Americans are predominantly ugly, Simonyan added that they are extraordinarily stupid. With a chutzpah that only be displayed by an utterly shameless propagandist, she blamed what she called the "dumbification" of the people by the US media.

In this way, she explained, "normal people" like Greene were vilified and instead of being lauded, they are labeled as "conspiracy theorists." (Among other things, Taylor Greene famously suggested in 2018 that California wildfires were started by covert space lasers operated by mysterious group of powerful people and has argued Ukraine is killing priests.) It should be noted that Russia's state media mocked Greene until her usefulness to the Russian cause became apparent.

But other than some words of support for the Georgia congresswoman, most of the response was pure rage and insult directed at the United States. Boris Yakemenko, who hosts a show called *Morning Z* on the Solovyov Live, channel described Americans with their "melting pot" as a bunch of disrespectful mutts with no history or national pride. He claimed that America is a brazen gopnik—an expression reserved for members of a delinquent subculture in Russia.

Beneath the seething anger is an unspoken truth—that the enormous US aid package seriously complicates Russia's realistic path to victory and ensures yet more tens of thousands of young Russians will suffer death and dismemberment. The evidence of enormous casualties is available for all to see in the swelling graveyards of the homeland.

Despite the boasting and bluster, Russians are suffering under the weight of Putin's war of aggression and the cracks are starting to show. Appearing on *The Evening With Vladimir Solovyov* last week, Karen Shakhnazarov urged fellow propagandists to start telling the truth about Russia's internal struggles and its many problems. Instead, others on the panel simply warned the viewers that hard times were coming and there was no resolution in sight, but Russia would certainly win in the end.

One of the visual demonstrations of this dichotomy was provided by host Yulia Vityazeva, who mocked Ukrainians for receiving American "handouts," and in the same breath asked fellow citizens to keep sending donations to supply Russian troops with a long list of urgently needed items, which the government still fails to provide.

Afterword

My readers and the viewers of my channel, Russian Media Monitor, often point out that observing the Russian media sphere in its natural habitat forever changed their prior perception of the country.

This is not the land of Tolstoy, Pushkin and Dostoevsky. Putin's Russia is dominated by violent, genocidal power mongers, serving a wannabe emperor—who resembles a mobster more than he does a Tsar.

It might be tempting for some to look away, as though it was as simple as changing the channel, but whether or not you're interested in Russia—Russia is interested in you. Whether or not you're watching Russia, Russia is watching you.

Putin's ultimate goal is to end the rules-based world championed by the West. This intended unseating of the current global leaders can't happen *sua sponte*: it requires constant meddling and behind-the-scenes plotting.

Conveniently, some of it spills out in the open, when Russian government officials, lawmakers, experts and opinion leaders plot to undermine the West, destroy domestic opposition, subjugate or eliminate their neighbors—live, on-air.

This book documents this eliminationist rhetoric and genocidal plotting for all the world to see, which will eventually become instrumental in future trials and tribunals of Putin, his henchmen, and his state-sanctioned propagandists. Perpetrators and promoters of genocide will be condemned by their own words.

Watching and analyzing what's happening on the airwaves of a state-controlled Russian television is important not only to understand how the Kremlin sees us, the aims it plans to pursue, the disinformation toolkit it uses and the views it is instilling in Russia's current and future generations.

It's also crucial to witness and fully understand what can happen to a country when it abandons even the pretense of a democracy—so we can avoid becoming that kind of a country ourselves.

UKRAINIAN VOICES

Collected by Andreas Umland

1   Mychailo Wynnyckyj
    Ukraine's Maidan, Russia's War
    A Chronicle and Analysis of the Revolution of Dignity
    With a foreword by Serhii Plokhy
    ISBN 978-3-8382-1327-9

2   Olexander Hryb
    Understanding Contemporary Ukrainian and Russian Nationalism
    The Post-Soviet Cossack Revival and Ukraine's National Security
    With a foreword by Vitali Vitaliev
    ISBN 978-3-8382-1377-4

3   Marko Bojcun
    Towards a Political Economy of Ukraine
    Selected Essays 1990–2015
    With a foreword by John-Paul Himka
    ISBN 978-3-8382-1368-2

4   Volodymyr Yermolenko (ed.)
    Ukraine in Histories and Stories
    Essays by Ukrainian Intellectuals
    With a preface by Peter Pomerantsev
    ISBN 978-3-8382-1456-6

5   Mykola Riabchuk
    At the Fence of Metternich's Garden
    Essays on Europe, Ukraine, and Europeanization
    ISBN 978-3-8382-1484-9

6   Marta Dyczok
    Ukraine Calling
    A Kaleidoscope from Hromadske Radio 2016–2019
    With a foreword by Andriy Kulykov
    ISBN 978-3-8382-1472-6

7   Olexander Scherba
    Ukraine vs. Darkness
    Undiplomatic Thoughts
    With a foreword by Adrian Karatnycky
    ISBN 978-3-8382-1501-3

8   Olesya Yaremchuk
    Our Others
    Stories of Ukrainian Diversity
    With a foreword by Ostap Slyvynsky
    Translated from the Ukrainian by Zenia Tompkins and Hanna Leliv
    ISBN 978-3-8382-1475-7

9   Nataliya Gumenyuk
    Die verlorene Insel
    Geschichten von der besetzten Krim
    Mit einem Vorwort von Alice Bota
    Aus dem Ukrainischen übersetzt von Johann Zajaczkowski
    ISBN 978-3-8382-1499-3

10 Olena Stiazhkina
    Zero Point Ukraine
    Four Essays on World War II
    Translated from the Ukrainian by Svitlana Kulinska
    ISBN 978-3-8382-1550-1

11 Oleksii Sinchenko, Dmytro Stus, Leonid Finberg (compilers)
    Ukrainian Dissidents
    An Anthology of Texts
    ISBN 978-3-8382-1551-8

12 John-Paul Himka
    Ukrainian Nationalists and the Holocaust
    OUN and UPA's Participation in the Destruction of Ukrainian Jewry, 1941–1944
    ISBN 978-3-8382-1548-8

13 Andrey Demartino
    False Mirrors
    The Weaponization of Social Media in Russia's Operation to Annex Crimea
    With a foreword by Oleksiy Danilov
    ISBN 978-3-8382-1533-4

14 Svitlana Biedarieva (ed.)
    Contemporary Ukrainian and Baltic Art
    Political and Social Perspectives, 1991–2021
    ISBN 978-3-8382-1526-6

15 Olesya Khromeychuk
    A Loss
    The Story of a Dead Soldier Told by His Sister
    With a foreword by Andrey Kurkov
    ISBN 978-3-8382-1570-9

16 Marieluise Beck (Hg.)
    Ukraine verstehen
    Auf den Spuren von Terror und Gewalt
    Mit einem Vorwort von Dmytro Kuleba
    ISBN 978-3-8382-1653-9

17 Stanislav Aseyev
    Heller Weg
    Geschichte eines Konzentrationslagers im Donbass 2017–2019
    Aus dem Russischen übersetzt von Martina Steis und Charis Haska
    ISBN 978-3-8382-1620-1

18 Mykola Davydiuk
    Wie funktioniert Putins Propaganda?
    Anmerkungen zum Informationskrieg des Kremls
    Aus dem Ukrainischen übersetzt von Christian Weise
    ISBN 978-3-8382-1628-7

19 Olesya Yaremchuk
    Unsere Anderen
    Geschichten ukrainischer Vielfalt
    Aus dem Ukrainischen übersetzt von Christian Weise
    ISBN 978-3-8382-1635-5

20 Oleksandr Mykhed
    „Dein Blut wird die Kohle tränken"
    Über die Ostukraine
    Aus dem Ukrainischen übersetzt von Simon Muschick und Dario Planert
    ISBN 978-3-8382-1648-5

21 Vakhtang Kipiani (Hg.)
    Der Zweite Weltkrieg in der Ukraine
    Geschichte und Lebensgeschichten
    Aus dem Ukrainischen übersetzt von Margarita Grinko
    ISBN 978-3-8382-1622-5

22 Vakhtang Kipiani (ed.)
    World War II, Uncontrived and Unredacted
    Testimonies from Ukraine
    Translated from the Ukrainian by Zenia Tompkins and Daisy Gibbons
    ISBN 978-3-8382-1621-8

23 *Dmytro Stus*
Vasyl Stus
Life in Creativity
Translated from the Ukrainian by
Ludmila Bachurina
ISBN 978-3-8382-1631-7

24 *Vitalii Ogiienko (ed.)*
The Holodomor and the
Origins of the Soviet Man
Reading the Testimony of
Anastasia Lysyvets
With forewords by Natalka
Bilotserkivets and Serhy
Yekelchyk
Translated from the Ukrainian by
Alla Parkhomenko and
Alexander J. Motyl
ISBN 978-3-8382-1616-4

25 *Vladislav Davidzon*
Jewish-Ukrainian Relations
and the Birth of a Political
Nation
Selected Writings 2013-2021
With a foreword by Bernard-
Henri Lévy
ISBN 978-3-8382-1509-9

26 *Serhy Yekelchyk*
Writing the Nation
The Ukrainian Historical
Profession in Independent
Ukraine and the Diaspora
ISBN 978-3-8382-1695-9

27 *Ildi Eperjesi, Oleksandr Kachura*
Shreds of War
Fates from the Donbas Frontline
2014-2019
With a foreword by Olexiy
Haran
ISBN 978-3-8382-1680-5

28 *Oleksandr Melnyk*
World War II as an Identity
Project
Historicism, Legitimacy
Contests, and the (Re-)Con-
struction of Political Commu-
nities in Ukraine, 1939–1946
With a foreword by David R.
Marples
ISBN 978-3-8382-1704-8

29 *Olesya Khromeychuk*
Ein Verlust
Die Geschichte eines gefallenen
ukrainischen Soldaten, erzählt
von seiner Schwester
Mit einem Vorwort von Andrej
Kurkow
Aus dem Englischen übersetzt
von Lily Sophie
ISBN 978-3-8382-1770-3

30 *Tamara Martsenyuk, Tetiana Kostiuchenko (eds.)*
Russia's War in Ukraine
During 2022
Personal Experiences of
Ukrainian Scholars
ISBN 978-3-8382-1757-4

31 *Ildikó Eperjesi, Oleksandr Kachura*
Shreds of War. Vol. 2
Fates from Crimea 2015–2022
With an interview of Oleh
Sentsov
ISBN 978-3-8382-1780-2

32 *Yuriy Lukanov*
The Press
How Russia Destroyed Media
Freedom in Crimea
With a foreword by Taras Kuzio
ISBN 978-3-8382-1784-0

33 *Megan Buskey*
Ukraine Is Not Dead Yet
A Family Story of Exile and
Return
ISBN 978-3-8382-1691-1

34 *Vira Ageyeva*
Behind the Scenes of the Empire
Essays on Cultural Relationships between Ukraine and Russia
With a foreword by Oksana Zabuzhko
ISBN 978-3-8382-1748-2

35 *Marieluise Beck (ed.)*
Understanding Ukraine
Tracing the Roots of Terror and Violence
With a foreword by Dmytro Kuleba
ISBN 978-3-8382-1773-4

36 *Olesya Khromeychuk*
A Loss
The Story of a Dead Soldier Told by His Sister, 2nd edn.
With a foreword by Philippe Sands
With a preface by Andrii Kurkov
ISBN 978-3-8382-1870-0

37 *Taras Kuzio, Stefan Jajecznyk-Kelman*
Fascism and Genocide
Russia's War Against Ukrainians
ISBN 978-3-8382-1791-8

38 *Alina Nychyk*
Ukraine Vis-à-Vis Russia and the EU
Misperceptions of Foreign Challenges in Times of War, 2014–2015
With a foreword by Paul D'Anieri
ISBN 978-3-8382-1767-3

39 *Sasha Dovzhyk (ed.)*
Ukraine Lab
Global Security, Environment, and Disinformation Through the Prism of Ukraine
With a foreword by Rory Finnin
ISBN 978-3-8382-1805-2

40 *Serhiy Kvit*
Media, History, and Education
Three Ways to Ukrainian Independence
With a preface by Diane Francis
ISBN 978-3-8382-1807-6

41 *Anna Romandash*
Women of Ukraine
Reportages from the War and Beyond
ISBN 978-3-8382-1819-9

42 *Dominika Rank*
Matzewe in meinem Garten
Abenteuer eines jüdischen Heritage-Touristen in der Ukraine
ISBN 978-3-8382-1810-6

43 *Myroslaw Marynowytsch*
Das Universum hinter dem Stacheldraht
Memoiren eines sowjet-ukrainischen Dissidenten
Mit einem Vorwort von Timothy Snyder und einem Nachwort von Max Hartmann
ISBN 978-3-8382-1806-9

44 *Konstantin Sigow*
Für Deine und meine Freiheit
Europäische Revolutions- und Kriegserfahrungen im heutigen Kyjiw
Mit einem Vorwort von Karl Schlögel
Herausgegeben von Regula M. Zwahlen
ISBN 978-3-8382-1755-0

45 *Kateryna Pylypchuk*
The War that Changed Us
Ukrainian Novellas, Poems, and Essays from 2022
With a foreword by Victor Yushchenko
Paperback
ISBN 978-3-8382-1859-5
Hardcover
ISBN 978-3-8382-1860-1

46 *Kyrylo Tkachenko*
Rechte Tür Links
Radikale Linke in Deutschland, die Revolution und der Krieg in der Ukraine, 2013-2018
ISBN 978-3-8382-1711-6

47 *Alexander Strashny*
The Ukrainian Mentality
An Ethno-Psychological, Historical and Comparative Exploration
With a foreword by Antonina Lovochkina
Translated from the Ukrainian by Michael M. Naydan and Olha Tytarenko
ISBN 978-3-8382-1886-1

48 *Alona Shestopalova*
From Screens to Battlefields
Tracing the Construction of Enemies on Russian Television
With a foreword by Nina Jankowicz
ISBN 978-3-8382-1884-7

49 *Iaroslav Petik*
Politics and Society in the Ukrainian People's Republic (1917–1921) and Contemporary Ukraine (2013–2022)
A Comparative Analysis
With a foreword by Mykola Doroshko
ISBN 978-3-8382-1817-5

50 *Serhii Plokhy*
Der Mann mit der Giftpistole
Eine Spionageschichte aus dem Kalten Krieg
ISBN 978-3-8382-1789-5

51 *Vakhtang Kipiani*
Ukrainische Dissidenten unter der Sowjetmacht
Im Kampf um Wahrheit und Freiheit
Aus dem Ukrainischen übersetzt von Christian Weise
ISBN 978-3-8382-1890-8

52 *Dmytro Shestakov*
When Businesses Test Hypotheses
A Four-Step Approach to Risk Management for Innovative Startups
With a foreword by Anthony J. Tether
ISBN 978-3-8382-1883-0

53 *Larissa Babij*
A Kind of Refugee
The Story of an American Who Refused to Leave Ukraine
With a foreword by Vladislav Davidzon
ISBN 978-3-8382-1898-4

54 *Julia Davis*
In Their Own Words
How Russian Propagandists Reveal Putin's Intentions
With a foreword by Timothy Snyder
ISBN 978-3-8382-1909-7

55 *Sonya Atlantova, Oleksandr Klymenko*
Icons on Ammo Boxes
Painting Life on the Remnants of Russia's War in Donbas, 2014-21
Translated from the Ukrainian by Anastasya Knyazhytska
ISBN 978-3-8382-1892-2

56 *Leonid Ushkalov*
Catching an Elusive Bird
The Life of Hryhorii Skovoroda
Translated from the Ukrainian by Natalia Komarova
ISBN 978-3-8382-1894-6

57 *Vakhtang Kipiani*
Ein Land weiblichen Geschlechts
Ukrainische Frauenschicksale im 20. und 21. Jahrhundert
Aus dem Ukrainischen übersetzt von Christian Weise
ISBN 978-3-8382-1891-5

58 Petro Rychlo
„Zerrissne Saiten einer
überlauten Harfe ..."
Deutschjüdische Dichter der
Bukowina
ISBN 978-3-8382-1893-9

59 Volodymyr Paniotto
Sociology in Jokes
An Entertaining Introduction
ISBN 978-3-8382-1857-1

60 Josef Wallmannsberger
(ed.)
Executing Renaissances
The Poetological Nation of
Ukraine
ISBN 978-3-8382-1741-3

61 Pavlo Kazarin
The Wild West of Eastern
Europe
ISBN 978-3-8382-1842-7

62 Ernest Gyidel
Ukrainian Public
Nationalism in the General
Government
The Case of Krakivski Visti,
1940–1944
With a foreword by David R.
Marples
ISBN 978-3-8382-1865-6

63 Olexander Hryb
Understanding
Contemporary Russian
Militarism
From Revolutionary to New
Generation Warfare
With a foreword by Mark Laity
ISBN 978-3-8382-1927-1

64 Orysia Hrudka, Bohdan Ben
Dark Days, Determined
People
Stories from Ukraine under
Siege
With a foreword by Myroslav
Marynovych
ISBN 978-3-8382-1958-5

65 Oleksandr Pankieiev (ed.)
Narratives of the Russo-
Ukrainian War
A Look Within and Without
With a foreword by Natalia
Khanenko-Friesen
ISBN 978-3-8382-1964-6

66 Roman Sohn, Ariana Gic
(eds.)
Unrecognized War
The Fight for Truth about
Russia's War on Ukraine
With a foreword by Viktor
Yushchenko
ISBN 978-3-8382-1947-9

67 Paul Robert Magocsi
Ukraina Redux
Schon wieder die Ukraine ...
ISBN 978-3-8382-1942-4

68 Paul Robert Magocsi
L'Ucraina Ritrovata
Sullo Stato e l'Identità Nazionale
ISBN 978-3-8382-1982-0

Book series "Ukrainian Voices"

Coordinator
Andreas Umland, National University of Kyiv-Mohyla Academy

Editorial Board
Lesia Bidochko, National University of Kyiv-Mohyla Academy
Svitlana Biedarieva, George Washington University, DC, USA
Ivan Gomza, Kyiv School of Economics, Ukraine
Natalie Jaresko, Aspen Institute, Kyiv/Washington
Olena Lennon, University of New Haven, West Haven, USA
Kateryna Yushchenko, First Lady of Ukraine 2005-2010, Kyiv
Oleksandr Zabirko, University of Regensburg, Germany

Advisory Board

Iuliia Bentia, National Academy of Arts of Ukraine, Kyiv
Natalya Belitser, Pylyp Orlyk Institute for Democracy, Kyiv
Oleksandra Bienert, Humboldt University of Berlin, Germany
Sergiy Bilenky, Canadian Institute of Ukrainian Studies, Toronto
Tymofii Brik, Kyiv School of Economics, Ukraine
Olga Brusylovska, Mechnikov National University, Odesa
Mariana Budjeryn, Harvard University, Cambridge, USA
Volodymyr Bugrov, Shevchenko National University, Kyiv
Olga Burlyuk, University of Amsterdam, The Netherlands
Yevhen Bystrytsky, NAS Institute of Philosophy, Kyiv
Andrii Danylenko, Pace University, New York, USA
Vladislav Davidzon, Atlantic Council, Washington/Paris
Mykola Davydiuk, Think Tank "Polityka," Kyiv
Andrii Demartino, National Security and Defense Council, Kyiv
Vadym Denisenko, Ukrainian Institute for the Future, Kyiv
Oleksandr Donii, Center for Political Values Studies, Kyiv
Volodymyr Dubovyk, Mechnikov National University, Odesa
Volodymyr Dubrovskiy, CASE Ukraine, Kyiv
Diana Dutsyk, National University of Kyiv-Mohyla Academy
Marta Dyczok, Western University, Ontario, Canada
Yevhen Fedchenko, National University of Kyiv-Mohyla Academy
Sofiya Filonenko, State Pedagogical University of Berdyansk
Oleksandr Fisun, Karazin National University, Kharkiv
Oksana Forostyna, Webjournal "Ukraina Moderna," Kyiv
Roman Goncharenko, Broadcaster "Deutsche Welle," Bonn
George Grabowicz, Harvard University, Cambridge, USA
Gelinada Grinchenko, Karazin National University, Kharkiv
Kateryna Härtel, Federal Union of European Nationalities, Brussels
Nataliia Hendel, University of Geneva, Switzerland
Anton Herashchenko, Kyiv School of Public Administration
John-Paul Himka, University of Alberta, Edmonton
Ola Hnatiuk, National University of Kyiv-Mohyla Academy
Oleksandr Holubov, Broadcaster "Deutsche Welle," Bonn
Yaroslav Hrytsak, Ukrainian Catholic University, Lviv
Oleksandra Humenna, National University of Kyiv-Mohyla Academy
Tamara Hundorova, NAS Institute of Literature, Kyiv
Oksana Huss, University of Bologna, Italy
Oleksandra Iwaniuk, University of Warsaw, Poland
Mykola Kapitonenko, Shevchenko National University, Kyiv
Georgiy Kasianov, Marie Curie-Skłodowska University, Lublin
Vakhtang Kebuladze, Shevchenko National University, Kyiv
Natalia Khanenko-Friesen, University of Alberta, Edmonton
Victoria Khiterer, Millersville University of Pennsylvania, USA
Oksana Kis, NAS Institute of Ethnology, Lviv
Pavlo Klimkin, Center for National Resilience and Development, Kyiv
Oleksandra Kolomiiets, Center for Economic Strategy, Kyiv

Sergiy Korsunsky, Kobe Gakuin University, Japan
Nadiia Koval, Kyiv School of Economics, Ukraine
Volodymyr Kravchenko, University of Alberta, Edmonton
Oleksiy Kresin, NAS Koretskiy Institute of State and Law, Kyiv
Anatoliy Kruglashov, Fedkovych National University, Chernivtsi
Andrey Kurkov, PEN Ukraine, Kyiv
Ostap Kushnir, Lazarski University, Warsaw
Taras Kuzio, National University of Kyiv-Mohyla Academy
Serhii Kvit, National University of Kyiv-Mohyla Academy
Yuliya Ladygina, The Pennsylvania State University, USA
Yevhen Mahda, Institute of World Policy, Kyiv
Victoria Malko, California State University, Fresno, USA
Yulia Marushevska, Security and Defense Center (SAND), Kyiv
Myroslav Marynovych, Ukrainian Catholic University, Lviv
Oleksandra Matviichuk, Center for Civil Liberties, Kyiv
Mykhailo Minakov, Kennan Institute, Washington, USA
Anton Moiseienko, The Australian National University, Canberra
Alexander Motyl, Rutgers University-Newark, USA
Vlad Mykhnenko, University of Oxford, United Kingdom
Vitalii Ogiienko, Ukrainian Institute of National Remembrance, Kyiv
Olga Onuch, University of Manchester, United Kingdom
Olesya Ostrovska, Museum "Mystetskyi Arsenal," Kyiv
Anna Osypchuk, National University of Kyiv-Mohyla Academy
Oleksandr Pankieiev, University of Alberta, Edmonton
Oleksiy Panych, Publishing House "Dukh i Litera," Kyiv
Valerii Pekar, Kyiv-Mohyla Business School, Ukraine
Yohanan Petrovsky-Shtern, Northwestern University, Chicago
Serhii Plokhy, Harvard University, Cambridge, USA
Andrii Portnov, Viadrina University, Frankfurt-Oder, Germany
Maryna Rabinovych, Kyiv School of Economics, Ukraine
Valentyna Romanova, Institute of Developing Economies, Tokyo
Natalya Ryabinska, Collegium Civitas, Warsaw, Poland
Darya Tsymbalyk, University of Oxford, United Kingdom
Vsevolod Samokhvalov, University of Liege, Belgium
Orest Semotiuk, Franko National University, Lviv
Viktoriya Sereda, NAS Institute of Ethnology, Lviv
Anton Shekhovtsov, University of Vienna, Austria
Andriy Shevchenko, Media Center Ukraine, Kyiv
Oxana Shevel, Tufts University, Medford, USA
Pavlo Shopin, National Pedagogical Dragomanov University, Kyiv
Karina Shyrokykh, Stockholm University, Sweden
Nadja Simon, freelance interpreter, Cologne, Germany
Olena Snigova, NAS Institute for Economics and Forecasting, Kyiv
Ilona Solohub, Analytical Platform "VoxUkraine," Kyiv
Iryna Solonenko, LibMod - Center for Liberal Modernity, Berlin
Galyna Solovei, National University of Kyiv-Mohyla Academy
Sergiy Stelmakh, NAS Institute of World History, Kyiv
Olena Stiazhkina, NAS Institute of the History of Ukraine, Kyiv
Dmitri Stratievski, Osteuropa Zentrum (OEZB), Berlin
Dmytro Stus, National Taras Shevchenko Museum, Kyiv
Frank Sysyn, University of Toronto, Canada
Olha Tokariuk, Center for European Policy Analysis, Washington
Olena Tregub, Independent Anti-Corruption Commission, Kyiv
Hlib Vyshlinsky, Centre for Economic Strategy, Kyiv
Mychailo Wynnyckyj, National University of Kyiv-Mohyla Academy
Yelyzaveta Yasko, NGO "Yellow Blue Strategy," Kyiv
Serhy Yekelchyk, University of Victoria, Canada
Victor Yushchenko, President of Ukraine 2005-2010, Kyiv
Oleksandr Zaitsev, Ukrainian Catholic University, Lviv
Kateryna Zarembo, National University of Kyiv-Mohyla Academy
Yaroslav Zhalilo, National Institute for Strategic Studies, Kyiv
Sergei Zhuk, Ball State University at Muncie, USA
Alina Zubkovych, Nordic Ukraine Forum, Stockholm
Liudmyla Zubrytska, National University of Kyiv-Mohyla Academy

Friends of the Series

Ana Maria Abulescu, University of Bucharest, Romania
Łukasz Adamski, Centrum Mieroszewskiego, Warsaw
Marieluise Beck, LibMod—Center for Liberal Modernity, Berlin
Marc Berenses, King's College London, United Kingdom
Johannes Bohnen, BOHNEN Public Affairs, Berlin
Karsten Brüggemann, University of Tallinn, Estonia
Ulf Brunnbauer, Leibniz Institute (IOS), Regensburg
Martin Dietze, German-Ukrainian Culture Society, Hamburg
Gergana Dimova, Florida State University, Tallahassee/London
Caroline von Gall, Goethe University, Frankfurt-Main
Zaur Gasimov, Rhenish Friedrich Wilhelm University, Bonn
Armand Gosu, University of Bucharest, Romania
Thomas Grant, University of Cambridge, United Kingdom
Gustav Gressel, European Council on Foreign Relations, Berlin
Rebecca Harms, European Centre for Press & Media Freedom, Leipzig
André Härtel, Stiftung Wissenschaft und Politik, Berlin/Brussels
Marcel Van Herpen, The Cicero Foundation, Maastricht
Richard Herzinger, freelance analyst, Berlin
Mieste Hotopp-Riecke, ICATAT, Magdeburg
Nico Lange, Munich Security Conference, Berlin
Martin Malek, freelance analyst, Vienna
Ingo Mannteufel, Broadcaster "Deutsche Welle," Bonn
Carlo Masala, Bundeswehr University, Munich
Wolfgang Mueller, University of Vienna, Austria
Dietmar Neutatz, Albert Ludwigs University, Freiburg
Torsten Oppelland, Friedrich Schiller University, Jena
Niccolò Pianciola, University of Padua, Italy
Gerald Praschl, German-Ukrainian Forum (DUF), Berlin
Felix Riefer, Think Tank Ideenagentur-Ost, Düsseldorf
Stefan Rohdewald, University of Leipzig, Germany
Sebastian Schäffer, Institute for the Danube Region (IDM), Vienna
Felix Schimansky-Geier, Friedrich Schiller University, Jena
Ulrich Schneckener, University of Osnabrück, Germany
Winfried Schneider-Deters, freelance analyst, Heidelberg/Kyiv
Gerhard Simon, University of Cologne, Germany
Kai Struve, Martin Luther University, Halle/Wittenberg
David Stulik, European Values Center for Security Policy, Prague
Andrzej Szeptycki, University of Warsaw, Poland
Philipp Ther, University of Vienna, Austria
Stefan Troebst, University of Leipzig, Germany

[Please send requests for changes in, corrections of, and additions to, this list to andreas.umland@stanforalumni.org.]

ibidem.eu